PLATO AND THE ENGLISH ROMANTICS

PLATO AND THE ENGLISH ROMANTICS

διάλογοι

E. Douka Kabitoglou

Routledge
London and New York

First published 1990
by Routledge
11 New Fetter Lane, London EC4P 4EE

Simultaneously published in the USA and Canada
by Routledge
a division of Routledge, Chapman and Hall, Inc.
29 West 35th Street, New York, NY 10001

© 1990 E. Douka Kabitoglou

Data converted to 10/12 Times by Columns of Reading
Printed in Great Britain by
TJ Press (Padstow) Ltd, Padstow, Cornwall

All rights reserved. No part of this book may be reprinted or reproduced or utilized in any form or by any electronic, mechanical, or other means, now known or hereafter invented, including photocopying and recording, or in any information storage or retrieval system, without permission in writing from the publishers.

British Library Cataloguing in Publication Data
Kabitoglou, E. Douka
Plato and the English Romantics.
1. Philosophy related to literature
I. Title
100

ISBN 0–415–03602–X

Library of Congress Cataloging in Publication Data
Kabitoglou, E. Douka
Plato and the English Romantics: dialogoi/E. Douka Kabitoglou.
p.   cm.
Includes bibliographical references.
ISBN 0–415–03602–X
1. English poetry–19th century–History and criticism.
2. English poetry–Classical influences.   3. Philosophy, Ancient, in literature.   4. Romanticism–England.   5. Plato–Influence.
I. Title.
PR590.K25   1990
821'.709–dc20   89–39160

If we reach and enter that course, it will lead thinking into a dialogue with poetry, a dialogue that is of the history of Being
      Martin Heidegger, *Poetry, Language, Thought*

CONTENTS

Preface ix

Acknowledgements xiii

1. THE DIALOGUE FORM: APOLLO AND
   DIONYSUS IN DISCOURSE 1
   Being and Forms in Plato 1
   The Mythos of Logos: Plato and Heidegger 13
   Platonic Dialogue as Play 27
   The Hermeneutics of the 'Ode on a Grecian Urn' 49

2. EROS IN LOGOS: SYMPOSIA ANCIENT AND
   MODERN 72
   The Symposium *as 'Amorous Romance'* 72
   The Triumph of Life: *Shelley's 'own Symposium'* 83
   Lamia *as Keats' Symposium* 125

3. TRANS-FORM-ATION: THE DIALECTICS OF
   ΠΑΘΟΣ AND ΠΟΙΗΣΙΣ 136
   The Logos of Mythos: 'Instant' Metamorphosis 136
   Plato on Πάσχεῖν/Ποιειν 151
   The Romantics on Passion/Poetry 168

4. ΠΑΘΗΜΑ AND ΠΟΙΗΜΑ: BEING IN THE
   ROMANTIC TEXTS 188
   The Prelude 188
   The Rime of the Ancient Mariner 205
   Prometheus Unbound 225
   Hyperion/The Fall of Hyperion 247

CONTENTS

5. ON RE-COLLECTION — 274

Notes — 296
Bibliography — 309
Index — 318

PREFACE

The present work is an exercise in intertextual hermeneutics. In accepting that literature and philosophy form a continuous text, it attempts to provide the space where the dialogue among texts, as well as that between 'reader' and 'text', can be carried out. It is not primarily an investigation of sources and influences, though it is an exploration into origins – the presuppositions conditioning the cultural span inhabited by the works under examination; such are basic Greek words, οὐσία, λόγος, ἔρως, ποίησις, ἀνάμνησις (etymology often acting as a point of departure into ontological linguistics). The underlying structure is the contradiction between 'identity' (Limit/Same) and 'difference' (Unlimited/Other) which, translated into mythological terms evinces the 'love-play' or 'discourse' of the Apollonian and Dionysian forces, and transferred into rhetorical tropes elicits 'metaphor'.

The ardent post-modern debate concerning the 'end' of metaphysics has triggered the urge to revisit the original site, the textual τόπος where metaphysics has its 'beginning', the Platonic *Dialogues*. Roaming about the discursive and imaginative landscape that provides the point of origination for the flight from the sensuous – Plato's alleged privileging of the transcendental signified over the empirical signifier – one realizes that what the text 'says' (despite what its characters sometimes 'speak') is a full immersion into the daily business of living. In their venture to grapple with the immediate problems of existence, the Platonic dialogues remain firmly set in the to and fro of 'everydayness' – the 'passion', the 'action', the 'discourse'. So I would argue that 'metaphysics' never really happens at the point of its supposed genesis, where physical desire (ἔρως) grounds meta-physical cognition; it is rather to be found in the 'interpretations' of subsequent commentaries, beginning with Aristotle.

My reading of Plato, emphasizing the 'dynamic' aspect of his ontology, is based on his own definition of Being (οὐσία) as 'power to act or suffer' – an assessment that has paradoxically been muted or 'marginalized' in the general tendency of western philosophical tradition which looks upon the Platonic notion of the real as something static, permanent and invariant. The argument discloses the possible kinship between Platonic metaphysics and Romantic aesthetics in the centrality of the ποιεῖν/πάσχειν model, which makes of 'poetry' and 'passion' the dialectical forces that constitute reality and creativity. The approach taken traces a common 'deep structure' in *logos* (dialectical procedure) and *mythos* (imaginative process), in the presence of μανία (intensified awareness) – the daemonic ἔρως that bridges the ontological gap between mortal and divine and the epistemological split of subject and object; it reads metamorphosis in the Romantic texts (the 'marriage' of Self and Other) in the light of Plato's anamnestic recognition. Such is the close intimacy with 'what is', the impassioned perception (νοῦς ἐρῶν) that deconstructs habitual consciousness (dissolution of ego or 'subject'), effecting a passage from 'ignorance of knowledge' to 'knowledge of knowledge', through 'knowledge of ignorance'. It is my basic contention that Platonic dialectic, in breaking the limitations imposed by imperceptible habits of perception or forestructures (shadows), suspending all that was formerly held true and taken for granted, is the forerunner of such modern practices as Heideggerian 'destruction' or Derridean 'deconstruction'.

The cohabitation of Platonic philosophy and Romantic poetry in the same textual abode is not intended primarily to support (the much disputed nowadays) Romantic Platonism; on the contrary, intertextuality works backwards, attempting the rather unprecedented task of turning Plato into a Wordsworthian. In my demarcation of a field of research that is interdisciplinary, diachronic, and cross-cultural, Heidegger's thought has become a central point of reference, among other things for presenting the possibility of a convergence between Greek philosophy and Romantic poetry, turning my attention towards the hidden resources of my language – that language which is privileged with the 'speaking of being'. I believe that despite Heidegger's professed anti-Platonism (a possible result of his reading

Nietzsche reading Plato), there are strong similarities in their logo-centric reality models, beginning with the dominance of the ontological question (τὶ τὸ ὄν). Heidegger's partiality for the dialogue form alerted me to the fact that the dialogical exchange in its 'playful' dramatization of everyday situations, 'says' as much about Plato's 'truth' as his expressed utterances. In the adoption of the dialogic / dramatic form, the author-ial voice is dissolved and (like Dionysus) parcelled out among the personages of the Platonic θίασος. And here I need to borrow Gadamer's words, who undertakes to remind us all in the concluding statement of his *Philosophical Apprenticeships* (1985), 'that Plato was no Platonist and that philosophy is not scholasticism'.

The literary reading of (Platonic) philosophy and the philosophical reading of (Romantic) poetry has been facilitated by the tracing of their lost foundation in ritualistic practices – Plato's depiction of the philosopher's condition not as a matter of theorizing and propositional thinking, but a form of 'madness' (τῆς φιλοσόφου μανίας καὶ βακχείας), still aware of the Dionysian origins of the 'discipline' he practises. Plato and the English Romantics may be seen as samples of a pre-post-Christian discourse, offering rival myths of interpreting 'being' and introducing formal explanations or metaphysical propositions operating outside the Judaeo-Christian historical, ideological, or imaginative context. The Romantic movement does not so much initiate an innovation in ontological models, I think, but the 'recollection' of a forgotten or 'suppressed' typology. The dominant Judaeo-Christian myth of patriarchal authority, centred on a rationalizing (logo-centric) and controlling 'ego' – Ἐγώ εἰμί Κύριος ὁ Θεός σου – ceases to be the only mode of experiencing, and expressing, human transactions with reality. From that point of view, the 'mistrust' of textuality that has been detected in western tradition (beginning with Plato) may be ascribed to a 'questioning' of the dogmatic authority and finality of 'script-ure' which, by providing ready answers, dulls (or lulls) sensitivity and erotic attentiveness to the event of 'being'.

Plato was the first to set down the dialogical situation as the condition of hermeneutics – inter-personal, in-personal, and trans-personal communication – which even in its 'written' form escapes the fixity and uniformity of the omniscient author. As practised in the present undertaking, hermeneutics has functioned not only as a stance of 'astonishment' and openness to 'textual' being. Next to gaining 'right understanding from the texts themselves' (to paraphrase Heidegger), the actual experience of involvement into an interpretative 'dialogue' with the Platonic and Romantic work has led to the inevitable realization that, much as I wished to achieve the presuppositionless stance of phenomenology, my readings could only be those dictated by my culture and my sex: the ἑρμηνεία of a Greek female.

E.D.K.

ACKNOWLEDGEMENTS

I should like to thank Christopher Salvesen whose initial interest and continued encouragement enabled me to carry this project to a successful conclusion. No less a gratitude should be expressed to the late Geoffrey Matthews who was 'there' at the beginning, and with unfailing care initiated me into the intricacies of Romantic 'poetic thinking'. I also wish to acknowledge the generous assistance given to me by my colleague and friend Jina Politi, whose readiness to listen and talk provided the mental stimulation and emotional steadying 'back home', that saw me through this work. I am particularly grateful to my friends Rothanthi and Lia Milioni who, in the hour of need, placed at my disposal that modern 'deus ex machina', the word-processor, which miraculously solved all practical difficulties.

My greatest personal debt goes to my family – my husband Mercos and my sons John and George – whose loving patience and precious support allowed me to transfer a large part of my attention and devotion to matters intellectual. Last, but not least, I deeply thank my mother who bore the burden of my absence.

Acknowledgement is due to the following for permission to reproduce copyright material: Oxford University Press for permission to quote lines from *Wordsworth: Poetical Works*, ed. T. Hutchinson, rev. edn E. de Selincourt; *Coleridge: Poetical Works*, ed. E. H. Coleridge; *Shelley: Poetical Works*, ed. T. Hutchinson, corr. edn G. M. Matthews; *Keats: Poetical Works*, ed. W. H. Garrod; and extracts from *S. T. Coleridge: Biographia Literaria*, ed. J. Shawcross; *The Letters of P. B. Shelley*, ed. F. L. Jones. Faber & Faber Ltd for permission to quote lines from T. S. Eliot, *Collected Poems, 1909–1962*, and *Murder in the Cathedral*. A. P. Watt Ltd for permission on behalf of Michael

ACKNOWLEDGEMENTS

B. Yeats and Macmillan London Ltd to quote lines from *The Collected Poems of W. B. Yeats*. Harvard University Press for permission to quote material from *The Letters of John Keats, 1814–1821*, ed. Hyder Edward Rollins. Penguin Books Ltd for permission to quote lines from *The Bacchae and Other Plays* by Euripides, trans. Philip Vellacott. And D. H. Reiman for permission to quote from his book *Shelley's 'The Triumph of Life': A Critical Study*.

My thanks are also due to the editors of *The Wordsworth Circle* for permission to reprint material which first appeared in this periodical (XIX/3, Summer 1988) under the title, 'Problematics of gender in the nuptials of *The Prelude*'.

1

THE DIALOGUE FORM
Apollo and Dionysus in Discourse

BEING AND FORMS IN PLATO

Form is factitious *Being*, and Thinking is the Process. Imagination the Laboratory, in which Thought elaborates Essence into Existence. A Psilosopher, i.e. a nominal Ph. without Imagination, is a *Coiner* – Vanity, the *Froth* of the molten Mass, is his *Stuff* – and Verbiage the Stamp & Impression. This is but a *deaf* Metaphor – better say, that he is guilty of Forgery – he presents the same ⟨sort of⟩ *Paper* as the honest Barterer, but when you carry it to the *Bank*, it is found to be drawn on – Outis, *Esqre*. His Words had deposited no Forms there, payable at Sight – or even at any imaginable Time from the Date of the Draft/ . . .

. . . Λογος ab *Ente* – at once the ~~essential~~ existent Reflection, and the Reflex Act – at once actual and real & therefore, filiation not creation / Thought *formed not fixed* – the molten *Being* never cooled into a *Thing*, tho' begotten into the vast adequate Thought. Est, Idea, Ideation – *Id* – inde, HOC et *illud*. Idea – *atio*, seu *actio* = Id: iterum, ⟨Hoc + Id, & then⟩ Id + Ea (i.e. Coadunatio Individui cum Universo per Amorem) = Idea: Idea + actio = Ideatio, seu αγιον πνευμα, which being transelemented into we are mystically united with the *Am – Ειμι –*.

(Coleridge 1962: II, 3158; 3159)

The 'spontaneous overflow' of Coleridge's thought as manifested in the above passage contains in embryonic form, or rather formlessness, the Romantic endeavour to deal with the epistemological and aesthetic problems and perplexities bequeathed to them by an age-long tradition and controversy, that 'series of footnotes to Plato' which constitutes, in A. N. Whitehead's view, western philosophy. Drawing his metaphors from chemistry (or alchemy), minting, banking practice, Coleridge immerses himself into a questionable etymological exploration of the term 'idea', to conclude with a twisting (so common of Coleridgean habits in the structuring of his arguments as well as his poems) that terminates intellectual or imaginative tensions by translating them into the accepted dogmas of Christian theology. His reading of 'ideas' as energies of thinking rather than mental concepts, in that 'an idea is deeper than all intelligence', although retaining the ontological primacy of the term, infuses it with the Romantic dynamics of the 'will' and turns its, supposedly, fixed nature into a tensive field of action.

How far is the inherent 'dynamism' that Coleridge attributes to the Platonic Ideas, and which seems to contradict traditional views of the Forms as 'static' configurations of reality, justified by the use of the term – and the concept – in the Platonic text itself? Or, is the notion of form a constriction and imprisonment of 'being', as J. Derrida affirms: 'It might then be thought that the *sense of being* has been limited by the imposition of *form* – which in its most overt function, and ever since the origin of philosophy, would, with the authority of the *is*, have assigned to the sense of being the closure of presence, the form-of-presence, presence-in-form, or form-presence' (1973: 127).

The 'classical' definition of forms is given in the *Parmenides* where, after Parmenides' assertion that a 'form' is a thing thought of as being one and always the same, Socrates expands the hermeneutical horizon by adding further details which exemplify the essence and function of forms; very tentatively, induced by his interlocutor,[1] he admits that 'these forms [εἴδη] are as it were patterns fixed in the nature of things [παραδείγματα ἑστάναι ἐν τῇ φύσει]' (132d).[2] Whatever activity or energy forms are allowed is in their relationship to each other, and their transactions with the sensible world; forms relate to one another, as things in the visible world relate to one another (*Parm.*, 129d–e). A greater amount of dynamism is displayed in the encounter of 'forms' and the 'formless' receptacle which exists before all shapes and colours and sounds appear, for 'that which is to receive perpetually and through its whole extent the resemblances of all eternal beings ought to be devoid of any particular form' (*Timaeus*, 51a); the universal mould receiving all Ideas, always the 'same' and open to impressions,

> is stirred and informed by them, and appears different from time to time by reason of them. But the forms which enter into and go out of her are the likenesses of eternal realities modeled after their patterns in a wonderful and mysterious manner, which we will hereafter investigate.
>
> (*Tim.*, 50c)

So forms in a way exhibit a simultaneous dynamic and static quality in sending forth 'representatives' that come and go into the maternal mould, while they themselves remain aloof, undisturbed. The manner of interaction between forms and receptacle is given in the *Timaeus* through the metaphor of 'visitation' (forms 'enter into' and 'go out of her') in what appears to be an open thoroughfare, neither inviting nor detaining them. Plato's 'formless' receptacle of forms is the material χώρα, the space where forms arise and vanish. For, if 'that which is to receive all forms should have no form', 'the mother and receptacle of all created and visible and in any way sensible things', the matrix of creation, 'is an invisible and formless being which receives all things and in some mysterious way partakes of the intelligible, and is most incomprehensible', (50e–51b). It is the 'marriage' of 'form' and 'space' that gives birth to 'image' or phenomenal reality observed by the senses; conversely, the formlessness of χώρα 'is apprehended, when all sense is absent, by a kind of spurious reason' and a 'dreamlike sense' (52b–c). So 'image' (or 'generation') is distinguished from 'space' (the 'nurse of generation'), and both are differentiated from 'idea', thus forming a triptych of existents. Yet when it comes to that, the metaphysical distinction dominating the Platonic strongly dualistic ontology – the difference between that spiritual 'place [τόπον] beyond the heavens' where 'true being dwells, without color or shape, that cannot be touched' (*Phaedrus*, 247c), 'the form which is always the same . . . invisible and imperceptible by any sense, and of which the contemplation is granted to intelligence only' (*Tim.*, 52a), and the sheer materiality of 'space [χώρας]', 'that must be always called the same' (*Tim.*, 50b), 'an invisible and formless being' (*Tim.*, 51a) – seems to be an extremely subtle noetic, and experiential, operation.

'Participation' of things in forms often bears traces of the exercise of violence. In the *Phaedo*, for instance, the language of the text introduces 'occupation' and 'enforcement' as conditions that are 'suffered' by a thing and resulting from its association with form. Confrontation of 'form' and 'thing' is not only hierarchical but may lead to unpredictable consequences, as 'they are things which are compelled by some form which takes possession of them to assume not only its own form but invariably also that of some other form which is an opposite' (104d). Such an assumption would uncover 'forms' to be not mere 'energies' but 'powers' in the full sense of the word, leading to a 'political' rather than 'scientific' reading of Platonic cosmology, easily discerning the relationship of oppressor / oppressed in the ontological transactions between the spiritual and the material. A similar observation can be made concerning the central activity in Plato's creation myth in the *Timaeus*, the famous, or infamous, 'Mind, the ruling power, persuaded necessity to bring the greater part of created things to perfection' (48a). Since the – anyway ethically ambiguous – technique of persuasion, even in its most innocent form of verbal persuasion or rhetoric, is often condemned by Plato as a misleading and enchanting practice (of which poetry is a type), the proposition perhaps implies that the whole Platonic edifice of a moral universe (the cause 'endowed with mind' working out 'things fair and good') is based upon misappropriation of power. D. F. Krell attempts to decipher the mechanics of persuasion that brings a 'cosmos' out of a 'chaos': 'Timeaus's craftsman', he contests, 'possesses only one *technē* and that one is *poiēsis*, production. We know nothing about his capacities in wooing and love-making. If he is the *logos* that cannot be persuaded', the critic wonders, how can he come to terms with the *alogon*? 'If he fears and despises *anankē* can he bring himself to lie with her – or induce her to lie with him?' In an attempt to clarify the relationship of ἔρως and λόγος, Krell protests: 'If he cannot be persuaded how will he learn the art of persuasion? Does not persuasion involve the give and take of dialogue and dialectic? Unless he does a bit of wandering himself how can *logos* persuade the *planōmenon*?' (1975: 415).

The activity of Ideas receives a milder presentation in the *Republic*, in Plato's effort to safeguard, once more, the 'uniqueness' and self-identity of each form, while justifying its pluralistic manifestations:

And in respect of the just and the unjust, the good and the bad, and all the ideas or forms, the same statement holds, that in itself each is one, but that by virtue of their communion with actions and bodies and with one another they present themselves everywhere, each as a multiplicity of aspects.

(V, 476a)

Moving in a reverse process, man must understand the language of forms, passing from a plurality of perceptions to a unity gathered together by thinking; the vision of forms presupposes, as is often stressed by Plato, a prior 'unification' and 'collectedness'. This highest stage, the final θεωρία, is prepared for by the preliminary phases of the dialectical process, which effect an 'intellectual' purification that cleanses the mind from preconceptions, opinions, conditioning (as well as an 'ethical' one that kills the pride of intellect) and allows a 'naked' contact of the soul with reality as it is (τὸ ὄντος ὄν), the original state of what is 'there' – or 'here'. Seen from within the perspective of the dialectical method, the Idea (Ideas) is that which *is* before we project our concepts (ὑποθέσεις) onto it. And although such a view tends to de-transcendentalize traditional interpretations concerning the nature of Platonic forms, I agree with the suggestion supporting the 'this-worldliness' of Plato's attitude rather than his so-called 'escapism', the view expressed by L. A. Cosman that 'the luminous world of forms is this world seen aright. That seeing (itself fugitive) is accomplished by a katharsis which makes appearance transparent, which allows the world itself to shine through its appearances' (1976: 67). One could even go as far as making paradoxical statements of the nature that Ideas can only be reached by a mind free from 'ideas'. Such subtle interplay of terms would be made meaningful if we turn to the root signification of the Greek word ἰδέα which is 'to observe, to see'; the implication might be that one refuses to see reality *as it is* by making an abstraction out of it, turning it into an 'idea' or 'picture' – in the sense the term is used by later philosophers.

Plato does not actually refer to Ideas as living powers but reserves the notion of 'dynamism' for the idea of 'being' – ὄν or οὐσία (deriving from οὖσα, participle feminine of εἰμί / am). The most thorough and extensive argument about the 'empowered' nature of the real appears in the *Sophist* where the definition (λόγος) of 'being', whether in an embodied or bodiless state, is set down as 'power' (δύναμις): 'I am proposing as a mark to distinguish real things that they are nothing but power' (247e). This 'power' that constitutes the essence of 'being' is further defined as power to 'affect' (ποιεῖν) or 'be affected' (πάσχειν). Having established the characteristic mark of reality as 'the presence in a thing of the power of being acted upon or of acting' (248c), the 'dramatis personae', the Eleatic Stranger and Theaetetus, carry on the discussion which was actually initiated earlier, by bringing face to face the two diametrically opposite positions concerning the nature of the real – that of the materialists (the exponents of flux) and that of the so-called idealists (the 'friends of forms').[3] In his usual philosophical practice Plato literally 'throws' on the ground the binary opposition and, like an interested but detached observer, follows the undulatory motion of the argument wherever it leads – which is usually 'nowhere'.

Beginning with the assumption that 'reality is just as hard to define as unreality', he sets down the basic premises of the parties involved in this 'quarrel about reality' like 'a battle of gods and giants'. The hypotheses of both contestants, materialists and idealists, receive due attention and presentation – in their most extremist positions (246a–249c). The task facing the Stranger and his interlocutor is to challenge each party in turn, Theaetetus undertaking to act as their spokesman. The seeming deadlock into which the either / or dialectical process ultimately corners itself is miraculously resolved by Plato (in the persona of the Stranger) offering not only one but two possible solutions: (a) the neither, and (b) the both / and:

> On these grounds, then, it seems that only one course is open to the philosopher who values knowledge and the rest above all else. He must refuse to accept from the champions either of the one or of the many forms the doctrine that all reality is changeless, and he must turn a deaf ear to the other party who represent reality as everywhere changing. Like a child begging for 'both,' he must declare that reality or the sum of things is both at once – all that is unchangeable and all that is in change.
>
> (249c–d)

The acceptance of both 'unchangeability', i.e. rest, and 'change', i.e. motion, as equally real, rather than posing the problem of the contradictory nature of οὐσία, facilitates the wrenching of reality from the clusters of either 'rest' or 'motion': instead of 'being' rest or motion, reality 'embraces' rest and motion – or rest and motion partake of reality which is then raised (or lowered) to a 'third' category or form. Reality or 'being' is neither motion nor rest, nor yet motion-and-rest at once, but 'different' or 'other' than motion or rest, in which, however, both κίνησις and στάσις (equally real) participate; the real is a 'third thing' neither static nor kinetic (250b–d).

Defining reality in a negative manner – not by what it is, but by what it *is not* – the argument concludes itself in characteristic Platonic ironic fashion by leaving the speakers – and readers – as perplexed as in the opening situation. To make matters worse, in an attempt to 'force a passage through the argument with both elbows at once' (251a), the Stranger introduces the 'linguistic' aspect, the multiplicity of names by which any given thing is called. The issue of the distinction between 'being' and its 'name' is discussed in the *Sophist* a little before the point where our intrusion into the text was made; the relation of 'word' to 'thing' is presented in equivocal terms leading, one way or the other, to a logical impossibility. The 'non-existence' of language is expounded as follows: if one assumes that the name (of reality) is different from the thing (i.e. reality) then he is surely speaking of *two* things, i.e. the name as other-than-reality. If, on the other hand, one assumes that the name (of reality) is the same as the thing (reality itself), 'either he will have to say it is not the name of anything, or if he says it is the name of something, it will follow that the name is merely a name of a name and of nothing else whatsoever' (244d).

The notion of 'pluralism' of names by which reality can be called,[4] necessarily creates the appropriate intellectual climate for the surfacing into the discussion of the concept of 'blending' (κοινωνία) of forms, which is a corner-stone in Platonic thought. The metaphor through which the ontological problem of the 'mixing' of forms is read, is a linguistic one: as with the letters of the alphabet so with the forms of reality, i.e. some are blendable and some are not. Dialectic science, or the 'grammar of reality', is the art responsible for pointing out which forms 'are consonant and which are incompatible with one another', and the dialectician is the one who can 'see clearly' this possibility (253b–e). Having confirmed the potentiality – indeed the necessity – of 'blending', the next step in the argument proposes that 'being' or 'existence' is the form which intermingles invariably with 'rest' or 'motion' since they both 'exist' without being 'existence' itself (254d); such subtle differentiation establishes the original three forms, each of which is *different* from the other two, and the *same* as itself. This further discrimination multiplies the number of original forms from 'three' to 'five', while it acknowledges that these two newly discovered Ideas, 'sameness' (ταὐτόν) and 'difference' (θάτερον) are, like 'existence', blendable with all other forms (255a–e).

The next argumentative step is to take a form, 'motion' for example, and to indicate that although it partakes in other forms such as 'being', 'sameness', and 'difference', *as such* it is heterogeneous to all other three; having existence (οὐσία) yet it *is not* existence, and 'In fact, it is clear that motion really is a thing that is not [existence] and a thing that is, since it partakes of existence' – hence, 'It must, then, be possible for "that which is not" [i.e. is different from existence] to be [to exist], not only in the case of motion but of all other kinds' (256d). The conclusion to which the dialogue had been oriented from its beginning is that *non-existence* (difference) *exists* in that it is 'different from' and not 'opposite to', existence; it is present in every form, including existence itself, and is an indispensible ingredient of any created thing which at the same time *is* and *is not*. Thus Plato has furnished a logical framework to support a really absurd proposition and to refute the central premise of Parmenides, that 'Never shall this be proved, that things that are not, are' (258d), by equating *nothingness* with *difference*: 'When we speak of "that which is not," it seems that we did not mean something contrary to what exists but only something that is different' (257b). This proposition, τὸ μὴ ὂν εἶναι, marks a turning point of momentous significance for the evolution of western thinking because it admits of the existence of a form 'other than being' – an 'otherness' – parcelled out among created beings; it attributes to 'no-thing' a measure of reality (where certainly 'things' or 'something' *can* come from 'nothing' – despite assertions to the contrary, as for instance King Lear's famous privative utterance: 'Nothing will come of nothing' (I, i, 89)):

So, when it is asserted that a negative signifies a contrary, we shall not agree, but admit no more than this – that the prefix 'not' indicates something different from the words that follow, or rather from the things designated by the words pronounced after the negative.

(*Soph.*, 257b–c)

Having effected the 'parricide' of father Parmenides, and having identified the nature of not-being as 'otherness' (rather than 'non-existence'), and after locating its presence 'parceled out over the whole field of existent things', and having 'dared to say that precisely that *is really* "that which is not" ' (258d–e), Plato orientates the inquiry into human discourse – both as an object of investigation and as significant metaphor – with the intention to prove that 'non-being' can be spoken, i.e. false articulation exists. This premise, whose target is to expose the falsity of sophistry in that it is capable of making statements – 'speaking' – different from (or other than) the things that 'are', is modified in a very interesting manner in the *Cratylus* by the assertion that 'falsehood may be spoken [λέγειν] but not said [φάναι]' (429e) – which places Plato before Heidegger in the distinction of logos into 'speaking' and 'saying'.

The analogical relation between language (λόγος) and reality (οὐσία) is a constant point of reference throughout the dialogues, and functions on two levels: (a) it traces the parallel operations of λόγος and οὐσία in a blending of simple elements into complexes, and (b) it recognizes a 'natural' affinity between the 'thing' and the 'word' in 'naming' (or a similarity of syntactical patterns in 'predicating'), in that the structures assumed by combinations of letters or syllables are 'imitations' of the way the elements of reality blend or 'weave' together. In the *Sophist* (261d–262d) Plato argues that the signs we use in speech (φωνῇ) to signify 'being' (οὐσίαν) are of two kinds, one called 'names', ὀνόματα, the other 'verbs', ῥήματα. The presence of both sorts of signs in interaction with each other (συμπλοκή) is a presupposition of λόγος, whereas the stringing together of elements from the same category never makes up a statement. As the intersection of blendable sounds produces meaningful names, so the weaving together of verbs with names 'states' something. The concept of 'fitting' and combination of simple elements is equally fundamental in Plato's linguistic as well as ontological universe.

In the *Cratylus*, the problem of the relation between reality and language arises in its 'naming' (etymological) rather than its 'predicating' (logical) aspect. The question of whether imitation of the essence of a thing is made by syllables and letters – τοῖς γράμμασι καὶ ταῖς συλλαβαῖς τοῦ ὄντος (424a–b) – leads to a close examination of the blendability of 'letters' (vowels, consonants, mutes), an operation seen as analogical to the mixing of 'words' to form sentences. The principle that underlies all these activities seems to be: as with 'being' so with 'predicating' and 'naming'. The initial assumption (to be later subverted within the same dialogue) is that 'the essence of the thing remains in possession of the name and appears in it' (393d). The word ὄνομα (name), to begin with,

> seems to be a compressed sentence, signifying ὂν οὗ ζήτημα (being for which there is a search), as is still more obvious in ὀνομαστόν (notable), which states in so many words that real existence is that for which there is a seeking (ὂν οὗ μάσμα).
>
> (421a)

So the root meaning of 'name' uncovers the essence of language as a pursuit after 'being' (ἡ τοῦ ὄντος θήρα) and justifies the definition of 'naming' as an art whose artificers are the 'legislators', in possession of the knowledge of how to put the 'natural' name of each thing into sounds and syllables – for 'as his name, so also is his nature [κατὰ φύσιν τὸ ὄνομα εἶναι]' (395a).

Assuming that the authenticity of such a statement can be provisionally accepted – if not on epistemological then on mythological grounds, as revelatory not of the 'being' of things but of the Platonic (and Greek) model concerning the nature of reality – then the following etymological investigations may be taken as valid in their own right, within the context that produced them:

> For example, that which we term οὐσία is by some called ἐσσία, and by others again ὠσία. Now that the essence of things should be called ἐστία, which is akin to the first of these (ἐσσία = ἐστία), is rational enough. And there is reason in the Athenians' calling that ἐστία which participates in οὐσία. For in ancient times we too seem to have said ἐσσία for οὐσία, and this you may note to have been

the idea of those who appointed that sacrifices should be first offered to ἑστία, which was natural enough if they meant that ἑστία was the essence of things. Those again who said ὠσία seem to have inclined to the opinion of Heraclitus that all things flow and nothing stands; with them the pushing principle (ὠθοῦν) was the cause and ruling power of all things, and was therefore rightly called ὠσία. Enough of this, which is all that we who know nothing can affirm.

(401c–e)

Socrates' ironic admission of ignorance concerning the nature of reality, although it 'deconstructs' the attempted definition while yet making it, yet in the recognition of the phonetic similarity of ἐσσία / ὠσία / οὐσία it allows to emerge in the name, if not the characteristic 'being' of the thing, two of its properties – its 'fireness' and its 'fluidity' – both of which can be attributed to the Heraclitean conception of reality, where not only things are in unceasing flow but the permanent λόγος within, below, or beyond things is that of 'fire' (Heraclitus 1979: 45–7).

The 'fiery' quality of 'being' is only mentioned once in the *Cratylus* in the passage quoted earlier, but its 'flowing' aspect receives a greater emphasis, in that it appears as the essential component of reality in a second attempt made by Socrates to get to the root meaning of the words ὄν / οὐσία: Ὄν and οὐσία are ἰόν with an ι broken off; this agrees with the true principle, for being (ὄν) is also moving (ἰόν), and the same may be said of not-being, which is likewise called not-going (οὐκίον or οὐκὶ ὄν = οὐκ ἰόν)' (421b–c). The concept of 'motion' appears to be the fundamental principle not only of 'reality' but also of 'truth', as in precisely the same passage and prior to the identification of 'being' with 'motion', ἀλήθεια is viewed as 'divine wandering' (421b).[5] Plato indulges in this spirit of apotheosis of movement by stressing that whatever facilitates κίνησις is good, whatever impedes it evil (419a–e); 'necessity' (the Platonic material element) is that which resists and obstructs motion (420d–e), ἐπιστήμη (knowledge) indicates that the soul 'follows (ἕπεται) the motion of things, neither anticipating them, nor falling behind them' (412a), and σοφία (wisdom) itself, although very dark and of foreign origin, is found out to mean '*touching the motion or stream of things*' (412b).

The counter-argument in the *Cratylus*, which follows in the usual Platonic practice of contra-diction, and endeavours to refute the position that supports the 'natural' signification of language by 'likeness', and to establish instead the theory of conventional representation by any 'chance sign,' is sustained (and the fallacy of the naturalness of 'names' exposed) through the reduction to absurdity of the 'naming' / 'moving' relationship. Reverting to their former discussion and getting Cratylus to admit their earlier argument, that 'in the names which have just been cited the motion of flux or generation of things is most surely indicated' (411c), Socrates (actually Plato) twists, I believe, both the process of the syllogism and its conclusion and – probably relying on Cratylus' weak memory – translates the assumption that language speaks of motion as that which is good and hindrance of motion as that which is evil (419a–420e) into 'all things are in motion . . . and this idea of motion is expressed by names' (436e) – silencing the evaluation principle. This obvious 'sophistry' of Socrates, probably justified by the Platonic argumentative principle of always bringing in the 'other' side of the issue, extends to a few paragraphs only compared to the thirty-or-so pages that the opposite exposition covers. It undertakes to prove the conventionality of language by disclosing the self-contradictory state of mind of the primal legislator (divine or human) who 'made some names expressive of rest and others of motion', thereby exhibiting his ignorance about the nature of reality and the possibility of its depiction in language, and allowing for the suspicion to creep in of 'one of the two not to be names at all' (438c).

The demolition of the theory that supported the presentation of 'being' in 'name' begins with the word ἐπιστήμη again – this time its etymology traced not to ἕπεται (following the motion) but, ambiguity taken into account, in the suggestion of 'stopping the soul at things than going round with them'; then μνήμη (memory) is given as an example expressing 'rest in the soul, and not motion' (437a–b). A few other illustrations associating 'motion' with evil and 'rest' with good are introduced, thus effecting a complete transvaluation of these two states of being (437b–c). Shortly after this rather thinly disguised effort to include the opposite or 'conventional' theory of language, the dialogue ends on an uncertain note admitting that knowledge of names does not yield knowledge of things, and cognition of things in themselves is impossible since they (unlike names) are in a state of intermittent flux: 'Must not the same thing be born and retire and vanish while the word is in our mouths?' (439e). Socrates incites Cratylus to reflect well and when he has found the truth to come and tell him. In a masterful open-endedness that leaves the question alive and fresh as in the opening situation – only more compact and precise – the text has circled back to its own beginning in an, apparently, futile gesture; the problem, brought to the frontier of the realm of speculation, has exerted human intellectual capacity to its limits. The argument, having moved forward in the form of a bridge (a dual one) towards a possible answer, suddenly stops with no opposite shore in sight. Questioning its own voice, its own assumptions and premises (τὰς ὑποθέσεις ἀναιροῦσα), it reveals itself to be not a bridge, after all, but a jetty, thrusting itself forward into the unknown, and allowing the participants – and the readers – a glimpse into the dark waters of ontological linguistics that awaits the investigation of the 'unaided mind'.

Plato's scepticism about the relation of λόγος to οὐσία seems to be absent from the phenomenology of logos as expressed in Heidegger's 'logocentric' ontology: 'Language is the precinct (*templum*), that is, the house of Being. The nature of language does not exhaust itself in signifying, nor is it merely something that has the character of sign or cipher'. Turning away from the 'semiotic' towards the 'symbolic' or 'mythic' function of human utterance, Heidegger asserts that 'It is because language is the house of Being, that we reach what is by constantly going through this house'; consequently, 'Thinking our way from the temple of Being, we have an intimation of what they dare who are sometimes more daring than the Being of beings. They dare the precinct of Being. They dare language' (1971a: 132).[6]

THE MYTHOS OF LOGOS: PLATO AND HEIDEGGER

Plato's recognition of the archetypal character of 'conversation' becomes manifest in the indisputable priority that 'discourse' receives in his text, in a multiplicity of forms and functions: the actual dramatic mode adopted as a means of presenting philosophical inquiry after truth; 'dialectic' as the methodology applied to such enquiry; the 'psychological' colloquy of mind's interior dialogue with itself as the prototype for 'speech' (or vice versa); the interaction of Logos–Mythos, which constitutes the basic structure of the Platonic writings; a compendium of dynamic relations between opposite forms such as Limit / Unlimited, Same / Other, Ideas / Receptacle, Nous / Eros, in conciliatory interplay or ironic tension; and finally, the textual correlation of two rhetorical practices, philosophic and poetic, abstract and concrete, that are hardly found as co-habitants in theoretical prose since,[7] portraying the living interplay between Concept and Image – which still leaves open the question (so arbitrarily settled in later years) of their proximity to truth.

Plato's use of figurative or metaphorical language is, I believe, a parallel to his dialectical method; the collapsing of barriers between linguistic categories in metaphor mirrors the exercise of 'disputation' and 'confutation', tearing the known world into pieces, and leading to a 'violent distrust' of all that had formerly been 'held true' (*Republic*, VII, 539c). Companion to a technique of direct questioning – which breaks down not only the interlocutor's but also the reader's sense of order – the metaphorical process, through the open trafficking that it effects between classes formerly sealed, becomes the embodiment of the unrealized connections of things, i.e. a linguistic representation of unapprehended structures, or 'ideas'. A. Fletcher recognizes and expands the operation of metaphor in Platonic thought from a linguistic to an ontological function: 'The ironic mode of the Platonic dialogues appears to follow from Plato's epistemology. With him things are an allegorical imitation of ideas, or, in another formulation, appearances are the allegorical equivalence of a higher reality'; as a result, 'The Platonic distrust of sense experience has a positive consequence, for while he would say that such experience is merely a model of the truth (he calls it a "shadow"), Plato is yet left with the idea of a model' (1964: 232–3).

I would argue that Plato's formal irony is less epistemological (since the continuity between 'perception' and 'idea' is guaranteed through the $\mu\acute{\epsilon}\theta\epsilon\xi\iota\varsigma$ – participation – of ideas in the world of generation) than methodological. 'Irony' as such is the starting and finishing point of the Platonic dialogue; the rest is symbolism, or 'romance'. If 'irony' is seen as a statement of irreconcilables, a trope which permits opposite points of view to be included – but not integrated – then it presides over the dialectical process in two ways: in the Socratic admission of 'knowledgeable ignorance', ἓν οἶδα ὅτι οὐδὲν οἶδα, and in the perception of contradiction and paradox as the essential presupposition for the 'awakening' of the type of thinking that tends to draw the mind to reality:

> The experiences that do not provoke thought are those that do not at the same time issue in a contradictory perception. Those that do have that effect I set down as provocatives, when the perception no more manifests one thing than its contrary, alike whether its impact comes from nearby or afar.
>
> (*Rep.*, VII, 523b–c)

Perceptions that stimulate reflection, setting the mind on the dialectical quest after 'being', are of things that 'impinge upon the senses together with their opposites' (VII, 524d), i.e. expound a questionable identity, where unity is subverted by the presence of opposition. In the case of an object whereby 'some contradiction is always seen coincidentally with it, so that it no more appears to be one than the opposite', the soul, being 'at a loss', is alerted to thinking and 'thus the study of unity will be one of the studies that guide and convert the soul to the contemplation of true being' (VII, 524e–525a).

Irony also operates as a principle of structure in most Platonic dialogues, where inconclusiveness or refusal of 'closure' leaves the argument where it began, *in medias res*; the Socratic incitement to his pupils to go home and think, and if they find the truth to come and tell him, renders the open-endedness of the (spoken or written) discourse into an invitation for embarking on a solitary, exploratory hunting after 'being'. The Platonic sense of an ending in its manifestly ironic mode, at once affirms and subverts the possibility of communicating the truth about 'reality'. In his distinction between Socratic and Platonic irony, P. Friedländer differentiates precisely between what I consider as the 'methodological' and 'structural' use of the ironic register in the Platonic text: Socrates begins the dialectical process with a professing of ignorance; Plato ends the dialogue with a presentation of multiple viewpoints (sometimes as many as the interlocutors), and a willing suspension of judgement. In Friedländer's words, 'And thus Platonic irony, incorporating the whole teaching and magic of the figure of Socrates, is revealed as veiling and protecting the Platonic secret. However, as in a Greek statue the garment not only serves as a veil but at the same time reveals that which it veils, so is Plato's irony also a guide on the path to the eternal forms and to that which is beyond being' (1958: 153).

So the 'real' question in the Platonic dialogues is the uncertainty of the dialogue form which, rather than providing definitive axioms, becomes an invitation to further exercise in 'thinking'. Plato's philosophy is an ironic mode of polarized tensions, surfacing not only in his ontological premises and methodological practices, but pointing to a conflict of contradictions within the author's ψυχή – an instance of which can be glimpsed in his simultaneous attraction / repulsion towards poetry, that ends in its ruthless persecution (*Rep.*, X, 603a–608b) – a frustrating conjunction of contrarities and a glaring example of self divided against itself. The ironic discourse is only one aspect in the multifaceted construction that the Platonic text *is*. Plato the artist manages to join and fuse 'irony' with 'romance', a simultaneous rejection and acceptance of the possibility of 'reconciliation of opposites', which makes for the paradoxical coexistence in the text of 'openness' and 'closedness' – the spiral and the circle. The nominally antithetical modes are seen as possible variants or expressions of the scission into two and unification into one, the clash of forces that is at the root of all existence. The question as to whether 'contraries' can be friendly is posed at a very early stage in the Platonic dialogues (*Lysis*, 216ff); in the work of his maturity, the *Laws*, Plato introduces the distinction between 'friendship' and 'love', the former expressing the affinity of similars, the latter the attraction between opposites (VIII, 837a–d).

What constitutes, I believe, the major target of Plato's conciliatory dynamics, is the engrafting of the binary opposition on to psychology, an aspect of which is the soul–body interaction. Contrary to what may be believed about the 'philosopher of transcendence', the human body holds a most central position in both the discursive and imaginative parts of the dialogues, and is the 'root' metaphor on which transcendence is built (as with body so with soul). The harmonious relation of the two existents has the topmost importance of all symmetries, and the statement that 'the due proportion of mind and body is the fairest and loveliest of all sights to him who has the seeing eye' (*Tim.*, 87d), indeed echoes its modern analogue of 'unity of being' best expressed by Yeats in 'Labour is blossoming or dancing where / The body is not bruised to pleasure soul' ('Among School Children', VIII).

The tension of the unresolved dialectic in the soul is, in Plato's view, the cause of all evil; he recognizes an internal condition of 'civil war' between various 'powers' which meddle and interfere with one another's 'functions' (*Rep.*, IV, 444b), a continual reassertion of polarities for the purpose of confrontation. Consequently, 'as in the domain of sight there was faction and strife and he held within himself contrary opinions at the same time about the same things, so also in our actions there is division and strife of the man with himself (X, 603c–d). The rhythm of dialectical progression that overcomes the principle of ambivalence in the soul bears exactly the same pattern as that of the formal process of the method of dialectic: διαίρεσις and συναγωγή, or 'discrimination' and 'mixing'. The structural devices for psychic integration that Plato introduces are rendered metaphorically through familiar, humble, menial, 'feminine' household occupations – such as sifting, straining, winnowing, threshing, carding, spinning, adjusting the warp and woof – in all of which there is implied a notion of division.[8] Such is the art of discerning and discriminating: 'In all the previously named processes, either like has been separated from the like or the better from the worse'; every distinction or differentiation of the second kind is called purification – καθαρμός (*Soph.*, 226d).

The art of reconciliation of opposites is called by Plato the 'royal art', or 'political art', and its allegorical equivalent is the activity of 'weaving'. Paradoxically, the pair of opposites to be 'woven' together is none other than a 'pair of virtues', which are 'in a certain sense enemies from of old, ranged in opposition to each other in many realms of life' (*Statesman*, 306b–c). The 'virtues' engaged in a perennial relation of contradiction are courage and moderation, or the 'brave' and the 'gentle'. The royal weaving process combines them into a unity, not only in the individual soul, where 'it is meet for a good man to be high-spirited and gentle, as occasion requires' (*Laws*, V, 731d), but also in the state. Thus Plato, inverting the metaphorical analogy he had used in the *Republic*, of 'as in the state so in the soul', establishes a model of 'as in the soul so in the state'; the preoccupation of the statesman is to achieve a reconciliation of opposites – the 'kingly weaver' must effect the 'web of state', a fabric enfolding 'all who dwell in the city, bond or free, in its firm contexture' (*Statesm.*, 311b–c). The 'weaving' metaphor is as central within Platonic iconography as that of 'blending'; both are expressive of the necessity of bringing together dialectical opposites in the spheres of ontology, sociology, psychology, linguistics; and both are 'arts', i.e. teachable, transferable, conscious activities of the mind. The 'textile' process is the enterprise that underlies language production – in other words looming is the correlative of λόγος, a complex fabric of 'names' and 'verbs'; signification depends on combination of names:

> Because now it gives information about facts or events in the present or past or future; it does not merely name something but gets you somewhere by weaving together verbs with names. Hence we say it 'states' something, not merely 'names' something, and in fact it is this complex that we mean by the word 'statement' [τῷ πλέγματι τούτῳ τὸ ὄνομα ἐφθεγξάμεθα λόγον].
>
> (*Soph.*, 262d)

Plato's attitude to *logos* is as much indicative of the inherent ambivalence in his thought as any of the more pronounced paradoxes of his text. He defines the οὐσία λόγου (essence of language) as συμπλοκὴ ὀνομάτων, an 'intertwining', 'complication' (possibly carrying hints of the 'other' meaning of the word, 'close struggle', or 'engagement') of 'names' (ὄνομα being both the generic term for 'word' and the specialized term for 'noun' as distinguished from 'verb'). Λόγος, composed of substantive and verbal parts, is only one of the three 'significations' through which cognition of reality can be achieved, the other two being 'name' and 'image' (*Letters*, VII, 342a–b). In the *Laws*, Plato repeats this triadic scheme, somehow eliminating the imaginal and concentrating instead on the ontological and linguistic components: 'I mean, for one, the reality of the thing, what it *is*, for another the *definition* of this reality, for another, its *name*. And thus you see there are two questions we can ask about everything which is' (X, 895d). The same conception is put forward in the *Cratylus*, as we have seen, that imitation of the essence of a thing is made by 'syllables' and 'letters' (423e), this time emphasizing not the product but the process of the imitative operation. The suppression of the component 'image' as a viaduct to knowledge is justified by a long, and firmly sustained, argumentation in the *Statesman*: the higher form of reality has no perceptual correspondent, and therefore can only be apprehended through λόγος (286a–b). The exultation of 'rationality' and propositional thinking – that which 'gets you somewhere by weaving together verbs with names' (*Soph.*, 262d) – occurs in several parts of the dialogues. For instance, in the *Timaeus*, Plato asserts that 'the river of speech [λόγων νάμα], which flows out of a man and ministers to the intelligence [ὑπηρετοῦν φρονήσει], is the fairest and noblest of all streams' (75e). Plato's voice, however, becomes uncertain in the *Republic*, where the supremacy of 'words' over 'things' or 'actions' is questioned: 'Is it possible for anything to be realized in deed as it is spoken in word, is it the nature of things that action should partake of exact truth less than speech, even if some deny it?' (V, 473a). The equivocation of λόγος is brought forth in the *Cratylus* by exploring the relation between language and its patron god, Hermes: 'I should imagine that the name Hermes has to do with speech, and signifies that he is the interpreter (ἑρμηνεύς), or messenger, or thief, or liar, or bargainer; all that sort of thing has a great deal to do with language [λόγου]' (407e–408a).

The utter degradation of λόγος, however, manifests itself in Plato's late dialogues and the *Letters*; in the *Laws* we read that 'He who deems he is advancing his soul by speech [λόγοις], gifts, or compliances, and all the while makes it no better than it was before, may dream that he shows it honor, but in truth does it none' (V, 727a). And finally, in the *Seventh Letter*, having admitted that he has never composed a work on the subject to which he has devoted himself, because he thinks that 'there is no way of putting it in words like other studies', Plato repudiates λόγος as incompetent to illustrate the essential reality of things, 'because of the inadequacy of language [διὰ τὸ τῶν λόγων ἀσθενές]':

> Hence no intelligent man will ever be so bold as to put into language those things which his reason has contemplated [τὰ νενοημένα], especially not into a form that is unalterable – which must be the case with what is expressed in written symbols [καὶ ταῦτα εἰς ἀμετακίνητον, ὃ δὴ πάσχει τὰ γεγραμμένα τύποις].

(343a)

In a manner less grave but equally equivocal – in that a proposition is put forward which carries within it its own defeat, as it is immediately proved untenable – we read in the *Cratylus* again that if knowledge of things is not to be derived from language (names), things must be studied and investigated in themselves (439b). This might well sound like a progenitor of the empiricist exhortation 'to the things themselves' (which liberated modern philosophical and scientific thinking from its subservience not to Plato but to Aristotle), except that the inexorable remark of Socrates as to how can a thing be known if it is ever in motion and flux, blows up the whole artifice and leaves a gaping whole in the argument that sends all participants home to 'reflect well'.

To look into the middle dialogues where the precarious correlation between οὐσία (being) and λόγος (propositional language) is still valid, the common denominator of cognition and language seems to be the possibility of 'splitting up' and 'reassembling'. In the *Theaetetus*, it is closely argued that a thing has an account (λόγον) when it can be broken down into its component parts; conversely, an element, because it cannot be further divided, has no account and is therefore unknowable (202a–c). The signs used in speech to signify 'being' (οὐσίαν), as has been noted earlier, are of two types: names and verbs; by 'verb' is meant an expression which is applied to actions, and by 'name' the term refers to what performs these actions (*Soph.*, 261e–262a). That Plato's linguistic distinction of performer / performance (meant to 'signify' 'being') does not actually correspond to the binary opposition which *is* the λόγος of 'being' ('power to act or suffer') but concentrates on and analyses the one pole of the antithetical alternatives (thus effacing the 'receptivity' aspect), shows, I believe, a 'distancing' already intervening between his conception of reality and its representation in language.

The reciprocity of οὐσία and λόγος that, despite aberrations, constitutes one of the corner-stones of Platonic thinking, is reinstated with extreme forcefulness in modern times through Heidegger's 'ontological linguistics'. Not only in the seminal proposition which recognizes language as the 'house' of 'being', but throughout his work and especially in *On the Way to Language* and *Poetry, Language, Thought*, the correspondence between *being* and *logos* is given as an unshakable premise. Emphasizing that the relation between reality and language has been an object of investigation from the beginning of western thought, Heidegger concludes that the word *logos* 'speaks simultaneously as the name for Being and for Saying' (1971b:

80).⁹ In *Poetry, Language, Thought*, this self-evident relation is temporarily (and superficially) questioned: does grammatical syntax reflect ontological syntax? 'Or could it be that even the structure of the thing as thus envisaged is a projection of the framework of the sentence?' (1971a: 24). Heidegger's argumentation follows close upon the Cratylian paradigm, in a dual exposition of the 'natural' and 'conventional' theories of the origin of language: 'What could be more obvious than that man transposes his propositional way of understanding things into the structure of the thing itself?'. In subverting the notion which detects the projection of mental procedures onto natural processes, Heidegger resorts to professing scepticism: 'It even remains doubtful whether in this form the question is at all decidable' (1971a: 24). Despite his admission of ignorance Heidegger, in a manner quite unlike Plato's, continues with providing an answer by bypassing the question. He refers to a 'third' reality, the origin of 'sentence' and 'thing' as the source of both, which might be said to correspond to the Platonic idea, common sub- or super-structure of φαινόμενα and λόγος. Actually, he elaborates, 'Both sentence and thing-structure derive, in their typical form and their possible mutual relationship, from a common and more original source' (1971a: 24). The shared ground that Heidegger detects as underlying both semantics and pragmatics, appears to be a modern version of German Romantic philosophy – particularly that of Schelling – which recognizes the original identity of the 'one' activity producing world and mind; 'In any case', Heidegger avows, 'this unfamiliar source once struck man as strange and caused him to think and to wonder' (1971a: 24).

Within the sphere of *logos*, Heidegger distinguishes between the 'communicative' and 'revelatory' function of the linguistic utterance; the former, he argues, does not incorporate the whole potential of language, nor does it exhaust its resources – and resourcefulness – because 'language is not only and not primarily an audible and written expression of what is to be communicated' (1971a: 73). Such conceptual or 'everyday language is a forgotten and therefore used-up poem, from which there hardly resounds a call any longer' (1971a: 208), whereas in its pristine function 'Language, by naming beings for the first time, first brings being to word and to appearance. Only this naming nominates beings *to* their being *from out of* their being' (1971a: 73). Plato is less cryptic than Heidegger about this 'naming' of language; in fact, in making a definite distinction between *naming* and *stating*, he expressly differentiates the operation of λέγειν which 'gives information about facts or events in the present or past or future' and achieves all that 'by weaving together verbs with names', from the function of 'merely naming' or ὀνομάζειν (*Soph.* 262d). Despite his efforts at discrimination, however, the Greek language itself (Heideggerian fashion) 'speaks' ambiguously; the reason being the use of the term ὄνομα to denote both the generic εἶδος – 'word' – and the species, 'noun' (versus 'verb'). It is worth tracing a little further, I believe, this distinction between λέγειν and ὀνομάζειν in the Platonic text, with side-glances at Heidegger's parallel differentiation between *speaking* and *naming* (or *saying*). For Plato, the operations of λέγειν and ὀνομάζειν although distinct are homologizable, in that they both rely on the activity of 'blending' or 'weaving', and in that they reflect the coalescence of Ideas.

The art that regulates 'naming' is the γραμματικὴ τέχνη (art of letters); that which presides over 'being' is the διαλεκτικὴ τέχνη, the art of 'gathering' and 'dividing', the method conducive to the vision of the Ideas. The logistics of the argument in its simplest form should go something like this: as with γραμματικὴ τέχνη (the art of blending sounds) so with διαλεκτικὴ τέχνη (the art of blending – or recognizing the blending of – Ideas). Speaking about the εἴδη, the Stranger in the *Sophist* admits that 'since some will blend, some not, they might be said to be in the same case with the letters [γράμματα] of the alphabet. Some of these cannot be conjoined; others will fit together' (252e–253a). The analogy of 'forms' to phonemes (or letters) having been established, an art, or science, parallel to 'grammar' (or phonology) is sought to facilitate the inquiry into the ways in which Ideas interfuse with one another – 'harmony' being the determining factor in both cases. Investigation into the dynamic inter-penetration of forms discloses the necessity of 'method', or a codifying system that will serve as a compass in the exploration of 'being' undertaken through 'logos'; consequently, the Stranger urges,

> is not some science needed as a guide on the voyage of discourse [τῶν λόγων], if one is to succeed in pointing out which kinds are consonant, and which are incompatible with

one another – also, whether there are certain kinds that pervade them and connect them so that they can blend, and again where there are divisions [separations], whether there are certain others that traverse wholes and are responsible for the division?

(253b)

These 'connecting links' the grammar of letters uncovers to be the 'vowels', which are 'specifically good at combination', and a kind of 'bond' pervading all sounds ('letters of the alphabet'), 'so that without a vowel the others cannot be fitted together' (253a). The analogue to 'vowel' that the art of dialectic discovers – the connecting medium between Ideas – is 'being' (ὄν, existence) and its 'other', 'non-being' (as ἕτερον or difference) (254b–e). Furthermore, if γραμματική is the art of 'naming' (blending of sounds) and διαλεκτική the art of 'being' (blending of forms), there is yet a third 'skill' that conduces to the exploration of reality, the art of language proper or λόγος, i.e. ῥητορικὴ τέχνη. The field of this art / science of rhetoric is 'words [περὶ λόγους]' (Gorgias, 449d), and the objective of this τῶν λόγων τέχνη is 'a kind of influencing of the mind by means of words' (*Phaedr.*, 261a); the methodology to be employed by the verbal art, if it aspires to success, is precisely the same gathering / dividing practice of the dialectical method (273d–e). The root metaphor of 'blending' or 'weaving' that underlies 'being', 'naming', and 'speaking' emphasizes a common ground or structural analogy between the ontological and the two linguistic modes. 'Name' and 'definition' are two corresponding and complementary ways of 'speaking' reality (*Laws*, X, 895d). Nevertheless, ὄνομα plays an enigmatic role, in that whereas it is a component of λόγος, it is itself a complex of sounds ('unit' and 'compound' simultaneously). Plato's assertion that a thing has an account (λόγον) only when it can be broken down into its constituents, and the paradoxical assumption that the indivisible is unknowable, seems to place 'letters' (i.e. phonemes) as well as Ideas beyond the range of 'logical' cognition.

It is characteristic of the manner in which Plato approaches 'naming' that on all occasions when the γραμματικὴ τέχνη receives attention, the condition of 'unreality' is introduced as a significant context – as for instance in the archaic myth of the Egyptian Theuth, father of logos (*Philebus*, 18b–d) or in the

Theaetetus. Socrates' discussion of 'grammatology' is set within a realm of 'dream' and *différance* – twice removed from the original – in that his utterance is a reported speech, and what is more, conditioned by the unreliability of a subjective impression:

> If you have had a dream, let me tell you mine in return. I seem to have heard some people say that what might be called the first elements of which we and all other things consist are such that no account can be given of them. Each of them just by itself can only be named; we cannot attribute to it anything further or say that it exists or does not exist, for we should at once be attaching to it existence or non-existence, whereas we ought to add nothing if we are to express just it alone.
>
> (*Theaet.*, 201d–202a)

The introduction of predication, Plato alleges in the *Theaetetus*, creates a complex situation which falsifies the simplicity and uniqueness of a first principle. Hence,

> there is no formula in which an element can be expressed; it can only be named, for a name is all there is that belongs to it. But when we come to things composed of these elements, then, just as these things are complex, so the names are combined to make a description (λόγος), a description being precisely a combination of names.
>
> (202b)

Here the double function of ὄνομα is emphasized as both 'unit' and 'complex' – unknowable as a particle (of the sentence) yet knowable as a compound (of letters); it is a paradoxical, ineffable cognition, a 'true notion' yet unspeakable, an 'unbeknown' thought – which drives a wedge between 'truth' and 'exposition' as much as between 'thinking' and 'knowing':

> Accordingly, elements are inexplicable [ἄλογα] and unknowable, but they can be perceived, while complexes ('syllables') are knowable and explicable, and you can have a true notion [δόξῃ] of them. So when a man gets hold of the true notion of something without an account [ἄνευ λόγου], his mind does think truly of it [ἀληθεύειν], but he does not know it [γιγνώσκειν δ' οὔ], for if one cannot give and receive an account [λόγον] of a thing, one has no

knowledge of that thing. But when he has also got hold of an account, all this becomes possible to him and he is fully equipped with knowledge [ἐπιστήμην].

Does that version represent the dream as you heard it, or not?

(202b–c)

The assertion that only that which has 'parts' can be known (knowledge presumably consisting in the capacity of dismantling and reassembling the thing – the precise operation of dialectic), turns the thinker into a puzzle player who deals with 'unknown' units that he can only shift around and thus find out how they fit, or mis-fit.

Conclusively, whereas the knowledge conveyed through λέγειν is secure and irrefutable, as the 'giving overt expression to one's thought by means of vocal sound with names and verbs, casting an image of one's notion on the stream that flows through the lips, like a reflection in a mirror or in water' (206d), ὀνομάζειν still remains very much in the twilight realm of dreaming and hearsay. The *Theaetetus* ends in suspended judgement, subverting all proposed 'definitions' of knowledge as 'mere wind eggs and not worth the rearing' (210b). Socrates' farewell message to Theaetetus is to 'conceive afresh' his 'embryo thoughts' in the barrenness of the intellectual waste land where he has been plunged – which will procure self-knowledge in humility, having dispersed the fallacy that he knows what he does not know. As Socrates leaves for the court to make his apology and arranges a meeting with the group for the following morning, he expounds the infinite possibilities as well as the limitations of yet another 'art', the μαιευτικὴ τέχνη, the midwife's or the teacher's craft:

> For that, and no more, is all my art can effect; nor have I any of that knowledge possessed by all the great and admirable men of our own day or of the past. But this midwife's art is a gift from heaven; my mother had it for women, and I for young men of a generous spirit and for all in whom beauty dwells.
>
> (210c–d)

If on the whole, competent handling of the 'divisions' and 'collections' of *logos* gives man the power to speak and to think (*Phaedr.*, 266b), the art of *naming*, also dealing with the 'spoken' word, is presented in a light that both grants and withholds meaning from its utterances. The true 'artists' of 'naming' are the legislators (*Crat.*, 389a), while dialecticians are only 'users' of names (*Crat.*, 390c–d); and it only takes a statement like Shelley's that 'Poets are the unacknowledged legislators of the world' (1954: 297), to make the transition from the Platonic ὀνομάζειν to the Heideggerian 'naming' which, I believe, is not only its distant echo, but illuminates the double discourse in Plato's dialogues – the alternation of the rational and the mythical as a 'weaving' of λέγειν and ὀνομάζειν, 'thinking' and 'poetizing'.

For Heidegger, the poet 'names' what is holy. Such 'naming' he also defines as a 'saying', the 'speaking names' where the speaker is language itself rather than its 'user', man (1971a: 198). This 'saying' is 'song' or 'poetry: 'For the God Orpheus, who lives in-finitely in the Open, song is an easy matter, but not for man', he contests (1971a: 139). Man's everyday speaking or language production 'stands in the assertion of calculating propositions and of the theorems of the reason that proceeds from proposition to proposition. The realm of self-assertive unshieldedness is dominated by reason', Heidegger thus pronounces the 'fall' of language (1971a: 132–3). Human 'speaking' (logos) can be transferred to 'saying' (naming) when a 'venturing' with language is attempted, Heideggerian linguistics sustains. This 'daring' into language is a penetration into the precinct of Being, whose 'house' language is (1971a: 133–4). Such 'conversion of consciousness' is what Heidegger calls the realm of the 'Open' (1971a: 106) and the realm of 'poetry'. We are not prepared for the interpretation of poems, he states, 'since the realm from which they speak, in its metaphysical constitution and unity, has not yet been sufficiently thought out in terms of the nature of metaphysics'; so the difficulty with poetry arises 'because we barely know the nature of metaphysics and are not experienced travellers in the land of the saying of Being' (1971a: 98). Poetry as the 'saying' of 'being'[10] (I believe the structural ambiguity that renders Being both subject and predicate is intentional) must be approached cautiously, 'because the realm in which the dialogue between poetry and thinking goes on can be discovered, reached, and explored in thought only slowly. Who today', Heidegger asks, 'would presume to claim that he is at home with the nature of poetry as well as with the nature of thinking and, in addition, strong enough to bring the nature of the two into the most extreme discord and so to establish their concord?' (1971a: 98).

It is my firm conviction that this is precisely what the Platonic text does: it embodies a commerce and discourse of thinking and poetry, 'speaking' and 'saying', λέγειν and ὀνομάζειν, or λόγος and μῦθος ('likely story' which cannot define what things 'are' but what they are 'like'). As such, the Platonic text fully fulfils the Heideggerian postulate for a discourse that unravels the 'story' of Being: 'That is the course of the history of Being. If we reach and enter that course, it will lead thinking into a dialogue with poetry, a dialogue that is of the history of Being' (1971a: 96). The lost cohabitation that Heidegger seeks (both conceptually and stylistically) finds its last philosophical manifestation in the Platonic 'dialogues', to be forgotten since. 'Presumably part of the reason is that the two kinds of utterance *par excellence*, poetry and thinking, have not been sought out in their proper habitat, their neighborhood. Yet', Heidegger attempts to elicit significance out of a commonplace expression, 'we talk often enough about "poets and thinkers." By now, this phrase has become a vacuous cliché. Perhaps the "and" in "poetry and thinking" ', he tentatively formulates the cognitive possibilities of syntax, 'will receive its full meaning and definition if we will let it enter our minds that this "and" might signify the neighborhood of poetry and thought' (1971b: 81).

PLATONIC DIALOGUE AS PLAY

Plato's methodological approach to the 'saying' of 'being' encompasses precisely a double level of communication, an interplay between analytical argument and mythical event; the vast horizon of Platonic 'drama' houses argumentative conversation and fictional narration under the same textual roof. This phenomenon can partly be accounted for, I believe, by what H.-G. Gadamer says about the thinking habits of the Greeks: 'They did not seek to base the objectivity of knowledge on subjectivity. Rather, their thinking always saw itself as an element of being itself'; more specifically, 'The dialectic, this expression of the logos, was not for the Greeks a movement performed by thought, but the movement of the object itself that thought experiences' (1975: 418). Awareness of the object-in-motion (which is precisely Plato's definition of σοφία, wisdom), the follow-up of what is actually happening, careful observation of things coming and going – the sharp consciousness of what *is* focusing on the object with a balanced and relaxed mind – bring 'logical thinking' and 'mythical narrative' into a close relation of two parallel motions, a 'dialogue' of λόγος and μῦθος (or Apollo and Dionysus) that is a reciprocal or 'significant conversation'.

That the movement of thought is a tracing (unwavering observation) of 'object' or ὄν, means a constant sensitiveness to the event of present 'being', or noticing the flow of things. This confluence of processional imagery and silent awareness, of the 'narrating' and 'witnessing' mind, becomes, I believe, the underlying energy of the Platonic text, and the highest form of intelligence which the text expounds. Even the distinction between λόγος as true story and μῦθος as fiction is blurred in the *Dialogues*; not only is the word 'mythos' wherever it appears almost invariably accompanied by 'logos', but the relation between the two is not clearly established as one of antithesis. When challenged by Phaedrus to confess whether he believed a story (μυθολόγημα), Socrates in his usual manner makes an equivocal answer of belief / disbelief, admitting that he should be quite in the fashion if he dismissed the story (as the men of science do) while professing willingness to give a scientific account – just like those who, sceptical about the 'truth' of myths, try all the time to reach the 'real truth',

> about the appearance of centaurs and the Chimera, not to mention a whole host of such creatures, Gorgons and Pegasuses and countless other remarkable monsters of legend flocking in on them. If our skeptic, with his somewhat crude science, means to reduce every one of them to the standard of probability, he'll need a deal of time for it. I myself have certainly no time for the business, and I'll tell you why, my friend. I can't as yet 'know myself,' as the inscription at Delphi enjoins, and so long as that ignorance remains it seems to me ridiculous to inquire into extraneous matters. Consequently I don't bother about such things, but accept the current beliefs about them, and direct my inquiries, as I have just said, rather to myself, to discover whether I really am a more complex creature and more puffed up with pride than Typhon, or a simpler,

gentler being whom heaven has blessed with a quiet, un-Typhonic nature.

(*Phaedr.*, 229d–230a)

Despite Socrates' apparent admission of indifference, the Platonic text 'says' about the relevance of myth to self-knowledge through the metaphorical utterances it makes. And even without modern testimony – as for instance C. Jung who claims that myth and psyche are co-extensive, or that the soul's mode of expression is a dramatic narrative of images – the invitation of the Delphic oracle inciting human consciousness to self-examination, encapsulates the fundamental imperative of Greek culture: the γνῶθι σαυτόν, the conscious return to the unconscious, or the 'unnoticed'. Socrates answers the call in realizing that always and ultimately, every affair is an affair with self; 'knowing oneself' seems to be the foremost occupation for him, i.e. using the known self to learn about and relate to the unknown selves, the various parts that constitute the structure of the soul. Socrates / Plato recognizes that the self knowing itself, the subject which is its own object, the fusion of being and knowing, is the greatest of all mysteries; it is the 'mythos' of logos – or 'logos' of mythos.

The opening of the *Timaeus*, the Platonic myth par excellence, is a statement of cosmological fable which, bypassing what Socrates' 'sceptics' would have called 'scientific' truth, points towards both psychological and spiritual reality. Within the narrative plot of the Platonic dialogues, the *Timaeus* follows upon the *Republic*, so in the opening scene Socrates not only counts the people who having been his guests the day before are to be his entertainers today, but refers to the basic theme of the *Republic* as the 'mixing' of opposites in the soul, the 'gentle' and the 'fierce' (*Tim.*,18a). He admits that drafting the 'structure' of the ideal city has left him unsatisfied, and that what he longs for is to see the pattern 'dramatized':

> I might compare myself to a person who, on beholding beautiful animals either created by the painter's art, or, better still, alive but at rest, is seized with a desire of seeing them in motion or engaged in some struggle or conflict to which their forms appear suited – this is my feeling about the state which we have been describing.
>
> (19b–c)

As a sequence to his *logos* Socrates demands a *mythos*, a 'logos' translated into 'play' – or better 'motion-picture'.

The verbal entertainment offered to Socrates – not a 'formal design' but a cinematic 'moving image' according to his wish – is an ancient oral tradition (παλαιᾶς ἀκοῆς); it is simultaneously a 'monument of gratitude' to the instructor by his pupils, and a hymn to the goddess (Athena) 'on this her day of festival'. Between the original source of the story and the present narration – as is usual with Plato – intervene a number of mediators that distance the 'now' from the primal event. The story itself is the myth of Atlantis and the 'archaeology' of the city of Athens founded by the goddess who, in the Egyptian priest's words, 'is the common patron and parent and educator of both our cities' (23d). Critias, the speaker, terminates his account by drawing attention to the fact, the 'mysterious coincidence' of how the social stratification of the Socratic utopian republic 'agreed in almost every particular with the narrative of Solon' (the class division of Egyptian society into priests / warriors / artificers), which really 'answers' Socrates' request for a histrionic counterpart to his static city (25e–26a). Critias announces that he is ready now to tell 'the tale': 'The city and citizens which you yesterday described to us in fiction [ἐν μύθῳ] we will now transfer to the world of reality' (26c). The transposition from the 'ideal' to the 'historical', from the utopian πολιτεία to the ancient city of Athens, inheres an element of displacement, and the metaphorical transfer becomes a willing projection of belief that blurs the semantic boundaries of the 'logical' and the 'mythical'. To Critias' question if this narrative (λόγος) is suited to the purpose, Socrates makes the following reply: 'And what other, Critias, can we find that will be better than this which is natural and suitable to the festival of the goddess, and has the very great advantage of being a fact [ἀληθινὸν λόγον] and not a fiction [πλασθέντα μῦθον]?' (26e). So whereas fictional μῦθος corresponds to the discursive presentation of social and psychic structure in the *Republic*, the term λόγος is applied to archaic or mythical events.

The telling of the story of the ancient city of Athens never materializes, as the 'prelude' to it, Timaeus the astronomer's undertaking to 'begin at the beginning' and recount the creation of the world, seems to occupy the whole time – and space. The issue raised by Timaeus before he begins his κοσμογονία is the problem of the reliability of language to render meta-physical events. Timaeus exhibits no scepticism in his unwavering conviction that language is 'related' to reality (29b–d), in full agreement with the Cratylian argument that 'names are natural and not conventional' (*Crat.*, 383a). So μῦθος is the linguistic rendering of the moving image of eternity that is 'apprehended by reason and mind [λόγῳ καὶ φρονήσει περιληπτόν] and is unchangeable' (29a). Here the distinction between λόγος and μῦθος – both equally true 'to themselves' – is made on the grounds of motion and stasis. No matter how justified the correlation of motion / mythos may be, however, logos as that which 'gets us somewhere' could never be seen in static terms. As the whole range of the Platonic dialogues proves, the citing of 'probability' is as much the province of λόγος as of μῦθος, both bearing an exegetical relation to reality.

In his discussion of the relation between logos and mythos in the Platonic text, Gadamer examines the nature of dialectics which 'even within the dialogue it often explicitly assumes a hermeneutical character', not failing, however, to look into 'the reverse situation, namely the extent to which Plato's own myths belong to the dialectic and hence themselves bear the character of interpretation' (1975: 487). The critical moments when Plato chooses to introduce μῦθος into the dialogic process should mark myths as paradigmatic (i.e. eidetic) rather than eventful stories, an attitude which probably induced Aristotle to place poetry (the way of mythic utterance) on a status higher than that of history. Plato seems to resort to the analogical method of mythical expression when rational argument reaches the limits of its capacity. Myth somehow 'breaking in upon the logic of the Dialogue' (Stewart 1905: 83), makes logos 'leap' as it were beyond its own limitations; and if the certainty of the mythical images is often made questionable in the end, so is the seemingly unerring dialectical procedure. If we are to remember that Plato was the first to introduce 'gradations' of reality to the effect that for every level of cognition there is a corresponding level of 'being' that is known, then μῦθος and λόγος may simply be considered as conveying various cognitive modes, sharing however in the common character of 'motion' – οὐσία ὄντως οὖσα being 'beheld' neither by λόγος nor by μῦθος but by νοῦς (*Phaedr.*, 247c).

That Plato's myths, despite their seemingly archaic content, are attempts to render into pictorial terms man's dealings with himself – iconographies of the soul or stages in the process of self-knowledge – is supported by two of the most original, in my view, Platonic readers, Gadamer and J. H. Randall who in his *Plato: Dramatist of the Life of Reason* asserts: 'Platonic myths are not ways of stating what is hard to say in literal words – they are not allegories. Plato is perfectly capable of stating in precise terms what he wants to state'. Randall distinguishes between propositional and imaginative utterances as alternative approaches to cognition: 'Plato's myths are rather ways of making us *see* something; and of expressing and communicating what the seeing does to us' (1970: 199). Gadamer views the Platonic appropriation of mythical stories as an expression of 'the inner certainty of the soul' and as 'linked to the truth which the soul discovers in philosophizing'; as such Gadamer's treatment of the relation of μῦθος to λόγος in the Platonic dialogue stresses what I would call the analogy of the 'mytho-logical' to the 'logical' – a relation not of kinesis to stasis, but of movement to a 'premise', an Archimidean τόπος wherefrom the flow of a pictorial narrative can be observed: 'But the fact that this Socratic knowledge of one's own self is expressed in the form of a play of mythical images', Gadamer proposes, is an indication that 'Socrates encounters in his soul something inexplicable which resists illumination by the enlightenment that had succeeded in clearing up and destroying mythology' (1980: 68–9). Through this open trafficking, the to and fro movement from λόγος to μῦθος and vice versa, Plato hints at the nature of the philosophic quest itself: when the philosopher as logician comes up against an enforced silence, the philosopher as mythologist resorts to a different form of utterance in order to remain within the 'competence' of language. Having of necessity abandoned discursive speech and thought, and having gone as far as he can with the dialectical mode, Plato ventures into the twilight realm of the Orphic myth of the soul and its nature; his choice of a direct dramatic language, I believe, is dictated by the fact that myth is not an explanation but a re-enactment, a dramatized story – not a rational account but perhaps an 'account' (λόγος) in the Heraclitean sense of the word, which simultaneously invites and discourages self-knowledge, in stating that 'You will not find the limits of the soul by going, even if you travel over every way, so deep is its report [βαθὺν λόγον ἔχει]' (Heraclitus 1979: 44–5).

THE DIALOGUE FORM

The suggestion that the mind's (or soul's) colloquy with 'self' may lead to a dialogue with 'other' is present both in the Platonic text and in the texts of some of its interpreters. Gadamer, raising the question in connection with what he calls the historical transformation of *logos* from a linguistic to a metaphysical modality, opens the query into the semantics of conversation: 'It cannot be simply the Greek logos, the dialogue that the soul conducts with itself', he argues. 'On the contrary, the mere fact that logos is translated both by ratio and verbum is an indication that the phenomenon of language will become more important in the scholastic elaboration of Greek metaphysics than was the case with the Greeks themselves' (1975: 381) – of which, I believe, ample proof is that the cornerstone of Platonic philosophy is the ἰδέα (something to be seen) rather than the λόγος (something to be spoken). Gadamer traces the evolution of *logos* from the Greek human communication to the Christian divine manifestation: 'Is not the very antithesis between intuition and discursiveness in the way here? What is common to the one and the other "process"?' (1975: 383), he wonders.

It is precisely this historically accredited antithesis between the intuitive and the discursive approaches to reality that the Platonic διαλέγεσθαι – the soul's dialogue with self not as mental chatter but as a philosophical 'method' to 'truth' – undertakes to reconcile. As Gadamer puts it, 'Plato described thought as an inner conversation of the soul with itself, and the infiniteness of the dialectical effort that he requires of the philosopher is the expression of the discursiveness of our finite understanding' (1975: 382). Plato seems to maintain throughout that the culmination of vigorous focused 'thinking' leads to an immediately experienced vision of the ὄντως ὄν (that which really is) thus introducing a qualitative change in the manner of apprehension; he places the dialectician on an 'upward path' which is not a mere dialogic process but an intellectual – and emotive – discipline that results in knowledge. No matter how paradoxical it may sound, Platonic dialectic is a suppression of 'normal' dialogue. It begins, as already emphasized with 'absence', the subversion of well-known and established hypotheses about life and truth, and ends with 'knowing' truth as an unmediated 'presence'; its methodology 'division' into two and 'reconciliation' into one – a scientific or 'artistic' (dialectic being defined as an 'art') procedure that is a replica of cosmic processes.

Dialectic can be defined as the technique which begins by

inverting the traditional hierarchy of question and answer, and ends with an unquestionable recognition of the nature of reality that transcends all questioning. Its starting location is a 'conceptual dying', its finishing point 'perceptual rebirth'; its method: a relentless refutation of all accepted concepts, values, configurations. In his account of what he calls 'the hermeneutical priority of the question', Gadamer – unavoidably – begins with a discussion of the model introduced by the Platonic dialectic. He underlines the radical repudiation that marks the initiatory stages of the process, 'the famous Socratic docta ignorantia which opens up the way, amid the most extreme negativity of doubt, to the true superiority of questioning'. Gadamer recognizes that one of the greatest insights that Socrates as a dramatis persona of the Platonic dialogues affords is that, contrary to common sense assumptions, it is more difficult – and perhaps more important – to ask questions than to answer them. Socrates' awkward and seemingly unanswerable queries not only create a climate of comic relief, but reveal a basic absurdity which must be taken into consideration – together with the desire to deal with it. As he puts it, 'In order to be able to ask, one must want to know, which involves knowing that one does not know'; irony of structure and comedy of situation (and, why not, the tragedy of humiliation or injured pride) fuse. Evidently, 'Discourse that is intended to reveal something requires that that thing be opened up by the question' (1975: 326).

This 'opening up' or bringing into the open is in fact a bringing into the void, the state of indeterminacy and insecurity that marks the first stage of the dialectical process. The eradication of intellectual assurance and the spirit of conceit that it entails (in the one who supposes he knows and does not know) is the objective of the dialectical confutation or ἔλεγχος:

> For as the physician considers that the body will receive no benefit from taking food until the internal obstacles have been removed, so the purifier of the soul is conscious that his patient will receive no benefit from the application of knowledge until he is refuted, and from refutation learns modesty; he must be purged of his prejudices first and made to think that he knows only what he knows, and no more.
> (*Soph.*, 230c–d)

The Socratic – and Platonic – realization is that consciousness, very much like a sick body, must first be cleansed of prefabricated concepts and preconceived notions. In a sense, firm convictions about things create a world of 'shadows' that obscure one's clarity of vision; a mind full of presuppositions or 'habits' is a mind 'chained' to a world of thoughts and mental constructs, mistaking shadows or projections for reality itself. This veil of categorizations must be exploded, and an emptying of consciousness from its referential grounds achieved, as a necessary prerequisite to any further quest after truth – Plato definitely believing 'in a reality independent of our beliefs' (White 1976: 228). Dialectic begins in a complete breaking with security, recognizable patterns, old ways of thinking; gradually, the condition of utter scepticism and doubt is superseded, and from that initial uncertainty grows certainty, clarity. Because, Gadamer asserts, 'the art of testing is the art of questioning. For we have seen that to question means to lay open, to place in the open. As against the solidity of opinions, questioning makes the object and all its possibilities fluid. A person who possesses the "art" of questioning', he specifies, highlighting the linguistic / political aspect of the issue, 'is a person who is able to prevent the suppression of questions by the dominant opinion' (1975: 330).

Finding out all about the machinery, the network of habit, necessitates a 'letting go' or a 'letting flow', like a river which is moving; abandoning oneself to the inquiry to be carried along seems to be the Platonic dialectical secret of arriving somewhere: 'if we are completely baffled, then, I suppose, we must be humble and let the argument [τῷ λόγῳ] do with us what it will, like a sailor trampling over sea-sick passengers' (*Theaet.*, 191a). It is precisely this 'activity' of complete surrender to the inscrutable workings of language, where λόγος 'speaks' man rather than vice versa, that lurks behind not only the Platonic statement above, but also the Heraclitean axiom 'τοῦ λόγου δ' ἐόντος ξυνοῦ ζώουσιν οἱ πολλοὶ ὡς ἰδίαν ἔχοντες φρόνησιν (Although the account is shared, most men live as though their thinking were a private possession)' (Heraclitus 1979: 28–9), and the Heideggerian assumption that language is the 'master' of man. Heidegger still writes from within what Derrida calls the 'logocentric' tradition that has dominated western metaphysics since Plato,[11] in his assumption that language, and particularly Greek, can 'speak Being'. As we see, however, the problem is placed by Heidegger – and Plato – in a way that recognizes not only the primacy of speech over writing (a hierarchy that Derrida's deconstructive policy attempts to subvert – or, better, to invert) but the supremacy of the 'word' over its 'user' (philosophical subject). For Heidegger *language speaks* and man 'participates' in the speaking of language. The 'speaking' of language (in the full ambiguity of the proposition which echoes the similar Platonic practice of syntactical indeterminacy) is for Heidegger a simultaneous 'call' and an answer. Attempting a definition of λόγος, he comes up with the tautology that 'language is language'; this λόγος of λόγος, although not 'getting us anywhere' literally, and leaving us suspended in mid air, *does* however uncover a frame of reference: 'Language speaks. If we let ourselves fall into the abyss denoted by this sentence, we do not go tumbling into emptiness. We fall upward to a height', he professes, transposing the traditional scientific and religious parameters, in that 'Its loftiness opens up a depth' (1971a: 190–2).

The German philosopher gets close to the Platonic dialectical tactics, or the process whereby λόγος leads to ἰδέα, in the identification of 'saying' and 'showing' – where the 'vocal' and the 'visionary' become interchangeable terms (Coleridge's 'A light in sound, a sound-like power in light' ('The Eolian Harp', l. 28)): 'To say and to speak are not identical', he enunciates, launching into a desynonymization of verbal utterances: 'In order to find out, we must stay close to what our very language tells us to think when we use the word. "Say" means to show, to let appear, to let be seen and heard'. Escaping from the tautological definition of language, he ventures into a proper description of the 'being' of language, stressing its phenomenological character: *'The essential being of language is Saying as Showing'* (1971b: 122–3). Heidegger[12] emphasizes the latent dynamics of λόγος, which renders language not only the 'house' of being but also a 'bridge' towards it. By maintaining that speech is the vocalization of thought, he retains (while reversing) the Platonic definition of thought as inner speech (*Theaet.*, 189e–190a), and adds the dimension of self-directionality to language that we also find lurking both in the Socratic dialectical method and in the Platonic textual practice: 'Speaking is known as the articulated vocalization of thought by means of the organs of speech. But speaking is at the same time also listening'. The paradox that such a seemingly conventional proposition generates is in the displacement of the transmitter / receiver communicative model; here the speaker listens / speaks and the activity, or 'passivity', of listening precedes or coincides rather than follows upon verbal utterance: 'Speaking is of itself a listening. Speaking is listening to the language which we speak. Thus, it is a listening not *while* but *before* we are speaking' (1971b: 123).

This 'speaking' of language (as a 'subject') is presented by Plato through the 'organic' metaphor (a very Romantic choice indeed) of λόγους ἔχοντες σπέρμα; as used by the art of dialectic which is the 'serious treatment' of language, words are allowed to 'speak', i.e. to fully develop their inner dynamic or potential:

> The dialectician selects a soul of the right type, and in it he plants and sows his words founded on knowledge, words which can defend both themselves and him who planted them, words which instead of remaining barren contain a seed whence new words grow up in new characters, whereby the seed is vouchsafed immortality, and its possessor the fullest measure of blessedness that man can attain unto.
>
> (*Phaedr.*, 276e–277a)

In all this, Platonic dialectic as an earnest encounter of man with λόγος (although the precise term used by Plato is παιδιά and παίζειν – playing, a verbal game – and the word rendered as 'serious' in the English translation is καλλίων, comparative of καλός – beautiful) appears not merely as an abstract method of reasoning but something expressing the philosopher's absorption – with his entire personality, intellectual and emotional – into the dialogic activity. Plato often emphasizes the exertion required in dialectical thought, which brings 'conversation' to the farthest reaches of mental capacity – and beyond:

> In like manner, when anyone by dialectic attempts through discourse of reason and apart from all perceptions of sense to find his way to the very essence of each thing [διὰ τοῦ λόγου ἐπ' αὐτὸ ὃ ἔστιν ἕκαστον ὁρμᾶν] and does not desist till he apprehends by thought [νοήσει] itself the nature of the good in itself, he arrives at the limit of the

intelligible, as the other in our parable came to the goal of the visible.

(*Rep.*, VII, 532a–b)

The dialectical process is marked, as already pointed out, by two crucial transitional points or *rites de passage* (to use the language of mythos): a wound to self-confidence and loss of self-composure at the very beginning of the intellectual 'ordeal', and a condition of amazement and confusion that the communication with a 'concealed' reality stimulates in the initiate; such is the 'perplexity' of the *Meno* (84a–c) and the 'amazement' in the *Phaedrus* (250a), that once more stress the affinity between philosophic 'madness' and the poetic 'enthusiasm' as expressed in the *Ion* (533e–534c).

Platonic dialectic is an 'art' that ultimately secures a relationship between a 'known' and an 'unknown', or, to make the terms of the relationship more complex but closer to the situation as it 'really is', between an 'unknowing knower' and an 'unknown known'. It begins as a trans-personal dialogue that conduces to arduous 'in-personal' exercise, and then reaches into the unfamiliar region where one listens to – or looks at – more than the echo of his own solitary being. It effects a 'rapport' with a forgotten 'knowledge' and in that it is re-cognition; as such, it bears the mark of authentic dialogue, i.e. dialogue in which other than just the ego is doing some of the 'listening' and 'talking', where 'new' information filters into the horizon of habitual awareness. So the dialogue of the mind with self extends to a dialogue of the mind with otherness (an 'unremembered' modality of being). Mind-as-thinker is finally transformed to mind-as-observer when διάνοια, the to and fro motion (διά indicating movement through, over), turns to νόησις – the vision of Ideas. Here spiritual development is not a matter of suppressing anything but a re-discovering what is there, through a process of un-learning preconceptions and relinquishing the emotional 'aura' that surrounds them, deconstructing customary attitudes of relating to the world. The mode of being contemplated by the power of dialectic is 'something truer and more exact than the object of the so-called arts and sciences whose assumptions are arbitrary starting points' (*Rep.*, VII, 511c). The strategy of dialectic is a method of undoing; through the motion of λόγος) all δόξες – concepts, stereotyped patterns of thinking, the labelling of phenomena – come to an end; dialectic is 'the only process of inquiry that advances in this manner, doing away with hypotheses, up to the first principle itself in order to find confirmation there' (VII, 533c). The dialectical exercise allows the practitioner to begin being aware of the experiential, non-conceptual level of things as they are, free from accepted conventions or 'hypotheses' about them; it leads to the viewing of reality, the perception of something beyond thought – as Plato puts forward in what he calls an 'indisputable proposition', that there is no 'other way of inquiry that attempts systematically and in all cases to determine what each thing really is' (VII, 533b).

While all the other arts and sciences are 'dreaming about being', dialectic only affords 'the clear waking vision' (VII, 533b–c) that allows things to be as they are. The mind of the philosopher is a mind entirely unfettered by presuppositions, conclusions, concepts – it uncovers what actually is, not a utopian 'should be'; it deals with the whole complex problem of 'being', i.e. of living. Coming upon truth can only be achieved through the 'purifying' (or annihilating) procedure which renders mind the clarity needed to perceive – beyond any assumption – what is, τὸ ὄντως ὄν; seeing things as they are entails an imaginative leap that Plato defines as 'a blaze kindled' in the soul which brings 'the nature of things to light [τὴν φύσιν εἰς φῶς πᾶσιν προαγαγεῖν]' (*Letts.*, VII, 341c–d). Despite his great reluctance to speak about such matters, he avows that 'sudden' enlightenment comes only after a long period of familiarity and 'dwelling' with the 'object', and is immediately preceded by a state of exhaustion; finally, this stage falls away exposing the luminous quality of Form. In the absence of hypotheses, the brilliance of *what is* is immediately perceived by a mind that is very precise and vivid (VII, 344b); it is the light, the peace, the repose, the coolness that supersedes the intensity of the intellectually erotic or erotically intellectual stage.

Plato leaves no room for doubt as to the epistemological / ontological priority of the question form, the chief tool of his dialectical art; the emergence of consciousness (of the Ideas) is concomitant upon the practice of questioning. Question, ἀπορία, generates awareness; answer, certitude, establishes boundaries and produces stasis, stagnation. Statements, definitions anaesthetize consciousness, whereas anything that is in a question form alerts (and alarms) the mind in that it points towards an 'unknown', a mystery. Answers 'freeze' reality, whereas questions permit it to flow freely again. Thus, it is not at all surprising that Plato should adopt a textual stylistics whereby the 'question' itself remains alive in the answer (Friedländer 1958: 136) and breaks through the finality of the static format of the written text, by adopting the conversational or dramatic method. As W. Pater very pertinently observes, the Platonic dialogues present 'a paradox, or a reconciliation of opposed tendencies: on one side, the largest possible demand for infallible certainty in knowledge . . . yet, on the other side, the utmost possible inexactness, or contingency, in the method by which actually he proposes to attain it'; stressing Plato's fascination with the word 'κινδυνεύει "it may chance to be" ', Pater proclaims that 'The philosopher of Being, or, of the verb "to be," is after all afraid of saying, "It is" ' (1925: 188–9). Translated into modern philosophical terms, the problem might sound something like this: 'The question Was Plato a Hume or a Kant? is an open question' (Ryle 1966: 7).

The dialogue appears to be the only kind of writing which undermines the rigidity of the 'book' and keeps surfaced the struggle between dialectical tensions.[13] It allows Plato to present contradictory points of view in a tentative manner 'without being personally committed to their content'; indeed, many of the dialogues 'wear an outer face of enigma' (Findlay 1974: 5). Such methodology makes philosophic literature an 'event' rather than a conceptual exposition.[14] Above all, Plato seeks the dialogue form in order to maintain παρουσία, precisely the (human) 'presence' for which Derrida has severely criticized the logocentric tradition whose origins he detects in the Platonic text. The 'dialogue' is a formal reproduction of a belief (or knowledge) that 'truth must live in present consciousness and cannot live anywhere else' (Murdoch 1977: 21); it portrays a basic attitude of being present right here. The goal is also the technique, the truth, the method: staying grounded in the present moment – in the asking, the answering, the discourse. Learning entails being active in the present, engaged 'in dialogue' with 'being'; and that is not possible when the mind is 'burdened' with all the ὑποθέσεις of given knowledge. Allowing oneself to be submerged in the living situation of what is, involves a 'letting be' of the play of actual circumstances, free from the fixed conditioning patterns.

The Platonic dialogues testify to what it means to be in the actuality of the present as process and interaction. Written in a form of 'play' – in the full multi-dimensional sense of the word – they display the inseparability of playfulness and seriousness, or rather the transvaluation of what we normally attribute to 'important' work and 'trivial' play. Having asserted that 'man's life is a business which does not deserve to be taken too seriously' (*Laws*, VII, 803b), Plato not only makes the strange proposition that man has been 'constructed as a toy for God' – which in fact is 'the finest thing about him' – but demands a 'complete inversion of current theory', a radical transformation of social practices that will permit 'men – and women' to perform their 'role' and spend life in making their *play* as perfect as possible:

> What, then, is our right course? We should pass our lives in the playing of games – *certain* games, that is, sacrifice, song, and dance – with the result of ability to gain heaven's grace, and to repel and vanquish an enemy when we have to fight him.
>
> (*Laws*, VII, 803d–e)

In Plato's sense of the word, 'play' is ritual and exploration; it is also experimentation as a dealing with reality in both its 'spiritual' and 'martial' aspects. My proposition is that this 'power of play' or 'play of power' is engrafted into the text through the dramatic (Dionysian) method employed; one can trace in the *Dialogues* the parallel development of formal dialectical practices and ritual enactment techniques, which result in the paradoxical coexistence of a full daylight consciousness along with a submerged, 'twilight' state of mind. Play and playfulness are deeply valued by Plato not only in his recognition of the sacredness of ceremonial 'representation' but in his own employment of the dramatic form, which renders to philosophic prose the Bacchic state of exultation, the μανία that delivers mind from its conditional bonds; the difference being that this release leads not to ἔκ-στασις but to ἔν-στασις, a conscious 'standing within', an awareness of simultaneous positioning in-and-out of (human) time.

Gadamer defines the subtleties of this ecstatic / enstatic alternative in terms of the 'presence' of the spectator who is part of the play of art: 'To be present, as a subjective act of a human attitude, has the character of being outside oneself'; forgetfulness of self, he explains, 'is anything but a primitive condition, for it arises from the attention to the object, which is the positive act of the spectator' (1975: 111). 'Ritual' and 'dialectic' meet in the Platonic concept of θεωρία which carries the sense of sacral communion (θεωρός being a state ambassador to the oracles or games) even when used as a 'looking upon' the Ideas. Gadamer expounds the full range of vision / participation or 'passive activity' that the term inheres; θεωρία seems to be simultaneously passive action or active passivity in its essential character of receptivity / attention. 'Theoria', he contends, 'is a true sharing, not something active, but something passive (pathos), namely being totally involved in and carried away by what one sees. It is from this point that people have tried recently to explain the religious background of the Greek idea of reason' (1975: 111). 'Theoretical' involvement implies a synchronicity of attachment / detachment; an alteration of consciousness which, with an appropriate meditative approach, can be 'consciously' experienced. It can be directed into a devotional, formalized representation by giving full attention to an extended 'play' while retaining the aloofness of spectator. The Platonic text, through its dramatic structure, both imparts and demands this kind of theoretical vision. In staging for us 'philosophical dramas', Plato not only partly fulfils his youthful attraction to the writing of tragedies; his 'theatrical' presentation of philosophy reflects his awareness of life as a dramatic play, as θέατρον (theatre in Greek meaning a place for seeing, or a possible show of / for the divine, due to the vocal proximity of θέα, view, and θεός / θεά, god / goddess). So the dramatic technique is not a mere literary device in the dialogues but is in fact an essential part of Plato's philosophy; it sets down 'drama' as the structural model of ontological / psychological / textual reality and, one might argue, the norm of philosophical prose from which there has been a gradual alienation. Plato's dramatic method employs the language of common speech, the words of everyday human concern, and elevates them into an 'organon' for the hunting of 'being'. The dialogues themselves reveal that for Plato the location of 'being' is the field of discourse and human experience, in both its external and internal forms.[15]

'Aeschylus, Sophocles, and Euripides depicted the dramatic qualities of human emotions, the play and conflict of his passions', Randall argues; 'They held them up for contemplation, as a spectacle for *theōria*. Plato, it can be said, depicts the dramatic qualities of man's thinking, the play and conflict of his ideas, the spectacle of his mind. Plato', he emphasizes, 'raised the Greek passion for seeing life as it is to the level of philosophy, to the vision of the realm of ideas – which has its abode, not in some impossible Heaven, but in the discourse of men – in men talking – in the drama of the Life of Reason' (1970: 3). Plato, I believe, both supports and refutes Randall's critical estimate when in the *Phaedo* he asserts the 'drama of consciousness' as a ψυχομαχία, an inner debate not of 'ideas' but of antithetical emotional polarities, where the whole – ψυχή – is 'conversing with the desires and passions and fears as though it were quite separate and distinct from them' (94d). The Platonic psychodrama, unlike its contemporary tragedies, may be seen as a conscious, earnest and devoted play or discourse not 'between' but 'with' the antagonistic forces that rage in the human soul. The possibility of impassively 'conversing' with passions, the contemplation of the 'drama of personality' enacted on the inner stage, gives to the 'Platonic tragicomedy' a dimension absent from its contemporary counterparts: it incorporates the 'spectator' component into the dramatic text itself, not in self-forgetfulness but in full attentive awareness. Relating to or interacting with passions is different from and contrasted to the usual approach of acting them out – or suppressing them; such bearing witness to psychic structure implies an actual encounter with emotional tensions, a working with them, a getting to know their 'texture', their power-graph, their 'idea'. It is neither an escape nor a releasing, but rather an actual experience of mental states *as they are*. What Plato suggests is that the (tripartite) psychic compound is a given, and can be dealt with or modified only by accepting it and attending to it. Play or conversation mobilizes and harmonizes the powers of the psyche; it gives 'form' to raw energy, in fact it uncovers the fundamental nature of passions *as* energy, and the possibility of relating with energy, the δύναμις that is the λόγος of οὐσία.

The soul teeming with countless self-contradictions (*Rep.*, X, 603c–d) is a fragmented – and tormented – entity, laying emphasis on one function and disregarding the other segments, which ultimately leads to conflict and great confusion, because each aspect (sensuous, affective, intellectual) demands a 'space' for self-expression; out of that faction and disharmony tragedy arises. Plato gives his clearest 'symbolic image of the soul' in the *Republic*:

Mold then, a single shape of a manifold and many-headed beast that has a ring of heads of tame and wild beasts and can change them and cause to spring forth from itself all such growths. . . . Then fashion one other form of a lion and one of a man and let the first be far the largest and the second second in size. . . . Join the three in one, then, so as in some sort to grow together. . . . Then mold about them outside the likeness of one, that of the man, so that to anyone who is unable to look within but who can see only the external sheath it appears to be one living creature, the man.

(IX, 588c–e)

The reality of 'maniness' hidden under the appearance of 'one' must be reckoned with, 'played' with, or 'discoursed' with. The outcome of such dealings with the underground creatures is 'justice' (δικαιοσύνη) which does not at all refer to interpersonal transactions but to the inner harmony of the soul, whereby each of the three principles is allowed to perform its work without interference by the others. Thus 'having linked and bound all three together and made of himself a unit, one man instead of many' (IV, 443e), 'he will have but one allotted portion, even as he has reduced the manifold within himself to unity, and in it will be happy, wise, blessed, all in one' (*Epinomis*, 992b); so he reproduces or rather re-collects the state of contemplation of true being, when man was 'initiated into that mystery which is rightly accounted blessed beyond all others', being 'whole and unblemished' (*Phaedr.*, 250b–c).

How is the overcoming of fragmentary existence to be effected by a mind that has broken up its 'steady' flow into divisible compartments and functions? How is such awareness of the totality of psyche to emerge, the looking at the whole of consciousness completely – which means to be a unified being in a simultaneous holding of plurality? Holistic observation, inclusive in that it recognizes and accepts the internal manifold (the snake-like and the lion-like), and in 'accepting' opening up the possibility of interplay among alienated forces, is described by Plato as the condition of the soul that concentrates itself by itself (*Phaedo*, 67c–d); because sense perception allowing a view of the external 'case' only but not the inner complexity, the Platonic philosophy points out that αἴσθησις is deceptive, and urges the soul to refrain from using the senses, but to collect and bring itself together – αὐτὴν δὲ εἰς αὑτὴν συλλέγεσθαι καὶ ἀθροίζεσθαι (83a). Change of attitude and total attention to the goings-on within is defined not only in terms of 'gathering' and 'concentrating', but also as μεταστροφή (a turning from one thing to another) and περιαγωγή (a going round, a revolution). The soul 'collects' the many fragments in perpetual conflict with one another, and observes itself as a complete and indivisible whole. Such inclusive apprehension circumscribes contradictions with their destructive energy, and allows a totally new modality of being to emerge. The mind that has turned upon itself in a maximum of attention and intensity suffers no fragmentation or 'wasting' of energy; 'like the scene-shifting periactus in the theater' the organ of knowledge is turned around, 'until the soul is able to endure the contemplation of essence and the brightest region of being [εἰς τὸ ὂν καὶ τοῦ ὄντος τὸ φανότατον]. And this, we say, is the good, do we not?' (*Rep.*, VII, 518c).

The indwelling power that comes to the forefront of consciousness when the incessant generative motion of 'ideas' subsides, Plato metaphorically defines as an 'eye', a kind of intuitive perception, a basic ground of awareness; this all-seeing eye is 'other' than the fragmented ego-eye. Ego is transmuted into a primordial intelligence that shines through in the vision of that which is 'good' – not a moral good as the opposite of evil, but an ontological good that knows no opposition in that it transcends categorial distinctions. The final truth accessible to 'turned around' soul is the awareness of παρουσία, that conscious 'presence' in which 'becoming' (looking and listening) occurs, in which 'being' dwells. In this witnessing presence that is ἐπέκεινα τῆς οὐσίας, there seems to be a great clarity, a brightness where the soul discovers the unchanging ground of its being. It is only on account of the direction of attention again and again towards becoming (what is to become), Plato argues, that mind fails to notice what is nearer and clearer, 'essence and the brightest region of being', that spacious stage in which images appear. Heidegger also refers to the reciprocity between 'light' and 'being' in the following terms: '*Enargeia*, which has the same root as *argentum* (silver), means that which in itself and of itself radiates and brings itself to light. In the Greek language', he explains, 'one is not speaking about the action of seeing, about *videre*, but about that which gleams and radiates'; still, he adds, 'it can only radiate if openness has already been granted' (1972: 66).

The Platonic dialogues are not portrayals of the life of the mind only, in the narrow 'intellectual' sense that the word denotes. By exhibiting a phenomenology of the soul whereby the possibility of a dialectic of transcendence is established (transcendence not by suppressing actuality but by probing deeper into it), the Platonic text hints towards a condition of total understanding of the anatomy of existence with all its extraordinary complexity. To this 'closed circle of meaning' Gadamer attributes the term 'drama'; life and art are realized as forms of play, homologizable versions of non-teleological movement: 'In these cases, in which reality is understood as a play, there emerges what the reality of play is, which we call the play of art. The being of all play is always realization, sheer fulfilment, energeia which has its telos within itself' (1975: 101).

In his effort to retrieve the question of artistic truth that, as his conviction is, has been superseded by scientific knowledge, Gadamer begins Chapter II of Part One, Truth and Method, entitled 'The ontology of the work of art and its hermeneutical significance', by investigating the concept of 'play' as a 'clue' to ontology and aesthetics (1975: 91–119) – an interpretation 'trailing clouds of glory', I believe, from the cryptic fragment of Heraclitus, that 'Lifetime is a child at play, moving pieces in a game. Kingship belongs to the child' (1979: 71). Adopting the binary opposition of serious / playful, Gadamer makes a distinction between the 'player' whose attitude is precisely marked by a lack of seriousness, and the 'play' itself which has its own, separate relation to what is essential. In undertaking to play, the player is aware of a deviation from the usual worldly occupations marked by earnestness of purpose; but it is paradoxically in this loss of intentionality that a relatedness with what is significant is established.

The 'mode of being' of play and the 'mode of being' of the work of art, Gadamer asserts, are similar in function in inverting the subject / object polarity. Initiative is withdrawn from its expected location, the human 'subject', and is conferred upon what is normally considered as the 'object' or event. Launching into an investigation of the 'nature' of play, Gadamer identifies the common denominator that underlies its various manifestations, as 'the to-and-fro movement which is not tied to any goal which would bring it to an end'. So play is motion, non-purposive in that it lacks a target of attainment, a destination that, once reached, cancels the activity itself. The 'subject' as such becomes irrelevant as the 'play' is the performance of the movement; 'play' precedes 'player', since the characteristic state of the 'playing consciousness' is an indeterminacy that fails to distinguish 'between belief and non-belief'.[16] This is the inherent structure of a number of play variations such as animal play, child play, or sacred play (ritual) – all acknowledging the primacy of the activity over the volition of the participant: 'The ease of play', Gadamer contends, 'which naturally does not mean that there is any real absence of effort, but phenomenologically refers only to the absence of strain, is experienced subjectively as relaxation'. With a wording that sounds remarkably close to Wordsworth's 'lightening' of the 'burthen of the mystery', Gadamer goes on to analyse this lack of pressure: 'The structure of play absorbs the player into itself, and thus takes from him the burden of the initiative, which constitutes the actual strain of existence' (1975: 91–4).

Derrida in *Writing and Difference* approaches the question of play from another perspective, which in identifying play with 'absence' shifts its ontological basis from symbolism to semiotics: 'Being must be conceived as presence or absence on the basis of the possibility of play and not the other way round'. Despite differences of approach Derrida, like Gadamer, recognizes the hermeneutical affiliation between play and interpretation, although his identification of play as an activity of deferment and distancing from 'beginnings', places him at the opposite pole from Gadamer's logocentric standpoint. Derrida proposes two attitudes to 'play': the one attempting to escape the play of *différance* by deciphering truth or origin; the other, 'which is no longer turned toward the origin, affirms play and tries to pass beyond man and humanism, the name of man being the name of that being who, throughout the history of metaphysics or of ontotheology – in other words, throughout his entire history – has dreamed of full presence, the reassuring foundation, the origin and the end of play' (1978: 292).

For Gadamer, play is structure and structure is presence, inherent in a holistic view of reality. The elementary characteristic of play, the 'to-and-fro movement', is found primarily in the 'mobile form of nature' into which human or artistic play is embedded. Such an interrelation, or action / counter-action, requires, Gadamer continues his exposition, the presence of another. What he calls 'the primacy of the game over the players', introduces an infringement of the players' freedom of choice (or will), and an admission of / submission to 'possibilities'; in that sense 'all playing is a being-played', and as such it engenders risk. This mastery of play over players is seen as an exercise of 'spell' that draws them into activity and keeps them there; thus the 'area' of play, both literally and metaphorically, becomes what I would call – translating into Greek Gadamer's concept of 'sacred precinct' – a *τέμενος*, a place of seclusion, or a field closed to the 'world of aims'. The 'refusal' of play to fulfil goals outside itself, the keeping out of touch from any 'purposive context', i.e. its non-utilitarian nature, defines its essential condition as self-manifestation. The difference between child play (a self-engrossed act that does not necessitate an audience) and the artistic production, e.g. the performance of a theatrical drama, is only superficial and apparent, Gadamer believes. The actuality of a dramatic performance, however, while equally embracing players and audience, is only fully revealed not to the 'actor' but the 'spectator': 'In him the game is raised, as it were, to its perfection'. Gadamer calls this transition of human play from the self-absorbing child play to the artistic audience-oriented play, a 'transformation into structure'; the nature of this metamorphosis is an *excursus* from the world of daily reality into another dimension, that of 'play' (1975: 94–100).

Precisely at this point Gadamer introduces an argumentative 'twist' that takes the reader by surprise. Having emphasized a complete segregation between art and life, he re-examines the issue from an entirely opposite perspective, i.e. not the relation of art to life, but of life to art; his mediating tool becomes Plato, 'the most radical critic of the high estimation of art in the history of philosophy', who, however, appears to make no distinction between the drama of life and the drama on stage; for, Gadamer fully endorses the Platonic stance, 'this difference disappears if one knows how to see the meaning of the game that unfolds before one. The pleasure offered in the spectacle is the same in both cases: it is the joy of knowledge'. Thus the 'enclosure' of play is enlarged enough to incorporate life, and the transformative 'action' becomes a matter of 'perception'. In this new visualisation that sees life *as* play, apparently nothing is left outside, in that everything is encompassed within the order and movement of the play itself. A mode of awareness that could embrace life as a whole would transfer 'reality' into a 'drama' – a play on stage (1975: 101–2).

So, Gadamer implies, the relation of art to reality is not one of copying; art, by uncovering the 'structures' of life, transforms it into the truth it already is; this inverted form of mimesis displaces 'recognition' from the common assumption of identification with something already known. It is evident by now that the labyrinthine movement of the argument has reached a familiar junction. The mind's re-cognition of a forgotten mode of being takes us nowhere else but into the heart of Platonic metaphysics and epistemology: the theory of Ideas (or structures of the real), and 'recollection' as the method of their recovery from oblivion. In Gadamer's words: 'This is the central motif of Platonism. In his theory of anamnesis Plato combined the mythical idea of remembrance with his dialectic, which sought in the logo, ie the ideality of language, the truth of being' (1975: 103). Gadamer extends his notion of 'play' from the aesthetic to the linguistic realm which receives extensive treatment in the third part of *Truth and Method*, entitled 'The ontological shift of hermeneutics guided by language'. He contests that language is closer to a natural force – not an expressive formation but an ontological game which precedes man, and whose movement one submits to. Logos, dialogue, conversation are a to and fro motion which holds and carries forward the participants in the discourse – a premise that sounds analogous to the Platonic admission of utter surrender to the dynamics of logos. For Gadamer the conversational mode engages the participants not as agents but rather as patients; the implication made here, I think, is that the 'act' of verbal communication is more of a $\pi\acute{\alpha}\theta\eta\mu\alpha$ (to use the Platonic term), a procedure to which the mind submits rather than wilfully directing it. Such differentiation between 'parole' and the 'creative' mind eventually turns the speaking subject into an object 'spoken through' (1975: 345–51).

THE HERMENEUTICS OF THE 'ODE ON A GRECIAN URN'

'The basis of the systematic significance which the linguistic nature of conversation has for all understanding we owe to German romanticism' (1975: 350), Gadamer admits. It was the

Romantic movement in Germany that simultaneously posed the problem of hermeneutics and recognized (or *in* recognizing) the importance of the Platonic text as the most ancient exponent of 'significant conversation'. So the Romantic period is seminal both for the reappraisal of Plato, and the casting forward of an interpretative trend known in philosophical / critical circles as 'hermeneutics', or the dialogue between reader and text. For the Romantics – philosophers and poets – the dialogue as a form of discourse exemplifies not only the act of 'construction' of a poem (i.e. the 'conversation' between consciousness and unconsciousness, as formulated for instance in Schelling's system of transcendental idealism), but also the 're-construction' that is achieved during the exegetical process. Thus hermeneutics is an operation itself that 'completes' the work of art in interpreting it. Schleiermacher's presupposition that the interpreter (Greek ἑρμηνεύς) understands the poem better than its author, may be seen as an aspect of the whole Romantic tendency of probing into what was considered to be organic or spontaneous creativity, the 'knowing' of the 'unknown'. The reproduction process, it was believed, brings to the surface, to the understanding, structural forms and patterns employed by the author without being 'noticed', and therefore latent in the text in not being 'pronounced'. The reception of a work of art 'improves' upon its production in a way that Plato would call a 'transition' from poetry to philosophy, from ἐνθουσιασμός to τέχνη. 'We must remember this especially in regard to the interpretation of poetry', Gadamer holds; 'There too it is necessary to understand a poet better than he understands himself, for he did not "understand himself" at all when he formed the construct that is his text' (1975: 170) – an assumption often verified by artists who confess, with Yeats, that man can embody truth but he cannot know it.

Hermeneutics, I would contend, 'states' what the poem 'names'; it is the transformation of ὀνομάζειν into λέγειν, thus establishing a new relationship between the old contestants of μῦθος and λόγος. Gadamer recognizes that although Romanticism tries to invert the hierarchical priorities introduced by the Enlightenment, in asserting a model whereby mythos precedes logos, yet it is still working within the conceptual postulates established by the eighteenth century in retaining the conflict between the 'logical' and 'mythical' apprehension of reality. The principle equally shared by Romanticism and Enlightenment,

Gadamer remarks, is the traditional awareness of 'the conquest of mythos by logos'. Thus Romanticism is seen to have played the historical and epistemological game according to the rules established in the age of 'reason', by ironically reversing a given hierarchy whose terms it fully endorses (1975: 242–3). I would argue that rather than simply transposing the Enlightenment polarity of logos / mythos, or concept / image, Romanticism is attempting to maintain the precarious balance between the logical and the mythical – a relation that Plato the 'dogmatist' so ruthlessly attacks whereas Plato the 'author' so carefully salvages. I would also call Romanticism the first endeavour in modern times to re-establish a 'dialogue' between these two modes of knowledge. Wordsworth's life-long concern to produce a 'philosophical poem', Coleridge's ultimate sacrifice of poetry to metaphysics, Shelley's oscillation between thinking and poetizing, and Keats' unfailing awareness of the demands of 'old' or 'cold' philosophy – despite his professed allegiance to a life of sensations rather than thoughts – are only samples of the Romantic attempt to 'heal' the quarrel between philosophy and poetry that, although not begun with Plato, finds its paramount expression (*Rep.*, X, 607b–c) – and its simultaneous subversion – in the Platonic work.

The Romantic assumption that poetry and philosophy are equally important in the cognitive process, and that imagination is a third state between, or outside, perception and conception – in creating the 'symbolic forms' through which experience becomes transcendent – is best summarized in E. Cassirer's assertion that 'To poeticize philosophy and to philosophize poetry – such was the highest aim of all the romantic thinkers' (1944: 156). The Romantics attempt to achieve the resolution of an enmity that is far older than the eighteenth century and – if we are to take Plato's testimony for it – which is fundamentally grounded in a conflict between a religious and a non-religious view of reality (*Laws*, XII, 967c–d); they reject dualism in establishing the fact that both poetry and philosophy play a crucial role in the quest for truth. Taking, I suppose, poetry to be the utterance or 'naming' of 'being', and philosophy the correlative 'statement' about 'being', they should have no difficulty in accepting that the two cultural forms can go hand in hand. The crucial problem for Romantic poetics is how to give a satisfactory account of the commerce between percept and concept, image and idea; in that respect, the new rhetoric of poetry, as is well known, aspires not only to become an epistemological tool of a status equal to philosophy, but to supplant the place left vacant through the reduction of theological certainty. The essential difference of method that poetry and philosophy employ in their search into reality or 'what is', did not prevent the Romantics from recognizing that although the two verbal configurations start in opposite directions, they coincide in their final goal – which is more or less what the Platonic text 'says' in the elaboration of a perfect balance of these two 'forms' – and despite what Plato himself 'speaks' of their radical opposition.

Writing in a post-logical period, the rehabilitation of the primacy of mythical consciousness was not only subverted from without by coming into open opposition with the dominant ideology of the time but – and this is most important – from the writers of Romanticism who are in a state of constant friction with social, conceptual, and linguistic codes – the 'given' beliefs and assumptions concerning the validity of imagination as a cognitive process. Gadamer illustrates this lack of epistemological – and ontological – confidence for which the best term is 'Romantic irony',[17] with the following observation: 'There is the related point that even the contrast between genuine mythical thinking and pseudo-mythical poetic thinking is a romantic illusion which is based on a prejudice of the enlightenment: namely, that the poetic act, because it is a creation of the free imagination, is no longer in any way bound within the religious quality of the myth'. He traces the tensive origin of the problem to 'the old quarrel between the poets and the philosophers in the modern garb appropriate to the age of belief in science' (1975: 243).

Keats' reiterated aversion to 'consequitive' thought is not an expression of settled conviction but of obsessive inner conflict between the 'dreamer' and the 'sage'. The relevant passages in his letters do precisely this – assert the imaginative activity as a familiar cognitive mode, and question, while paradoxically accepting, that 'other' way to truth, of which he professes ignorance:

> The imagination may be compared to Adam's dream – he awoke and found it truth. I am the more zealous in this

affair, because I have never yet been able to perceive how any thing can be known for truth by consequitive reasoning – and yet it must be – Can it be that even the greatest Philosopher ever ‹when› arrived at his goal without putting aside numerous objections – However it may be, O for a Life of Sensations rather than of Thoughts!

(1958: I, 185)

His distinction is between the discursive and imaginative modes of knowing, the logical process that moves from one thought to another through analysis versus the synthetic integration that operates through recognition of hidden relationships or similitudes. W. H. Evert, after defining the two mental functions as the 'logical' and the 'analogical', offers a possible explanation for Keats' intellectual and artistic dilemma: 'Inclined toward speculative activity and a basically religious view of life, yet out of sympathy with the dominant metaphysical mode of organizing experience [Christianity] in that culture to which he must address his poetry, how was he to proceed?'. Evert recognizes the extensive historical dimensions of the poet's personal problematic and the solution adopted by Keats in his return to 'the very origins of western cultural history', where he found 'a ready-made vocabulary and symbolism of those natural forces and ideal concepts on the balance of which he believed the cultural health of the individual to depend, and which he thought to be artificially stifled by the prevailing Christian culture' (1965: 13–14).

The most readily available symbol in which to embody the symbiosis of philosophy and poetry is for Keats the god Apollo who is already established in Greek culture as the divine presider over the poetic and the prophetic / philosophic activities, the upholder of harmony and luminous order. The poet's letter to the George Keatses for March 1819 not only betrays an awareness of the uneasy relationship and questionable hierarchy between the imaginative and discursive faculties – which inverts the value system he appears to endorse – but expresses his full consciousness that in adopting Apollo as his key mythical figure he aspires precisely to this: the reconciliation of the logical and the analogical (or meta-logical) aspects of experience:

> This is the very thing in which consists poetry; and if so it is not so fine a thing as philosophy – For the same reason that

an eagle is not so fine a thing as a truth – Give me this credit – Do you not think I strive – to know myself? Give me this credit – and you will not think that on my own accou[n]t I repeat Milton's lines

> "How charming is divine Philosophy
> Not harsh and crabbed as dull fools suppose
> But musical as is Apollo's lute" –
>
> (1958: II, 80–1)

A reference to Socrates immediately preceding the passage quoted, leaves no doubt as to the identity of the 'divine Philosophy' whose 'music' is metaphorically assimilated to the Apollonian song; what is less clear is the syllogism through which Keats arrives at this identification. There is a kind of irresolution in his thinking, a sense of indeterminacy, a striving in the darkness where any terms of reference, codes, or opinions are absent – a process that indeed sounds very close to the formal dialectic itself. Although Keats is entirely unaware of method in pursuing what he calls an 'instinctive course', yet his conclusion of distrust of proverbs – 'Nothing ever becomes real till it is experienced' – what he elsewhere calls 'axioms' or abstractions, sets the very presupposition of the Platonic practice. Through the image of concentric circles – where 'man' looks upon 'animals' while himself perceived by 'superior beings' – Keats establishes a relation of ontological correspondence, whereby what he (man) appreciates in physical motion – even in its vulgar expression of a street fight – may be equally appreciated (by spiritual entities) in man's intellectual, even if oftentimes faulty, procedure: namely 'energy' which, whether displayed in its ugly or beautiful aspects, is 'fine'.

It is apparently 'energy-at-play', the polarized 'rapport' of opposites or 'to and fro motion', the creative (or destructive) process itself that fascinates Keats whether in its 'philosophical' or 'poetic' form. Directly relating to the play of situations or the play of mind is Keats' grasping of life, a surrendering process that goes beyond conceptualization. Every action perceived has some spiritual implication automatically, a 'dynamic' aspect to its 'massive' phenomenal nature which, the poet admits, is 'fine' – not in the sense of a 'good' opposite to a 'bad' but in the sense of 'excellence'. Quarrel, aggression, anger are expressions of energy with which the poet wants to communicate; searching out the 'power' aspect of existence, working with it, generates in him the passion to find out, to get acquainted with the 'essence' of things. As Keats' poetry attempts to convey, the involved human observer develops new depths of insight through direct communication with the 'energies' within the actuality of the phenomenal world, the vividness and beauty of the universe. What is given in this letter in 'seed' form receives amplification in a multiplicity of imaginative formulations. Power called 'grace' or 'beauty' is recognized as that which abides in the heart of all beings, self-existing soul sustaining life. This indestructible δύναχις gives impetus to both acceptable and unacceptable (by conventional standards) states of mind – and of 'being'; it is seen as the driving force of violence and confusion, but also of love and wisdom. To translate abstract concepts into the concrete Greek – and Keatsian – imaginative symbols, it is the Dionysus that empowers Apollo, while 'controlled' by him.

The conjunction of opposites constitutes, I believe, the metaphysical motif of Keats' poetry and thought; it represents, in all its expressions, a transcendence of the phenomenal – and conceptual – activity, abolishment of all experience of duality, a 'negation' (to use the Hegelian term) or 'destruction' of the given cosmos. It is only by grasping the dialectical interplay between what are considered to be mutually exclusive conditions, that mind can avoid the splitting off of the one pole from the other. This nostalgia for the primordial completeness and bliss, is what animates and informs all the techniques that lead to the reconciliation of opposites in one's own being – burning / cooling, pain / happiness, tension / release: 'Just when the sufferer begins to burn, / Then it is free to him; and from an urn, / Still fed by melting ice, he takes a draught' (*Endymion*, IV, 533–5). In the 'Cave of Quietude' the whole range of antithetical mental and physical activity – 'Happy gloom! / Dark Paradise!' – becomes extremely clear, and many of the things which were below the normal threshold of awareness, much of what is called subconscious material, is illuminated and integrated more fully into the mind. Silence appears as energy-giver. It creates a clarity in which all the aspects of consciousness are distinctly seen by those 'brightest eyes', experiencing fully all the pains and aches, all the blissful sensation, all the restlessness and boredom. 'Quietude' provides the space of solitude in which all of this can be made visible.

The image of the 'urn' introduced in the above citation serves a dual function: first it suggests that 'den' and 'urn' are possibly 'isomorphic', i.e. translatable into each other as emblems of delimited space – the one natural, the other cultural, 'form'; second, it introduces the 'cooling' effect of water-drinking to the 'burning' thirst of the 'sufferer', not only hinting ahead to the cryptic correlation of 'Cold Pastoral' in the 'Ode on a Grecian Urn', but also bringing once more to the surface the *coincidentia oppositorum* that haunted Keats' physiological metaphysics as much as Shelley's: the conjunction of 'hot' and 'cold'. A tentative excursion into the Keatsian text reveals an intense concern, almost obsession, with the polarity of the sensations of 'heat' and 'coldness', which may have to do with the condition of his bodily ailment (his usually feverish state), but also points toward an awareness of bodily states of excitation (in either extremity) that do not necessarily derive from 'pathological' causes. A 'burning' man is not only one who suffers from tuberculosis, but also, as many religious and magical practices reveal, a man in communion with the deity, in 'divine possession' – rage or μανία. Coldness, on the other hand, may be the natural symptom of perspiration, or the tranquillity, peace of soul, absence of passion, relief from suffering, designating the 'extinguishing' of 'fire', the anger, the fever – in short the 'heat' engendered by divine or daemonic powers (Eliade 1958: 85–7).

Even a very brief and tentative 'statistical' investigation of the correlation of heat / cold in Keats' poetry would discourage us, I believe, from following the normal evaluation process of associating 'heat' with 'good', i.e. positive aspects of existence such as life, feeling, love; and 'cold' with the opposite code of 'death' and its cognates – emotional sterility, indifference, fear. Value systems are as much blurred as ontological, psychological, and physical borders in that primary experiential continuum on which evaluation judgements rest. 'Cold' may indicate the lifelessness of corporeal death, but also the 'coolness' of spirituality – as 'enchantments cold' so clearly manifests. 'Heat' may denote severe suffering, sexuality, or a purgatory effect, a 'fire' of extinction which consumes ignorance so that life takes on a new meaning, when all previous attitudes are burned up; it can also be 'an external fierce destruction', the ravaging energy at the core of things into which Keats had cast a terrified glance, as he confesses in his friendly epistle 'To J. H. Reynolds, Esq'. After such knowledge, what happiness? – the poet laments the loss of innocent outlook:

> Away, ye horrid moods!
> Moods of one's mind! You know I hate them well.
> You know I'd sooner be a clapping Bell
> To some Kamtschatcan Missionary Church,
> Than with these horrid moods be left i' the lurch.
>
> (ll. 105–9)

The Christian 'attitude' of keeping things neatly compartmentalized, offers a position of security to the poet's disturbed imaginative insight, literally into the 'nature' of things; unable to bear such an 'unmediated' vision of reality, he seeks a convenient division into irreconcilable oppositions, which uses concepts as 'filters' to screen the mind from a direct perception of destructive fierceness. Keats sees 'through' semantic categories, and 'into' the defence system that provides 'protection' by means of comforting classifications. As he writes to his friend, he is acutely conscious of the illusion, but also of the terrors that the escape from illusion brings along. Awareness of having lived a whole life in a structure of 'habit' makes the 'deconstruction' of the mechanism of habit a morally ambivalent operation:

> and so philosophize
> I dare not yet! Oh, never will the prize,
> High reason, and the lore of good and ill,
> Be my award! Things cannot to the will
> Be settled, but they tease us out of thought;
> Or is it that imagination brought
> Beyond its proper bound, yet still confin'd,
> Lost in a sort of Purgatory blind,
> Cannot refer to any standard law
> Of either earth or heaven? It is a flaw
> In happiness, to see beyond our bourn, –
> It forces us in summer skies to mourn,
> It spoils the singing of the Nightingale.
>
> (ll. 73–85)

Or conducts to the 'nightingale'.

The playful yet malicious imaginative 'teasing out of thought', subverting familiar ways of thinking 'good and ill' (the repetitive, stereotyped ethical patterns), is as much feared as desired.

Clinging to conventional habits of ideation provides an escape whose 'escape', Keats seems to be well aware, leads into uncharted territories, where a 'shock' may be experienced that jars man out of his comfortable life-style. The 'out-of-thought' condition, the non-discursive, non-dualistic approach to things, the dreadful 'unlearning' of preconceptions, the giving up of solid points of reference, the stealing out from a continuous activity of comparison, division, identification is, Keats insinuates, an experience that repels as much as it attracts – a fascination with abomination.[18] A little earlier on in the poem, he had wished for an objective correlative that could become a visible carrier of these imaginative states, bringing into the open the phenomenology of mind:

> O that our dreamings all, of sleep or wake,
> Would all their colours from the sunset take:
> From something of material sublime,
> Rather than shadow our soul's day-time
> In the dark void of night. . . .
>
> (ll. 67–71)

Such a 'material sublime' is, I believe, the 'form' of the Grecian Urn.

Written in March 1818, the 'epistle' to Reynolds precedes the 'Ode on a Grecian Urn' dated 'May 1819' in Dilke's transcript by over one year. Besides the obvious analogy to the condition of 'thoughtlessness' that is central in both poems, there are further allusions, or rather 'post-allusions', easily recognizable in the earlier work. The opening lines of the 'epistle' bear the mark of a confessional tone, as it should be expected in a letter addressed to a close, and trusted, friend: 'Dear Reynolds! as last night I lay in bed, / There came before my eyes that wonted thread / Of shapes, and shadows, and remembrances, / That every other minute vex and please' (ll. 1–4). The peculiar clarity of his imaginative vision that makes unexpected 'metaphorical' associations, as for example 'Old Socrates a-tying his cravat', turns from isolated instances of paradoxical figures to a narrative in images, a pictorial story, an unfolding of 'spatial' realities in 'time':

> The sacrifice goes on; the pontiff knife
> Gleams in the Sun, the milk-white heifer lows,
> The pipes go shrilly, the libation flows:
> A white sail shows above the green-head cliff,

Moves round the point, and throws her anchor stiff;
The mariners join hymn with those on land.
(ll. 20–5)

The 'mythos' – in both senses of the word, as 'story' and verbal aspect of a ritual event – is very close to that of the 'Ode on a Grecian Urn'; 'sacrifice' is an essential motif in both poems, the sense that certain things must be ended before new things can develop, a needful 'dying' to thought, prior to the 'dying into life' that in the epistle is tainted by a touch of moral equivocalness.

Closer to the 'Grecian Urn' than the epistle to Reynolds, lies the 'Ode on Indolence' – another 'urn' construct probably written in May 1819 – at some chronological point 'around' the 'Grecian Urn'. The poem is of interest to our investigation less for its thematic concern with Love, Ambition, Poesy and more for its mood of indolence, the twilight state that sustains the appearance of 'Phantoms', shapes of delight or of horror. The figures are not static but in motion, and their movement is faithful to the, realistically valid, approach to an urn that is 'turned round' to see the 'other' or hidden side. Keats does not provide any indication as to the specific rotatory pattern employed, or make any comment on the possible signification of the 'direction' and 'speed' of the revolution. He furnishes, however, a detailed account of the effect of the rotating vision upon his psychological make-up, as producing an intermediary zone between waking and sleeping, in which the customary activity of the conscious mind is absent – the state of reverie where 'marvels' are revealed[19] if consciousness can sustain its 'negative capability' or 'willing suspension of disbelief': 'my pulse grew less and less; / Pain had no sting, and pleasure's wreath no flower: / O, why did ye not melt, and leave my sense / Unhaunted quite of all but – nothingness?' (ll. 17–20). 'Pain' and 'pleasure' deprived of their meaning indicate a condition of annihilation (or reconciliation) of opposites. The imaginative shapes themselves are experienced by the poet as a middle ground, an intrusion, an interference that prevents the oncoming of the wished-for frame of mental 'nothingness', the emptiness out of – or 'space' into – which the visions of waking-dreaming arise. The phantoms refuse to obey his bidding and withdraw, to leave his mind empty, void, naked; they continue to occupy his attention and his concern, until they are recognized as the dominant forces regulating his life – love, ambition, poetry. Caught between the 'burning' desire to follow them in order to penetrate into their essential nature, and the 'coolness' of his indolent state of suspended animation, the poet exorcises the 'three ghosts' from his field of imaginative vista: 'Vanish, ye Phantoms! from my idle spright, / Into the clouds, and never more return!' (ll. 59–60).

Taking into consideration the possible chronological coincidence between the 'Ode on Indolence' and the 'Ode on a Grecian Urn', the 'phantoms' *do* return, or have been *there* all the time – at least the ghost of 'poetry' and certainly that of 'love'. The question that hovers about the 'Grecian Urn' – and throughout the Keatsian text – is the one that received its clearest formulation in *Endymion*, characteristic of the inquiring spirit and uncertainty with which the whole matter is treated; the relevant passage follows close upon Endymion's rejection of ambition for worldly recognition and social acceptance: 'Wherein lies happiness? In that which becks / Our ready minds to fellowship divine, / A fellowship with essence; till we shine, / Full alchemiz'd, and free of space' (I, 777–80). Keats uses the term 'fellowship' or 'friendship', which usually characterizes intersexual rather than trans-sexual relationships, to define the encounter between the human and the divine. Yet the 'method' of approach to this 'fellowship' bears unmistakable signs of an heterosexual, erotic involvement: 'Just so may love, although 'tis understood / The mere commingling of passionate breath, / Produce more than our searching witnesseth: / What I know not' (I, 832–5). The question – which is one of the constants underlying the poetic thoughts of Keats – reduced to its 'naked' form, reveals the poet's enquiry as to whether the spiritual can be attained through indulgence in the sensual, rather than in abstinence from it. Put into mythical terms, it uncovers itself in the dramatization of the Dionysian process, or the method of how Dionysus may be transfigured to Apollo.

The 'Ode on a Grecian Urn' is an instance of Apollo and Dionysus in discourse, in all the varied implications of such a statement. The possibility of establishing an openness and interchange between the forces represented by the two gods is exemplifed not only by Greek culture (whose 'sample', the urn, Keats has undertaken to explore) that dedicated the Delphic oracle to the worship of both deities, but in the thematics and formal structure of the Platonic work itself constituting a 'textual' manifestation of the Greek 'achievement' of combining moderation, control, balance, and Apollonian grace with the reality below and beyond explanation and rational synthesis. Apollonian 'prophecy' and Dionysian 'mysticism' are indeed only aspects of the same root-madness, the frenzy which is also the source of 'poetry' and 'love' (*Phaedr.*, 265b). Plato's assumption that all these 'forms' of μανία are homologous in structure as well as analogous in function is, I think, the basic presupposition of Platonic philosophic thought. The possibility of union – or a dialectical maintenance of discord – between Apollonian finiteness and Dionysian infinitude, enters into Plato's conception of the nature of reality, 'the whole tragicomedy of life' (*Phil.*, 50b). Despite the professed 'Apollonianism' of the Platonic dialogues, it is to Dionysus that the right 'mixing' of life is entrusted (*Phil.*, 61b–c) – and that contending Nietzsche's claim, who looks upon Socrates (and presumably Plato) as 'that *second spectator* who did not comprehend and therefore did not esteem the Old Tragedy', being the 'opponent of Dionysus'. Nietzsche sees this contest as 'the new opposition: the Dionysian and the Socratic – and the art of Greek tragedy was wrecked on this', when 'the one great Cyclops eye of Socrates fixed on tragedy, an eye in which the fair frenzy of artistic enthusiasm had never glowed. To this eye was denied the pleasure of gazing into the Dionysian abysses' (1967: 82–9). M. Krieger in discussing the 'classic vision' or 'retreat from extremity', sets the structural framework necessary for the experiencing of the two gods, in that 'the Apollonian and Dionysian motives could be defined only in terms of each other and would become seriously corrupted when not maintained dialectically in an opposition that is a tensional union'; he points out that the Apollonian, left to itself, becomes the 'ethical'; the Dionysian 'on its own and without the overpowering imposition of a transcendent order, becomes the Titanic worship of the unrelieved darkness of chaos, unredeemed tragic existence free of its containing frame in tragedy' (1971: 4–5).

That Dionysus was not actually a Titan, but was 'feasted on' by the Titans and reborn from Semele, as the myth goes, complicates even more the moral aspects of the relation of the 'dionysian' to the 'titanic', because man, rising from the ashes of the sinful Titans, may be said to incorporate in him 'evil Prometheanism and the good Dionysian element' (Bloom 1973: 116). Like his Titanic consumer, however, Dionysus is associated with the iconography of 'fire' – as he is characteristically born 'in fire' and is often referred to as the 'torch-bearer' (which is possibly what Προμηθεύς means).[20] The Dionysian version of the myth of the Fall is presented as a 'devouring' and dispersion of the unity of the 'immortal body' into the multiplicity of earthly sojourn, ultimately restored to unity by Apollo. In this exposition of the archaic story (Harper 1961: 228–9), Dionysus and Apollo, rather than being antithetical entities, are taken as instances of unification, of a *pro-*, and *meta-*fragmentary existential condition. So their alleged antagonism may be seen as ultimately a 'love-play', and the tension between them as generating the dynamic of life.[21]

An alternative view, which deserves incorporation, is presented by Derrida when he refers to 'the fallen Dionysianism' not in its mythical but its historical dimension: 'The divergence, the *difference* between Dionysus and Apollo, between ardor and structure, cannot be erased in history, for it is not *in* history. It, too, in an unexpected sense, is an original structure: the opening of history, historicity itself'. Paradoxically, Derrida places *difference* in a no man's land, outside the motion of empirical existence as well as the form of metempirical essence: '*Difference* does not simply belong either to history or to structure. If we must say, along with Schelling, that "all is but Dionysus," we must know – and this is to write – that, like pure force, Dionysus is worked by difference. He sees and lets himself be seen. He tears out (his) eyes. For all eternity, he has had a relationship to his exterior, to visible form, to structure, as he does to his death. This is how he appears (to himself)' (1978: 28–9). Finally, Cassirer relegates the myth to the various 'forms' of Greek culture, the poetry and art that encompass it: 'Like all great vegetation cults, that of Dionysus' induces 'the "ecstasy" by which the soul bursts the fetters of the body and of individuality, to become united once more with universal life'. He makes a clear differentiation between the mythical / ritualistic and the artistic views in their respective attitudes to subjectivity, the former looking upon personal identity as a severance from primordial unity, whereas the latter accepts the 'ego' as a necessary self-integration that transforms chaos into order; 'For this view a definite plastic outline becomes the first guarantee of perfection. And perfection demands the finite; it calls for fixed determination and delimitation' (1955b: 197).

As a verbal construct that interprets a plastic object that represents the paradigmatic gestures of ceremonial dance, love, and sacrifice, the 'Ode on a Grecian Urn' integrates into 'one' the linguistic, artistic, and mythical configurations towards 'being', thus holding together by a unity of meaning the diversity of what Cassirer recognizes as 'symbolic forms'. A hermeneutic chain is set up as the linguistic sign 'speaks' the artistic 'image' which has 'looked' at the action of the original mythical 'event'. Thus the poem seems to reproduce the essential elements of ritual summed up in the formula uttered by the initiate in the Eleusinian Mysteries: 'I saw, I said, I did'; this phrasal model sets down the stages of transformation as sensuous perception, vocal expression, and dramatic re-enactment.[22]

Considered as the prototype for both poetry and art, ritual is perhaps the most effective of cultural 'forms' for evoking and transmuting 'power', in its potency to elicit unconscious formations and unleash energies which easily overwhelm the individual ego's capacity for rational choice-making and reflection; hence ritual has historically been the prerogative of authorial government and organized religion. By an intense stimulation of all the senses – sight through colour, hearing through singing, smell through fragrance, taste through herbs, touch through dancing – a whole 'psychic mechanics' for the exploration of 'being' is set afoot. Ritual knowledge is not necessarily additive and discursive but rather transformative, causing a qualitative change within the organism. Ritual practice has traditionally been the means of maintaining human activity in conscious accordance with the laws of nature, making the human individual a more receptive agent of cosmic forces by initiating him / her into an expanded and intensified participation in the workings of the cosmos. Identifying oneself with divinity (the Platonic ὁμοίωσις θεῷ) is equivalent to awakening the sacred 'presence' that is believed to lie asleep in man; as this is not a purely intellectual exercise, 'personality' becomes the vehicle of tension and suffering that must be sacrificed. In Eliade's words, 'Every ritual repetition of the cosmogony is preceded by a symbolic retrogression to Chaos'. Stressing the archaic belief that 'a state cannot be changed without first being *annihilated*', Eliade affirms that metaphorically speaking, 'Initiatory death provides the clean slate on which will be written the successive revelations whose end is the formation of a new man' (1958: xiii). Ritualistic 'dying' is necessarily followed by a 'rebirth' process. It is for the sake of this birth to another modality of being that the participant 'sacrifices' everything that, on the level of 'profane' existence, seems important. This 'detachment' from the ego and its intentions, being enticed 'out of thought', effects a transformation of mundane activities into rites, into the archetypal gestures and postures of a perfectly accomplished act (probably the Aristotelian πράξεως σπουδαίας καὶ τελείας – the act serious and perfect of which tragedy is a 'mimesis'). By the power of ritual some ordinary object incorporates the sacred; in a 'synecdochic' process a part coincides with the whole, the οὐσία τῶν ὄντων.

The Grecian urn may indeed be such a 'ritual object' itself – besides a 'space' where ceremonial activity is contained. I would also tend to support the view that the poem brings together ritual and meditation as two planes that are homologizable.[23] And if ritual may be said to connect man with cosmic processes, meditation may be seen to open up commerce with the same processes in one's own body; the poem's 'argument' expounds that, starting from any level we can establish communication with the other. The urn is firmly held within the observer's attention and becomes the focus of intense concentration. It is the reduction of multiform awareness to a 'point' and the increase of 'con-centred' sensitiveness, that not only makes it correspondent to the excessive emotionalism of ritual participation, but allows penetration into the deeper aspects of the object – getting its inner 'power-graph' (or ἰδέα) properly imaged in a consciousness that is maximally roused. The anchoring of meditational experience on a concrete 'thing', an isolated 'fragment' that comes to represent the reality of the whole cosmos, can only be rendered possible by intensively reducing normal perception of reality. Such absorptive involvement with a single 'object' may be experienced as an 'assault' *on* – or *by* – 'being', as Plato's testimony of ἡ τοῦ ὄντος θήρα manifests – and Keats', who experiences the 'reading' of the urn as an act of violence, a sexual enforcement, a 'rape'.

'Thou still unravished bride of quietness', discloses a simultaneous realization and expectation in the ambiguity of 'still' – the muteness of the work of art to be interpreted; this points to the 'hermeneutic' character not only of art but reality itself (enhanced by the paradoxical 'silence' of an urn that blasts with sound),[24] and the 'as yet' sexual act of initiation that is to be performed (the aggressiveness of the speaker possibly due to the conditioning of a culture that looks upon sexuality as a form of self-assertion). My argument would be that the poem traces a transformative inversion of 'rape',[25] in that violation 'intended' ultimately becomes violation 'suffered', as the 'still unravished bride' finally 'teases' the wilful assailant 'out of thought', out of himself, out of his 'will'.

The initial attempt to de-code the urn's 'meaning' is made through the 'rhetorical' route of using three metaphors: the urn is 'bride', 'child', and 'historian'. The 'nuptial' image of the opening line gives its place to the 'procreative' one of child – or 'foster-child' (reminiscent of both Wordsworth's Nature / nurse in the 'Immortality Ode', and Plato's 'mother' or nurse of generation, the second cause of creation). 'Silence' and 'slow time' are not only the condition that allowed the initial creation of the artistic object, but the context of its 're-cognition' by the speaker. The 'silence' and 'slow time' images echo a mental emptiness or 'nothingness', and the deceleration of pulse beats mentioned in the contemporary 'Ode on Indolence'. Subsequently – 'intentions' and 'origin' having been investigated – 'function' becomes the target of attention: the urn is a narrator of a 'vegetative' nature (literally and metaphorically), unfolding its *mythos* in a pictorial rather than verbal form of discourse, faithful to the mythological – or 'imaginal' – stage of human evolution that it represents:

> What leaf-fring'd legend haunts about thy shape
>   Of deities or mortals, or of both,
>   In Tempe or the dales of Archady?
>   What men or gods are these? What maidens loth?
>   What mad pursuit? What struggle to escape?
>   What pipes and timbrels? What wild ecstacy?
>
> (I)

The seven 'what-questions' (supplemented later in the poem by two more 'what' interrogations, one 'who', and one 'why') introduce, I believe, a historical transition 'from ritual to romance',[26] highlighting the quest, the conscious effort of a seeker who dares to penetrate beyond the surface of things and ask 'What is the meaning of it all?'. What we have here is a series of ceremonial or magical questions, not 'about' the 'cup' of the Grail legend, but addressed to the container, the 'vessel' itself in its archaic pre-Christian form, the all-round ἀμφορεύς (shortened version of ἀμφι-φορεύς, bearer on both sides).

The urn is the shape, the receptacle of forms, the χώρα; though itself a 'form', its formal character and boundary line are gradually blurred, until it becomes open 'space' for the action to unfold. It seems as if the urn's solidity as a marble vase (the most dense of existing things imaginable) that delimits it as a separate entity, is gradually lost, and 'form' as an observable thing, a tangible 'otherness', turns into fluidity, the waving of sound. Open space unfreezes the action, the rigidity, and allows a basic freedom, a spacious quality in which the natural flow of the 'imprisoned' dynamism can be experienced: the condition becomes one of infinite expansion in which the mould landscapes – people, streets, houses – are unravelled. Percepts and fantasy images prove to be mutual reflections, an experiential indeterminacy that does not clearly distinguish between inner and outer happenings. The Dionysian character of Stanzas II and III has already received enough attention by Keats scholars to need any further exemplification, although statements like the one suggesting that the first three stanzas manifest 'the convergence of the mortal and immortal, or the Dionysian and Apollonian' (Wasserman 1953: 32–3), might meet with Keats' own disapproval, who, far from correlating 'dionysianism' with 'mortality' addresses the 'god' Dionysus as a most awesome initiator into the mysteries of universal knowledge (*End.*, I, 285–9), entreating him to ' "Be still the unimaginable lodge / For solitary thinkings' that 'dodge / Conception to the very bourne of heaven, / Then leave the naked brain' (I, 293–6).

I should like, instead, to concentrate on syntax, on the enigmatic dialectic of never / ever,[27] negation-and-affirmation in time. The flooding of negative adverbs, the nine 'nots' and 'nevers' of Stanza II, is gradually reduced to two in Stanza III, two in Stanza IV, which makes a total of thirteen. In such a syntactic 'drama', the 'forever' seems to be contingent upon the 'never'; the 'arrested' or 'frozen' action on the urn's surface depicts not only the iconography of immortality, but its presupposition. What the poem appears to celebrate is not consummation of physical love or abstention from it, but a 'middle' state, a possible erotic equivalent to the poetic 'negative capability', or perhaps the rendering into sexual terms of a 'willing suspension' not of disbelief but of desire – a *coitus reservatus*.

The question that underlies the poem – although not openly pronounced – the question that has been haunting Keats ever since *Endymion*, 'if this earthly love has power to make / Men's being mortal, immortal' (I, 843–4) – to which the earlier 'romance' gives a positive answer – seems to receive here not only confirmation (in the Platonic manner) but also a methodology. Sensual excitation forever poised on the verge of attainment, a 'foreverness' of passionate intensity to which releasing fulfilment is denied, is imaginatively suggested as a means of transcending the hedonistic or procreative ends of normal sexuality, and its transformation into an immortalizing process of death and rebirth. The preventive action itself is given as the cause of the displacement of consciousness and, ultimately, of transcendence. In its transition from the 'not' of Stanza II, to the 'ever' of Stanza III, to the sacrificial emptiness of Stanza IV, the poem seems to trace a succession of stages, whose pattern marks a transposition of erotic self-dissolution into self-extinction in sacred 'otherness', through 'resistance' to – or the surmounting of – sexual pleasure.

The indissoluble bond between the forces of sensuous desire and religious emotion in the Bacchic mania is a well-known fact, present in all manifestations of the cult of Dionysus and surviving in artistic or linguistic remnants that have been preserved from those times. The vehemence of the orgiastic passion – a compound of sexuality and spirituality – shows that through 'ecstasis', pagan ritual acknowledges the 'presence' of supra-personal power, as well as its capacity to influence human behaviour in an act of mutual assertion and surrender. This 'stepping' from the ritual to the spiritual is effected in the poem between Stanzas III and IV, a passage from the 'burning' condition to the 'mystery', 'emptiness', and 'desolation' of the sacrifical rites. In Stanza V, the 'wild' energy that has manifested itself as 'haunting' about the urn, is gradually constellating back into 'shape' – and finally 'form':

> O Attic shape! Fair attitude! with brede
>   Of marble men and maidens overwrought,
> With forest branches and the trodden weed;
>   Thou silent form, dost tease us out of thought
> As doth eternity: Cold Pastoral!
>
>   (V)

When the orgiastic frenzy has settled down into a decorative pattern, the urn becomes again 'shape', 'attitude', 'silent form'. Ecstatic identification with 'passion' is succeeded by the aesthetic distancing from passion, 'energy' transformed to new 'openness', the enstasis of a silent mind whose conceptual storage has been burned by the intensity of the passionate experience. The urn is the field of awareness in which 'forms' are situated, an open dimension of heightened consciousness in which there is no conflict, no time, and no thought, the much wished for state of 'nothingness' of the 'Ode on Indolence'.

Heidegger, in his essay on 'The Origin of the Work of Art', depicts not the 'production' but the 'consumption' of art, in terms strikingly similar to those used by Keats in his hermeneutics of the urn: 'The more solitarily the work, fixed in the figure, stands on its own and the more cleanly it seems to cut all ties to human beings, the more simply does the thrust come into the Open that such a work *is*, and the more essentially is the extraordinary thrust to the surface and the long-familiar thrust down.' The forceful blow that the art object exercises on the mind that contemplates it, Heidegger continues, is paradoxically deprived of unpleasant extremities, in that it transmits its dynamism, the energy stored into it, with an immediacy that is analogous to the work's proximity to reality. Such existential 'appraisal' rather than 'transcendence' of the habitual, Heidegger defines in the following terms: 'To submit to this displacement means: to transform our accustomed ties to world and to earth and henceforth to restrain all usual doing and prizing, knowing and looking, in order to stay with the truth that is happening in the work'; an arrest or suspension that is identifiable to the condition of being 'teased' out of thought, uncovers for Heidegger the essential nature of the object of art, in that 'Only the restraint of this staying lets what is created be the work that it is' (1971a: 66).

As the internalizing process of ritual and myth reaches its culmination, the artistic object has fully performed for Keats its function of 'empowerment', as a link in the chain that Plato had described in the *Ion* – the 'power divine' which, like a magnet, impels the interpreter and inspires to him the divine 'possession' and enthusiasm experienced by the original artist: 'No, when once they launch into harmony and rhythm, they are seized with the Bacchic transport, and are possessed – as the bacchants, when possessed, draw milk and honey from the rivers, but not when in their senses' (533e–534a).[28] In the 'Ode on a Grecian Urn' Keats is twice removed from the primal event, placing himself in the role of an 'interpreter of interpreter', in a distance not only of historical but also of formal *différance*. His 'reading' of the urn's text, however, points towards the potentiality inherent in the 'cultural form' to both contain and transmit the authentic experience that brought it into being, a frozen 'competence' that, given the appropriate 'receiver' (or perceiver), may unfreeze into the released flow of 'performance'. The 'Cold Pastoral'[29] is more 'like a flame transformed to marble' (*Adonais*, l. 447), retaining the full potential for a 'de-marblization' back into the impassioned condition that produced it – and which its 'flowery tale' depicts; an intermittent trafficking between the states of 'burning' and 'freezing', that is captured not only by a 'Grecian' urn, but by the Greek language itself in rendering 'life' in two 'forms': as ζωή (deriving from ζάω, possible analogue of ζέω, to boil, seethe) and ψυχή (derivative of ψύχω, to breathe, cool).

The poem's end is an aberration from the norm of Keats' structural pattern, in that it portrays no 'journey homeward to habitual self' (*End.*, II, 276); 'Thoughts of self', do not come to disturb the 'teasing out of thought' that the urn has effected. Yet enough 'thought' or new insight has been gained to propel the poet into philosophical speculation that is closer to Apollonian 'prophecy' than to the 'consequitive reasoning' he so despised. His hermeneutics of the Dionysian experience results in the celebrated pronouncement of ' "Beauty is truth, truth beauty" ', which repeats the Platonic identification of ontology and aesthetics, i.e. it points towards an artistic or 'poetic' epistemology of 'being'. In accordance with the Romantic philosophy of his time, Keats appears 'to hold up art as the source of the highest form of wisdom' (Wasserman 1953: 49); a wisdom that is probably inherent in a mode of perception which certainly does not see 'different' things but sees things 'differently', a frame of mind that expounds readiness for observation, choiceless and non-interfering awareness, an almost erotic gazing at things as they are. In this respect, the urn's preaching is a 'reminder' (ὑπόμνησις) of a way of looking – and listening – 'forgotten' by humanity who, blinded with 'woe' and personal concerns, cannot see the beauty of natural or human forms, having lost touch with 'sensations' and tending exclusively to develop intellectual capacities. The art form operates as a kind of 'stimulation' that bridges the contact with nature – and ultimately with 'being'; having 'seen' what it is like to 'see', it transmits this mode of perception, this 'fair attitude', this precision of vision that is unrelated to the accomplishment of any end other than the perception itself.

The problem of eroticism and its relation to poetry, as has already been indicated, is discursively set and imaginatively resolved within the compass of *Endymion*. There, 'fellowship divine / A fellowship with essence', i.e. friendship and reconciliation, succeed the 'grand battle', and give birth to a 'lullaby', an Orphic song: 'But there are / Richer entanglements, enthralments far / More self-destroying, leading by degrees, / To the chief intensity' (I, 797–800). However, the proposition that the spiritual may be attained by sexual intoxication is simultaneously affirmed and questioned; recognized as 'A hope beyond the shadow of a dream' (I, 857), it seems to have haunted Keats throughout his life. John Bailey, his close friend and partner in conversation, expresses his horror about the thematics of *Endymion* and Keats' unorthodox views on sexuality to John Taylor, the poem's publisher, making the relevant comparison to Shelley's similar fascination with abomination:

> The approaching inclination it has to that abominable principle of Shelley! – *that sensual love is the principle of things*. Of this I believe him to be unconscious, and can see how by process of imagination he might arrive at so false, delusive and dangerous conclusion . . . If he be attacked on these points, and on the first he assuredly will, *he is not defensible*.
>
> (Pettet 1957: 144)

Keats was not 'unconscious' of the problem but demanded a philosophical, axiomatic sanctioning beyond its experiential and imaginative versions. In his marginalia on Burton's *Anatomy of Melancholy*, he gives vein to his obstinate – and overwhelming – questioning in a most characteristic manner:

> Here is the old plague spot: the pestilence, the raw scrofula. I mean that there is nothing disgraces me in my own eyes so much as being one of a race of eyes, nose and mouth beings in a planet called the earth who all from Plato to Wesley

have always mingled goatish, winnyish, lustful love with the abstract adoration of the deity. I don't understand greek – is the Love of God and the Love of women expressed by the same word in Greek? I hope my little mind is wrong – if not I could – Has Plato separated these loves?

(Gittings 1954: 140)

The confusion and perplexity that torture Keats concerning the ambivalence of ἔρως – as heated lust and luminous worship – indeed reflects an ontological duality between the 'human' and the 'divine' aspects of the experience, and is rightly addressed to Plato as the originator – at least in western metaphysics – of the mysteries of love, τὰ ἐρωτικά.

2
EROS IN LOGOS
Symposia Ancient and Modern

THE *SYMPOSIUM* AS 'AMOROUS ROMANCE'

The *Symposium* may be considered Plato's supreme 'conversation poem' for a number of reasons that operate at various levels, thematic, structural, imaginative, mythical, psychological, metaphysical. Ἔρως unites the human and divine in (the) dialogue; in fact the continuity of erotic experience and the vision of Ideas, exemplifies – discursively and poetically – the philosophy of sexual attraction that has been the object of Keats', and Shelley's, uneasy investigations. The dialogue is also 'conversational' in that it stages the real or actual form of the community (society of Plato's time, rather than a fictional – utopian or fabulous – representation), and what is more, in a language 'which is uttered by men in real life, under the actual pressure of those passions, certain shadows of which the Poet thus produces, or feels to be produced, in himself'.[1] In depicting 'reality' not as a separate modality of being but as true ordinariness, as something very extraordinarily ordinary, Plato implies that the strangeness derives from the experience of discovery, the defamiliarization of familiar, everyday events: it is love that 'unites us in such friendly gatherings as this – presiding at the table, at the dance, and at the altar . . . in toil or terror, in drink or dialectic' (*Symp.*, 197d–e).

In this dialogue Plato touches upon the 'is-ness' of what is 'there' – 'being' precisely as experienced in daily transactions; it portrays a very accurate way of seeing the world, the actual life of things and people as they are, and the possibilities not of its 'transcendence' but of its 'transformation'. He works with real situations, with the existential condition of man, keeping his mind sharply focused on the temporal and topical in order to catch its essence, its simplicity – what man really is and does without any distortion (or idealization). In observing life as it is, neither justifying nor criticizing it, Plato discovers the relationship between activity and silence, the paradoxical discourse of time and that which is timeless. Absorption into 'what is' uncovers the common source of the erotic and the spiritual, the inextricable affinity between the philosophy of Eros and amorous experience, within the specific cultural context of ancient Athens. Randall notices that 'In Plato himself, in the dialogues, the "Ideal" does not appear as a realm apart, an isolated abode of detached essences, as the conventional tradition has it. Plato presents it dramatically rather as the sum of possible perfectings of existent natural and human materials' (1970: 142).

The paradoxical condition of the dialogues and especially the *Symposium* is that you only arrive at the place 'beyond', the realm of 'true being' (οὐσία ὄντως οὖσα) when you finally realize that essence and existence are the same, as the common term for 'being' (οὐσία / ὄν) implies. In other words, having ascended the steps to that place χωριστά, the seeker after 'truth' realizes that he has been 'there' all along. Thus the events of the dialogue – exchange of question and answer, actions, emotions, setting, characters, the coming and going – have an essential part in the economy of Platonic philosophy, and are not to be dispensed with as soon as θεωρία of the Ideas is achieved – which is 'dramatically' impressed rather than 'theoretically' expressed. The more aware the reader becomes of the archetypal conflict or merging of Ideas – portrayed in the 'praxis' of a dialogue that remains earthbound – the more he is likely to 'participate' (κοινωνεῖν) in the philosophic ritual, and to realize that philosophy is inseparable from the daily experience of human activity – and discourse. 'The Platonic Dialogue may be broadly described as a Drama in which speech is the action, and Socrates and his companions are the actors', J. A. Stewart asserts (1905: 24). The chase for 'being' (ἡ τοῦ ὄντος θήρα) is not an abstract reasoning of disembodied concepts, but is placed in the full dynamic context of life situations suffused not only with 'divine madness' but with the more ordinary human emotions of pride, prejudice, wonder, frustration, jealousy, expectation, friendship – the whole range of affectivity that constantly intrudes upon the 'ideal' and conditions its signification. The correspondence between the 'drama' of Ideas – their collision or reconciliation in συμπλοκή εἰδῶν (the Greek word virtually carrying both meanings) – and the actual dramatic events, establishes a symbolic parallelism that allows Plato to operate on two levels of communication at once: the analytic argument and the scenic occasion that conveys and accompanies it (Shelley's λογίζειν and ποιεῖν simultaneously). That 'Ideas have their being in discourse, in *logos*: they have a logical existence in human talk – and in the vivid emotional experience of aspiration or love' (Randall 1970: 197), may be said to find its sanction in Plato's own authority – and authorship – in the love ladder of ascent which brings λόγος to the doorstep of ἰδέα.

The *Symposium* as an 'Amorous Romance' (Parker 1666: 78) is an intellectual / erotic contest apparently typical of the Athenian philosophical circles; Plato places what he has to say in the festive conviviality of a drinking party, fully conscious of the 'continuity' between the existential and the ideal. Throughout the 'play' one notices that he is not rejecting, but coming to terms with physical ἔρως, which makes of speculative ideas – as much as Ideas – a matter of beginning in and working with the human condition as it is. Structurally, the *Symposium* is among Plato's most complex dialogues, a masterpiece of *différance*, as the original authentic occurrence is removed from the immediacy of the present situation not thrice but multiple times. Plato's object being to impress upon the reader a feeling of remoteness and extraordinary metaphysical revelation – paradoxically embedded within the familiar circumstance of a social gathering – he introduces again a perspectival approach through a series of reported speeches: Apollodorus narrates to a friend his conversation with Glaucon, who had been told the story by a participant in the banquet, Aristodemus (one of the 'dumb' figures), who in his turn transmitted Socrates' report of Diotima's initiation. Another way in which Plato conveys 'otherness' within 'sameness' is through the mental state in which the event is being recounted: Apollodorus, the actual narrator, is referred to as 'mad', an apellation which he fully endorses: 'My dear man, of course I am! And of course I shouldn't *dream* of thinking such things about myself or about my friends if I weren't completely crazy' (173e). Aristodemus was probably drunk when he related the story, since Plato persistently evokes the presence of Dionysus from the beginning of the dialogue to the end. Socrates, prior to his entry into the feast, 'fell into a fit of abstraction and began to lag behind' (174d), retreating into the next-door neighbour's porch – a habit of ἀποστασία or trance well known to his companions. Finally, in the representation of Socrates' speech as a revelation from a doubly 'other' (higher and feminine) authority, the philosopher's own personality is annihilated and is placed under the influence of a priestess-initiator in direct contact with the divine. The atmosphere of the 'unusual' however is fused with the sights and sounds of 'common' human enterprise where the actual, the intellectual, and the mystical blend.

Plato's whole conception in the *Symposium* depends upon the ultimate combining of abstract reasoning and ritual mystery of initiation in ἔρως, and to this end he metaphorically associates an unknown mental state (intuition of real beauty, ἐκεῖνο τὸ καλόν) to a well known occasion (the drunken condition of a banquet), by fusing them together artistically. It is this unprecedented sensuous approach to the spiritual which makes the *Symposium* so unique. Here, more than in any other of his dialogues, Plato works with 'life' as he saw it lived around him – and in him; he accepts physical passion as a prime mover of human conduct, and utilizes its energy in order to reach 'reality'; conversely, philosophic dispassionate discourse is 'caught up' in the total intellectual / emotional happening which begins with 'conversation' and uninterruptedly passes through a flow of stages that culminate in the climactic vision of the 'sea' (rather than 'sun') of beauty.

In its highly effective mirroring of a multiplicity of conceptions about love, before the Socratic revelation is made, the *Symposium* is thematically one of Plato's most integrated dialogues. Its peculiar dialectic consists of a series of extended speeches on different aspects and interpretations of the experience termed 'love'; Phaedrus appears to be the initiator of the erotic verbal game to be played, in proposing a research into the λόγος (definition) of ἔρως, since 'not one single poet has ever sung a song in praise of so ancient and so powerful a god as Love' (177a–b). The speakers are, in order of appearance, Phaedrus, Pausanias, Eryximachus, Aristophanes, Agathon, Socrates, and finally Alcibiades. The common denominator in their eulogies of ἔρως is the recognition of love as a δαίμων, binding and serving as a medium of communication and a unifying force, a means of bridging the ontological gaps in various realms or categories of being: bodily, natural, psychological, cosmic, divine.

Phaedrus' presentation stresses 'love' as a creative cosmological principle (178a–180b); Pausanias effects a division between sensual and spiritual love by introducing the concept of the 'two' Aphrodites, the Uranian (heavenly) 'sprung from no mother's womb but from the heavens themselves', and the Pandemus (earthly), daughter of Zeus and Dione (180d–e); in his discrimination, Pausanias disproves the conventional belief that associates eros and the instinct for reproduction, but his rigid boundary refuses any consecration to bisexual love. Odd as it may be for a feminine divinity, while Pandemus Aphrodite partakes of both the male and female natures, her Uranian counterpart possesses attributes that 'have nothing of the female, but are altogether male' (181c), and consequently excites the desire for 'vigorous and intellectual' intercourse that only male company can fulfil. Eryximachus confirms the ontological duality of Pausanias, and furnishes its 'medical' application in supporting that the 'right' sort of love is a principle of concord in the human body, harmonizing opposites and producing a condition of sympathy between them; while the division into 'two' kinds of love is retained, the origin of earthly love is attributed to Polyhymnia, the Muse of many songs, and its ethical devaluation is minimized in the assertion that both aspects of love, if justly and temperately consummated, may tend towards the good (186a–188d).

Aristophanes introduces the mythical notion of the 'hermaphrodite' – ἔρως seen as a unitary force that reintegrates the split parts of the originary 'whole' creature, 'a being which was half male and half female', 'globular in shape, with rounded back and sides', 'whirling round and round', descending from the Moon (189e–190b). By designating the primordial state prior to dual existence as male / female, Aristophanes reintroduces the indispensability of the 'feminine' which was ousted by the conception of the 'spiritual' as offered by Pausanias. Nevertheless, allowances are still made for homosexual practices in men and women on metaphysical grounds – the original creatures bisected by Zeus being not only hermaphrodite, but also pure male or pure female; thus the desire for wholeness in the descending 'halves' may equally be directed towards the same or the other sex (190a–b). Whatever the manner of division or the object of attraction, love is uniformly defined as the longing for 'that primeval wholeness' (193a) – the authentic 'being' whose symbol is the 'sphere' – a condition from which man has been alienated and to which he longs to return.

Agathon's oration transposes the discussion from the human to the cosmic level, describing love as a creative universal force; his presentation cancels the dualities of the former speakers, and somehow serves as a passage to the unitary aspect that is introduced by Socrates. Agathon, however, goes to an extreme of 'exclusiveness' in endowing ἔρως with positive characteristics only – gentleness, delicacy, suppleness, tenderness, loveliness, but also valour and inventiveness; in possessing the qualities of passivity and activity, love becomes the motive power of all creation (195c–197b). With Agathon's – fifth – definition, the absurdity of an intellectual situation that is not only pluralistic but contradictory and equivocal, makes itself strongly felt; the (informal?) exercise of the dialectical method has reached its 'zero' point in the admission of multiplicity and confusion, precisely the stage where many dialogues terminate with the Socratic admonition to his interlocutors to 'go home and think'. Here, however, instead of dismissing the assembly and inciting to introversion and meditative practice, Socrates invites all to participate in a communal ritual of initiative 'discourse'.

Socrates' speech introduces a fundamental shift in the exploration and understanding of the nature of ἔρως, in a number of ways. First, in the confession that his λόγος is not a reasoning process, a logical argument that is constructed in the present moment, but the recollection of a revelation disclosed by the Mantinean prophetess Diotima. Second, the displacement from historical to mythical time – 'once upon a time' (201d) – and the intervention of the female priestess, symbolically enact the simultaneous remoteness and immediacy of rites of initiation. The 'appearance' of Diotima introduces a revaluation of the image of the female mostly subverted in the earlier eulogies of love. In making Diotima a prophetess, and putting the kernel of his discourse into a framework borrowed from the Eleusinian mysteries, Plato re-establishes the bond between eros and woman, representing the feminine as an essential factor – or intermediary – in the experiential contact with divinity. There is a subtle and paradoxical relationship between the 'impoverished' celibacy of the priestess Diotima, and her account of the 'plenum' that the vision of the sea of beauty affords to the soul – the 'impregnation' of mind through desire inspired by the λόγοι σπερματικοί, and the final 'birth' that results from proximity to the beautiful. We pass from the primarily physical eros of a feasting party through the intervention of Diotima (who, incidentally, is the only female character in the Platonic 'plays') into the spiritual eros of the sacred, uninterruptedly. All along, the 'rite of passage' is tempered by an air of intemperance, merriment, exultation, but also intellectual alertness. The atmosphere of the event is manifested through the two presiding deities: Dionysus, god of wine and 'mystic' inspiration, and Eros, god of the 'fourth type' of madness, 'declared to be the highest'; yet Apollo is also present through the 'prophetic' utterances of Diotima, and 'poetic' enthusiasm is constantly referred to, thus completing the 'fourfold' phenomenology of θεία μανία (*Phaedrus*, 265b).

Mediation and dialectical interaction are the elements that condition Socrates' speech. His definition of love is given in very precise terms, beginning with function and origin. As a δαίμων, 'halfway between god and man', envoy and interpreter 'between heaven and earth', Ἔρως conducts the traffic between the mortal and immortal modalities of being, merging the two states 'into one great whole', and effecting the transition through which 'man can have any intercourse, whether waking or sleeping, with the gods' (202d–203a). If the human is to have converse with divine reality, eros is the power to generate such communion by bridging the ontological interstice between the two existent conditions. As a μεταξύ, psychic 'energy' or intensity of desire, love becomes 'the connecting link between the creative factors and the creature – it is a principle of betweenness, the bond between the absolute and the relative. The *Eros* is only another word for the causal energy exhibited in the total scheme' (Demos 1939: 15).

The myth of Eros' origination differs from the traditional one presenting him as the child of Aphrodite; in Plato's fable, the drunken Πόρος (resource, ferry) copulating with Πενία (poverty, need) symbolizes the 'rapport' between the states of plenum and void. And although the dynamic of eros is set in motion by the perception of physical, human beauty, its longing is not 'for the beautiful itself, but for the conception and generation that the beautiful effects' (206e); beauty creates the optimum context that terminates 'labour' and facilitates birth of 'an immortal something in the midst of man's mortality which is incompatible with any kind of discord' (206c). So both love and beauty are seen as mediatory factors, the one promoting 'conception', the other 'delivery'. The possibility of expanding such psychological 'obstetrics' into a metaphysical model of self-reflexiveness, is suggested in Cosman's interpretation of Platonic love: 'That human eros is most properly auto-erotic is only an instance of the fact that for Plato the world itself is auto-erotic' (1976: 61). Diotima's exposition proceeds from 'the more elementary mysteries of Love' to the 'final revelation', constituting what is traditionally known as the Platonic ladder of ascent from the 'bodily' to the 'essential' through various stages of sublimation, by transmuting sexual desire into a propellant that precipitates the soul up to the presence of beauty. An unexpected relation of ἔρως and λόγος is established even at the initial stage of physical attraction, which seems to justify the statement that 'The exciting thing about Plato, the reason why he deserves our most alert and sympathetic attention after all these centuries, is that he alone has tried to spell out all the consequences, ethical, political, epistemological, and metaphysical, of the assumption which we evidently still believe: that without love neither thought nor activity is profitable or perhaps even possible' (Gould 1963: 17).

The conjunction of ἔρως / λόγος becomes the constant that underlies the transformative process from sensory through contemplative to spiritual reality. As Diotima enunciates, 'the candidate for this intiation' should wait for the ripe time when his instruction can begin, and only then 'he will fall in love with the beauty of one individual body, so that his passion may give life to noble discourse' (210a); the companionship of ἔρως and λόγος, desire and language, continues up to the last but one rung of the ladder, where the disciple,

> turning his eyes toward the open sea of beauty, he will find in such contemplation the seed of the most fruitful discourse and the loftiest thought, and reap a golden harvest of philosophy, until, confirmed and strengthened, he will come upon one single form of knowledge, the knowledge of the beauty I am about to speak of.
>
> (210d)

Passing from 'beauty' to 'beauty', from the open sea of panoramic vision to the singleness of form, suddenly 'there bursts upon' the initiate into the 'mysteries of Love', 'that wondrous vision which is the very soul of the beauty he has toiled so long for' (210e–211a); yet, this is not the final stage of a progression that seems rather an infinite regress, as the candidate carried 'so far that the universal beauty dawns upon his inward sight, he is almost within reach of the final revelation' (211b), about which Diotima remains silent. What Diotima's initiation reveals – between the lines – is the ontological conjunction of ἔρως, λόγος, and κάλλος. Similarly, in the *Cratylus*, the etymological root of καλόν is traced to the verb καλῶ – to call, summon – and the principle of beauty is affirmed to be 'mind', 'because she does the works which we recognize and speak of as the beautiful' (416c–d), which apparently stops short before the non-verbal, and hence ineffable, final revelation.

The last word in the *Symposium*, however, is not spoken by Diotima or Socrates; as the 'instructed instructor' interweaves the transcendent with the utilitarian, by giving utterance to his 'conviction' that if we are to make the 'gift' of immortality our own, 'Love will help our mortal nature more than all the world' (212a–b) – thus establishing the intimate relationship between the religious, philosophic, and erotic experience – 'suddenly there came a knocking at the outer door, followed by the notes of a flute and the sound of festive brawling in the street' (212c). The generic, continuous relationship between the physical, intellectual, and mystical love is shown to work both ways, in the possibility of gradual or abrupt transition from one stage to the other – whether in an anagogical or catagogical movement – proving the truth of the Heraclitean saying 'ὁδὸς ἄνω κάτω μία καὶ ὠυτή (The way up and down is one and the same)' (Heraclitus 1979: 74–5).

As Dionysian frenzy bursts upon Apollonian stillness and harmony, 'transformed' sexual energy redescends the ladder to the bottom rung of carnality, when Alcibiades, 'very drunk', decorated with 'an enormous wreath of ivy and violets sprouting on his head' (212d–e) – the very image of a sylvan Dionysus – enters the room and sits unknowingly (blinded by his wreath) between Agathon and Socrates who moved aside to make room for him. The moment Alcibiades notices the unsuspected presence of the 'third' one, he accuses Socrates of playing on him 'The same old game of lying in wait and popping out at me when I least expect you' (213b–c);[2] he continues with remarks heavily charged with eroticism, to which Socrates responds by admitting what a 'dreadful thing' it is 'to be in love with Alcibiades' (213c). This unexpected 'deflation', the return of sublimated passion to its subliminal origins, to the 'foul rag-and-bone shop of the heart' where 'all the ladders start' (Yeats, 'The Circus Animals' Desertion', III), is carefully noted by Randall in the following words: 'Plato lets Socrates transform a passion of the body into a vision of the soul; and then he abruptly confronts love as an imaginative experience with love as an animal fact. The effect', the critic emphasizes, 'is to convince us that love is not to be seen as a vision of perfection alone, nor yet merely as Alcibiades creeping under the cloak of Socrates. Love is to be seen truly only when you can behold both, in the dramatic and irrational juxtaposition of life itself' (1970: 129).

The final speech in the dialogue, delivered by Alcibiades, is not a praise of 'love' as a logical abstraction – or even an imaginative representation – but a eulogy of the 'lover', the concrete, tangible, actual human personage, the stimulator of all this talk, Socrates. The relationship of Alcibiades and Socrates seems to portray a sensuous / educational / social basis more or less shared by all members of the group, as Alcibiades admits:

> And looking round me, gentlemen, I see Phaedrus, and Agathon, and Eryximachus, and Pausanias, and Aristodemus, and Aristophanes, and all the rest of them – to say nothing of Socrates himself – and every one of you has had his taste of this philosophical frenzy, this sacred rage [τῆς φιλοσόφου μανίας καὶ βακχείας]; so I don't mind telling *you* about it because I know you'll make allowances for me – both for the way I behaved with Socrates and for what I'm saying now. But the servants must put their fingers in their ears, and so must anybody else who's liable to be at all profane or beastly.
>
> (218a–b)

As Alcibiades continues his exposition of Socratic 'eccentricities' stressing the uniqueness of his erotic partner and instructor, he makes a second, this time allegorical, reference to Dionysian 'madness' by proclaiming that 'you'll never find anyone like Socrates', unless you 'compare him, not with human beings, but with sileni and satyrs – and the same with his ideas' (221c–d). Philosophical and figurative *μανία* are finally transformed into an actual orgy, and the dialogue concludes with ἔρως, an uncontrollable Dionysian force, bursting into the enclosed space of λόγος, as,

> all of a sudden, just as Agathon was getting up to go and sit by Socrates, a whole crowd of revelers came to the door, and finding it open, as someone was just going out, they marched straight in and joined the party. No sooner had they sat down than the whole place was in an uproar; decency and order went by the board, and everybody had to drink the most enormous quantities of wine.
>
> (223b)

The dialectic of 'calm' and 'rage', philosophical solemnity and vulgar hedonism – the characteristic structural pattern of Apollo and Dionysus in discourse, expressive of the mixed quality of life as lived – is finally rendered in artistic / poetic terms as the 'blending' of the comic and tragic genres, in that 'the same man might be capable of writing both comedy and tragedy – that the tragic poet might be a comedian as well' (223d).

The ending of one of the greatest erotic – and why not 'romantic' – texts of literature, is as prosaic and factual as any plain account of common, domestic, daily affairs. At daybreak, everybody having fallen asleep, Socrates left followed by Aristodemus; later 'after calling at the Lyceum for a bath, he spent the rest of the day as usual, and then, toward evening, made his way home to rest' (223d). In calling the *Symposium* Plato's dramatic masterpiece, Randall exposes the Platonic methodology of achieving its climatic effects through the paradoxical or 'metaphorical' confrontation of 'events' whose latent interconnectedness has remained unapprehended. The re-creation of the dramatic experience itself, the 'drama' of life, 'is the supreme example of what philosophy can do. It takes a very unpromising material, and proceeds to show its imaginative possibilities. Then it confronts these possibilities, that imaginative vision, with the bare facts, and makes us "see" – it generates *theōria*'[3] (1970: 127), a remark that comes very close to Shelley's claim for 'poetry' which 'compels us to feel that which we perceive, and to imagine that which we know' (1954: 295).

Plato's vision in the *Symposium* begins as near as possible to go very far; it investigates, inquires, looks into things that are very close to us, our everyday life with all its conflicts, contradictions, pleasure-seeking, pain-shunning, desire, and anxiety. There is no artificial division between what 'should be' and what 'is', which seems to be a most deceptive way of dealing with life, existence, οὐσία. Tackling actual, physical situations, and particularly the phenomenon called 'love', the mind becomes more sensitive and receptive to the patterns and qualities of reality (its 'Ideas'), and sees more clearly the meaning in life experiences. Such an open attitude towards 'phenomenal' events allows, Plato suggests, the birth of an intuitive perception which really sees things as they are, ὅτι τὸ ὄν. This insight, this recollection, at the beginning might be rather vague – only a glimpse of what is – a very dim glimmer compared with the darkness and confusion. But darkness and confusion, 'indecency' and 'disorder' are not conditions to escape from into some fake, constructed, 'ideal' notion of existence; what is needed, Plato implies, is a staring straight into the dialectic of life, the hard ordinary ground. The 'turning around' (περιαγωγή) is a looking back up into the place whence the spontaneous overflow of experienced reality is coming; then one can see life as it really is. The 'transcendence' is in the seeing.

THE TRIUMPH OF LIFE: SHELLEY'S 'OWN SYMPOSIUM'

One manifestation of the attraction the Platonic theory of love as 'cognition' exercized on the Romantic mind, is Shelley's avowed fascination with the *Symposium* (Notopoulos 1949b: 98–102); R. G. Woodman stresses that he 'considered it the most beautiful and perfect among all the works of Plato' (1960: 504). The *Symposium* 'saga' may be taken to begin with a note made by Shelley around August 1817, expressing not only his early enthusiasm for the work, but the inner dialectic that Plato's λόγοι σπερματικοί engendered in his soul, a process which would ultimately lead him to write a 'Symposium of his own':

> THE WONDERFUL description of Love in Plato, Sympos. p. 214 – particularly 214, 1.8 – 1. *ultima, et passim* 218.
>
> I should say in answer, that Ἔρως neither loved nor was loved, but is the cause of Love in others – a subtlety to beat Plato.
>
> *Agathon*, a poem.
(Notopoulos 1949a: 461)

Shelley translated the *Symposium* in the summer of 1818, an operation which lasted about a week, from 9 July to 17 (Shelley 1954: 216); the project, and its justification, was mentioned in a letter to John and Maria Gisborne on 10 July:

> I am employed just now having little better to do, in translating into my fainting & inefficient periods the divine eloquence of Plato's Symposium – only as an exercise or perhaps to give Mary some idea of the manners & feelings of the Athenians – so different on many subjects from that of any other community that ever existed. –
> (1964: II, 20)

In its matter-of-factness, the passage somehow subverts the poet's reasons for interest in the work, as well as his intentions for translating it – acquainting his wife with the 'mores' of ancient Athens, or as a skill acquisition. Yet, the frequency with which references to the work's progress are made in his correspondence, attest to the importance the whole undertaking acquired for Shelley.

In fact, the translation of the *Symposium* has its own 'dramatic' story within the Shelleyan canon: the translation itself, Mary's transcription, the author's indulgence in speaking – and writing – about it, the manuscript's loss, the eager search after it, and its ultimate recovery on the threshold of death, are all indicative of an obsessive preoccupation with the Platonic text. Godwin is informed of the poet's occupation on 25 July, together with his primal admiration for the dialogue, 'The Symposium of Plato, seems to me, one of the most valuable pieces of all antiquity', yet articulating his uneasiness concerning 'some differences in sentiment between the antients & moderns with respect to the subject of the dialogue' (1964: II, 22). Peacock also hears about it on the same day: 'I have lately found myself totally incapable of original composition. I employed my mornings, therefore, in translating the *Symposium*, which I accomplished in ten days. Mary is now transcribing it, and I am writing a prefatory essay' (26).[4] Shelley was acutely sensitive to the careful handling that the topic of homosexual love and its justification on historical grounds enforced upon him, to the extent that he was prepared to observe restrictions of expression – 'delicate caution' – which deviated from his normal treatment of such matters. In a second letter to Peacock for 16 August, he announces the completion of the translation, and its transcription, as well as his fears for its public reception, 'considering the subject with reference to the difference of sentiments respecting it, existing between the Greeks and modern nations' (1964: II, 29).[5]

During the same period of July–August 1818 Shelley wrote an introductory piece to the translation itself, dealing not with the thematics of the dialogue but with a safer subject, its artistic perfection and linguistic competence: 'The dialogue entitled "The Banquet" was selected by the translator as the most beautiful and perfect among all the works of Plato'. An appreciation which he enhances by exulting the textual dialectic between 'subtle logic' and 'Pythian enthusiasm', and the interconnection of discourse and music in the 'rhetorical' texture of its language, 'which hurry the persuasions onward, as in a breathless career. His language is that of an immortal spirit rather than a man'. Finally, Shelley gives a synopsis of the dialogue to which he attributes the term 'Ἐρωτικός, or a Discussion upon Love', forbearing however from defining the specific nature of that love. He deals with safer aspects such as setting, time, characters, of what he specifies as the 'drama (for so the lively distinction of character and the various and well-wrought circumstances of the story almost entitle it to be called)', portraying 'the most lively conception of refined Athenian manners' (1954: 335–6). Shelley's recognition of the dramatic quality of the dialogue duplicates his statement in the *Defence*, which discerns in Plato's linguistic and structural devices the resistance of closure and 'determinate forms' (1954: 280); the implication that structure is meaning indicates Shelley's awareness – together with his fellow Romantics – of the paradox of an 'erotic romance' cast in the language of irony. Behind the innocent phrase 'refined Athenian manners' is hidden the poet's embarrassment at a phenomenon that simultaneously interests and repels him, an occurrence whose cultural necessity he recognizes, but whose phenomenology – as expressed in the Platonic dialogues – he finds alien not only to the conventions of his time, but also to his own emotional make-up. What he needs, in fact, is a *Symposium* rewritten in a manner that will efface the accidents of history, and allow its essential paradigm, its 'deep structure', to shine through. Meanwhile, over a year later, he informs Leigh Hunt of his translation of the dialogue 'which is the delight and astonishment of all who read it; I mean the original, or so much of the original as is seen in my translation, not the translation itself' (1964: II, 153).

For almost two years nothing is heard of the *Symposium* or its translation until in a letter to Thomas Medwin written in Pisa on 22 August 1821, we find the postscript 'P.S. – I think you must have put up by mistake a Ms translation of the Symposium of Plato. – If so pray contrive to send it me' (1964: II, 342).[6] In the October of the same year Shelley makes a belated announcement of his translation to Thomas Hogg, without mentioning its disappearance, adding, 'I have employed Greek in large doses, & I consider it the only sure remedy for diseases of the mind. I read the tragedians, Homer, & Plato perpetually' (1964: II, 360). The allusion to Plato this time is not initiated by Shelley himself but provoked by Hogg who refers to his own recent readings in Plato, and particularly the *Gorgias* which he finds the best of the philosopher's 'wonderful' works; recommending that it should be translated and published with notes, Hogg continues: 'Plato is unfortunately little read, even by scholars, which is much to be regretted, as he is, perhaps, the most edifying of the Greeks, and his style is so easy and simple. That he should be shunned at Universities is natural enough' (1964: II, 359). The terminal reference to the manuscript is made in the last letter Shelley wrote to Mary from Pisa on 4 July 1822; in a postscript he notes, 'I have found the translation of the Symposium' (1964: II, 444), that in its laconic, factual briefness hides, I believe, a triumphant exultation at the re-collection of a long lost companion – an ἀναγνώρισις in the Homeric sense or ἀνάμνησις in the Platonic.

On the same day that Shelley wrote the epistle to Hogg, 22 October 1821, acknowledging his compliance with his friend's advice to study the *Gorgias* which 'is now open before me, and I shall read it with double interest from the views you suggest about it' (1964: II, 360), he composed another letter to John Gisborne where he made a triple reference to Plato; the first (actually last in the text) is an obvious transcription of his 'reading' situation: 'I read the Greek dramatists & Plato forever' (364). The middle mention of the Greek philosopher carries not erotic but political overtones, in the assessment 'What Godwin is compared with Plato & Lord Bacon we well know', which interprets the current hostile attitude towards Godwin as 'full evidence of the influence of successful evil & tyranny' (364). The note on Godwin is preceded by a statement on his own poetic occupations, 'I am just finishing a dramatic poem called *Hellas* upon the contest now waging in Greece', following upon an attempt at 'hermeneutics' of his recently published work, *Epipsychidion*, (published anonymously in London by C. & J. Ollier), and a hint at a prospect for future undertakings:

> The Epipsychidion is a mystery – As to real flesh & blood, you know that I do not deal in those articles, – you might as well go to a ginshop for a leg of mutton, as expect any thing human or earthly from me. I desired Ollier not to circulate this piece except to the Σύνετοι [cognoscenti], and even they it seems are inclined to approximate me to the circle of a servant girl & her sweetheart. – But I intend to write a Symposium of my own to set all this right.
>
> (1964: II, 363)

The chances that *The Triumph of Life* might be Shelley's 'own Symposium'[7] – an attempt to probe into the mysteries of ἔρως disengaged both from its homosexual and heterosexual / vulgar aspects – are very high indeed, since it is the only substantial piece of work the poet produced between the writing of this comment on 22 October 1821, and his death on 8 July 1822. A look at his correspondence in this period reveals his usual concerns with the reception of his published works, 'I am especially curious to hear the fate of Adonais. – I confess I should be surprised if *that* poem were born to an immortality of oblivion' (1964: II, 365); his exhilaration at the Greek war of independence, 'The news of the Greeks continues to be more & more glorious' (368), and the parallel annoyance at the critical articles on *Hellas*, 'The reviews & journals they say continue to attack me' (379). On 25 January 1822, there is a note concerning his creative work at the time, 'I am at present writing the drama of Charles the 1st, a play which if completed according to my present idea will hold a higher rank that [than] the Cenci as a work of art' (380) – a piece already designed in 1818. The unenthusiastic response of the public to *Adonais* seems to have stifled his poetic creativity, 'I can write nothing, & if Adonais had no success & excited no interest what incentive can I have to write?' (382).

Writing appears to have become very difficult for him, his past verbal effluence drying up: 'I write nothing but by fits. I have done some of Charles I. but although the poetry succeeds very well I cannot seize the conception of the subject as a whole yet, & seldom now touch the *canvas*' (388). The 10th of April becomes an extraordinarily productive day, if not in poetic composition, in the writing of three epistles simultaneously, to Claire Clairmont, Leigh Hunt, and a long one to John Gisborne where, although no mention is made of his own writing, there are significant references to the literary works that occupied his attention at the time. After the reiterative anxieties about reviews and critical reception, of the type 'Tell me how you like Hellas & give me your opinion freely', or 'I know what to think of Adonais, but what to think of those who confound it with the many bad poems of the day, I know not', he turns to more imaginative matters:

> I have been reading over & over again Faust, & always with sensations which no other composition excites. It deepens the gloom & augments the rapidity of the ideas, & would therefore seem to be an unfit study for any person who is a prey to the reproaches of memory, & the delusions of an imagination not to be restrained. – And yet the pleasure of sympathizing with emotions known only to few, although they derive their sole charm from despair & a scorn of the narrow good we can attain in our present state, seems more than to cure the pain which belongs to them. – Perhaps all discontent with the *less* (to use a Platonic sophism) supposes the sense of a just claim to the *greater*, & that we admirers of Faust are in the right road to Paradise. – Such a supposition is not more absurd, and is certainly less demoniacal than that of Wordsworth – where he says –
>
> > This earth,
> > Which is the world of all of us, & where
> > *We find our happiness or not at all.*
> >   (1964: II, 406)

To the strange conglomeration of Goethe, Plato, and Wordsworth is added yet more paradoxical company, that of Rousseau: 'Do you remember the 54th letter of the 1st part of the Nouvelle Heloise? [Faust *cancelled*] Göthe in a subsequent scene evidently had that letter in his mind, & this etching is an idealism of it. – So much for the world of shadows' (1964: II, 407).

On 18 June Shelley writes another extended letter to John

Gisborne, with references to his permanent concern with the fate of his recent poetic productions, the *Adonais*, *Hellas*, and *Epipsychidion* which, he avows, he 'cannot look at'; this radical change of attitude is effected by his disillusionment with the prototype of the heroine: 'the person whom it celebrates was a cloud instead of a Juno'. He admits, however, that the poem as such conveys something of his past – and present – state of 'being':

> It is an idealized history of my life and feelings. I think one is always in love with something or other; the error, and I confess it is not easy for spirits cased in flesh and blood to avoid it, consists in seeking in a mortal image the likeness of what is perhaps eternal.
>
> (1964: II, 434)

Yet, his way of thinking paradoxically reveals an intense focusing on the 'present', an attitude that, despite recognition of the 'idealized history' of past experience, refrains from living in temporal dimensions outside the 'moment' and rejects a view of life coloured by the expectation of achieving an 'ideal' goal: 'Jane brings her guitar, and if the past and the future could be obliterated, the present would content me so well that I could say with Faust to the passing moment, "Remain, thou, thou art so beautiful" ' (1964: II, 435–6).

The two remarks taken together indicate the regret for a past 'future' projection (idealism) – as that which is 'to be' but never 'is' – and the recognition that in this expectation one possibly misses the precision, openness, and beauty of the 'now'. The implications of his realization are that, being fascinated and overwhelmed by an idealized objective, the mind becomes indifferent and insensitive to the actual moment, because it is living too much in the future (or the past). The value of the 'passing moment', the 'nowness', the immediacy of living, is referred to as a kind of perilous freedom of whose significance Shelley seems to have become fully aware both imaginatively and intellectually. This direct and clear perception of what *is now*, which need not be mysterious or mystical, has induced a point-present consciousness free from memory and desire. Such vision, unmediated by associative barriers arising from past remembrances or future anticipations, the seeing directly what is 'there', creates for Shelley a condition of 'emptiness' which, in its rejection of relational loci, terrifies as much as it thrills him: 'I stand, as it were, upon a precipice, which I have ascended with great, and cannot descend with *greater*, peril, and I am content if the heaven above me is calm for the passing moment' (1964: II, 436).

In the last letter he posted from Lerici to Horace Smith, his utter disillusionment with all principles and doctrines, preconceptions and models of what man is and how he should conduct himself, finds express utterance. The radical contradiction between fictitious abstractions – 'ideas' and theories – with what every individual man 'is', surfaces the raging conflict in Shelley's mind between 'system' and human 'reality'. And it has been a life-long conviction of the poet's (though 'conviction' may be the wrong word to use in such a context) that the individual contributes to this 'evil' by being submissive to a 'conditioning' which prevents direct contact with anything in life – seeing things, people, relationships as they actually are – and obstructs communication through the falling of the veil, or 'Shadow':[8]

> It seems to me that things have now arrived at such a crisis as requires every man plainly to utter his sentiments in the inefficacy of the existing religions no less than political systems for restraining & guiding mankind. Let us see the truth whatever that may be. –
>
> (1964: II, 442)

This letter is shortly to be followed by the one to Mary sent from Pisa in which the recovery of the *Symposium* translation is celebrated, and a last short note to Jane posted on the same day, 4 July, where Shelley informs her 'I return to Leghorn tonight & shall urge him [Williams] to sail with the first fair wind without expecting me' (1964: II, 445), to which she replied two days later, adding in a postscript: 'Why do you talk of never enjoying moments like the past, are you going to join your friend Plato or do you expect I shall do so soon?' (445). Although the remark is somehow cryptic, the allusion to death – or immortality – is probably indicative of the discussions between Shelley and Jane, a sample of which was filtered into the Gisborne letter that has been referred to.

A look into the biographical data[9] of Shelley's last months has revealed the intellectual and emotional context that surrounds the writing of *The Triumph of Life*: the literary presence of Plato, the Greek dramatists, Goethe, Wordsworth, and Rousseau; an extreme discontent with all ideologies and idealisms; and an intense absorption in the 'here and now' that is metaphorically transcribed as an 'ascent', not on the Platonic 'ladder' however, which implies the security of 'measured' upward motion – and the even greater reassurance of a safeguarded descent – but on a 'precipice', an image which utterly eliminates all sense of certainty and confidence in its immediacy to danger and fear.

The first, almost over-simplified questions that confront the prospective interpreter of *The Triumph of Life* concern the character of the nominal (if not grammatical) subject: 'what life?', and the nature of the absent, yet implicit, object: 'over what?'. Shelley's choice of two nouns whose conceptual content is so limited precisely by being so extensive, creates a title appropriate for a poem which becomes a representation of the interplay of pure energies, a poem about the dialectical structure of 'being' as light and shadow. As R. Cronin puts it, 'The crucial nouns of the poem are "shape", "shadow", "figure". This is no accident', he admits; 'Shelley carefully chooses nouns in which the referential function is reduced to a minimum'; in the critic's view, 'meaning resides in the proposition rather than as an aggregate of the meanings of the individual words of which the proposition is composed. It is only by concentrating on the syntax of the poem that a limited meaning will emerge' (1981: 218).

Without wishing to undermine the above contention, I believe that 'meaning' also resides in the work's texture, and that the hermeneutical horizon of the poem can be enriched by examining instances of the imaginative and conceptual context in which the word 'life' appears in its various occurences in the Shelleyan canon. In *Queen Mab* we find an early example of a multifaceted relation that is one of the metaphysical constants in Shelley's work, the correlation of 'life' and 'love' in a situation where ' "All things are recreated, and the flame / Of consentaneous love inspires all life' (VIII, 107–8). In *The Revolt of Islam* the invocation to the divine source of the created world includes an equation of 'life' with 'being', and 'light' with 'beauty': ' "O Spirit vast and deep as Night and Heaven! / Mother and soul of all to which is given / The light of life, the loveliness of being' (V, 2197–200). The Promethean activity is presented in a cluster of metaphors that evoke a chain of dialectical reactions, while stressing the affective, almost Dionysian, quality of life: 'and

Love he sent to bind / The disunited tendrils of that vine / Which bears the wine of life, the human heart' (*Prometheus Unbound*, II, iv, 63–5). In the well-known lyric – the hymn to love sung by 'Voices' – Asia is invoked as 'Life of Life' making 'the cold air fire', 'Child of Light' whose 'limbs are burning', 'Lamp of Earth' dressing with 'brightness' the 'dim shapes' of the visible world (II, v, 48–71); Prometheus addresses Asia as 'light of life, / Shadow of beauty unbeheld' (III, iii, 6–7). At the close of Act III, liberation (from violence, aggression, pain, and fear), delivery (from every form of dependence, slavery, acceptance, and conformity), freedom (to doubt and question everything, that ultimately conduces to a passionate, intense, and vigorous existence) are presented metaphorically through the rending of the 'painted veil' (of culture, tradition, and authority 'called life') which allows the human individual 'to be'. Gone is the condition of ignorance and captivity under which the nations of the world suffered,

> Flattering the thing they feared, which fear was hate, –
> Frown, mouldering fast, o'er their abandoned shrines:
> The painted veil, by those who were, called life,
> Which mimicked, as with colours idly spread,
> All men believed or hoped, is torn aside;
> The loathsome mask has fallen . . .
>
> (iv, 188–93)

The introduction of the modifier 'call' in 'called life' throws a shadow or veil of nominalism between 'name' and 'thing', language and reality, together with a hint of misappropriation and wrong usage. An identical image, and verbal phrasing, commands a sonnet written at approximately the same period, yet incorporating a radical difference of outlook, as the unconditional enthusiasm of *Prometheus Unbound* concerning the experience of what lies 'behind' the veil, is tempered by scepticism and ambivalence. The suggestion here is that if perception on this side of the curtain is altered, Fear is still present (in a mutual relation with Hope), a fear which by being unnamed – and probably unnameable – thrusts with an attack of greater terror the blinded soul that, standing over the 'precipice', must perform the delicate job of interconnecting or reconciling extremities of emotion; so, 'Lift not the painted veil which those who live / Call Life' (ll. 1–2). What the sonnet expressly suggests is that the lifting or rending of the veil, appropriately or inappropriately named 'life', does not automatically guarantee access to 'light' and 'truth'. The imaginative content of the poem represents a passage from a world of 'shadows' to a world of further 'shadows', where the only 'bright' spot is paradoxically the inquiring spirit of the quester. It is not at all a condition where 'All things are void of terror' (*Queen Mab*, VIII, 225), as penetration through the veil of perception appears to necessitate a visit to the (Demogorgon) realm of gloom, darkness, and 'power' – through the uncomfortable dialectic of hope and fear. In *Epipsychidion,* the equation of loving / living that seems to be the alternative to calling / living, emphasizes not only that the 'being' of 'life' is 'love' but also the sad incompetence of language to portray this reality, and even the destructive intrusiveness of speech. Here the 'veil' metaphor operates in a peculiarly integrative as much as separatist function, effecting the necessary distancing that creates the τέμενος, the holy spot of seclusion. The relevant scene 'speaks' the transition from the condition of 'twoness' to that of desired 'oneness': 'till to love and live / Be one' (ll. 551–2).

The interaction of loving / living and calling / living, or simply the dialectic of 'life' and 'life', is presented in the short lyric 'O world! O life! O time!' within a 'historical' perspective (both personal and communal), as a transition from one set of signifieds – glory / joy – to another – fear / grief – for which world / life / time are common signifiers. The condition of 'glory' that the poem commemorates only to negate in its utter bleakness, is precisely the mode of 'being' whose absence is lamented in a much earlier, though admittedly not so absolutist, work, the 'Hymn to Intellectual Beauty' of 1816. Here the extraordinary presence in 'this various world' of a 'light' which is in fact 'The awful shadow of some unseen Power'

> like mist o'er mountains driven,
> Or music by the night-wind sent
> Through string of some still instrument,
> Or moonlight on a midnight stream,
> Gives grace and truth to life's unquiet dream.
> (ll. 32–6)

The experience of Beauty as a bright, awful shadow of Power, consecrates the 'vale of tears' which otherwise remains 'vacant and desolate' – where 'fear and dream and death and birth' cast 'gloom' upon 'the daylight of this earth' and forbid the 'sunlight' to 'weave rainbows'. The equation of 'life' to an 'unquiet dream' or nightmare is further amplified in the poem in a dual metaphor that extends the mode of 'darkness' from 'life' to 'death', in the hopeless finality of a transition from 'death-in-life' to a death that *is* 'life-in-death':

> Thou – that to human thought are nourishment,
> Like darkness to a dying flame!
> Depart not as thy shadow came,
> Depart not – lest the grave should be,
> Like life and fear, a dark reality.
>
> (ll. 44–8)

'Dark reality', the common denominator of 'life' and 'fear' (though different from the 'darkness', the 'awful unknown' that feeds human thought) allows, I think, the construction of an analogue to the calling / living model of life – that of fearing / living,[10] more appropriate antithesis to its loving / living polar opposite.

What, I expect, this imaginative wandering through Shelley's text in search of 'life' situations has showed, is the value ambivalence that all three words – 'life', 'light', 'darkness' – carry, terms on which *The Triumph of Life* is built. This semantic and moral ambiguity is carried into the 'life' – and 'death' – images in *Adonais*, the poem which, with the exception of *Hellas*, lies closest to Shelley's last poetic composition. Here 'life' is the chthonic, dynamic, creative force that animates the wintry landscape:

> Through wood and stream and field and hill and Ocean
> A quickening life from the Earth's heart has burst
> As it has ever done, with change and motion,
> From the great morning of the world when first
> God dawned on Chaos . . .
>
> (ll. 163–7)

The poem exhibits a consistency in its chiatus inversion of the binary oppositions of dreaming / waking, living / dying, night / day: 'Peace, peace! he is not dead, he doth not sleep – / He hath awakened from the dream of life –' (ll. 343–4), which leads to the extremely unconventional proposition, ' 'tis Death is dead, not he' (l. 361). In Adonais' absorption into 'oneness' with Nature – the Power 'Which wields the world with never-wearied love' (l. 377) – he participates in Spirit, the loveliness (or intellectual beauty) that 'bursts' from natural and human forms. The 'veil' metaphor is appointed here to the condition of being dead, 'death is a low mist which cannot blot / The brightness it may veil'; 'loving' and 'living' are given as conflicting, mutually exclusive experiences in an either / or pattern of reversible transformation, 'When lofty thought / Lifts a young heart above its mortal lair, / And love and life contend in it' (ll. 391–4).

Adonais of course contains the celebrated statement which identifies 'life' with the multiplicity, transiency, darkness, and colourfulness of 'becoming' as opposed to the oneness, permanence, light, and whiteness of 'being':

> The One remains, the many change and pass;
> Heaven's light forever shines, Earth's shadows fly;
> Life, like a dome of many-coloured glass,
> Stains the white radiance of Eternity,
> Until Death tramples it to fragments. . . .
>
> (ll. 460–4)

The extremity of the allegorical statement – of a 'life' fragmented and fragmenting and a 'death' unitary and holistic – as appears in the line 'No more let Life divide what Death can join together' (l. 477), is however subverted by the imaginative overtones of the passage, where it is death that 'tramples to fragments' the beauty of the 'many-coloured glass' which may stain 'the white radiance of Eternity', but is itself a 'dome', traditional symbol of glorification and transcendence. The equivocalness with which Shelley treats 'life' even in a saying considered typical of his 'life-destructive' tendencies, indicates, I believe, not his confused view about life, but the constant presence in his mind and poetry of what I called earlier the dialectic between 'life' and 'life' – loving / living and fearing / living (which is as much a hating / living). The paradoxical unity of the 'maniness' in the many-coloured glass before it is dispersed into fragments expresses, I think, Shelley's awareness of the always identical form of the world process, the 'function' that never dies, the flow of energy that is the self-nature of all, sameness and difference, 'being' and 'non-being' (which, according to Plato *is*), irrespective of mental games of commitment that label things under categorial distinctions such as 'life' or 'death'.

That the 'immortalizing' death-experience is not a static but a dynamic one, cognizance of the flow of impermanence, apprehension of the transitory, temporal nature of all phenomena – the fluidity of reality that cannot be contained in the fixity of classes like 'one' and 'many' – is, I think, rendered in the gradual modification of the names of the 'real' in Stanza LIV of *Adonais*, which betrays the ascendancy of the dynamic component over its static counterpart: the Light, which is Beauty, which is Benediction, which is Love, finally becomes the Fire 'for which all thirst'. The devouring action of fire, 'destroyer and preserver', the poet admits, 'now beams on me, / Consuming the last clouds of cold mortality' (ll. 485–6). In the last stanza, the elemental energy of 'fire' is further transmuted into that of 'wind' whose tempestuous breath shakes the 'bark' as it is 'born darkly, fearfully, afar'. Earth, air, water, and fire – the 'life' elements – far from being annihilated or 'transcended', are impressively present in a fourfold conjunction. It seems that access to the 'One', to 'Eternity' (which exhibits a puzzling pluralism, as designated by the verb form employed – 'are') is initiated by a rousing to the highest pitch of all the faculties which become the raw material for transformation into 'enlightenment', reconverted into the pure energy from which they all originated.

The 'breath' of the final stanza of *Adonais* parallels in more than one ways the 'breath of Autumn's being', the 'Wild Spirit' of the 'Ode to the West Wind': the 'spirit's bark is driven' as 'the leaves dead / Are driven', and 'cold mortality' is quickened like the seeds that 'lie cold and low, / Each like a corpse within its grave'; the 'spheréd skies are riven' resembling 'the steep sky's commotion', and the 'tempest given' recalls 'Angels of rain and lightning'; 'Death is dead' in the 'dirge / Of the dying year', and life, a 'dome of many-coloured glass' will be annihilated by the wind which 'this closing night / Will be the dome of a vast sepulcre, / Vaulted with all thy congregated might / Of vapours'. The wild energy of pneuma, the 'uncontrollable', 'Spirit fierce', 'Like the bright hair uplifted from the head / Of some fierce Maenad' is invoked 'by the incantation of this verse', as a 'prayer' in the hour of 'sore need'; the effects upon the human mind and body of the encounter with 'power' are rending, burning, lacerating – elevating and crashing: 'O, lift me as a wave, a leaf, a cloud! / I fall upon the thorns of life! I bleed!' (ll. 53–4).

The structure of *The Triumph of Life* introduces a 'distancing' or 'difference' very similar to the one employed in the Platonic dialogues and specifically the *Symposium*: the 'sober' eye of the Poet observes the condition of trance that brings forth Rousseau looking upon, and 'interpreting', life. In these gradations of vision, the poem establishes a series of concentric circles, or better, because of its open-endedness, the semi-circular rows of an amphitheatre that progressively focus on the δρώμενα, what is going on on stage, the 'drama' of life. The language of irony that the poem adopts, the uneasy and vacillating dialogue, is never so simple as to amount to a debate between the 'ideal' and the 'real' as many Shelley critics contend;[11] there is an inherent contradiction, I think, within the terms themselves that deconstructs their traditional connotations and value, and lends to an evasiveness that defeats all logic and patterned approach. R. Cronin's association between idea / imagination / absence, interprets 'ideality' as a projection of value upon the 'real', a quality attributed by the eye of the percipient rather than inherent in the object perceived: 'An ideal is an imaginary construct that has its existence in both the past and the future because the two are imaginary constructs'. With his suggestion that the 'ideal' can exist only as a substitute to and in the absence of the 'actual' that is being idealized, the critic moves from the idealized object to the idealizing subject itself: 'An ideal is the imaginary construct of the individual, but the notion of individuality is a fiction. . . . The poem, as we have it, stresses the delusory nature of the ideal' (1981: 220–1).

It is precisely this tentative proposition of the fictionality of the individual 'ideal subject' that I believe underlies all questions of 'ideality' and 'reality' in the poem. By reproducing a speaking voice that is 'Absorbed like one within a dream who dreams / That he is dreaming, until slumber seems / A mockery of itself' ('Ginevra', ll. 44–5), Shelley poses the problematic that has been perplexing him all along, the great paradox which is, of course, who is dreaming whom in this life? Is man in his own manifestation, which he considers 'real', someone else's dream? Is he 'dreamed' in the same way that he dreams the characters of his own 'dramatic' dreams? Is human existence relative to the existence of a larger 'dreaming' (or imagining) entity? The poem, I think, is an exploration similar to the one attempted in

Prometheus Unbound into the 'idea' of personality, the 'I' or 'ego', the suggestion of its possible (or rather highly probable) ficticity, and the consequences from its 'preservation' (as *Prometheus Unbound* traces the effects of its 'effacement').

The Triumph of Life presents instances of refusal to perceive the present 'absence' of ego, while constantly 'drumming' at the background the latent potentialities inherent in the movement of life – a 'self' unfrozen from the fixity of self-centredness which is the 'coldness' that imprisons flow into stasis. Space solidity is concomitant to time concretization – the projections into past and future that introduce the dimension of 'ideality'. The poem may be read as a dual proposition: the necessity of recognizing the conceptual nature of 'ego', realizing its 'reality' to be an 'idea' or ideal, an intentional fallacy inscribed onto phenomena. It is also a commentary on the state of confusion that results from human reluctance to reject the 'principle of self' (1954: 293)[12] – which seems to be securely continuous and solid – and become submerged in the play or 'dance' of life, in which the 'I' appears as a transitory, discontinuous event. *The Triumph of Life* is, in my view, one more dramatic embodiment of the Shelleyan 'monomyth', the suggestion that perhaps the most deeply ingrained concept – the one that has kept mankind longest in the cave of shadows or illusions – is the 'idea' of self, the conviction that there is 'someone' behind the experiential flow, some permanent individual 'subject', constantly defended by a 'calculating' mechanism.

The poem's celebrated lack of clarity, both thematic and stylistic, is rooted in the ambiguity of the situation it is attempting to portray – a simultaneous posing of the problem and its solution (whose imaginative conception so distinctly grasped by the poet, proves as yet so ineffectual in its worldly application). The 'confusion' is also largely methodological (very much in the Platonic fashion of unwillingness to commit to writing subjects to which one becomes devoted) rather than ontological or hermeneutical; from this perspective, P. de Man's comment seems the right thing to say for the wrong reason: 'Light covers light, trance covers slumber and creates conditions of optical confusion that resemble nothing as much as the experience of trying to read *The Triumph of Life,* as its meaning glimmers, hovers and waves, but refuses to yield the clarity it keeps announcing' (1984: 106). Derrida in 'Living On' places Shelley's problematic work within his own basic interpretative model of deconstructing the metaphysics of presence: in his view, the poem 'belongs in many ways to the category of the *récit*, in the disappearance or overrun that takes place the moment we wish to close its case after citing it, calling it forth, commanding it to appear' (1979: 85). And J. H. Miller sees it as equally lending itself to 'univocal' or 'deconstructionist' readings, since '*The Triumph of Life* contains within itself, jostling irreconcilably with one another, both logocentric metaphysics and nihilism' (1979: 226). In fact the poem is, I think, the most express statement within the horizon of English Romanticism of the ontological (ironic) interplay between 'light' and 'shade', the founding symbolism of western (and why not eastern) hermeneutics of existence. Shelley's particular version of this 'light' metaphysics in the poem presents luminosity not only as symbolic of an imageless truth, but as the essence of 'being', motion, flow – as well as the principle of frozenness and arrest of flow.

Shelley puts the light / dark family, which is the archetypal metaphor in rhetoric, to the specific uses that the poem's inner logic dictates. The metaphysics of light as a metaphysics of beauty has its origin, as so much else, in the Platonic text: 'Beauty it was ours to see in all its brightness in those days when, amidst that happy company, we beheld with our eyes that blessed vision' (*Phaedr.*, 250b). Beauty is luminous and hence it is primarily by beautiful objects that the soul is fired to desire, to reposses itself in the metempirical vision of reality. Plato not only constantly uses the analogy between 'light' and 'beauty', but characterizes this light / beauty, this 'shining' of objects (or the shining of the 'beautiful' through objects) as a property by virtue of which things make us 'mad' (249d–e), a 'call' of, or from, 'being' – a particular kind of perception which sets the soul on the journey of recovery or recollection of the Ideas: 'for beauty alone this has been ordained, to be most manifest to sense and most lovely of them all' (250d). Plato distinguishes two classes of men, those who 'see' and those who, although looking, are insensitive to the perception of 'presence' (250e–251a). The initial stage of beauty's confrontation in a human (male) body is succeeded by a series of physiological symptoms, manifesting the transformation that the experience of light / beauty engenders in the soul / body: following upon the sudden shivering, 'a strange sweating and fever seizes' the 'lover' (or 'philosopher'), the reason being 'warmth' caused by the 'stream of beauty entering in through his eyes'; this heating causes a melting in the 'roots' of the soul's wings 'which for long had been so hardened and closed up that nothing could grow'. Plato continues to describe the spiritual ascent in metaphors that are overtly sexual, the culmination of the ordeal and anguish given in images of simultaneous 'evacuation' and 'replenishment', as the soul 'lets the flood pour in upon her, releasing the imprisoned waters; then has she refreshment and respite from her stings and sufferings, and at that moment tastes a pleasure that is sweet beyond compare' (251b–e).

The 'shining forth' of the beautiful in the object (human form, i.e. the body) is experienced as a 'streaming in' whose name (in human linguistics) is Ἔρως, 'so called because flowing in (ἐσρῶν) from without' (*Cratylus*, 420a) or (in divine linguistics) Πτέρος – the winged one (*Phadr.*, 252b). Thus, in the Platonic text the metaphysics of light is associated not only with the metaphysics of beauty, but also with the metaphysics of sex. The double naming Ἔρως / Πτέρος (streaming / flying) is indicative of the functional use of 'eroticism' that serves as a vehicle towards 'enlightenment' or 'sublimation': the raising of desire to its highest ('apocalyptic') pitch, and the consequent transformation of this powerful sensuous / emotive charge to a spiritual rocket-fuel. The psycho-physical organism, rather than being suppressed or ignored, becomes the propulsion mechanism which, heightened to a fine intensity, is re-converted into the original state of 'being', or 'dwelling', with beauty – and truth. The final stage of the perception of beauty represents a condition of direct experiencing of 'light', the interfusion of forces as they dissolve beyond time, the condition of pure dynamism, the δύναμις (essence of οὐσία) from which all originate. The regressive climb into the 'source' of time and space is achieved through the inquiring attitude (ἀπορία) which reverses the act of creation by staring straight into the incessant process of generation. The key word is, as we have seen, περιαγωγή, turning around and looking into and beyond the move of fleeting experience.

That 'optics' and 'temporality' are closely related (often antithetically) in Shelley's poetry, becomes evident in the second Act of *Prometheus Unbound*; the concept of time having been inverted, from a past-to-present sequence to a present-to-past motion (an unfolding 'from out of' the present moment), the anti-clockwise direction is realized in Asia's 'enchanted' speech:[13] 'We have passed Age's icy caves, / . . . / Through Death and Birth, to a diviner day' (II, v, 98–103). In Act IV 'time' is standing still, i.e. annihilated: 'Once the hungry Hours were hounds / Which chased the day like a bleeding deer, / And it limped and stumbled with many wounds / Through the nightly dells of a desert year'; yet, now, the invocation comes, 'Let the Hours, and the spirits of might and pleasure, / Like the clouds and sunbeams, unite' (ll. 73–9). Redemption of time as an ontological / psychological presupposition to the oncoming of 'light', is manifest in Asia's song of retrogression to that 'diviner day', translated from temporal to spatial terms – into 'A paradise of vaulted bowers', a dome 'Peopled by shapes too bright to see' (II, v, 104–8).

In *The Triumph of Life* 'light' undergoes four metamorphic gradations: the physical 'sun' that shines upon the perceptual world, 'Rejoicing in his splendour' and lifting 'the mask / Of darkness' from 'the awakened Earth', surrenders to the 'blinding light' of the 'wondrous trance' presided over by the hooded, deformed Shape, which in turn is subdued by that 'light diviner than the common sun', the 'Shape all light' that finally wanes in the outburst of 'new vision, never seen before'. The physics of light (natural sun) is superseded by three successive conditions of meta-physical illumination – light experienced progressively as 'cold glare', 'fierce splendour', and 'chrysolite of sunrise'. The dialectic of transformation from sight to vision, the passage into the stage of 'waking dream', is signalled by the enigmatic presence of a light-like shade and the sense of 'coldness' that initiates trance, suggestive of the physical symptom of perspiration (in its severe form as chilling and shuddering) that alludes not only to the phenomenology of divine visitation as presented in the Platonic *Phaedrus,* but to the 'wondrous cold' world of the *Ancient Mariner,* and the Keatsian 'Cold Pastoral'; the state of suspension between 'height' and 'depth' also evokes the imagery of the Snowdon episode in *The Prelude*:

>   the deep
> Was at my feet, and Heaven above my head, –
> When a strange trance over my fancy grew
> Which was not slumber, for the shade it spread

> Was so transparent, that the scene came through
> As clear as when a veil of light is drawn
> O'er evening hills they glimmer; and I knew
>
> That I had felt the freshness of that dawn
> Bathe in the same cold dew my brow and hair,
> And sate as thus upon that slope of lawn.
>
> (ll. 27–36)

The texture of the ecstatic condition is composed of 'frozenness' and 'motion', and the imaginative rendering is identical to that of the 'Ode to the West Wind':

> And as I gazed, methought that in the way
> The throng grew wilder, as the woods of June
> When the south wind shakes the extinguished day,
>
> And a cold glare, intenser than the moon,
> But icy cold, obscured with blinding light
> The sun, as he the stars. . . .
>
> (ll. 74–9)

Meta-physical 'cold' light succeeds the physical 'warmth' of the natural sun. The structure of trance is that of confused activity, a constant streaming forward that incorporates numerous 'side' movements – 'hurrying to and fro'. The scene of what seems to be purposeless and futile agitation is presided over by the self-motion of a chariot – 'Of its own rushing splendour' – drawn by invisible but distinctly audible 'shapes', driven by a 'Shadow', and inhabited by a hooded, veiled 'Shape' – blood-brother (or sister), it seems to me, to that 'veiled form' confronted by Asia and Panthea, the 'mighty darkness / Filling the seat of power, and rays of gloom / Dart around, as light from the meridian sun' (*Prom.*, II, iv, 2–4); that 'terrible shadow' which, floating up from its throne, ascends the car pulled by the 'terrified' winged horses, driven by the 'ghastly charioteer', the 'Spirit with a dreadful countenance' (II, iv, 142–55). In *The Triumph of Life*, the Shape of gloom

>   a Shape
> So sate within, as one whom years deform,

> Beneath a dusky hood and double cape,
> Crouching within the shadow of a tomb;
> And o'er what seemed the head a cloud-like crape
>
> Was bent, a dun and faint aetherial gloom
> Tempering the light. . . .
>
> (ll. 87–93)

The presence that paradoxically 'dims the sun' in its shadowy devastating process, is trans-formed into 'another' luminosity, as the Poet's trance deepens and the mediation of Rousseau conducts him from the light of darkness to the 'Shape all light'. Light and sound intermingle again but in a different texture, weaving 'the mystic measure / Of music, and dance, and shapes of light' (*Prom.*, IV, 77–8), as optical and auditory perceptions fuse in the synaesthesia of an intense awareness which tramples the 'many-coloured' scarf of Iris, and reveals the 'white radiance' of the female form carrying the 'crystal glass, / Mantling with bright Nepenthe' (*Triumph*, ll. 358–9), suffused with 'nepenthe, love' (*Prom.*, IV, 163). Unlike the 'cold' of the previous vision, the main property of Iris, goddess of dawn, is a 'heat' that burns away the light of common day; she is a 'light diviner than the common sun', accompanied by 'magic sounds', and standing amid a sun intensely bright that 'burned on the waters' with 'emerald fire' ('emerald' pointing at least in three 'textual' directions – the 'emerald throne' of *The Witch of Atlas*, the ice 'green as emerald' of the *Ancient Mariner*, and the Emerald Table of Hermes Trismegistus).[14] The flatness of the ground on which the Shape of 'fierce splendour' stands, but also its commotion, is specifically suggested through the image of 'vibrating / Floor of the fountain, paved with flashing rays' (ll. 350–1) that inevitably gestures forward to those 'Marbles of the dancing floor' of Yeats' Byzantine imperial palace, where 'flames begotten of flame' die into a dance, 'An agony of trance, / An agony of flame that cannot singe a sleeve' ('Byzantium').

The 'Shape all light' is doubly occupied, dropping dewy freshness on the earth with her left hand and upholding the 'cup of love' with her right one. The 'fierce splendour' of the luminous form contrasts with the 'cold glare' of the first stage of the Poet's initiation into the experience of 'radiance' – first 'gloomy' and then 'bright'. The Shape possesses self-motion in 'partly treading the waves', but is also carried along by the movement of the stream; the whole of nature is harmonized into a 'ceaseless song', a 'measure new'. In her constant fluidity, the exquisite female dancer whose rhythmical mobility weaves the fabric of the world, teases the mind 'out of thought'[15] and inverts the properties of illusion and reality:

> 'And still her feet, no less than the sweet tune
> To which they moved, seemed as they moved to blot
> The thoughts of him who gazed on them; and soon
>
> 'All that was, seemed as if it had been not;
> And all the gazer's mind was strewn beneath
> Her feet like embers; and she, thought by thought,
>
> 'Trampled its sparks into the dust of death.
>
> (ll. 382–8)

Lines 375–423 contain four metaphors which testify to the speaker's difficulty to render his experience conceptually – emphatically choosing the method of εἰκὸς λόγος in speaking of what the thing is *like* rather than what it *is*. The dance, 'measure new', is translated into terms of light, 'as on the summer evening breeze, // "Up from the lake a shape of golden dew / Between two rocks, athwart the rising moon, / Dances i' the wind' (ll. 378–81). The extinction of thought and annihilation of memory is again imaginatively compared to the dawning of day, 'As day upon the threshold of the east / Treads out the lamps of night, until the breath // "Of darkness re-illumine even the least / Of heaven's living eyes' (ll. 389–92). Rousseau's initiation into the mystery of life, his address to the Shape coming from 'the realm without a name' – the deep, imageless truth – is answered by an invitation to drink from the 'cup' of love, archetypal symbol not only in 'romance' (the Grail myth) but also in 'ritual' – as Shelley's own reference in *Prometheus Unbound* suggests, in an apostrophe made by the Moon to her lover Earth:

> I, a most enamoured maiden
> Whose weak brain is overladen
> With the pleasure of her love,
> Maniac-like around thee move
> Gazing, an insatiate bride,
> On thy form from every side
> Like a Maenad, round the cup

Which Agave lifted up
In the weird Cadmaean forest.
(IV, 467–75)

In *The Triumph of Life* the effect of drinking the magic potion of 'love' is rendered figuratively through the use of two image clusters: those of erasure / chase and veil / star. The two symbolic compounds are distanced by an interlude of a few lines, which announces the revelation of a novel visionary experience, a brighter light that obscures the radiance of Iris: 'so on my sight / Burst a new vision, never seen before, // "And the fair shape waned in the coming light' (ll. 410–12). The first image, just preceding this annunciation, depicts the 'subject's' state of mind 'as sand // "Where the first wave had more than half erased / The track of deer on desert Labrador; / Whilst the wolf, from which they fled amazed, // "Leaves his stamp visibly upon the shore, / Until the second bursts' (ll. 405–10). The other image portrays the transmutation happening in the 'object', the quality of light itself, as the 'Shape of light' is gradually fading in the advent of a brighter light: 'As veil by veil the silent splendour drops / From Lucifer, amid the chrysolite // "Of sunrise, ere it tinge the mountain-tops' (ll. 413–15); the metaphor attempts to convey the 'new vision', the 'coming light', as a transition from dawn / twilight to full daylight – from Lucifer / Iris to 'Sun': 'And as the presence of that fairest planet, / Although unseen, is felt by one who hopes // "That his day's path may end as be began it, / In that star's smile, whose light is like the scent / Of a jonquil when evening breezes fan it' (ll. 416–20).

Lines 424–38 present, I think, the greatest imaginative difficulty, in that they contain the whole variety of forms of light appearing in the poem, in a manner of indistinct relationship – as the one highlights the other, or conversely fade into each other. It is the 'fourth stage' light (starting the counting with the physical sun at the beginning of the poem) that renders 'knowledge' of the mobile 'Shape all light':

> 'So knew I in that light's severe excess
> The presence of that Shape which on the stream
> Moved, as I moved along the wilderness,
>
> 'More dimly than a day-appearing dream,
> The ghost of a forgotten form of sleep;
> A light of heaven, whose half-extinguished beam

> 'Through the sick day in which we wake to weep
> Glimmers, for ever sought, for ever lost;
> So did that shape its obscure tenour keep
>
> 'Beside my path, as silent as a ghost;
> But the new Vision, and the cold bright car,
> With solemn speed and stunning music, crossed
>
> 'The forest, and as if from some dread war
> Triumphantly returning, the loud million
> Fiercely extolled the fortune of her star.
>
> (ll. 424–38)

'That light's severe excess' serves as a catalyst which renders cognition of the Shape's 'presence' *as* a 'ghost', the recollection of a forgotten existence. Although the syntactic ambiguities of the passage permit the possible identification of 'that light's severe excess' with 'that Shape', the distinction made between 'fair shape' and 'coming light' of l. 412 should, I think, be carried over into the reading of ll. 424–5, making 'light' the context of the Shape's 'knowledge', precisely as in the *Symposium* beauty is not sought for itself but because it facilitates τόκος ἐν καλῷ, the birth of new being.

Ambiguity also surrounds the expression 'light of heaven' which could be an attribute of the newly risen 'sun', the 'light's severe excess', or – by virtue of its 'half-extinguished beam' that continues the 'waning' metaphor – a property of the Shape glimmering, like Platonic beauty, through the objects of sense in the 'sick day'. The rhetorical conjunction of 'the new Vision' with 'the cold bright car' and the image of 'her star', somehow combines in a paradoxical manner all three modalities of metaphysical radiance in the poem – the 'cold glare', the 'fierce splendour', and the 'coming light'. The reappearance of the 'cold bright car' allows a re-entry from Rousseau's 'vision' into the Poet's 'trance' – with a difference: the inhabitant of the chariot is no longer the deformed Shape of gloom but the Shape all light, Iris / Lucifer, the morning star 'triumphantly returning',

> the loud million
> Fiercely extolled the fortune of her star.
>
> 'A moving arch of victory, the vermilion
> And green and azure plumes of Iris had
> Built high over her wind-wingéd pavilion,

'And underneath aetherial glory clad
The wilderness, and far before her flew
The tempest of the splendour, which forbade

'Shadow to fall from leaf and stone; the crew
Seemed in that light, like atomies to dance
Within a sunbeam; – some upon the new

'Embroidery of flowers, that did enhance
The grassy vesture of the desert, played,
Forgetful of the chariot's swift advance;

'Others stood gazing, till within the shade
Of the great mountain its light left them dim;
Others outspeeded it; and others made

'Circles around it, like the clouds that swim
Round the high moon in a bright sea of air;
And more did follow, with exulting hymn,

'The chariot and the captives fettered there: –
But all like bubbles on an eddying flood
Fell into the same track at last, and were

'Borne onward. . . .
                                    (ll. 437–60)

Summing up Shelley's depiction of the successive stages of 'enlightenment' in the poem we may discern a pattern that constellates the various types of luminosity, as a continuous process in which one form of light subsumes the other, or conversely a precedent light giving birth to the light that succeeds it through its own extinction – light begotten of light, to paraphrase Yeats again. At the first stage of the Poet's 'waking trance' that effaces the 'splendour' of the empirical sun, a vast light is realized associated with an intense experience of 'coldness' in the body, and the presence of a paradoxical 'radiant darkness' or black brilliance. At the second stage, initiated through the mediating intervention of Rousseau's narrative, and as the trance deepens, a 'Shape all light' marked by fierceness and intense heat, 'dawns' onto the speaker's consciousness. 'Obscurity' and 'chill' fade away, disclosing the luminous quality of 'form'; in this awakened state, the colourful properties of energy manifest themselves, as the filter (or veil) of confusion between the eye that sees and the object that is seen is suddenly removed and perception becomes precise and vivid.

Progressively, as the many-coloured scarf of the shape is drawn, a sort of naked energy and motion is experienced *as* brilliant light. That the appearance of the 'Shape all light' follows upon 'recognition' of the 'Shape of gloom' is possibly indicative of Shelley's expressive awareness (here as well as in *Prometheus Unbound*) that we cannot have the experience of light as long as we are involved with escaping the darkness; in fact, it appears that the very involvement with what Shelley calls 'the principle of self' (1954: 293) blocks the light. So finding out about this 'self', 'which obscures and distorts that which should be beautiful' (1954: 281), is a preliminary step to awareness; when it has been realized what this is and how it has come about, then the energy is set free to transform. Transformation to selflessness, in Shelley's view, does not render man into an amorphous entity, but 'strips the veil of familiarity from the world and lays bare the naked and sleeping beauty, which is the spirit of its forms' (1954: 295). By becoming sensitive to the perception of the 'formless' and colourless light (of what Plato calls οὐσία ὄντως οὖσα), the Poet / aspirant has been able to destroy the personality aspects, so the transmuted life-force can enhance spiritual growth. Finally, 'knowledge' lights upon and enlightens experience – the 'presence of that Shape which in the stream / Moved' is made manifest in the 'sick day' of actuality; cognition as a re-cognition, a recollection that unveils the essence of life, does not produce anything; it only reveals reality immediately.

The first stage of a re-entry into time and historical existence in *The Triumph of Life* (ll. 439–60) is marked by a rebirth of sanctified life – a life made 'real' by the incorporation of the sacred – which turns the actual into the mythical. Images of splendour, playfulness, circularity, celebration, and unification accompany Iris / Lucifer / Shape all light 'triumphantly returning' in a 'moving arch of victory.' Life's 'passengers' being carried within the same natural flow, 'all like bubbles on an eddying flood', suggests that to be 'whole' is to be willingly and knowingly attuned to the great forces of the universe – to acknowledge and give thanks 'with exulting hymn'; this is the path of life, a life presided over by the Shape all light. Life moves by itself; it is 'that early Form / Which moved upon its motion' (ll. 464–5) and as long as we think that we have to make it move we delude ourselves, Shelley implies. Life flows – a stream bearing onward its 'captives' playfully, like bubbles. Life goes on – thoughts come and go, perceptions arise and vanish of themselves, actions materialize – without anyone claiming that he has 'been', 'thought', 'seen', or 'done' it. The scene conveys the experience of living as 'play' where life is non-teleological, has no purpose at all but its own purpose: it just *is*. And the perceived forms that appear and disappear, that surge up from the stillness of non-being and dissolve back into it, turn out to be something like a dance, 'like atomies to dance / Within a sunbeam' (ll. 446–7), where 'self appears as what it is, an atom to a universe' (1954: 294) – a story of the ever-new creation rather than 'a "panorama" ' of a 'modern Dance of Death' (Reiman 1965: 35).

The poem is circular in its structuring, in that it portrays growth as an unfreezing or 'de-freezing', the tremendous opening experience when 'life can flow freely again' around and through its participants – but also the reverse process of narrowing down, the 'en-freezing' into that 'cold light, whose airs too soon deform' (l. 468), effected through the growing awareness of ego, or 'impersonalization', and made manifest gramatically in the emphatic reiteration of the personal pronoun:

> I among the multitude
> Was swept – me, sweetest flowers delayed not long;
> Me, not the shadow nor the solitude;
>
> 'Me, not that falling stream's Lethean song;
> Me, not the phantom of that early Form
> Which moved upon its motion – but among
>
> 'The thickest billows of that living storm
> I plunged, and bared my bosom to the clime
> Of that cold light, whose airs too soon deform.
>
> (ll. 460–8)

Rousseau speaks. Why Rousseau? – is a question that tantalizes the ἑρμηνευτής of the poem with the same urgency as the puzzling interrogations the text poses: 'And what is this?', 'And is all here amiss?', or finally, 'Then, what is life?'. As the deformed / transformed initiator into the mysteries of 'life', Rousseau plays the role of Virgil to Shelley's Dante, Mephistopheles to Goethe's Faust – and, definitely, Diotima to the Platonic Socrates. We have seen in our perusal of Shelley's correspondence at the time, how closely Rousseau and Goethe become associated, always, of course, under the canopy of the poet's perennial concern with Plato and Greek drama. H. Bloom gives a very interesting account of Rousseau's appearance in *The Triumph of Life*, which I intend to use as a launching board for my interpretation of the function of the philosopher of Romanticism in the poem. 'Rousseau', he claims, 'has attained completely to the state of nature; grotesquely, he has become a part of what Blake calls the Vegetative universe, the state of Generation, the world in which only a vegetable is comfortably at home. Rousseau's metamorphosis is opposite to the metamorphoses which are accomplished by mythopoeia. A man has become an old root; rather than a natural object having been humanized, a human being has been naturalized' (1959: 255).

That Greek mythology teems with countless examples of 'naturalized' humans – men and women turned into trees, and birds, and animals – is enough evidence, I think, to refute Bloom's thesis. Certainly, the 'naturalization' of Rousseau, an 'old root' with 'grassy hair' and 'hollows' for eyes, his occupying a middle state between senseless vegetation and rational humanity – *and* speaking a language whereby 'the passions of men are incorporated with the beautiful and permanent forms of nature' (Wordsworth 1974: I, 125) – renders him an appropriate mediational figure to initiate the Poet into the mysteries and meaning of the universe – and life. Speaking from 'within' – himself 'deformed' and 'deluded' – he unfolds the history of 'this deep scorn' like a sufferer who, having been awakened to 'reality' performs his shamanic mission by opening up the visionary realms of 'life' to the uninitiated. His vision, the 'Shape all light', is a life force, a power that permeates all; expressed conversely, his vision reveals that all that exists lives, i.e. has a living dynamic within. Granted the 'magic' world view – which acknowledges a kinship among all aspects of nature – Rousseau's transformation into a plant is neither unnatural nor surprising. The special and sanctified awareness of the universe is codified in Rousseau's tale of the *mysterium* which is life; the sacred way of the 'wounded healer' (or, to put it into modern terms, the 'wounded surgeon') is the narrating of a transpersonal experience resulting from a crisis of death and rebirth, a transformation of profane existence into one that is sacramental (and in the specific instance of *The Triumph of Life*, a return to profaneness, yet 'trailing clouds of glory').

Accounts of the shaman's inner jouney of turmoil and distress through exposure to natural forces emphasize the danger, and often horrifying quality of the undertaking – an experience of 'destruction' through which comes 'instruction'.[16] Rousseau's 'paedeutics' to the near-silent auditor of the Poet falls into three parts: discursive presentation, imaginative revelation, followed by a third stage of discourse. The first step of (to use Shelley's terms) λογίζειν, prior to ποιεῖν, is 'negative' in character – in that it presents what has been neglected – and 'critical'; to the Poet's inquiry 'and who are those chained to the car?' Rousseau answers:

> 'The wise,
>
> 'The great, the unforgotten, – they who wore
> Mitres and helms and crowns, or wreaths of light,
> Signs of thought's empire over thought – their lore
>
> 'Taught them not this, to know themselves; their might
> Could not repress the mystery within,
> And for the morn of truth they feigned, deep night
>
> 'Caught them ere evening.' . . .
>
> (ll. 208–15)

The speaker's 'return' from the encounter with the 'fierce splendour' of the Shape, is rendered in language that refers to the experience in terms of a ritual νέκυια, or descent to the underworld, as the obvious identification with Dante suggests; now the message is 'positive' and 'emotive', unquestionably Dantesque but also Shelleyan:

> 'Before the chariot had begun to climb
> The opposing steep of that mysterious dell,
> Behold a wonder worthy of the rhyme
>
> 'Of him who from the lowest depths of hell,
> Through every paradise and through all glory,
> Love led serene, and who returned to tell
>
> 'The words of hate and awe; the wondrous story
> How all things are transfigured except Love.
>
> (ll. 469–76)

That 'love' should be both the ultimate 'good' beyond the

constant process of 'becoming', beyond the duality and conflict of opposites, and simultaneously a 'victimizer', is one of the paradoxes of the poem. Characteristically, it is Plato, the philosopher of love's celebration, that has fallen victim to the snares of apparently perverted, unsublimated passion for 'Aster' (the 'flower of heaven' encapsulating in its ambivalence the star-image and the Platonic reference to man as οὐράνιον φυτόν):

> 'All that is mortal of great Plato there
> Expiates the joy and woe his master knew not;
> The star that ruled his doom was far too fair,
>
> 'And life, where long that flower of Heaven grew not,
> Conquered that heart by love, which gold, or pain,
> Or age, or sloth, or slavery could subdue not.
> (ll. 254–9)

Plato's 'transgression' is apparently a 'wasting' of love and sexual energy in untransformed indulgence, rather than its employment as a creative impetus along the ladder of beauty – a failure, or unwillingness, to 'consider how nearly related the beauty of any one body is to the beauty of any other', which would 'set himself to be the lover of every lovely body, and bring his passion for the one into due proportion by deeming it of little or of no importance' (*Symp.*, 210b). Rousseau testifies to as great a 'crime' for himself: 'I was overcome / By my own heart alone, which neither age, // "Nor tears, nor infamy, nor now the tomb / Could temper to its object" ' (ll. 240–3).

Shelley's choice of Rousseau as an initiator into the mysteries of life, which to a large extent is an initiation into the mysteries of love – a close analogue to Diotima's ἐρωτικά – must have been dictated by his awareness of the primacy of passion, 'the quivering, the quick devouring fire more rapid than lightning', which Rousseau admits to having consumed away his life.[17] As he confesses in his *Confessions*: 'My passions are extremely strong, and while I am under their sway nothing can equal my impetuosity. I am amenable to no restraint, respect, fear, or decorum. I am cynical, bold, violent, and daring' (1953: 44). In its audacity, vehemence, and aggresiveness, Rousseau's depiction of the passionate state falls surprisingly close to Socrates' description of ἔρως in the *Symposium*, who, in his advances upon the 'beautiful' of which he is desperately 'needy' uses all of his resourcefulness, being 'gallant, impetuous, and energetic, a mighty hunter, and a master of device and artifice – at once desirous and full of wisdom, a lifelong seeker after truth, an adept in sorcery, enchantment, and seduction' (203d).

Rousseau recognizes the devastating presence of affectivity in his life: 'I was devoured alternately by desires and by fears', unalleviated 'permanent passion'; 'So I was burning with love for no object, and it is perhaps love of this sort that is the most exhausting', a love that repeatedly fails to lead to consummation: 'Physical pleasure! Is it the lot of man to enjoy it? Ah, if ever in all my life I had once tasted the delights of love to the full, I do not think that my frail existence could have endured them. I should have died on the spot' (1953: 210). Caught between 'earthly' and 'heavenly' Aphrodite – or such 'conceptions' of love – Rousseau seems suspended in a mental / physical agony that cancels both: 'No, Nature has not made me for sensual delight. She has put the hunger for it in my heart, but what might be ineffable pleasure turns to poison in my wretched head' (1953: 300), he admits despairingly. He gives intimate instances of erotic failure that, despite their documentary matter-of-factness, evoke an imaginative aura familiar to readers of Shelley's poetry:

> Do not attempt to imagine the charms and graces of that enchanting girl. You would not come near to the truth. Young virgins in the cloisters are not more fresh, seraglio beauties are not so sportive, the houris of paradise are less enticing. Never was such sweet pleasure offered to mortal heart and senses.
>
> (1953: 300)

Or even more emphatically: 'I entered a courtesan's room as if it were the sanctuary of love and beauty; in her person I felt I saw the divinity' (1953: 300). Without making any suggestions of influence or 'mimesis', one cannot help noticing the physical basis of rhetorical figures in this parallel reading of Rousseau's autobiography and Shelley's poetry. One could even argue that traces if not of a 'visionary' at least of an 'auditory' and 'kinetic' experience, evoking the 'magic sounds' and the 'vibrating floor' of Rousseau's trance in *The Triumph of Life*, can be read back into the autobiographical material that is presented in *The Confessions*:

> One morning . . . I felt a sudden, almost inconceivable disturbance throughout my whole body. I cannot describe it better than a kind of storm which started in my blood and instantly took control of all my limbs. . . . This was accompanied by a great noise in my ears of three or four different kinds: a dull, heavy buzzing, a sharper note as of running water, a very shrill whistling and the throbbing I have described, the pulsations of which I could easily count without feeling my pulse or touching my body with my hands. This internal noise was so loud that it robbed me of the fine ear I had once possessed.
>
> (1953: 217)

It is perhaps Rousseau's susceptibility to extra-ordinary sensuous experiences, coupled with his avowed veneration for love and beauty, that conditioned Shelley's choice of a historical figure uniting the functions of lover / philosopher, prophet, ceremonialist, and poet – thus containing in 'one' all four aspects of μανία or divine madness:

> And in the divine kind we distinguish four types, ascribing them to four gods: the inspiration of the prophet to Apollo [μαντικήν], that of the mystic to Dionysus [τελεστικήν], that of the poet to the Muses [ποιητικήν], and a fourth type which we declared to be the highest, the madness of the lover [ἐρωτικήν], to Aphrodite and Eros.
>
> (*Phaedr.*, 265b)

It is precisely this fourth type that in the *Symposium*, as we have seen, is called 'the philosophical frenzy' – τῆς φιλοσόφου μανίας καὶ βακχείας.

Rousseau perfectly fits into the role of a modern version of the manic / mantic philosopher – a Romantic equivalent, if not to Socrates, then to Plato; nor is it accidental, I believe, that Plato and Rousseau in *The Triumph of Life* are the only ones conquered by 'excess' of love rather than pride, power, thought, will, fame. Rousseau's distinction from the rest of the 'deluded crew' is that his 'wretchedness' is an illusion 'seen through' which translates victimization into awareness – even if such awareness is of 'The horror! the horror!'.[18] His 'botanical' appearance, paradoxically not only sustained but welcome, 'nor this disguise / Stain that which ought to have disdained to wear it' (ll. 204–5), identifies him to nature itself, a visible embodiment of the sacred forces that pervade the empirical world and a spokesman for their creative / destructive impact upon human life. Wearing the 'mask' of nature, Rousseau 'naturalized' is the iconography chosen by Shelley to portray the vegetative condition and the divinity that inhabits it – the Dionysian life force; Rousseau's metamorphosis 'speaks' of matter not only as alive but more especially as the reservoir of 'power', of its awakening and 'materializing'. Shelley's homologizing the human body with a plant, the suggestion that the cosmos is contained within a man's own physical structure, receives a clear imaginative utterance – which of course requires the painful recognition and acceptance of the existence of ambivalent forces within oneself. Rousseau admits to having been swept away by fear, love, hate, suffering (l. 200), but his very admission ratifies and transforms them. His – and Shelley's – attitude suggests that the purpose is not to suppress or eliminate these energies; to fully envision – and 'converse' with – the 'passions' or aspects of the soul which one is most afraid of confronting, seems to be the only way of overcoming them. No matter how terrifying or 'infuriated' the projections and visions of human fears may be, they are transformable; fully recognized, these 'execrable shapes' (*Prom.*, I, 449) are no longer destructive.

The gestures and motions of the multitude 'caught' by the chariot of life are controlled by 'fear': 'Mixed in one mighty torrent did appear, / Some flying from the thing they feared, and some / Seeking the object of another's fear' (ll. 53–5); they are also dominated by 'ignorance': 'All hastening onward, yet none seemed to know / Whither he went, or whence he came, or why / He made one of the multitude' (ll. 47–9). It is an ignorance of beginnings and ends, of the 'whither', 'where', 'what', 'why', 'how' – questions that are socially prohibitive, morally irrelevant, and religiously reprehensible. The population of the poem is trapped in a world of 'shadows', exhausted in the effort to secure and safeguard themselves, struggling to conquer and escape:

> Upon that path where flowers never grew, –
> And, weary with vain toil and faint for thirst,
> Heard not the fountains, whose melodious dew
>
> Out of their mossy cells forever burst;
> Nor felt the breeze which from the forest told
> Of grassy paths and wood-lawns interspersed

With overarching elms and caverns cold,
And violet banks where sweet dreams brood, but they
Pursued their serious folly as of old.
(ll. 65–73)

Persistent 'striving' and 'progressing' makes humans deaf ('heard not'), insensitive ('nor felt'), and blind to the 'presence' of nature.

The confused to and fro motion of the multitude growing wilder, as when 'the south wind shakes the extinguished day', rises in intensity and is paradoxically schematized enough to conceptually fit into the category of 'dance': 'The million with fierce song and maniac dance / Raging around' (ll. 110–11). In fact, dancing *is* the universal action of the poem: 'The wild dance maddens in the van',

To savage music, wilder as it grows,

They, tortured by their agonizing pleasure,
Convulsed and on the rapid whirlwinds spun
Of that fierce Spirit, whose unholy leisure

Was soothed by mischief since the world begun,
Throw back their heads and loose their streaming hair.
(ll. 142–7)

Although Shelley refrains from overtly 'naming' this exhibition of hysterical dance, its phenomenological character is sufficiently clear to allow its encoding under the experience known – in its Greek version – as 'maenadism'. In his book, *The Greeks and the Irrational*, E. R. Dodds explores both the sacred and the profane aspects of the phenomenon, contending that 'in Greece the ritual oreibasia at a fixed date may originally have developed out of spontaneous attacks of mass hysteria. By canalising such hysteria in an organised rite once in two years, the Dionysiac cult kept it within bounds and gave it a relatively harmless outlet'. What the chorus in the opening scene of Euripides' play *Bacchae* depicts is 'hysteria subdued to the service of religion; what happened on Mount Cithaeron was hysteria in the raw, the dangerous Bacchism which descends as a punishment on the too respectable and sweeps them away against their will. Dionysus', he informs us, 'is present in both: like St. John or St. Vitus, he is the cause of madness and the liberator from madness, Βάκχος and

Λύσιος'. This equivocalness is inherent in the nature of the god and must be recognized, Dodds asserts: 'To resist Dionysus is to repress the elemental in one's own nature; the punishment is the sudden complete collapse of the inward dykes when the elemental breaks through perforce and civilisation vanishes' (1951: 272–3).

We must keep this 'ambivalence' in mind, I believe, when we attempt to interpret *The Triumph of Life* – the poem, the Poet, the mediator, the action, the vision, the dance, the triumph, and the question about 'life' that rounds it all. In fact, it seems to me the ambiguity can be carried as far as the original 'conception' of the poetic construct that may be said to represent the figurative embodiment of Shelley's declaration: 'I read the Greek dramatists & Plato forever'; as I see it, it is not only Shelley's 'own Symposium' but a blending of the *Symposium* and the *Bacchae*,[19] presenting the dual possibilities of a 'triumph' of life: μανία integrated and transformed versus μανία thwarted and exploding. 'Wholeness' seen as unity of being must encompass the dark side of life as well: pain, suffering, tragedy, and death; wholeness and 'health' therefore do not exclude these negative phenomena but incorporate them. Transformation lies in the exploration and imaginative integration of the chthonic Dionysian forces through 'discourse', or an amplitude of 'panoramic' vision afforded by an Apollonian 'attitude'.

The importance of μανία as a source of divine inspiration, or more specifically as an experience of the 'participation' (κοινωνία) of the sacred in the empirical world, holds the centre not only of the Platonic dialogue but also of the Euripidean play. The message of Dionysus, as presented by the dramatist, is that the 'pride' of those convinced of the supremacy of reason will fall into confusion, and whoever resists the invitation of the god – a 'calling' to joy and communion with nature through the simplicity of sensation and emotion – is condemned to a condition of insanity, itself a manifestation of revenge of the neglected Dionysian spirit. In his attempt to account for the controversial function of the Dionysian forces in the *Bacchae*, Dodds refers to parallel examples from other cultures, which may 'enlighten' the destructive / creative experience of maenadism – the horrifying punishment of Pentheus and Agave, and the deeply gratifying knowledge expressed in the celebrating hymn of the chorus:

Blest is the happy man
Who knows the mysteries the gods ordain,
And sanctifies his life,
Joins soul with soul in mystic unity,
And, by due ritual made pure,
Enters the ecstasy of mountain solitudes;
Who observes the mystic rites
Made lawful by Cybele the Great Mother;
Who crowns his head with ivy,
And shakes aloft his wand in worship of Dionysus.
(ll. 74–83)

'In many societies', Dodds contends, drawing on external authority to support his argument, 'there are people for whom, as Mr. Aldous Huxley puts it, "ritual dances provide a religious experience that seems more satisfying and convincing than any other. . . . It is with their muscles that they most easily obtain knowledge of the divine." Mr. Huxley', Dodds continues, 'thinks that Christianity made a mistake when it allowed the dance to become completely secularised, since, in the words of a Mohammedan sage, "he that knows the Power of the Dance dwells in God." But the Power of the Dance is a dangerous power. Like other forms of self-surrender, it is easier to begin than to stop'. The hazards inherent in dancing, Dodds explains, are not only personal intoxication but transpersonal infection: 'As Pentheus observes at *Bacchae* 778, it spreads like wildfire. The will to dance takes possession of people without the consent of the conscious mind . . . Even sceptics were sometimes, like Agave, infected with the mania against their will, and contrary to their professed belief' (1951: 271–2).

That Dionysus never makes any sex or age discriminations of the type 'That is no country for old men' (Yeats, 'Sailing to Byzantium', I), is attested to by the Athenian in Plato's *Laws*, Tiresias in the *Bacchae*, and the Poet in *The Triumph of Life*: 'But when a man is verging on the forties, we shall tell him . . . to invoke the gods, and more particularly to ask the presence of Dionysus in that sacrament and pastime of advancing years – I mean the wine cup' (*Laws*, II, 666b–c). Furthermore, the Athenian refers to the equivocation surrounding Dionysus, the 'old unqualified censure of the gift of Dionysus as an evil thing', and the 'current of story and pious tradition' that explains the affliction of 'his victims with Bacchic possession and all its frenzied dancing, by way of revenge' (II, 672a–b). In a parallel manner, Tiresias protests: 'Not so; the god draws no distinction between young / And old, to tell us which should dance and which should not / He desires equal worship from all men: his claim / To glory is universal; no one is exempt' (*Bacchae*, ll. 206–9). Finally, Shelley exposes the phenomenon from its 'other' side, not of worship and self-surrender, but neglect and self-usurpation:

> Maidens and youths fling their wild arms in air
> As their feet twinkle; they recede, and now
> Bending within each other's atmosphere,
>
> Kindle invisibly – and as they glow,
> Like moths by light attracted and repelled,
> Oft to their bright destruction come and go.
> (ll. 149–54)

Also

> behind,
> Old men and women foully disarrayed,
> Shake their gray hairs in the insulting wind,
>
> And follow in the dance, with limbs decayed,
> Seeking to reach the light which leaves them still
> Farther behind and deeper in the shade.
> (ll. 164–9)

The paradoxical experience of fascination with abomination that the Shelleyan multitude seems to undergo in its frantic and ecstatic dancing, is attributed by Dodds to 'The culminating act of the Dionysian winter dance', which was 'the tearing to pieces, and eating raw, of an animal body, σπαραγμός and ὠμοφαγία', a practice that filled its participants with 'a mixture of supreme exaltation and supreme repulsion: it is at once holy and horrible, fulfilment and uncleanness, a sacrament and a pollution – the same violent conflict of emotional attitudes that runs all through the *Bacchae* and lies at the root of all religion of the Dionysiac type' (1944: xvi–xvii). The intense affective equivocalness that the experience of sacrality evokes in the human is also emphasized in the archaic designation of divinity, as expounded by Cassirer: 'The original mythical concept of holiness coincides so little with that of ethical purity that a remarkable opposition, a characteristic tension, can arise between the two. That which is hallowed in a mythical and religious sense has thereby become forbidden, an object of awe, hence unclean. This double meaning', he specifies, 'this peculiar ambivalence is still expressed in the Latin *sacer* and the Greek ἅγιος, ἅζεσθαί, for these terms designate both the holy and the accursed or forbidden, but in both cases something consecrated and set apart' (1955b: 79).

The conflict is not only present in the emotional attitudes of those who 'suffer' the visitations of the god, but also in the consequences that this in-dwelling effects, ranging between poles of ultimate extremity: pernicious practices rending the most tenable family and social bonds or acts of social edification – rituals which ground the mythological conceptions and explanatory systems that give significance and direction to human suffering. In the words of Tiresias again, 'this god is a prophet; the Bacchic ecstasy / And frenzy hold a strong prophetic element. / When he fills irresistibly a human body / He gives those so possessed power to foretell the future' (*Bacchae*, ll. 298–301). 'Dionysus' is as much a controversial figure in Euripides' play, as 'life' is an ambiguous concept – and image – in Shelley's poem; and 'revenge' lies at the heart of both as the 'triumph' of that which has been neglected, despised, scorned, combated – or simply ignored. 'The vengeance of Dionysus', Dodds asserts, 'is as cruel and undiscriminating as the vengeance of Aphrodite in the *Hippolytus*'; from the standpoint of human morality, Pentheus, the god's adversary and ritual victim may be considered as 'one of the martyrs of enlightenment'; yet Euripides, the critic modifies his proposition, has 'invested him with the traits of a typical tragedy-tyrant' (1944: xlii–xliii), characteristics which, in their enumeration, would certainly place him among Shelley's oppressors of mankind in *The Triumph of Life* and elsewhere, those whose wielding of power 'Taught them not this, – to know themselves; their might / Could not repress the mystery [mutiny] within' (ll. 212–13).

Self-knowledge or understanding 'other', both the play and the poem seem to suggest, necessitate a great deal of humility, care, and precision. Taking a journey of discovery into the most secret corners of our 'being' (or the 'soul' as Plato would put it), is like stepping on the razor's edge. It is essential to relate to oneself, to one's own experience, to unpleasant or dark facets, 'really'. If one cannot connect to oneself, to the δαίμονα σύνοικον ἑαυτῷ (*Timaeus*, 90c), then the life path becomes dangerous. 'As the "moral" of the *Hippolytus*', Dodds remarks, 'is that sex is a thing about which you cannot afford to make mistakes, so the "moral" of the *Bacchae* is that we ignore at our peril the demand of the human spirit for Dionysiac experience'; whether the surfacing of Dionysus will prove creative or destructive largely depends, in the critic's view, on the quality, or 'attitude', of the consciousness that is to receive him: 'For those who do not close their minds against it such experience can be a deep source of spiritual power and εὐδαιμονία. But those who repress the demand in themselves or refuse its satisfaction to others transform it by their act into a power of disintegration and destruction, a blind natural force that sweeps away the innocent with the guilty'. The inexorable and inflexible 'necessity' of the phenomenon cannot be stressed too forcibly, Dodds warns us: 'When that has happened, it is too late to reason or to plead: in man's justice there is room for pity, but there is none in the justice of Nature; to our "Ought" its sufficient reply is the simple "Must"; we have no choice but to accept that reply and to endure as we may' (1944: xlv).

The end of Shelley's poem, although equally invoking the fact that life cannot be fooled, does not portray the tragedy but the misery of existence; it is simply the 'boredom', to the 'horror' of the *Bacchae*, and the 'glory' of the *Symposium* – to borrow Eliot's pattern of reading the human condition (1933: 106). There is no act of violence or expiation, but a lingering futility of 'living and partly living' (Eliot 1935: 62), as

After brief space,
From every form the beauty slowly waned;

'From every firmest limb and fairest face
The strength and freshness fell like dust, and left
The action and the shape without the grace

'Of life. . . .
(ll. 518–23)

'Shape without form, shade without colour / Paralysed force, gesture without motion' (Eliot, 'The Hollow Men', I), in a parody of living that signifies petrification – the emptiness of 'formality' deprived of ritual meaning which assimilates mortals to divinities, making all human actions sacred in the unity of life that throbs through all. Progressive diminution of energy, beauty, and joy is the theme of the poem's closing lines:

> thus on the way
> Mask after mask fell from the countenance
> And form of all; and long before the day
>
> 'Was old, the joy which waked like heaven's glance
> The sleepers in the oblivious valley, died;
> And some grew weary of the ghastly dance,
>
> 'And fell, as I have fallen, by the wayside; –
> Those soonest from whose forms most shadows passed,
> And least of strength and beauty did abide.
>
> (ll. 535–43)

In a literary construct whose texture is ironic rather than tragic, the inconclusive conclusion of its ultimate question may very well be seen as a rhetorical device rather than as a sign of incompleteness. Contrary to Shelley's expressed intentionality and despite the work's 'apparent' fragmentariness, I would contend that the poem is essentially completed, if unfinished; not only is *The Triumph of Life not* a fragment (certainly not in the way Keats' *Hyperion* and *The Fall of Hyperion* are), but the interrogative form that nearly closes it is the only manner in which a poem teeming with ambiguities and 'overwhelming' questionings *could* end,[20] precisely in the way the Platonic dialogues 'terminate' their dialectic. It is the question, the guest that suggests the mystery which is life. Answers close reality, questions open it anew. In his discussion of the hermeneutical priority of the question, as we have seen, Gadamer asserts that 'it is more difficult to ask questions than to answer them', because 'to ask a question means to bring into the open. The openness of what is in question consists in the fact that the answer is not settled' (1975: 326). The state of indeterminacy to which the question form leads is the state of irresolution that is simultaneously an admission of ignorance and an invitation to apocalyptic conversation; and 'To conduct a conversation', Gadamer has challenged, 'means to allow oneself to be conducted by the object' (1975: 330).

To the philosophical justification of the question form as the appropriate ending for a poem that ventures into the signification

– and significance – of 'life', one could add its mythical counterpart, thus enlisting both λόγος and μῦθος as supporters of the paradoxical assertion that the 'asking' is the 'answer'. In many myths and rituals having for their ultimate object the initiation into the unapparent sources of life – including most of the Grail romances – a question must be asked if the waters are to flow again, and the waste land is to be redeemed, 'the important Grail question which will end the Wounded King's pain' (Matthews 1984: 112). Usually there is no response to these ceremonial inquiries, but there is a transformative quality in their content and structure – passing from the causality of 'why' to the ontology of 'what'. The poem's final asking of what is the meaning of life is not only a thrust into the void but a definite progress, a minor(?) 'triumph' over the ineffable, in that it substitutes the earlier question asked – 'And what is this?' – by an interrogative type that partly contains its own answer, in the self-referentiality of the final question form. The answer is not something 'out there'; the answer to the one obstinate question of what it is all about, is necessarily the asking of it, the ἀπορία – the living and experiencing the perplexity. As Heidegger puts it, 'The true problem is what we do not know and what, insofar as we know it *authentically*, namely *as* a problem, we know only *questioningly*. To know how to question means to know how to wait, even a whole lifetime' (1959: 206).

It would be of interest to trace the question which terminates Shelley's poetic career to its early manifestation in an essay 'On Life' apparently composed in 1812–14; although 'speculative and metaphysical', in that it relies quite heavily on various trends of contemporary philosophy while attempting to distinguish them, the work introduces very clearly some of the nuclei thoughts and images that underlie Shelley's last poem – and all his work:

> What is life? Thoughts and feelings arise, with or without our will, and we employ words to express them. We are born, and our birth is unremembered, and our infancy remembered but in fragments; we live on, and in living we lose the apprehension of life. How vain is it to think that words can penetrate the mystery of our being! Rightly used they may make evident our ignorance to ourselves, and this is much. For what are we? Whence do we come? And whither do we go? Is birth the commencement, is death the

conclusion of our being? What is birth and death?

(1954: 172)

The passage speaks of thoughts, feelings, and language as the phenomenology of life, mental events are brought alongside physical events to which the mind is 'subjected'. Paradoxically, 'living on' obliterates awareness of life; in the gradual identification with the life process and thought process, the natural, effortless 'happening' of living is forgotten:

> Life and the world, or whatever we call that which we are and feel, is an astonishing thing. The mist of familiarity obscures from us the wonder of our being. We are struck with admiration at some of its transient modifications, but it is itself the great miracle.
>
> (1954: 172)

The 'mist of familiarity', an earlier version of the 'painted veil', estranges us from ourselves, Shelley implies, by establishing a mental condition where everything is 'known' or taken for granted, obliterating question, perplexity, observation. To understand anything one must live with it, care for it, know its content, its nature, its movement. Life, Shelley notes, is not a static state, but a living thing; and to live with a living thing, mind must also be alive and alert, free from the habitude of received opinions, ideologies, and values:

> Life, the great miracle, we admire not, because it is so miraculous. It is well that we are thus shielded by the familiarity of what is at once so certain and so unfathomable from an astonishment which would otherwise absorb and overawe the functions of that which is its object.
>
> (1954: 172)

In a statement that approximates Eliot's 'Human kind cannot bear very much reality' (1935: 55), Shelley's veil of familiarity is dressed in the ambiguous function of obstructing / protecting the encounter with 'what is' – the constant transiency and flow of existence where things arise and vanish momentarily. The 'Essay on Life' suggests an approach to reality, which sees impermanence as the great mystery; everything is changing in each moment – minds, bodies, situations; an attitude that stays 'fluid', free of 'familiar' concepts, self-images, and projections 'allows for' these changes with an openness that accepts phenomena as they are. Familiarity, Shelley urges, acts as a screen and becomes an obstacle to the discovery of 'nowness' by constantly referring the mind to past residue and future contrivance, memory and desire.

Much as Shelley has attempted a discourse on the problem of 'life' in conceptual terms, he has refrained, as already discussed, from giving a definitive answer in his poetic compositions, where the 'dialogue' between poetry and thinking expresses the dialectical rhythm of the experience itself – precisely as it underlies the movement of Plato's thought which *is* in a sense the process it describes – the *form* being the thing, and the *method* the truth. Shelley rephrases in poetic terms the Platonic concept of philosophy as the 'activity' of human mind, which makes of 'discourse' not just a theoretical thought process but a mythical 'event', an archetypal drama. Consciousness is the field where the 'play' is being performed, by entering into ambivalence and dialogue, posing the questions and 'waiting' for answers to emerge.

LAMIA AS KEATS' SYMPOSIUM

Before concluding my discussion on 'eros in logos' I should like briefly to touch upon yet another Romantic 'symposium' (as feast and dialogue), Keats' *Lamia*. In more ways than one, it may be considered not only a reproduction of the thematics of the original *Symposium* but also a commentary upon it. The subject of the poem, we are told, 'is taken from Burton's *Anatomy of Melancholy*; and Burton, while he speaks of the heroine as a serpent or Lamia and refers her to the general category of evil spirits, has nothing to say of the vampire-like proclivities ordinarily associated with lamias. Still less is there any hint of this side of her nature in Keats' rendering. Lamia is, to be sure, a snake-woman, a creature of enchantment' (Beach 1944: 125). It was on the margin of the Burton book, as we have already seen, that Keats jotted down his truly agonizing remark concerning the possible relation between the carnal and the spiritual eros, of which S. Sperry reminds us: 'In *Lamia* as (in a more diffuse way) in *Endymion*, the poetic and sexual themes, both broadly imaginative in their concern are inseparable'; he underlines that 'Nothing better illustrates this fact than part of the comment Keats penned into the margin of his copy of Burton's *Anatomy*'.

The critic believes that the annotation is apocalyptic of Keats' personal inner conflict, and touches upon 'the root of Lamia's ambivalence, a quality that the self-confident Hermes is able to ignore or take for granted but that proves fatal to the poet-scholar Lycius'; 'Throughout the poem', he recapitulates, 'the glance of dazzled wonder and the voyeur's piercing stare are increasingly at odds' (1973: 300–1).

I would argue that what is 'at odds' in *Lamia* is more than just two ways of 'seeing'; the perceptual distinction is an aspect of an ontological dialectic that in its mythic form is presented as the contention between the 'hero' and the 'dragon' – whose archetypal version (at least in the tradition from which Keats was drawing his materials) is the battle of Apollo and Python. The most archaic manifestation of the Delphic dragon – or better dragoness (Python's original sex being female) – appears in the Homeric Hymn to Apollo, where 'we find the earliest known record of Apollo's combat with a dragon at Delphi. Soon after his birth on Delos, Apollo crossed the sea and wandered over the mainland, looking for a good place in which to establish an oracular shrine'. J. Fontenprose continues his investigation by giving further details about the paradigmatic incident; it is likely, he postulates, 'that Apollo encountered her while he was at work on the foundations not more than a few yards from her spring. She was a monstrous creature, huge and savage, guilty of terrible violence against the people and the flocks of the land. To meet her meant death to any man' (1959: 13–14).

The correlation between the 'serpent' and Dionysus has been established in both mythical and historical terms. Not only does traditional symbolology employ the serpent form as one of the god's phenomenological configurations – 'The association of Dionysos with Python may not appear so strange, once we realise that Dionysos took the form of snakes and several kinds of beasts and was associated with them' (1959: 378) – but the attributes of the Dionysian and the serpentine are blended in the context of Delphic practices. The oracle's early name Πυθώ (from the snake's dual name Typhon / Python) survives into Πυθία. That both the prophetess and the oracle existed before the arrival of Apollo appears to be a common recognition in the ancient world. The ὀμφαλός was considered the serpent's tomb, and the presence of bones and skin around the tripod had to do with remnants of an earlier cult of Python. 'Now much the same statements were made about Dionysos', Fontenprose informs us, stressing that 'Dionysos spoke oracles at Delphi before Apollo did . . . his bones were placed in a basin beside the tripod', and 'the omphalos was his tomb'. Furthermore, it was widely known that 'Dionysos was second only to Apollo in Delphian and Parnassian worship; Plutarch, in fact, assigns to Dionysos an equal share with Apollo' (1959: 375).

Despite its mythical elimination, the historical presence of Dionysus at Delphi, only second, or perhaps equal to that of Apollo, and the fact that there appears to have been no competition between the two cults, testifies to a harmonious coexistence or the possibility of 'discourse' between the Apollonian and Dionysian in Greek culture – whose artistic expression has been recognized in Keats' reading of the Grecian urn, and whose linguistic formulation is dramatized, I believe, in Plato's own Συμ-πόσιον. The alternate worship of the two gods at Delphi, and the unobstructed periodicity of παιάν and διθύραμβος, divided the ritual year between the Olympian Apollo who presided over the 'light' months, and the Chthonian Dionysus who ruled in the 'dark' of winter. It is this underworld, daemonic nature of Dionysus, which, contrary to the Olympian 'apathetic' way, apparently establishes a commerce between the human and the divine; it also makes Dionysus a deity of 'darkness' and 'death', god of fertility and sterility alike, preserver and destroyer. 'This Dionysus at Delphi was a god of death and winter', Fontenprose reports; 'Nothing is more certainly known about him than that he was the center of Delphic worship for the three winter months, when Apollo was absent' (1959: 379).

That the 'slaying' of the Dionysian / Pythian 'old darkness' by Apollo, the 'new light god' – the first of a long series of heroic dragon killers – is more of a 'transformation' than 'annihilation' is fully documented, I think, by the historical cohabitation of the two gods at Delphi – which allows for the alternate sway of light and darkness. The Delphic practice 'signifies' – as in the Heraclitean dictum, according to which 'The lord whose oracle is in Delphi neither declares nor conceals, but gives a sign [ὁ ἄναξ οὗ τὸ μαντεῖόν ἐστι τὸ ἐν Δελφοῖς οὔτε λέγει οὔτε κρύπτει ἀλλὰ σημαίνει]' (Heraclitus 1979: 42–3) – that the magical level of consciousness need not be definitely effaced under the advent of enlightened rationalism, that μῦθος and λόγος can coexist in 'significant conversation'. Later versions and names for the original Delphian dragoness, the Delphyne Πυθώ who fought Apollo, Fontenprose maintains, enlist among its various manifestations those of Gorgo and Lamia, all bearing attributes of creative vitality and destructive energy, since 'the she-monster . . . has in her keeping the instrument of potency' (1959: 245). Thus we see that Greek mythology establishes an unquestionable 'blood' relationship between the figures of Dionysus, Typhon / Python, Gorgo, and Lamia, and their iconic representation through the 'snake' (1959: 284–8). It is characteristic of the metamorphosis of one mythic force into another that 'sex' remains indeterminate, hermaphroditic. The ambiguity playing around the Pythonic sex – and gender – exhibits a consistency in keeping the feminine component steadily in focus, if not as an attribute of the creature itself, then as the prominent aspect of its parentage: 'This frightful woman [Hecate, Lamia, Echidna] was spectre, ogress, vampire, snake, sea monster, several kinds of beast and various mixtures of them. Her various forms group themselves', Fontenprose specifies, 'about the realm of death, the sea, and the terrible or weird fauna of the earth, especially snakes' (1959: 117). The serpentine Dionysus is related to water and humidity, but also to fire; not only is the account of his birth in the opening scene of the *Bacchae* given in 'fiery' terms, 'From her womb the fire / Of a lightning-flash delivered me' (ll. 2–3), but the whole play teems with images of fireburning and earthquake volcanic eruptions.

Keats' *Lamia* is placed chronologically in *illud tempus*, the mythical or fairy tale once 'Upon a time'. The female protagonist is a creature of colourful radiance, a 'palpitating snake', 'a gordian shape of dazzling hue', 'some demon's mistress or the demon's self'.[21] 'Madness', 'torture', 'anguish', 'writhing', 'convulsion', 'scarlet pain' are the psycho-physiological symptoms that accompany the scene of her transfiguration into a 'woman's shape' or 'woman's form' – her original mien. As her many-coloured veil dropped, 'A deep volcanian yellow took the place / Of all her milder-mooned body's grace' (I, 155–6): 'So that, in moments few, she was undrest / Of all her sapphires, greens, and amethyst, / And rubious-argent: of all this bereft, / Nothing but pain and ugliness were left' (I, 161–4). Paradoxically the 'ugliness' is muted when, a few lines below, Lamia is referred to as 'a lady bright, / A full-born beauty new and exquisite' (I, 171–2), having left behind 'the serpent prison-house' (I, 203).

The meeting between Lycius and Lamia takes place in a 'Platonic' context, the liminal realm of reverie that Keats, rightly or wrongly, associated with Plato's practices: 'His phantasy was lost, where reason fades, / In the calm'd twilight of Platonic shades' (I, 235–6).[22] Not noticing her at first, 'he pass'd, shut up in mysteries, / His mind wrapp'd like his mantle' (I, 241–2), in self-reflective speculations from which the sound of her voice extracted him, thus looking at her 'not with cold wonder fearingly, / But Orpheus-like at an Eurydice' (I, 247–8) – a metaphor which bears overtones of a descent to Hades. The request that the 'cruel lady' makes, to be conducted to 'serener palaces, / "Where I may all my many senses please, / "And by mysterious sleights a hundred thirsts appease' (I, 283–5), throws Lycius into a fit of fainting and pain from which she delivers him with a kiss, ushering him into a miraculous state of awakened sleep as 'from one trance was waking / Into another' (I, 296–7). The third personage of the drama, 'Apollonius sage', is presented in imagery that stresses the 'penetrating' quality of his perception more than anything else; as the 'trusty guide' and 'good instructor' approaches 'With curl'd gray beard, sharp eyes, and smooth bald crown, / Slow-stepp'd, and robed in philosophic gown' (I, 364–5) – a description that fits an ascetic as much as a Socrates – his old age is obscured by his 'quick eyes'. The woman / love and old man / wisdom archetypes are posed not only as polar opposites, but as adversaries in the poem; unlike models (the Platonic or Dantesque) where woman / love leads the quester to wisdom, here Lycius / seeker is 'destroyed' by the composite action of wisdom and love.

Part II, the 'symposium' proper, begins with a commentary by the narrative voice, which brings together sexuality and asceticism in a manner that admits of their comparison while giving the ascendancy to the latter:

> Love in a hut, with water and a crust,
> Is – Love, forgive us! – cinders, ashes, dust;
> Love in a palace is perhaps at last
> More grievous torment than a hermit's fast: –
> That is a doubtful tale from fairy land,
> Hard for the non-elect to understand.
>
> (ll. 1–6)

The dialectic of radical opposition – which, in rejecting the possibility of a 'both / and' resolution and adopting the 'either / or', ends with 'neither' – is enacted in the poem in three rhetorical tropes: conceptual, mythical, dramatic. This conflict has been defined in Keatsian criticism as science vs. imagination, rationalism vs. emotionalism, spirituality vs. sensuality, historical vs. mythical consciousness, and so on. However, the clearest and exemplary formulation to which the imaginative structure conduces is, I believe, the mortal confrontation of Apollo and Dionysus – Dionysian ecstatic frenzy vs. Apollonian enstatic order.

The poem's logical nucleus is given in the 'theoretical' proposition: 'That but a moment's thought is passion's passing bell' (II, 39); the mythical version of the concept is introduced about forty lines below, in a metaphorical depiction of Lycius' 'rage' against Lamia's forbidding the intrusion of 'thought' and externality into the 'purple-lined palace of sweet sin':

> His passion, cruel grown, took on a hue
> Fierce and sanguineous as 'twas possible
> In one whose brow had no dark veins to swell.
> Fine was the mitigated fury, like
> Apollo's presence when in act to strike
> The serpent – Ha, the serpent! certes, she
> Was none. . . .
>
> (II, 75–81)

In its dramatic rendering the encounter between passion and thought, serpent and Apollo, or Lamia and Apollo-nius (a name that thinly covers the elect protagonist of the Keatsian lore), is placed in the setting of a 'symposium', a context associated with drinking, Dionysian frenzy, and – in its Greek version – religious ritual; the δαίς (banquet), whose etymological root is both 'to feast' and 'to blaze', allows the godlike in human nature to surface.

In terms strangely close to the Platonic deprecation of average humanity – the conviction that 'no serious man will ever think of writing about serious realities for the general public so as to make them a prey to envy and perplexity' (*Letters*, VII, 344c) – the narrative voice reproaches Lycius for exposing to the eyes of the vulgar multitude his 'serpentine' experience: 'O senseless Lycius! Madman! wherefore flout / The silent-blessing fate, warm cloister'd hours, / And show to common eyes these secret bowers?' (II, 147–9). The description of the party's advent is made in the same derogatory terms: 'The herd approach'd; each guest, with busy brain, / Arriving at the portal, gaz'd amain, / And enter'd marvelling'; remembering the street 'from childhood' (a Wordworthian hint?), 'they hurried all, maz'd, curious and keen' (II, 150–6). The sumptuousness of the occasion is depicted in great detail: 'The glowing banquet-room shone with wide-arched grace' (II, 121); and then again, 'Of wealthy lustre was the banquet-room, / Fill'd with pervading brilliance and perfume' (II, 173–4); sacred tripods were sending up fumes of spices, and wine and food were lavishly provided: 'Thus loaded with a feast the tables stood, / Each shrining in the midst the image of a God' (II, 189–90). The ceremonies of purification duly observed, the guests 'all mov'd to the feast / In white robes and themselves in order placed / Around the silken couches, wondering' (II, 195–8). That *Lamia* may be read as an inversion of the Συμπόσιον is supported by the formal sequence, where 'drinking' follows upon 'discourse' rather than the other way round; in the Platonic text – and 'ladder' – Διόνυσος and Ἔρως are both initiatory stages to λόγος, and then to κάλλος. Here, however,

>   Soft went the music the soft air along,
>   While fluent Greek a vowel'd undersong
>   Kept up among the guests, discoursing low
>   At first, for scarcely was the wine at flow;
>   But when the happy vintage touch'd their brains,
>   Louder they talk, and louder come the strains
>   Of powerful instruments . . .
>   (II, 199–205)

As λόγος is drowned in music and wine, and 'every soul from human trammels freed', 'Lamia's self' gradually loses its otherness and becomes familiar; 'Soon was God Bacchus at meridian height' (II, 213), and all participants were 'naturalized', garlanded with wreaths and flowers. Yet, the ominous presence of the word 'deflower'd' coupled with 'thought' (II, 216–18), marks the beginning of the 'count down'.

The combat between Apollo-nius and the serpent-woman is played in the field of 'optics' – hardly a fight, as she offers no resistance but merely 'suffers' his look: 'The bald-head philosopher / Had fix'd his eye, without a twinkle or stir / Full on the alarmed beauty of the bride, / Brow-beating her fair form, and troubling her sweet pride' (II, 245–8). For Lycius, who partakes in the experience, the visual perception is translated into the pathological symptoms of extremities of the tactile sense: 'the cold ran through his veins; / Then sudden it grew hot, and all the pains / Of an unnatural heat shot to his heart' (II, 251–3). For the onlookers, or θεωροί to the ritual drama enacted before their eyes – thrice removed from the original event – the significance is ethical as well as physical: 'A deadly silence step by step increased, / Until it seem'd a horrid presence there, / And not a man but felt the terror in his hair' (II, 266–8). Lamia is transfixed under a double gaze, Apollonius' gaze of 'recognition' and Lycius' gaze of appeal for 'signification'. Lycius 'gaz'd into her eyes', and 'more he gaz'd', 'and gazing again', while Apollonius' 'juggling eyes', 'demon eyes', 'his eyes still / Relented not, nor moved' (II, 256–76). What finally 'kills' Lamia – the serpent power – is the piercing glance of an active concentration, a 'holding' which forbids its object to escape from awareness, penetrating into its deeper aspects and getting its inner subtle essence clearly reflected in consciousness. The arrow-like single-pointedness of Apollo-nius' attentiveness, unscattered and non-diversified, dissolves the (apparently) illusory nature of the bride and the ignorance of the bridegroom – simultaneously. The intensive look initiates a stripping process which 'empties' them both; 'nakedness' falls upon them in the form of physical motionlessness that is called 'death':

> Then Lamia breath'd death breath; the sophist's eye,
> Like a sharp spear, went through her utterly,
> Keen, cruel, perceant, stinging: she, as well
> As her weak hand could any meaning tell,
> Motion'd him to be silent; vainly so,
> He look'd and look'd again a level – No!
> 'A serpent!' echoed he; no sooner said,
> Than with a frightful scream she vanished:
> And Lycius' arms were empty of delight,
> As were his limbs of life, from that same night.
>
> (II, 299–308)

The 'moral' of the poem is spoken by the narrator through whose 'eyes' the story is presented, in the interpretative interlude that precedes the dramatic climax; like the choric parts of a

Greek tragedy it provides a commentary upon the action, meant to guide the reader's response into a specific channel of understanding. In my view, the narrative voice grasps only a fragment of the drama enacted in equating the confrontation to that between (hot) imagination and 'cold' philosophy, or magic and science:

> Do not all charms fly
> At the mere touch of cold philosophy?
> There was an awful rainbow once in heaven:
> We know her woof, her texture; she is given
> In the dull catalogue of common things.
> Philosophy will clip an Angel's wings,
> Conquer all mysteries by rule and line,
> Empty the haunted air, and gnomed mine –
> Unweave a rainbow, as it erewhile made
> The tender-person'd Lamia melt into a shade.
>
> (II, 229–38)

The crux of this poetic composition seems to me to lie in the ambiguous nature not of Lamia (feminine, serpentine, chthonian, Dionysian) but of Apollonius (masculine, luminous, Olympian, Apollonian). Apollonius is not a scientist but a 'sophist', an artificer of rhetoric, closer – by virtue of culture and chronology – to the 'old' or 'divine' philosophy, ' "Not harsh and crabbed as dull fools suppose / But musical as is Apollo's lute" ' (1958: II, 81), rather than to Lockean empiricism or Newtonian cosmology. That Keats' own attitude to the problem of 'thinking' and 'poetizing' is far more complex than the simplistic condemnation of his narrator betrays, can be viewed, as already pointed out, in the oscillating dialectic that emerges in his letters: 'I have been hovering for some time between an exquisite sense of the luxurious and a love for Philosophy – were I calculated for the former I should be glad – but as I am not I shall turn all my soul to the latter' (1958: I, 271). Or the familiar evidence that exists side by side in the letter exulting the sensuous over the intellectual, 'O for a Life of Sensations rather than of Thoughts!', which enhances the 'complex Mind', that is a man 'who would exist partly on sensation partly on thought – to whom it is necessary that years should bring the philosophic Mind' (1958: I, 186).

I would argue that *Lamia* is one more case of Keats'

bewilderment or rather problematic relation with the figures, and modalities of being, that in Greek mythology have been exemplified as the Dionysian and the Apollonian, ἔκστασις and ἔνστασις, which is precisely the *con-fusion* – or lack of it – that prevented the completion of his Hyperion poems. In *Lamia*, the opposites are not only irreconcilable but mutually exclusive: male destroys female, mind (νοῦς) evaporates existence (οὐσία), stasis exterminates motion; the god of light, harmonious balance, and permanence dissolves the god of darkness, vitality, and transience. The Apollonian / Dionysian correspondence that had been celebrated in the 'Ode on a Grecian Urn' – and which forms the substratum of the Platonic *Symposium* – cannot be sustained here; rather than 'passion' generating 'thought', 'thought' obliterates 'passion'. The poem is built on Keats' one and only 'myth', the dramatization of the Dionysian process – or Dionysus transfigured into Apollo – the 'death' and 'birth' into life, the dialectical interplay between 'light' and 'darkness'. This polarity constitutes the metaphysical constant of Keats' poetic universe, yet his allegiance to 'things of light' renders his relationship with 'darkness' uncertain and ambivalent.

The ambiguity of the poem also rests on the narrator's interpretation of the Apollo-nian 'gaze'; fixedness of perception is not such stuff as science is made on, i.e. the conceptual categorization of reality presupposing a theoretical stance that compares, divides, contrasts, analyses, and classifies physical and psychomental life. The motionless attentiveness of the philosopher's look (that sees the essence or 'idea' of the serpent) is not the busy calculation of the scientific outlook; the deep concentration that absorbs Lamia and Lycius together – dynamic energy and normal awareness – is more of the nature of an Apollonian 'pure present', that is of a 'timelessness' beyond the time / thought process. But, as Cassirer informs us, it is precisely this point-present 'now', reducing consciousness of the world through anchoring perception on an isolated fragment – saturating the mind by a single sensation, a single image, a 'monoform' – that gives birth not to scientific λόγος but to imaginative μῦθος. Mythical thinking is entirely alien to the ramifications of intellectual activity, Cassirer asserts; for, in the mythical mode of consciousness 'thought does not dispose freely over the data of intuition, in order to relate and compare them to each other', but 'comes to rest in the immediate experience; the sensible present is so great that everything else dwindles before it'; the simultaneous 'exclusiveness' and 'intensity' of the occurrence is stressed, and empathic identification or dissolution of subject into object is the experiential outcome of such vehement focusing. This convergence of the whole psychic dynamism upon a single form is the condition, Cassirer emphatically states, that triggers mythical 'thought', which is more of the nature of 'presence' than 'representation': 'When, on the one hand, the entire self is given up to a single impression, is "possessed" by it and, on the other hand, there is the outmost tension between the subject and its object, the outer world; when external reality is not merely viewed and contemplated, but overcomes a man in sheer immediacy, with emotions of fear or hope, terror or wish fulfilment: then the spark jumps somehow across, the tension finds release, as the subjective excitement becomes objectified, and confronts the mind as a god or a daemon' (1946: 32–3).

Translating modern (Keats' 'cold') philosophy into its 'old' (or 'divine') equivalent, we come upon a similar pattern of 'knowledge' of a subject to which one 'devotes' oneself:

> Acquaintance with it must come rather after a long period of attendance on instruction in the subject itself and of close companionship, when, suddenly, like a blaze kindled by a leaping spark, it is generated in the soul and at once becomes self-sustaining [ἀλλ' ἐκ πολλῆς συνουσίας γιγνομένης περὶ τὸ πρᾶγμα αὐτὸ καὶ τοῦ συζῆν ἐξαίφνης, οἷον ἀπὸ πυρὸς πηδήσαντος ἐξαφθὲν φῶς, ἐν τῇ ψυχῇ γενόμενον αὐτὸ ἑαυτὸ ἤδη τρέφει].
> (*Letts.*, VII, 341c–d)

3

TRANS-FORM-ATION
The Dialectics of Πάθος and Ποίησις

THE LOGOS OF MYTHOS: 'INSTANT' METAMORPHOSIS

'Mythical thinking' as conceived by Cassirer and 'dialectical thinking' as exposed by Plato seem to share a common 'deep structure': the exclusiveness of 'living with', in 'close companionship' to the object of the mind's attention, an intense concentration which allows no interruption in the flow of that thought, no penetration of something else into it – which makes consciousness on both occasions single-pointed and one-form until the object 'does itself actually exist in the mind' (Wordsworth 1974: I, 149). The image 'held' becomes steady, and awareness being impenetrable by other objects stays uninterrupted and does not change its 'form'. A concentric thought, when composed of only one image without any intellective oscillation, is apparently able to express its intrinsic power, by which it gets translated into a living phenomenon – a fact (or Idea). In both accounts of the peak experience, innate restlessness is subdued and the mind can focus on a single existent, it can become open and receptive. Such recollected, intensified thought furnishes the context, and presuppositions, for the rousing process which on both occasions is described as a 'jumping' or 'leaping' spark – the transformative fire inducing a qualitatively different consciousness that can fully comprehend metaphysical truth. During retention, there seems to be effected a union between mind and thing; if mindfulness remains attached to the object, the object is restrained from instantly vanishing beyond awareness, and becomes 'known'.

This 'collecting' of thought force, the gathering of diversified mental powers to a point of maximum concentration, is for Heidegger the root meaning of the Greek λόγος as a process of revealing truth: 'For the Greeks, to tell is to lay bare and make appear'; μῦθος and λόγος, Heidegger enunciates, are not binary opposites, mutually exclusive rhetorical modes, but analogous or even homologous structures: 'The *mythos* is that appeal of foremost and radical concern to all human beings which makes man think of what appears, what is his being. *Logos* says the same; *mythos* and *logos* are not, as our current historians of philosophy claim, placed into opposition by philosophy as such; on the contrary, the early Greek thinkers (Parmenides, fragment 8) are precisely the ones to use *mythos* and *logos* in the same sense'. Opposition arises when the originary signification is lost, and Heidegger sees that happening in the Platonic text, locating the 'point' of schism within western metaphysics – and linguistics: 'Historians and philologists, by virtue of a prejudice which modern rationalism adopted from Platonism, imagine that *mythos* was destroyed by *logos*. But nothing religious is ever destroyed by logic; it is destroyed only by the God's withdrawal' (1968: 10). Supplementing Heidegger's argument, one could claim that, far from being antithetical to λόγος or destroyed by it, μῦθος is precisely the cultural form that 'speaks' the power of λόγος.

That the work of Plato does not portray the 'separation' of μῦθος and λόγος but their dialectical relationship – μῦθος becoming 'aware' of itself – sets, I think, the Platonic dialogues as a bridge from magical to rational functioning; in the Platonic text, the 'stream of consciousness' moves back and forth all the time between unitary awareness and logical categorization. It not only marks but embodies the transition from the Dionysian to the Apollonian modes of experience and, like the Delphic oracle, reverences them both. It shows acknowledgement of the fact that in order for light to prevail, the dark twin-force must be carefully propitiated – and 'incorporated'. The polarity that the Platonic dialogue introduces is, as has been repeatedly emphasized, still a 'twoness' of Apollo and Dionysus in discourse, where no estrangement has befallen as yet granting power to Apollo over Dionysus, as it happens with later authoritarian doctrines. In a process (rather than system) whereby philosophy is seen as the product of 'rage' (τῆς φιλοσόφου μανίας καὶ βακχείας) – the Dionysian dark side of existence, the destructive, non-rational, violent aspect effecting dissolution and transformation, is taken cognizance of. Qualitative change is as much the basic event of dialectic as the primary condition of myth; and θεωρία, the ultimate goal of Platonic quest after 'being', becomes imaginative insight into the life one lives, 'the vision, of what is worth knowing' (Randall 1970: 198). Shelley uses much the same terms referring not to μῦθος or λόγος, but to ποίησις which 'makes us the inhabitants of a world to which the familiar world is a chaos. It reproduces the common Universe of which we are portions and percipients, and it purges from our inward sight the film of familiarity which obscures from us the wonder of our being' (1954: 295).

J. A. Stewart names this condition 'transcendental feeling' and locates its rhetorical manifestation in the transfer from argumentative conversation to mythological expression within the Platonic text. The mythic core of Plato's dialogues marks the philosopher's attempt to exemplify an epiphany; the function of myth, far from being purely decorative, signifies the passage to a different modality of knowing / being. The experienced reader, Stewart argues, 'feels when the brisk debate is silenced for a while, and Socrates or another great interlocutor opens his mouth in Myth, that the movement of the Philosophic Drama is not arrested, but is being sustained, at a crisis, on another plane'; in a language strongly analogous to Plato's depiction of the lightning-like dialectical climax, Stewart continues with 'The Myth bursts in upon the Dialogue with a revelation of something new and strange' (1905: 25). In terms of the Platonic cognitive 'line', the transition might be said to represent the shift from διάνοια to νόησις – an imaginative leap beyond the activity of intellective inquiry into the nature of οὐσία, which must be carried on by constant occupation throughout a long period:

> Hardly after practicing detailed comparisons of names and definitions and visual and other sense perceptions, after scrutinizing them in benevolent disputation by the use of question and answer without jealousy, at last in a flash understanding of each blazes up, and the mind, as it exerts all its powers to the limit of human capacity, is flooded with light.
>
> (*Letters*, VII, 344b)

The last step on the way up the ladder is right mindfulness. This is involvement of consciousness, the ability to live intimately with the object, affectionately and 'without jealousy', caring for it without criticizing or justifying it; as concentration is developed it keeps the mind vigilant and collected in an exhaustive intensity of attention which is total energy, and that total energy (ἔρως), Plato suggests, induces the highest form of intelligence (νοῦς).

The dialectical process entails simultaneous awareness of 'collectedness' and 'separation'. As Plato exemplifies in his discussion of 'madness' in the *Phaedrus*, 'we bring a dispersed plurality under a single form, seeing all together' and then reverse the procedure dividing into forms, not like a 'clumsy butcher' (265d), but 'divide them according to their natural divisions as we would carve a sacrificial victim' (*Statesman*, 287c). Ceremonial collection and division thus become the tools of re-collection. 'Synchronicity' provides some ground, some room for exploration into experiential states like pleasure, pain, love, madness, virtue, knowledge, art, and so on; thus concentration furnishes the 'topic for exposition', and division is the methodological apparatus which looks around and locates all relevant terms. Συναγωγή is precision, focusing on a thing snatched from the existential flow; διαίρεσις is the searching and uncovering of all its possible ramifications. Gathering is the prelude to dispension; the mind flashes on a situation and then diffuses that one-pointedness into its manifold aspects, the 'many' that are contained in the 'one'. Assemblage and dissemination, as Socrates admits, are of the nature of λόγος:

> Believe me, Phaedrus, I am myself a lover of these divisions, and collections, that I may gain the power to speak and to think, and whenever I deem another man able to discern an objective unity and plurality, I follow 'in his footsteps where he leadeth as a god.' Futhermore – whether I am right or wrong in doing so, God alone knows – it is those that have this ability whom for the present I call dialecticians.
>
> (*Phaedr.*, 266b)

'As opposed to sophism', Gadamer contends, Platonic dialectic 'cultivates the ability to hold unerringly to that which one sees before one's eyes as true'; Socrates 'knows how to lead the way through confusion to unshakable knowledge, to use the former as a means to attain the latter' (1980: 11). The process of λέγειν is also defined by Heidegger as 'to collect oneself amid dispersion into the impermanent, to recapture oneself out of confusion in appearance'. Defining 'the essence of *logos*' Heidegger surprises us by unearthing the archaeology of the word λέγειν 'as gathering' which is 'related to the original togetherness of being, and because being means to come into unconcealment, this gathering has a fundamental character of opening, making manifest'. Λέγειν, in its signification as 'collecting' and 'revealing' is, he argues, also present in the Platonic work: 'Thus the *logos*, not only in Heraclitus but still in Plato, has the character of *dēloun*, making manifest'. However, Heidegger recognizes the Platonic (and Aristotelian) text as the τόπος (place) where the violation of λόγος took place, 'the vitiation of the meaning of *logos* that was to make logic possible'. Consequently, 'for two thousand years, these ties between *logos*, *alētheia*, *physis*, *noein*, and *idea* have remained hidden in unintelligibility' (1959: 169–71). The essentially revelatory nature of λόγος in its archaic usage is also shown in the Heideggerian 'apocalyptic' proposition enhancing the saying / showing nature of language: 'Its showing character is not based on signs of any kind; rather, all signs arise from a showing within whose realm and for whose purposes they can be signs' (1971b: 123); as an answer to the problematics of the relation between language and reality, Heidegger always reverts to the etymological origin of the Greek *logos*, which 'speaks simultaneously as the name for Being and for Saying' (1971b: 80).

The original bond between linguistics and ontology, the suggestion that the 'name' *is*, or evokes, the event – that the word is the 'seed' through which ontological essence can be appropriated – is propounded by Cassirer, and others, as the distinctive feature of the mental – and historical – state called 'mythical consciousness'. Examining the place of language and myth in the evolution of human culture, Cassirer begins with the Platonic *Phaedrus,* and the Socratic interpretation of the Delphic myth in terms of self-knowledge; he then poses the problem of what he calls the 'Faustian word', the coincidence of 'language' and 'reality': 'The notion that name and essence bear a necessary and internal relation to each other, that the name does not merely denote but actually *is* the essence of its object, that the potency of the real thing is contained in the name – that is one of the fundamental assumptions of the mythmaking consciousness itself'. This 'natural' rather than 'conventional' *logos*, Cassirer asserts, is not only reported as an immediate experience, but recognized as the basic characteristic of myth by any formal attempt to systematize mythical data, i.e. mytho-logy: 'the doctrine of the intimate relation between names and essences, and of their latent identity, is here set up as a methodological principle' (1946: 3). In the second volume of the *Philosophy of Symbolic Forms* where he examines myth as a form of thought, he attributes the inability of mythical thinking for conceptual signification to its peculiar relation to language: 'Myth and language are inseparable and mutually condition each other'; thus, 'Word and name do not designate and signify, they are and act'. Seen in its synoptic basis, Cassirer's contention is that in the mythical frame of mind all human utterances are ultimately – and potentially – speech acts: 'In the mere sensuous matter of language, in the mere sound of the human voice, there resides a peculiar power over things' (1955b: 40).

This is the logocentric dream of presence in metaphysics, the haunting of historical existence by the image of an archaic modality in which 'being' and 'speaking' were coextensive, yet repeatedly 'deconstructed' at various points in the western evolution of consciousness, until Derrida's recent assumption that the phonic signifier is as 'conventional' as the graphic. Conversely, 'logocentrism' has been recognized as a definitely antique spiritual technique whereby logos, or even unintelligible phonetic productions, awaken a profound inner echo in the human mind – 'sound' being the mode of apprehension of power-in-motion rather than latency, i.e. power 'manifest'. Thus the 'word' becomes a medium that 'calls' the thing, an external signal that activates inward potential. In his discussion of the basis on which lies the distinction between word as 'sign' and word as 'symbol', Gadamer recognizes the ontological chasm between the extremes of 'pure indication' and 'pure representation', as a pointing towards something that is absent versus a showing or manifestation of presence; his notion of representation stresses the evocative power of the 'proxy' rather than its displacing character. So 'taking the place' is not substitution but re-enactment: 'Thus the symbol takes the place of something in representing: that is, it makes something immediately present. Only because the symbol presents in this way the presence of what it represents, is it treated with the reverence due to that which it symbolises' (1975: 136). The notion of representation as 'presence' rather than 'absence' is also emphasized in Coleridge's definition of symbol, contrasted to the 'phantom proxy' of allegory:

> On the other hand a Symbol (ὁ ἔστιν ἄει ταυτηγόρικον) is characterized by a translucence of the Special in the Individual or of the General in the Especial or of the Universal in the General. Above all by the translucence of the Eternal through and in the Temporal. It always partakes of the Reality which it renders intelligible; and while it enunciates the whole, abides itself as a living part in that Unity, of which it is the representative.
>
> (1972: 30)

The original meaning of 'symbol' refers to the Pythagorean conjunction of the terms σύμβολα and ἀκούσματα, as phonemes expressive of states of consciousness 'cosmic' in structure and hence difficult to formulate in secular terminology. Within a mythical mode of awareness, symbols are not merely overdetermined concepts, but loaded with the energies of divinities (in religious terms) or archetypes (in psychological terms). The reality inherent in symbol may be experienced directly through participation, metaphorically through concentration, or dialectically though a consciously oriented technique which can approach energies (or Platonic Ideas) through an intellective process. All such procedures rely on a 'correspondence' model, on the assumption that a 'unity of life' allows for an inter-traffic between modes of being, and categories, that appear segregated.

The mythological world view recognizes a magical continuum where everything partakes of ψυχή and μανία. Everything is a manifestation of the holy; the sacred is not separated from matter, from the body, from physical activity or rhetorical properties. In this magical identity of an ἔνθεη φύσις, where the human and the divine have not yet been divorced, and the interaction of the containing field is relatively 'subjectless', Dionysus – or by whatever name the life-force is known, life as it is regardless of idealistic conceptualizations of what it should be – is realized as a manifestation of a powerful and unknowable 'presence' beyond man's control. It is this 'fluid' process in which modalities of being merge or are telescoped together, that allows the demoniacal interchange beween the linguistic and experiential forms. Under such conditions the relation of λόγος and μῦθος may be seen from a dual perspective: as the myth of the *logos*, which looks upon language as the 'house of Being', and as the logic of *mythos*, which, searching for an underlying structural form in mythical fantasy and mythical thinking, discerns the 'logos' – the theoretical or intellectual centre of myth – in the event of μεταμόρφωσις or transformation.

In his exploration of 'play' as a hermeneutical key to the nature of 'being', Gadamer makes a radical distinction between what appear to be synonymous terms – 'change' and 'transformation' (in a way that somehow recalls Coleridge's desynonymization between fancy and imagination). Change, he asserts, no matter how thorough it is, retains a recognizable portion of the old characteristics of the object and relates to the category of accidental aspects and not to the substance of the thing; transformation 'means that something is suddenly and as a whole something else, that this other transformed thing that it has become is its true being, in comparison with which its earlier being is nothing'. The basic difference between these two modes of alteration is that one happens 'in' time and the other in 'no' time: 'There cannot here be any transition of gradual change leading from one to the other since the one is the denial of the other' (1975: 100). Gadamer's term 'transformation into structure', as we have seen, entails observation of the game of life, the transitoriness of experience. So, looking at the drama of life, its constant fluctuation, generates a tremendous joy which paradoxically emerges when one is totally attentive to 'change', seeing the whole interplay and significance of the comedy and tragedy of existence. 'This gives the full meaning to what we called transformation into a structure', Gadamer asserts; 'It is not enchantment in the sense of a bewitchment . . . but it is itself redemption and transformation back into true being' (1975: 101).

The transformative potential of play-acting sets 'play' as the fundamental ritual of exploration and experimentation with reality. Entering into play with 'what is', i.e. recognizing the continual passing of one qualitative state into another as a primary ontological fact, obliterates solidity and dissolves the familiar conceptual order in which things are 'things' by virtue of fixed classifications; the confounding of categories, or deconstruction of habitual ways of thinking, introduces a state of indeterminacy that cannot sustain the old stable ego-other confrontation. Self-transformation, as the central mythical and artistic event, necessitates a 'dying' to the world of the old order, an emptying without which there is no room for renewal. Thus μεταμόρφωσις is not a 'growth' or additive process, but a condition requiring reduction and 'death'. The human being under the impulse of a regenerative drive seeks the experience of decomposition (the mythical dismemberment of Dionysus as a prelude to rebirth) to inaugurate newness. In psychological terms this implies that the relation between subject and object becomes uncertain, and ways of seeing – and 'being' – contradictory to common sense experience.

'Subjectivity' (particularly as viewed by the Romantic and Platonic mind) only means that the starting point for authentic experience is placed in the individual consciousness. The action becomes one of ego reflection, 'I' knowing 'me'. That the subject makes an 'object' of itself seems to be the crucial principle of the metamorphic operation, whereby ego knowing 'self' becomes ego knowing 'other' – or possibly 'ego' *known* by the 'other'; the ego's subject turns into the other's object. But in order to become an object to the 'other', the 'ego' must first become an object to itself by objectifying and watching self, the experiential flow. For transformation to set in, the subject must become an object to the 'Other' – god or daemon (Plato's σύνοικον ἑαυτῷ) – in other words aware of itself as an 'object', which induces consciousness of 'other' as 'subject'. Self-objectification, observation of the 'I's' impermanence, transience, and constant change, appears to be the essential condition of μεταμόρφωσις; the 'subject' dies objectively so that the 'object' may be subjectively born – and the logos irresistibly and inevitably draws again towards Heraclitus, whose saying 'Immortals are mortal, mortals immortal, living the others' death, dead in the others' life' (Heraclitus 1979: 71) points precisely in the direction of the reversibility (and mutual exclusiveness) of syntactic – and ontological – modalities.

The condition of a 'formless' reality, which allows for a multiform relation between the existential systems of ego / other – and the grammatical categories of subject / object – is recognized by Cassirer as the psychological presupposition that underlies the transformative mechanism of mythical consciousness. Asserting that 'mythical consciousness has its own category, its own specific view, of subjectivity as well as objectivity', he continues by supporting that in myth 'Reality – corporeal or psychic – has not yet become stabilized but preserves a peculiar "fluidity." Reality is not yet divided into definite classes of things with characteristics established once and for all . . . For here, too, the fundamental motif of myth – the motif of "metamorphosis" – prevails.' Resistance to, or ignorance of, taxonomy procedures primarily affects the ego's sense of separate, and separable, identity. 'Life is still a single unbroken stream of becoming, a dynamic flow which only very gradually divides into separate waves'; the archaic experience of life, Cassirer supports, knows no categories whatsoever, even primary distinctions like personal / impersonal, organic / inorganic, life / death (1957: 70–1). Such a mythical metaphysics of the subject's – and object's – dissolution within the pervading 'continuum' can also be detected, I think, in the Heraclitean 'shared' λόγος, power steering all things.

In its modern version, also rooted in the thought of Heraclitus, it re-emerges in the Heideggerian identification of λόγος and φύσις: 'Being in the sense of *physis* is the power that emerges' (1959: 125). Heidegger – after tracing the meaning of λόγος through the various fragmentary remnants of pre-Socratic thought, as a 'permanent gathering' that contains the conflict of opposites 'rooted in togetherness' – exposes the fundamental character of the Greek reality model in its acceptance of contradiction but rejection of randomness: λόγος as 'gathering' is never 'a mere driving-together and heaping-up. It maintains in a common bond the conflicting and that which tends apart. It does not let them fall into haphazard dispersion. In thus maintaining a bond, the *logos* has the character of permeating power, of *physis*' (1959: 134) – which makes phenomenal processes grounded in paradigmatic structures. In such modes of 'poetic thinking', before the later split into the scientific and the mythical, Heidegger discerns the confluence of thought and reality, best expressed in the Parmenidiean maxim ' "There is a reciprocal bond between apprehension and being" ' (1959: 145), a correspondence whose later disjunction is also traced by Cassirer as, on the one hand, 'scientific thinking' directed toward establishing causal relations in successive changes, and on the other 'mythical thinking' which does away with 'law', replacing causality with arbitrariness where 'anything can come from anything' in unpredictable metamorphosis. The dividing line between 'science' and 'myth' seems to be that the former experience lends itself to systematization and classification, whereas the latter can never be fully subjected to conceptual – hence repeatable and predictable structures – retaining an erratic or uncontrollable component: 'mythical thinking clings to the total representation as such and contents itself with picturing the simple course of what happens' (1955b: 46–7).

Although Cassirer recognizes mythical content as that of 'transformation' and mythical form as that of 'repetition', his interpretation of μεταμόρφωσις lacks the dimension of 'transformation into structure' that, as we have seen, is the central condition of Gadamer's artistic outlook, resulting precisely from 'picturing the simple course of what happens', the 'drama' and 'history' of life situations; such a view implies that permanence or structure is embedded in recurrence, in the perception of rhythm and pattern that turns random movement into play or dance. Without cancelling the mythical awareness of what Cassirer calls 'the constellation of things in the here and now', Gadamer exposes the meaningfulness or revelatory nature of 'contemporaneity', the mind's encounter with what is actually taking place, both in the religious and artistic experience. The moment of 'nowness' as 'parousia', absolute presence, delineates similarly the ontological mode of aesthetic being – the work of art – and 'the absolute moment in which a spectator stands', which is 'at once self-forgetfulness and reconciliation with self' (1975: 113). In his discussion of 'this strange experience of timelessness', G. Poulet affirms that the 'present' moment 'is so intensely experienced that it seems as if its transience gives way to everlastingness, as if time stands still and becomes eternity' (1954: 6).

Παρουσία, being-present, seems to be both the presupposition and the consequence of the mythical occurence, μεταμόρφωσις. At the magical or instinctual level only the here and now exists, all encompassing. Past, present, and future are not differentiated, and neither are body and soul, percipient and perceived, 'I' and 'other'. What rational consciousness has distinguished into inner and outer worlds is psychologically still equivalent and interchangeable. Space is what is concretely and immediately given, time is the current and directly experienced event. In the phase of intuitive existence, whether in personal or world history, Cassirer maintains, time and space are not categories, but are represented as a distancing from immediate presence, 'reduced to the simple distinction of near and far'. Such a simplistic relation to time operates under the plain archetypal opposition of light / darkness, or consciousness / unconsciousness (1955a: 217). Here Cassirer refers to a primitive mythical state of consciousness (personal or racial) prior to the development of memory and the mental function of abstraction or conceptualization.

Paradoxically, however, he comes to recognize 'presentness' as the fundamental quality of a historical phase which, although departing 'from the sphere of myth', still 'epitomizes the whole spirit of mythical creation peculiar to the Greeks and particularly to Plato' (1955b: 133). The transition effected is from the magical attitude accepting incidents (that cannot be rationally planned) as fated manifestations of forces beyond man's control, to a 'humanistic' code which places destiny, 'the meaning and centre of man's life' within the individual person. The transference is a 'noetic' rather than a 'realistic' one, a psychologizing of cosmology which 'reads' the gods and daemons of the magical phase into archetypal psychic structures (e.g. Plato's model of the soul). In the Greek 'path of the logos', Cassirer detects not a denial of change but a 'theory' of change, providing 'a solid intellectual substratum' for 'the world of sensuous phenomena', thus opposing (as in Plato's case) 'to temporal coming-into-being and passing away' a 'realm of pure timeless forms, in which all temporal existence participates' (1955b: 131).

The experience of eternity in the moment, which is precisely what Cassirer means by the expression 'speculative feeling of time and presence', is rendered in mythical / religious terms as the Apollonian timeless present or the realization of 'being' in time, the highest point of human consciousness. It is this absolute presence in the 'nowness', which turns profane or historical time (the Greek χρόνος of definite time) into speculative time (or Greek καιρός as the due measure, proportion, the right point of time), and transforms χρόνος, the 'moving image of eternity' (*Timaeus*, 37d) into αἰών, eternity itself. The 'pointness' and 'fitness' of καιρός as 'the exact or critical time', makes it instrumental to the transformative process of historical temporality into sacred 'timeless' time. The focusing and intensity suggested in this 'pointed' awareness, precisely being 'in' the moment, relating to the present rather than to a past remembrance or future prospect, is seen by Heidegger as the authentic condition of memory *as* concentration: 'Originally, "memory" means as much as devotion: a constant concentrated abiding with something – not just with something that has passed, but in the same way with what is present and with what may become. What is past, present, and to come appears in the oneness of its own *present* being' (1968: 140).

What such a concept of time suggests in its absolute 'presentness' is the abolition of 'historicity', of the assumption that things began at some initiatory point back in the depths of cosmic creation; instead, history (in the transpersonal) and memory (in the personal) level are seen as projected through a 'present' frame, which becomes the generator 'pouring out' the world of experience; within such a framework of interpreting 'creation', the causes of things should not be pursued 'out there' among an 'older' externality but in the propelling mechanism itself. Cognition of 'time', then, would entail knowledge of the present moment – a 'turning around' from historical awareness of extension into the past (*natura naturata*) and looking straight into the place from which experienced reality (*natura naturans*) emerges. An inverted, or 'introverted', perception into the 'chasm' or 'abyss' which ejects time and space, reverses all myths of immemorial genesis by implying the continuing act of creation; it may be defined as the περιαγωγή which looks through the flow of passing time to the 'present' point of its origination. Granted such a 'transformed' model, the only reality seems to rest on the 'living moment' – to use Wordsworth's expression; if everything is in flowing change, if nothing exists but momentarily in its present form, if one thing is transfused into another and cannot be grasped – as Plato so frequently and forcibly argued – solidity and continuity (historical or personal) appears to be an illusion, and experience threatens to reveal the transitoriness and contingency of 'humanity' – in fact of all existence. The 'myth' of permanence (temporal and spatial) veils the awareness that because each existent is in constant change, there is no stable identical 'self'; the actual nature of each 'being' seems to be nothing but change itself, the self-nature of all life. In discussing the conditions under which coming-to-be universally takes place, Plato testifies:

> Manifestly 'tis effected whenever its starting point has received increment and so come to its second stage, and from this to the next, and so by three steps acquired

perceptibility to percipients. 'Tis ever by such change and transformation of motion that a thing comes to be; it is in veritable being so long as it persists. When it has changed to a different constitution, it is utterly destroyed.

(*Laws*, X, 894a)

When this flux of impermanence is deeply sensed in the immediate recognition that every part of our being, body and mind, is in change – as Plato affirms in the *Symposium* (207d–e) – then possibly we begin to let go of our most deeply conditioned attachments to past and future, and we come into harmony with the fleeting flow of life, as Heraclitus suggests.

If experience consists in the arising and passing away of sensation (the Humean 'bundle of perceptions'), or the sequence of different thoughts (mind objects), then 'being' is the continuity of process. There is no abiding entity, no solid human 'subject' to which it is happening, because each 'subjective' consciousness and its 'objective' content arise and vanish together from moment to moment. So, getting out of the 'present' into past and future projections, is stepping out of reality into fictional dimensions. Within the moment, the 'now', however, the temporal 'phenomenon' does not change, does not move; in the next moment it 'dies', changes into something else, and another existent arises, is 'born'. Becoming 'present' to the 'present' seems to be the crux of the whole matter of time and eternity – awareness that not only perception is a 'present' experience, but memory (of the past) and anticipation (of the future) are only experienced *as* present events. To see remembrance and expectation as 'present' experiences is to collapse the boundaries that create the concept of time; with nothing before or ahead – that leaves only the (timeless) present consciousness, the ontological ἕν ἐστός of Parmenides (or the linguistic ἐνεστώς of the one and only present tense in Greek grammar). The mind's tendency to 'look away' from the current instant, to regret / relish the past or fear / hope for the future, is indicative of a pervasive reluctance to watch, and accept, things as they are just now. The human mind tends to 'turn its back to', withdraw awareness from what *is*, avoid the 'present' in all its forms, in order to toy with optical illusions, mental fabrications, images of pastness and futurity that place consciousness 'in time' rather than vice versa. It appears to be very difficult to stay grounded in the actual moment in 'attention'; as Wittgenstein puts it, 'If we take eternity to mean not infinite temporal duration but timelessness, then eternal life belongs to those who live in the present' (1961: 6.4311).

Heidegger's discussion of 'being' and 'time' traces western metaphysics to its origin 'in Greek thought', the Greek 'situation in regard to time', best developed, as he asserts, by Aristotle: ' "In being" means: being present. Beings are more in being the more present they are'. Having established the identity or synchronicity of 'is-ness' and 'presence', Heidegger probes into the meaning of this aspect of temporality: 'Since in all metaphysics from the beginning of Western thought, Being means being present, Being, if it is to be thought in the highest instance, must be thought as pure presence, that is, as the presence that persists, the abiding present, the steadily standing "now." Medieval thought speaks of *nunc stans*. But that is the interpretation of the nature of eternity' (1968: 101–2). At this point Heidegger introduces the hermeneutics of 'being' initiated by the German Romantic philosophers, and specifically Schelling who, after defining the essence of 'primal being' as 'willing', enumerates among its predicates 'eternity' as 'independence of time'. Western metaphysics in its fundamental postulate, Heidegger argues, seems to be inferring a split between Being and Time, if 'being' is eternal, motionless, and 'time' impermanent, transient. And yet, Heidegger notices, what has been forgotten in the various ramifications of philosophical thought, what has been misinterpreted and possibly misrepresented, is that original conjunction of 'Being' and 'Time', the Being / Presence, which determines as much the nature of 'time' as that of 'being'. Heidegger's reluctance to use terms like 'existence' and 'essence', which traditionally characterize being-in-motion and being-motionless, follows, I believe, if unintentionally, the Greek / Platonic practice of employing one term ὄν / οὐσία for all conceptualizations of reality. 'But what about that definition', Heidegger wonders, 'here left unattended, of Being itself as being present, even as the enduring presence?' (1968: 102–3). The inadequacy of the 'time concept' as recognized by Heidegger, actually hints at the deficiency of all ideas which remain fixed while reality is always in flux; the concept as a static view, looking at things from a historically conditioned point of view, distorts the phenomenon of existence.

'What about Being and Time, then?' Heidegger ἀπορεῖ in

Socratic fashion. 'Must not the one as much as the other, Being as much as Time – must not both become questionable in their relatedness, first questionable and finally doubtful?' That something of tremendous importance was left 'unthought', escaped notice, remained unattended, is, I think, Heidegger's way of speaking the Platonic contention of 'forgetfulness'; thus silence substitutes logos if 'The question "Being and Time" points to what is unthought in all metaphysics' (1968: 103). In concluding the chapter, Heidegger lays down the difficulty inherent in this thinking about 'Being', a puzzlement as much experienced by modern as expressed by ancient thinkers, such as Aristotle who implies in his *Metaphysics* that the 'Being of beings is the most apparent; and yet, we normally do not see it – and if we do, only with difficulty' (1968: 110).

PLATO ON ΠΑΣΧΕΙΝ / ΠΟΙΕΙΝ

We have already traced Plato's explorations into the Being of beings or οὐσία τῶν ὄντων; Plato has circumscribed – tentatively so – the realm of 'being' by numerous sporadic references not only to what it *is* but to what is *is not*. I sum up here his major definitions and interpretations for the sake of furthering the argument on 'time' and 'presence', which forms part of the inquiry into 'transformation' as the basic ontological event in λόγος and μῦθος. Plato maintains that because our minds are in a state of confusion as much about 'reality' as about 'unreality' we must begin by studying reality – ὅτι τὸ ὄν (*Sophist*, 243d). Names, descriptions, images, concepts 'do as much to illustrate' the particular quality, as the essential reality of things (*Letts.*, VII, 342e); even if imitation of the essence of a thing is made by syllables and letters (*Cratylus*, 423e), the mind perceives οὐσίαν by 'itself' and not through sensation (*Theaetetus*, 186a); in fact, intercourse with real being is effected by means of the soul though reflection (*Soph.*, 248a), since soul desires 'being' and hunts after it (*Phaedo*, 66a). Turning from ontology to epistemology, Plato affirms that soul 'knows', real being 'is known'; such contention is, however, subverted by the inquiry into the precise nature of cognition, which investigates whether 'knowing and being known' are actions or experiences, or one experience and the other action (*Soph.*, 248d). The question is partly answered in the proposition that there are four types of knowledge occuring in the soul – for which the term 'affections (παθήματα)' is used – corresponding to the four gradations of reality (*Republic*, VII, 511d–e). Reality is not only a fourfold, but exhibits simultaneously unity and multiplicity: the real is three, two, one – both one and many, in alternate states of peace and war (*Soph.*, 242c–243a); reality is also divided into three kinds: 'form' – same and uncreated – 'copy' of form – created, in motion – and 'space' – eternal, indestructible (*Tim.*, 50c–d).

Although the study of unity is one of the prospects that guide and convert the soul to the contemplation of true being (*Rep.*, VII, 524e–525a), the 'one' and 'being' are different from each other, since the 'one' *is not* 'being', but *has* 'being' (*Parmenides*, 143b). Nor is 'being' the same as the 'good', because the 'good' itself is not essence but transcends 'being' in 'dignity' and 'power' (*Rep.*, VI, 509b). Within a structure of ontological hierarchy, οὐσία ὄντως οὖσα surpassed by the 'good', itself rises above the sensible world, dwelling in that place beyond the heavens, devoid of colour, shape, or mass, and approached only by νοῦς, 'the soul's pilot' (*Phaedr.*, 247c). It is the philosophical nature that is attracted to this kind of knowledge which reveals to man something of eternal being, not what wanders between the poles of generation and decay (*Rep.*, VI, 485a–b). Essence (being) and generation (becoming) are offered as a pair of categorial opposites (*Philebus*, 54a), generation characterized by motion, whereas eternal being 'rests in unity' – it has no past and future (*Tim.*, 37d–e). As one of the four causes of the created world, however, οὐσία is a coming-into-being, resulting from the fusion of the 'limit' and the 'unlimited' (*Phil.*, 26d); the dispute over the 'static' or 'kinetic' nature of 'being' is tentatively settled in the recognition that even though movement and rest are real, reality is not motion and rest 'both at once', but something distinct from them, which makes of reality what is neither motionless nor moving (*Soph.*, 250c).

This paradoxical condition of 'otherness' is encountered again in the discussion of the 'instant' (τὸ ἐξαίφνης), the threshold through which the 'one' passes in and out of 'being', in and out of time:

> And since it cannot both have and not have existence at the same time, it can only have existence at one time and not have existence at another. And there must also be a time

when it comes to possess existence and a time when it ceases to possess it; it can possess a thing at one time and not at another only if there are times when it acquires that thing and loses it. Now acquiring existence [ονείας μεταλαμδάνειν] is called 'coming into existence,' and losing existence [άπαλλάττεσθαι ονείας] is called 'ceasing to exist.'

(*Parm.*, 155e–156a)

The 'birth' of the 'one', or its coming-into-being, and its 'death', or its passing out-of-being, arising into motion and vanishing into stillness, are made from the 'point', the no-man's-land of the 'moment'; this is the 'suddenness', the 'unawares' which is neither rest nor motion, neither impermanence nor permanence but pending between existence and non-existence (the moment equally out of time and out of timelessness). The transitional point, that 'queer thing', is the 'instant', ή έξαίφνης αύτη φύσις, άτοπος (strange, unwanted, extraordinary, unnatural, disgusting, foul, marvellous, absurd),[1] and έν χρόνω ούδενί ούσα (occupying no time):

> Accordingly, the one, since it both is at rest and is in motion, must pass from the one condition to the other – only so can it do both things – and when it passes, it makes the transition instantaneously; it occupies no time in making it and at that moment it cannot be either in motion or at rest.
>
> (*Parm.*, 156d–e)

To translate ontology into psychology, the 'moment' becomes the 'focus' through which the diversity of perception and intellection is transformed into the monoform, the 'oneness' of that which is beyond time and beyond being, έπέκεινα τῆς ούσίας – the contemplation of the 'good' itself.[2]

But to return to 'being' – and 'time'. Plato's closest attempts at a depiction of the 'essence' of being, as we have seen, relate it to fire (*Crat.*, 401c) and the principle of motion (*Crat.* 401c–d; 421b–c). The most reiterated definition, however, is that ούσία – whether embodied or bodiless – is 'power', δύναμις, to affect or be affected (*Soph.*, 247d–e). Thus the mind's confrontation with 'becoming' or 'being', as an intercourse between όντα, is the experiencing or producing an effect – πάθημα ή ποίημα – 'as the

153

result of some power, from things that encounter one another', the Stranger informs Theaetetus (*Soph.*, 248b). The same Theaetetus, who has already exhibited the sense of wonder, the 'mark of the philosopher' – τοῦτο τὸ πάθος, τὸ θαυμάζειν – (*Theaet.*, 155d), receives his initiation – τὰ μυστήρια – from Socrates who declares τὸ πᾶν κίνησις, everything is motion divided into two, power of acting – ποιεῖν – or being acted upon – πάσχειν: 'From the intercourse and friction of these with one another arise offspring, endless in number, but in pairs of twins' (*Theaet.*, 156a–b). The interrelatedness of the two modalities of 'power' is manifested in the following explanation: 'For there is no such thing as an agent until it meets with a patient, nor any patient until it meets with its agent'; so is the indeterminacy and unpredictability of the nature of the 'meeting': 'Also what meets with something and behaves as agent, if it encounters something different at another time, shows itself as patient' (*Theaet.*, 157a).

Soul and body are equally subject to παθήματα (impressions, experiences), Plato argues in the *Philebus*, sensation (αἴσθησιν) being the name of that movement which concurrently affects body and soul (34a). Affection and sensation are inextricably linked in a complicated manner which poses the problem of causality in either direction: 'In order, then, that the affections [παθήματα] may follow regularly after the elements, let us presuppose the existence of body and soul', Plato proposes in the *Timaeus* (61d), introducing a hypothesis in the form of metaphysical metaphor, which has conditioned western conceptions of reality ever since. It is the lower or mortal part of the soul, Plato contends, that is subject to terrible and irresistible affections (*Tim.*, 69d). In a secondary division within the mortal or irrational soul (ἄλογον), the 'black' of the two horses – according to the allegorical analogy introduced in the *Republic* – termed ἐπιθυμητικόν and described as ὀφεῶδες, of a snake-like nature (IX, 590b), is here related to vegetative life, positioned 'between the midrift and the navel' and pronounced to be always in a condition of passiveness (πάσχον γὰρ διατελεῖ πάντα), impervious to rational influence,

> having no part in opinion [δόξης] or reason [λογισμοῦ] or mind [νοῦ], but only in feelings [αἰσθήσεως] of pleasure and pain and the desires which accompany them. For this nature is always in a passive state, and is not endowed by

nature with the power of revolving in and about itself, repelling the motion from without and using its own, in such a way as to observe and reflect upon any of its own concerns. Wherefore it lives and does not differ from a living being, but is fixed and rooted in the same spot, having no power of self-motion.

(*Tim.*, 77b–c)

The irrational part of the soul, 'rooted' or tied down 'like a wild animal which was chained up with man', must be nourished if the human being is to exist and prosper. Positioned as far as possible from the headquarters – 'council chamber' – of the head, so that its disturbing intrusions might be minimized, it is impervious to reason, 'and even if attaining to some degree of perception would never naturally care for rational notions', but is only attracted by images and 'led by phantoms and visions' (*Tim.*, 69e–71a). Situated in the liver, it partakes of the sweet / bitter nature of this organ whose smoothness and brightness reflects as in a mirror 'the power of thought which proceeds from the mind [ἡ ἐκ τοῦ νοῦ φερομένη δύναμις]'. Noetic power translated into 'image' operates in two ways: it can either 'strike terror' into the desires by making use of the bitterness of the liver in a 'twisting', 'contracting', 'contorting', and 'closing' activity which 'causes pain and loathing'; or conversely, 'when some gentle inspiration of the understanding pictures images of an opposite character', the sweetness of the liver is employed to harmonize and smooth up everything, rendering 'the portion of the soul which resides about the liver happy and joyful, enabling it to pass the night in peace, and to practice divination in sleep inasmuch as it has no share in mind and reason [λόγου καὶ φρονήσεως]' (*Tim.*, 71b–d).

Thus balance or 'justice' is achieved, and the inferior part of the soul is allowed 'to attain a measure of truth', since the liver is appointed to be the seat of divination. Plato distinguishes between 'divination' and 'prophecy', the former being the reception of the 'inspired word' in an ecstatic state, the latter an act of 'interpretation' necessitating 'reason [λογισμῷ]' to 'signify [σημαίνει]' i.e. translate 'images [φαντάσματα]' into propositional discourse (*Tim.*, 71e–72a). The transition from 'vision' – or rather 'audition' – to 'signification' (as practised under the auspices of Apollo, patron of the first type of divine madness), entirely divorces the prophet / interpreter from the primal experience of the divine; Plato refrains from reproducing the model introduced in the *Ion*, where the interpreter of art (poetry) forms a link in the magnetic chain of divine power, equally subject to the original ἐνθουσιασμός – possessed alike with the poet and seized as 'with a Bacchic transport' (533d–e). Here, on the contrary, the return to the condition of φρόνησις is imperative; what is needed is the intervention of an ἔμφρων critic who will translate – or transcribe – inspiration into prophecy, embodied truth into known truth (*Tim.*, 72a–b).

Plato's assumption that the soul is divided into three parts or forms (εἴδη) generates the analogical model of soul / city correspondence, which makes of the *Republic* with its investigation into social structures, a 'blow-up', a 'capitalization' writ large for the indistinct stratification of the human psyche. As Socrates admits, the individual is expected 'to have these same forms in his soul, and by reason of identical affections [πάθη] of these with those in the city to receive properly the same appellations' (IV, 435b–c). The affections of the various parts of the soul, warring against each other, reduce man to a condition of utter helplessness and passivity in the hands of a force beyond human comprehension, encumbering free will and rational action – which for Plato as the 'preserver' of social order (rather than the 'destroyer' of intellectual / moral systems of conditioning) is identified with 'civil law' as early as the *Apology* (33a) and as late as the *Laws* (I, 644d–645a). It is precisely the experience of polarity in παθήματα, the unresolved dialectic of inner tensions or affective ambivalence, that gives rise to the theory of the tripartite soul. To the question whether intellection, aggression, and sensuality are attributes of 'the same thing or whether there are three things', Plato opts for a psychic multiplicity of functions, seeming to rest on an a priori maxim of non-contradiction but, as I see it, actually giving birth to it:

> It is obvious that the same thing will never do [ποιεῖν] or suffer [πάσχειν] opposites in the same respect in relation to the same thing and at the same time. So that if ever we find these contradictions in the functions of the mind we shall know that it was not the same thing functioning but a plurality.
>
> (*Rep.*, IV, 436b–c)

Even if we do not accept B. Jowett's[3] interpretation, which reads the phrase τἀναντία ποιεῖν ἢ πάσχειν not as 'the same thing will never do or suffer opposites', but as 'the same thing cannot act or be acted upon' – which makes of ποίησις and πάθος the irreconcilable polarity, Plato has furnished enough evidence throughout the dialogues to allow for such a presupposition.

Choosing examples from different points in his career confirms more forcibly the above hypothesis. In the *Phaedrus*, exploring the best way to reflect about the nature of a thing, Plato recommends that in the case of a 'complex' object, enumeration of its parts is the first stage of approach; in cases of 'simplicity' the course is 'to inquire what natural capacity it has of acting upon another thing, and through what means; or by what other thing, and through what means, it can be acted upon' (270d). In the *Philebus* it is admitted that 'those of them who consider themselves students of reality spend a whole lifetime in studying the universe around us, how it came to be, how it does things, and how things happen to it' (59a). In the *Laws*, a classification of 'motions' is attempted, and 'the condition under which coming to be universally takes place' (X, 893e) is investigated: generation is interpreted as a gradual passing through various stages or types of motion until enough impetus (or acceleration) is acquired to render 'perceptibility to percipients'; the propulsion behind all life, 'That which moves itself as well as other things – and finds its place in all doing [ποιήμασι] and all being-done-to [παθήμασι], is veritably called transformation [μεταβολήν] and motion [κίνησιν] of all that is [ὄντως τῶν ὄντων]' (X, 894c). In the *Seventh Letter*, the epistemological process of comparing names, descriptions, and images, is said to be universally applicable to all shapes and surfaces, concepts, bodies, elements, animals, qualities, 'and in respect to all states active and passive [περὶ ποιήματα καὶ παθήματα σύμπαντα]' (342d–e).

It would appear, then, that Plato violates the either / or model he establishes, exemplified in its ontological aspect in the *Sophist* – οὐσία being δύναμιν εἴτ' εἰς τὸ ποιεῖν . . . εἴτ' εἰς τὸ παθεῖν (247e) – and in its psychological version in the *Republic* as the axiom of non-contradiction – Δῆλον ὅτι ταὐτὸν τἀναντία ποιεῖν ἢ πάσχειν κατὰ ταυτόν γε καὶ πρὸς ταυτὸν οὐκ ἐθελήσει ἅμα (IV, 436b) – when he makes his monumental declaration in the *Symposium*: ποιητὴς ὁ Ἔρως (196e). In a statement of great metaphysical irony, the familiar conceptual order which identifies the 'actor' with the 'cause' – τὸ ποιοῦν καὶ τὸ αἴτιον ἕν (*Phil.*, 26e) – is undermined, and πάθος becomes the prime mover in both human and cosmic affairs:

> Love is himself so divine a poet that he can kindle in the souls of others the poetic fire, for no matter what dull clay we seemed to be before, we are every one of us a poet when we are in love. We need ask no further proof than this that Love is a poet deeply versed in every branch of what I may define succinctly as creative art, for, just as no one can give away what he has not got, so no one can teach what he does not know.
>
> And who will deny that the creative power [ποίησιν] by which all living things are begotten and brought forth is the very genius of Love?
> (*Symp.*, 196e–197a)

Yet, the doings of the 'needy' Ἔρως, and the effects of desire in the soul are not always presented in the light of the approval they receive in the *Symposium* or the *Phaedrus*. Plato seems to be fully aware of the destructive potential of 'the indwelling tyrant Eros' (*Rep.*, IX, 573d), and of the fact that 'there exists in every one of us, even in some reputed most respectable, a terrible, fierce, and lawless brood of desires, which it seems are revealed in our sleep' (*Rep.*, IX, 572b); not only is Ἔρως set free during sleep, but it endangers 'the democratic constitution of the soul' when, emancipated and set loose in daytime, it becomes the ruling passion – turning 'democracy' into 'tyranny' (*Rep.*, IX, 574d–575a). Thus 'the best and most reasonable parts' of the soul are enslaved 'while a small part, the worst and the most frenzied [μανικώτατον], plays the despot'; consequently, 'the tyrant soul must of necessity be needy and suffer from unfulfilled desire' (IX, 577d–578a), never finding rest and repose. In conclusion, Plato declares that the most distant from philosophy and reason (φιλοσοφίας καὶ λόγου) are the 'erotic and tyrannical appetites', fixed 'at the furthest remove from true and proper pleasure' (IX, 587a–b). The harmful results of an uncontrollable πάθος, that of anarchic Ἔρως, are also enumerated in the *Laws*, where man appears 'ready to scruple at no act whatsoever – innocent, sinful, or utterly shameful – so long as it promises to sate him, like some brute beast, with a perfect glut of eating, drinking, and sexual sport' (VIII, 831d).

The *Phaedrus*, with its 'right madness' (244e), occupies a middle position between the subversive exposition of passion as an utterly negative force in the *Republic*, and its exaltation in the *Symposium* where physical love is securely established as a point of departure for philosophical activity. This dialogue portrays the struggle between conflicting tensions, where the power of love to activate intelligence and perception of reality is presented but not safeguarded. The perils inherent in the operation of canalizing the aroused sexual drive, transforming sensual into spiritual energy, constitute an ironic dialectic between success and its deconstruction. The cohabitation of μανία and διαλεκτική, the two movements which lead to the vision of Ideas, is yet an uneasy one, and the achievement of the warm intellectualism of νοῦς ἐρῶν – the initial Platonic unity prior to the split into passion / reason – seems an adventurous undertaking. Socrates speaking in his own 'human' voice – by 'his own eyes inspired' – rather than reporting the mantic revelation of a priestess, is as sensitive to the aberrations that such erotic games may originate, as to their creative potential:

> So therefore glorious and blissful is the endeavour of true lovers in that mystery rite, if they accomplish that which they endeavour after the fashion of which I speak, when mutual affection arises through the madness inspired by love. But the beloved must needs be captured, and the manner of the capture I will now tell.
>
> (*Phaedr.*, 253c)

Although the whole argument is built on the assumption that 'If Love is, as he is indeed, a god or a divine being, he cannot be an evil thing' (242e) – radically contradicting the premise on which the *Republic* is constructed – the phenomenology of the erotic and initiatory consciousness as Socrates portrays it, is instinct with an ambiguity that makes the conversion of physical into meta-physical desire a questionable process. The metaphor employed throughout is that of the 'soul-chariot' that appears again in the *Republic*, and a detailed iconography of the irrational energy is given – the black ἄλογον of uncontrollable impulse – as 'crooked of frame, a massive jumble of a creature, with thick short neck, snub nose, black skin, and gray eyes; hot blooded, consorting with wantonness and vainglory; shaggy of ear, deaf, and hard to control with whip and goad' (253e). The bodily 'affections' resulting from this psychic dialectic are given in great detail through the interaction of 'driver' and 'horses', for the achievement of the Platonic oxymoron of 'rational passion' (253e–255a). The exposition of sexual metaphysics in the *Phaedrus* is an alternation of 'ifs' and 'buts', and the dual awareness of transcendence and its limitations emphasizes the fact that what is called in the *Republic* the 'tyranny of love' is at any moment threatening to overthrow, undermine, and subordinate all sublimation, leading instead to extremities of physical and moral degradation, an impoverishment of 'being'. Conversely – Socrates constantly admonishes his listeners – in the complete division between ἔρως and the instinct for reproduction, sex becomes a sacred ceremony that in its intensity releases the νοῦς from conditional bonds, and brings it into contact with the 'ideistic' substratum of reality. If physical gratification is resisted when lover and beloved 'lie side by side', and if 'the victory be won by the higher elements of mind guiding them into the ordered rule of the philosophical life, their days on earth will be blessed with happiness and concord' (*Phaedr.*, 256a–b).

In the *Symposium*, as has already been discussed, the 'erotic' or 'daemonic' as a μεταξύ is firmly established in Platonic metaphysics in the role of a mediating structural component. The dark and destructive aspects of love's possession are completely silenced, and ἔρως is presented as the means of bridging the ontological gap between immortals and mortals, μεταξὺ θεοῦ τε καὶ θνητοῦ. Diotima's mysterious 'intermediate space' inhabited by love, the interim between conception and generation, is a psycho-physiological transformation, a rebirth process that sounds as natural – and painful – as the physical birth to which it is likened. Although the outcome is an 'enlightened' human being, the initial stages seem to share the violence, helplessness, and shock that attend childbirth. Beauty as 'concord' facilitates parturition and releases 'immortality' or an altered form of consciousness that liberates man from the condition of impermanence; for,

> although we speak of an individual as being the same so long as he continues to exist in the same form, and therefore assume that a man is the same person in his dotage as in his infancy, yet for all we call him the same,

every bit of him is different, and every day he is becoming a new man [νέος ἀεὶ γιγνόμενος], while the old man is ceasing to exist.

(*Symp.*, 207d)

With a being always in flux, where not only body but mind is subject to constant mutation – emerging into and vanishing out of existence in variable forms – ἔρως is proposed as the only power that can turn 'change' into 'transformation'.

The organ of transmutation of energies and 'affections' is the mind-in-love that can reach 'sameness'; this is the Platonic identification of the 'good' with αὐτάρκεια (self-sufficiency) and cessation of desire, the 'repose' which signifies the consummation rather than the suppression of passion. The mapping out of the 'Platonic love' territory marks a procedure that begins with physical desire transformed into a longing for the psychic condition of 'beauty' (as harmony or balance), serving as a catalyst for birth into 'immortality'; such is a condition of 'sameness' or eternity, free from the continual flow of perceptual, emotional, and intellectual events flashing into the phenomenal world. In his doctrine Plato recognizes the common source of sexuality, creativity, and knowledge, making love not only a 'poet', as we have seen – ποιητὴς ὁ Ἔρως (*Symp.*, 196e) – but also a 'philosopher' – ἀναγκαῖον Ἔρωτα φιλόσοφον εἶναι (*Symp.*, 204b) – placed between wisdom and ignorance, yet an ignorance acutely aware of a sense of loss, absence, and unfulfilled potential. The Resource / Need combination in the parentage of Ἔρως designates the polarity of an unresolved dialectic of contrarieties whose creative tension signals an energy-producing scheme that, by retaining a high degree of intensity in consciousness, *catches* 'being' in it (ἡ τοῦ ὄντος θήρα) – thus transforming πάσχειν into ποιεῖν.

The conjunction of philosophy and poetry that is effected under the auspices of Ἔρως – ποιητής and φιλόσοφος – not only seems to be an instance of resolution of that 'ancient enmity' (*Rep.*, X, 607c) between the two cultural forms, but poses the very problem of human creativity, ποίησις, and its relation to the παθήματα of habitual consciousness, as well as the reality of 'beauty' that shines through empirical existence; for, 'wisdom is concerned with the loveliest of things, and Love is the love of what is lovely' (*Symp.*, 204b), as much as love 'can kindle in the souls of others the poetic fire' (*Symp.*, 196e). The aesthetic experience of 'beauty' is the denominator of both poetry and philosophy, and the road leading to it, its ποίησις, seems to be the way of πάθησις, that strange condition called creative suffering. From that 'passion' arises the whole question of creation, the passion that begins with an individual to become a πάθος for all existents. It is not surprising that the *Symposium* is one of the dialogues where the issue of creativity is raised, in the context of an argument about the 'other' madness, that of the lover / philosopher. What meaning must be given to ποίησις? What is creation, what is the creative mind? Is it a mind that suffers, and through that πάθησις has learned a 'truth' and a 'method' which it embodies in language (or other materials)? Is ποίησις the outcome of tension and intensity? The subject of poetry is introduced by Diotima immediately after the definition of Ἔρως as the 'lover' and its object as that of 'beauty' – in a seemingly casual fashion, while in a process of 'desynonymization' of words:

> For instance, poetry. You'll agree that there is more than one kind of poetry in the true sense of the word – that is to say, calling something into existence that was not there before, so that every kind of artistic creation is poetry, and every artist is a poet.
>
> (205b–c)

The official definition of poetry (i.e. a λόγος arrived at in the course of a dialectical process of collection and division) is given in the *Sophist,* in terms similar to those sketched in the random reference of the *Symposium*; the creative art is a 'power of producing', and 'He who brings to existence [εἰς οὐσίαν ἄγῃ] something that did not exist before is said to be a producer' (219b). Later in the dialogue, the definition is repeated with greater emphasis, and ποιητική is again interpreted as δύναμις 'that can bring into existence [γίγνεσθαι] what did not exist before' (265b). Plato is consistent throughout in asserting ποιητική to be a power, a gate through which things come from non-existence, nothingness, into οὐσία – which in the Platonic metaphysical geography would place poetry in the territory of the 'instant', between non-being and being, rest and motion. What seems to cause a series of contradictory statements, though, is the nature of this creative 'power', whether it is with λόγος, a product of θεός, or ἄ-λογος, a manifestation of φύσις. The problematic is posed in the *Sophist* again, following immediately upon the definition of poetry: 'Must we not attribute the coming-into-being of these things out of not-being to divine craftsmanship and nothing else? Or are we to fall in with the belief that is commonly expressed?' (265c). The answer arrived at is straightforward and contains none of the familiar Socratic ambiguity; it is firmly asserted that 'the products of nature, as they are called, are works of divine art, as things made out of them by man are works of human art' (265e). But once the edifice is constructed, the Platonic text furnishes the prospective 'deconstructor' with a host of 'weapons' to expose the essential irony of what seems to be an unshakable conviction. If divine art is defined as an analogue to human art, the relation can be inverted, and human art is seen as a spontaneous creation which, paradoxically, reconciles 'god' and 'nature' rather than presenting them as opposite forces – production coming 'not so much from science [τέχνῃ] as from a native instinct implanted by God [φύσει κατὰ θεόν]' (*Epinomis*, 975b).

The relation of 'art' to the irrational is a perpetual source of contradiction in the dialogues. The etymology of τέχνη as 'possession of mind' (*Crat.*, 414b–c), homologizes the ὄνομα with the λόγος (definition) of art, as that which introduces a norm or due measure into excess and deficiency; thus 'art' and 'measure' become interchangeable terms, as 'to deny either is to deny both' (*Statesm.*, 284d). Having identified art with 'measure' and 'reason', and having emphatically declared, 'I refuse the name of art to anything irrational' (*Gorgias*, 465a), Plato comes in the *Phaedrus* to call μαντική, inspired prophecy, the greatest of arts – καλλίστη τέχνη. It was precisely because 'the men of old who
gave things their names' considered 'madness to be a valuable gift, when due to divine dispensation, that they named that art as they did, though the men of today, having no sense of values, have put in an extra letter, making it not *manic* but *mantic*' (244b–c). The evolution of the argument about the 'superiority of heaven-sent madness over man-made sanity' (244d) introduces a duplication of the *Ion* position (542a–b) – that the poet is not an 'artist' but possessed by the divine epiphany – without however the ironic (not to say sarcastic) edge that lurks throughout the earlier

dialogue. The third form of madness originating in the Muses,

> seizes a tender, virgin soul and stimulates it to rapt passionate expression, especially in lyric poetry, glorifying the countless mighty deeds of ancient times for the instruction of posterity. But if any man come to the gates of poetry without the madness [μανίας] of the Muses, persuaded that skill [τέχνης] alone will make him a good poet, then shall he and his works of sanity with him be brought to nought by the poetry of madness, and behold, their place is nowhere to be found.
>
> (*Phaedr.*, 245a)

Plato's severe criticism of ποίησις[4] – not in the generic sense of 'creativity', but in the limited notion of a 'saying' with 'musical colouring' whose adornments 'rhythm, meter, and harmony' cast a mighty spell on the soul (*Rep.*, X, 601a–b) – lies at the threshold of western aesthetics, having provoked, as is widely known, a series of 'defences' of poetry – beginning with Aristotle and including those of Sidney and Shelley. Yet, the Platonic textual inconsistencies easily allow the construction of a defence of poetry from 'within', which deconstructs both the open attack launched in the *Republic*, and the more subtle subversion attempted in the *Ion*. It is the poets, Plato maintains, who first arouse the soul from its slumber and set it on its search for reality (ὄντος), by 'always dinning into our ears, that we neither hear nor see anything accurately' (*Phaedo*, 65b); for poets 'are as good as fathers and guides to us in matters of wisdom' (*Lysis*, 214a). No less a celebrity than Protagoras asserts that 'the most important part of man's education is to become an authority on poetry' (*Protagoras*, 339a), and together with Socrates embarks upon an animated critical appreciation of a poem by Simonides on the topic of 'virtue'. Poets, together with priests, are called in as witnesses to the immortality of the soul, the cornerstone of the Platonic doctrine of Ideas (*Meno*, 81a–b).

Sacred madness not only conducts to metempirical knowledge of permanence but renders a 'true' image of man's empirical existence, because poets 'singing as they do under the divine afflatus, are among the inspired and so, by the help of their Graces and Muses, often enough hit upon true historical fact' (*Laws*, III, 682a). Μανία, as a manifestation of 'rhythm' and 'melody' under any of its patron divinities (Apollo, the Muses, or

Dionysus), is a gift considered not as the revenge of the gods, or an 'evil thing' that drives the humans frantic, but as a 'medicine, to produce modesty of soul, and health and strength of body' (*Laws*, III, 672d). As such, ᾠδαί (songs) are 'spells' for the soul, not in the derogatory sense implied in the *Republic*, i.e. as the alienation of the soul from its true nature (X, 601b), but 'directed in all earnest to the production of the concord' (*Laws*, II, 659e) that is the most desirable condition for both the individual and the city. And if poets are denied the title of 'legislator' for being thrice removed from truth and reality – fabricators of phantoms – to whom no city owes its well-being and prosperity (*Rep.*, X, 599d–e), the poetic practice is used as the archetypal metaphor for the definition and interpretation of 'legislating'. If poets are not legislators, legislators *are* poets, not in the broad aspect of the term, but in the specific meaning of portraying the 'drama' of life; as legislators admit in an (imaginative) address to poets,

> we are ourselves authors of a tragedy, and that the finest and best we know how to make. In fact, our whole polity has been constructed as a dramatization of a noble and perfect life; that is what *we* hold to be in truth the most real of tragedies. Thus you are poets, and we also are poets in the same style, rival artists and rival actors, and that in the finest of all dramas, one which indeed can be produced only by a code of true law – or at least that is our faith.
>
> (*Laws*, VII, 817b)

In his metaphorical usage of the terms 'tragedy' and 'drama', Plato seems to overlook the fact that it is precisely for the reason of depicting opposition and conflict that poetic products are rejected from the ideal city, since the image of man presented in poetry is of a soul self-divided and torn with countless contradictions (*Rep.*, X, 603c–d). The oxymoron that characterizes the poetic condition as presented by Plato – of a mind that, seized with the Bacchic transport and launching into harmony and rhythm (*Ion*, 534a), should yet speak of disorder and strife (*Rep.*, X, 603c) – not only poses the paradox of 'orderly disorder', but introduces a tensive relation between content and form. That the poet 'knows nothing' of what he speaks (*Ion*, 534c), makes poetry a product of the 'daemonic' (which should automatically absolve the poet from any charge of mis-representation of the divine, that ultimately comes to be seen as a 'self-representation'), but also a communication of psychic chaos that reflects ontological chaos. The poet's capacity for passionate intensity, although, typologically, sharing the same substratum as that of the philosophic activity – in that each on its own plane indicates a particular way of transcending the 'profane' world and attaining to the world of the gods or Being – enjoys an equivocal status in the Platonic canon.

To the extent that it becomes a vehicle for contradiction and ambiguity, poetry is suspect of inducing a state of mind uncontrollable by civil law or social decorum. Ambivalence, or 'polyvalence', of signification as the linguistic expression poetry employs to denote indeterminacy and equivocation, is what distinguishes the polyphonic poet from the univocal legislator, since it is well known,

> that when a poet takes his seat on the Muse's tripod, his judgment takes leave of him. He is like a fountain which gives free course to the rush of its waters, and since representation is of the essence of his art, must often contradict his own utterances in his presentations of contrasted characters, without knowing whether the truth is on the side of this speaker or of that. Now it is not the legislator's business in his law to make two such statements about one and the same topic; he has regularly to deliver himself of one pronouncement on one matter.
>
> (*Laws*, IV, 719c–d)

But if the legislator's 'business' is to suppress ironic tensions of the co-presence of opposites, it is as much the philosopher's as it is the poet's to take cognizance of the phenomenon – as appears in Plato's own emphasis not only on the metaphysical but epistemological importance of 'irony'; it is coincidental contradiction, he tells us, that awakens reflection and sets the mind on the dialectical pursuit of 'being', stimulated by 'provocation' – things provocative of thought defined as those that 'impinge upon the senses together with their opposites' (*Rep.*, VII, 524d). Poetic 'provocation', however, unlike its philosophic counterpart, is feared as corruptive 'of the mind of all listeners who do not possess as an antidote a knowledge of its real nature' (*Rep.*, X, 595b). It is precisely in the lack of an antidote, φάρμακον (which is the word the Greek text uses), that the 'danger' of poetry lies. One, however, should not forget here that φάρμακον is itself an ambiguous term, denoting poison and medicine, enchantment and cure – 'the wounder (φάρμακος) shall heal', as a Delphic oracle pronounces, not to mention the attribute of φαρμακεύς that is ascribed to ἔρως (*Symp.*, 203d). Because 'it associates with the part in us that is remote from intelligence and is its companion and friend for no sound and true purpose', 'cohabiting with an inferior and engendering inferior off-spring', poetic μίμησις appeals to the lower part of the soul, and stimulates it by fashioning 'phantoms' and images removed from reality, destroying the 'rational' part and enhancing 'the senseless element that cannot discriminate the greater from the less, but calls the same thing now one, now the other' (*Rep.*, X, 603b–605c).

The subversive power of poetry, as Plato sees it, lies in the threat it poses to the established hierarchy of psychic and social structures, its assault on doctrine, ideology, and emotional constitution, introducing 'anarchy' in place of institutionalized codes of behaviour, law, and order. Poetic licence is condemned because it leads to reckless excess of liberty and disobedience to any form of rule – an 'emancipation from the authority' of opinion, habit, and tradition (*Laws*, III, 701b), which is as much to be feared in its 'poetical' manifestation as it is paradoxically welcome in its 'philosophical' version: that of the dialectical 'purificatory' process (*Soph.*, 230c–d) which, by doing away with all 'hypotheses' (*Rep.*, VII, 533c), leads to 'a violent distrust' of all that was formerly held true (*Rep.*, VII, 539c) – provoking an epistemological admission of total 'ignorance', an 'emptiness' that of necessity annihilates ethical values.[5] Such a condition of ἕν οἶδα ὅτι οὐδὲν οἶδα is in itself a deliverance from orthodoxy and system, putting an end to the old ways of thinking, acting, and living. The 'tale of approximation' that the Platonic text seems to 'say' (despite Plato's 'moral' pronouncements) is precisely this: the unconditional rapport of the poetic and philosophic practices – as 'ecstatic' and 'enstatic' modes – equally sharing an intensity of awareness that undermines habitual consciousness and exposes the transparency of concepts, so that 'labelling' no longer serves as a way of solidifying the image of the 'real'.

The Platonic dialogues constantly generate inner contradictions because of the author's refusal to admit, at times, the proximity of the categories – and experiences – of 'philosophy' and 'poetry', identified in certain places simply as two forms of μανία – the rage and heat engendered by a violent and excessive increase of 'consciousness'; it is the magical 'burning' of passion due to the manifestation of the divine or daemonic power – both conducing to an emergence from time and the abolition of 'history', despite their possible structural differences. In a text that teems with (intentional or unintentional) dialectical contrarieties, 'irony' seems to 'signify' (in the Heraclitean sense of neither 'declaring' nor 'concealing', but 'giving a sign') the Platonic enigma of the 'fury' that leads to heaven (as well as hell), a spirit or fire that becomes a tool, a bridge to the Being of beings. In providing a maximum tension that overwhelms normal mental operations and inaugurates divine possession, both poetic and philosophical exercises obviously opt for 'the madness that is of god' rather than 'the wisdom that is of man' (*Phaedr.*, 256b).

THE ROMANTICS ON PASSION / POETRY

The notion that the intellective / affective dualism is false, that thought and emotion are both aspects of the same capacity, that true 'intelligence' involves both functions simultaneously might be described as a constant of Romantic ideology. Coleridge's repetitive exclamation, 'O for some Sun that shall unite Light & Warmth', first appearing in the *Notebooks* between September and November 1799, and its later version of August–September 1802, 'O for some Sun to unite heat & ~~warm~~ Light!' (1957: I, 467; 1233), is clearly expressive of the desire – and the recognition – that the 'burning' of emotional intensity is inseparable from the 'light' of intellectual awareness. The blaze of passion as a presupposition to creativity is also evinced in Keats' aesthetic theory, where material things are 'burnt' into spirituality through the mind's extremity of experience; and although Keats' relation to 'fire' and 'burning' is ambivalent, as his treatment of Hyperion betrays, it is through excessive πάθος whereby the whole being is shaken that the transmutation into 'ethereality' is achieved. Both forms of πάσχειν, intensity and receptivity, are stressed by Keats as necessary conditions to poetic production, in statements like 'for I have the same Idea of all our Passions as of Love they are all in their sublime, creative of essential Beauty' (1958: I, 184), or 'let us open our leaves like a flower and be passive and receptive – budding patiently under the eye of Apollo' (1958: I, 232); in his search for the relation of 'suffering' to 'meaning' Keats recognizes that creative dejection is the acceptance of the necessary pain involved in the conflicts of empirical existence.

Whereas Keats is inclined to stress 'pain' as a condition and counterbalancing of 'delight', Wordsworth concentrates on 'joy' as the infallible evidence for the presence of transformation, the ποιεῖν that succeeds upon πάσχειν. The workings of 'passion' become operative from the 'dawn' of consciousness – or rather become instrumental *to* the arousal of consciousness (a stimulation apparently effected through the Platonic practice of συνορᾶν εἰς ἕν – integrate vision); the 'infant babe',

> who sleeps
> Upon his mother's breast, who, when his soul
> Claims manifest kindred with an earthly soul,
> Doth gather passion from his mother's eye.
> Such feelings pass into his torpid life
> Like an awakening breeze, and hence his mind,
> Even at the first trial of its powers,
> Is prompt and watchful, eager to combine
> In one appearance all the elements
> And parts of the same object, else detached
> And loth to coalesce. . . .
> (*Prelude*, 1805, II, 240–50)

Wordsworth recognizes that a dialectic interplay, a tension between acceptance and excitability, characterizes the logical structure of creativeness; when the poet attains to a state of receptive openness, a 'wise passiveness' ('Expostulation and Reply', l. 24), he becomes the embodiment and voice of an impassioned revelation of 'relationship' that remains hidden from the so-called rational perception of reality. Passion appears as an inner system of energy that not only establishes a connective between the 'res cogitans' and 'res extensa' of the Cartesian reality model, but is a 'producer' of art; as the Poet in *The Excursion* admits, through the operation of deep feelings he 'attained / An active power to fasten images / Upon his brain; and on their pictured lines / Intensely brooded, even till they acquired / The liveliness of dreams' (I, 144–8).

Dynamic concentration aims at single-pointedness of mind. The ability to surrender opinions and preconceived ideas, means being able to relax the mental process, to be, as Keats asserts, 'in uncertainties, Mysteries, doubts, without any irritable reaching after fact & reason' (1958: I, 193). This repose and receptivity of mind is a necessary prerequisite for obtaining cognizance of the workings of nature, or natural 'presences',

> for they speak,
> In these their invocations, with a voice
> Obedient to the strong creative power
> Of human passion. Sympathies there are
> More tranquil, yet perhaps of kindred birth,
> That steal upon the meditative mind,
> And grow with thought. . . .
> (*Ex.*, I, 478–84)

Transmutation of 'an agonizing sorrow', or 'resolution', is the bringing to completion, to closure, to a comprehensive ending, of unalleviated tension or conflict. Paradoxically, it is intensity that relieves from the fixation of tension and allows the merging of all the energies invoked. If polarized antagonism is maintained, Wordsworth seems to believe, then a new unity can come about; transformation occurs when the contradiction is resolved through intensive integration that annihilates any 'given' or formulated equilibrium; the 'sufferer'

> longs
> To realize the vision, with intense
> And over-constant yearning; – there – there lies
> The excess by which the balance is destroyed.
> Too, too contracted are these walls of flesh,
> This vital warmth too cold, these visual orbs,
> Though inconceivably endowed, too dim
> For any passion of the soul that leads
> To ecstasy; and all the crooked paths
> Of time and change disdaining, takes its course
> Along the line of limitless desires.
> (*Ex.*, IV, 175–85)

The characterization of 'passion' as 'highest reason' (*Prel.*, V, 40–1) is not only a deliberate con-fusion of terms that subverts the traditional binary opposition, but an admission of a puzzling relation between the two, not normally recognized in the separatist categorizations of conceptual thinking:

> The dangerous craft of culling term and phrase
> From languages that want the living voice
> To carry meaning to the natural heart;
> To tell us what is passion, what is truth,
> What reason, what simplicity and sense.
> (*Prel.*, VI, 110–14)

The questionable relation between 'passion' and 'reason' is portrayed in a later passage in *The Prelude*, where affectivity is presented as a 'possession' by the triple modality of nature / power / divinity, 'To yield myself to Nature, when that strong / And holy passion overcame me first, / Nor day nor night, evening or morn, were free / From its oppression' (X, 417–20). Passion acts as a mediator, a μεταξύ, that allows the intermingling of 'nature' and 'man', or 'passion' and 'passion' (XIII, 287–93), generating an extraordinary condition of wisdom – being 'wise in passion' (XI, 84) – a state 'not thoroughly understood / By reason' (XI, 87–8).

Wordsworth duplicates in inverted form the Platonic ποιητὴς ὁ Ἔρως, through his proposition 'Poetry is passion', appearing in the notes on 'The Thorn'; language is the meeting-ground of πάσχειν and ποιεῖν, a drama, an event where a discharge of energy is registered. 'If to the poetry of common speech / Faith may be given' (*Ex.*, V, 392–3),

> Words, a Poet's words more particularly, ought to be weighed in the balance of feeling, and not measured by the space which they occupy upon paper. For the Reader cannot be too often reminded that Poetry is passion: it is the history or science of feelings.
> (1904: 701)

Traditional thought formations depend on the intellect alone; the emotions are feared as destroyers and contaminators of thought, therefore 'discursiveness' requires the systematic extinction of excitability. Yet the creative process, the most compelling form of thought, appears to contain an element that makes all the difference: affective intensity which renders to λόγος its archaic potency, where poetry not only communicates the experience of an interaction between the individual mind and 'another' power, but *affects* it. To this effect Wordsworth notes 'the interest which the mind attaches to words, not only as symbols of the passion, but as *things*, active and efficient, which are of themselves part of the passion' (1904: 701). And although he evidently attributes to poetry a 'phenomenalism' that dissociates it from 'reality', in that the business of poetry 'is to treat of things not as they *are*, but as they *appear*; not as they exist in themselves, but as they *seem* to exist to the *senses*, and to the *passions* (1974: III, 63), his intention is really to draw a distinction between the conceptual ('pure science') and poetic apprehensions of existence – outside the habitual categories of spatial and temporal organization – as 'Enraptured Art draws from those sacred springs / Streams that reflect the poetry of things!' ('Humanity', ll. 19–20).

The suggested affinity between the poetic and religious activities, in 'Poetry is most just to its own divine origin when it administers the comforts and breathes the spirit of religion' (1974: III, 64), points towards the ritualistic power of the impassioned word to abolish multiplicity and fragmentation, to reintegrate, to unify, to make whole. The magical efficacy of the poetic λόγος is depicted in *The Prelude* where the speaker 'Content and not unwilling now to give / A respite to this passion' (I, 59–60), performs the hieratic ceremony of an 'echo' aroused in the deepest strata of the human being, upon his rediscovery of the 'message' hidden in verbal utterance:

> A prophecy: poetic numbers came
> Spontaneously to clothe in priestly robe
> A renovated spirit singled out,
> Such hope was mine, for holy services.
> My own voice cheered me, and, far more, the mind's
> Internal echo of the imperfect sound;
> To both I listened, drawing from them both
> A cheerful confidence in things to come.
>
> (I, 51–8)

The relation of πάσχειν, ποιεῖν, and λέγειν is for Wordsworth homological rather than analogical – all three modes of being seen as aspects or expressions of 'power', vehicles for archetypal experience, the primordial ground inherent in all life – when the mind 'With conscious pleasure opened to the charm / Of words in tuneful order, found them sweet / For their own *sakes*, a passion, and a power' (*Prel.*, V, 554–6). The intense stimulation of all the senses through 'The fermentation and the vernal heat / Of poesy' (*Prel.*, IV, 103–4) is the πάθος / ποίησις condition which transforms a creature of history into a creature of experience; it replaces a personal consciousness (nourished on one's own memorial contents) by a witnessing consciousness, which is pure lucidity and spontaneity. The reality of the present moment, 'Past, future, shrinking up beneath the incumbent Now' ('The Warning', l. 96), becomes the cross-section where the barriers of passion and poetry are collapsed 'In what alone is ours, the living Now' ('Memorials of a Tour in Italy', X, 14).

Coleridge seems to be most aware, both poetically and critically, of the dialectic of transformation inherent in the coexistence of πάσχειν and ποιεῖν, when he applies himself to the work of Wordsworth and its 'poetic thoughts', one of the 'high arguments' of the *Biographia Literaria*. He not only defines the essence of Wordsworth's poetry as the expression of intellectual emotions – that 'union of deep feeling with profound thought' (1907: I, 59), which exposes the fallacy of the thinking / feeling dualism – but attempts to render into both conceptual and imaginative terms the ποίησις that the πάθος of Wordsworth's λόγος engendered in him:

> The language was not only peculiar and strong, but at times knotty and contorted, as by its own impatient strength; while the novelty and struggling crowd of images, acting in conjunction with the difficulties of the style, demanded always a greater closeness of attention, than poetry (at all events, than descriptive poetry) has a right to claim. It not seldom therefore justified the complaint of obscurity.
>
> (1907: I, 56)

For the 'poetic' rendering of the experience of poetry to which Coleridge as 'interpreter' is subjected, he singles out one of the Wordsworthian 'sketches' which becomes simultaneously an emblem for the artistic *and* aesthetic experience – of the 'production' and 'consumption' of poetry. The poem's pattern of tension / release, the discharge of energy which makes of it a natural, psychological, and verbal 'drama', the imagery of fiery intensity and luminosity in a context of darkness, indicate that the condition of 'heat and light' are for once fulfilled for both 'poet' and 'reader':

> In the following extract I have sometimes fancied, that I saw an emblem of the poem itself, and of the author's genius as it was then displayed.

" 'Tis storm; and hid in mist from hour to hour,
All day the floods a deepening murmur pour;
The sky is veiled, and every cheerful sight:
Dark is the region as with coming night;
And yet what frequent bursts of overpowering light!
Triumphant on the bosom of the storm,
Glances the fire-clad eagle's wheeling form;
Eastward, in long perspective glittering, shine
The wood-crowned cliffs that o'er the lake recline;
Wide o'er the Alps a hundred streams unfold,
At once to pillars turn'd that flame with gold;
Behind his sail the peasant strives to shun
The West, that burns like one dilated sun,
Where in a mighty crucible expire
The mountains, glowing hot, like coals of fire."
(1907: I, 56–7)

What is given as the natural symbol of 'the poem itself', the condition of poetry, is the emission of power as 'overpowering light', or the ability of mind in a state of darkness to register the lightning-like and splendorous burst of creative energy. The 'spark' ignited by the 'heating' of passion is, in Coleridge's interpretation, a symptom of the phenomenology of both the passive / creative and passive / receptive consciousness. The transformative effects of such fire-like and light-like (as well as sound-like) events in the human mind and body, as a genesis of a new form of awareness, are set down by Coleridge in the statement that follows immediately upon the poem's 'reading', in his recognition that 'The poetic PSYCHE, in its process to full development, undergoes as many changes as its Greek namesake, the butterfly' (1907: I, 57).

The poem Coleridge himself composed after the recitation by Wordsworth 'of a poem on the Growth of an individual mind', shows in 'action' the Platonic 'magnet', the power divine impelling and attracting the ἑρμηνευτής as much as the original ποιητής (*Ion*, 533d): 'and what within the mind / By vital breathings secret as the soul / Of vernal growth, oft quickens in the heart / Thoughts all to deep for words!' ('To William Wordsworth', ll. 8–11). The interaction of ποιεῖν and πάσχειν, 'action' and 'suffering', is a characteristic experience not only of the perceptive faculty – 'When power streamed from thee, and the soul received / The light reflected, as a light bestowed' (ll. 18–19) – but also of intellection; so the 'poetic thought' of l. 21 is proportionable to the 'passionate thoughts' of l. 46: 'An Orphic song indeed, / A song divine of high and passionate thoughts / To their own music chaunted!' (ll. 45–7). 'Passionate' thought turns itself 'poetic' through the mediation of λόγος, language:

> Now poetry, Mr. Wordsworth truly affirms, does always imply PASSION: which word must be here understood in its general sense, as an excited state of the feelings and faculties. And as every passion has its proper pulse, so will it likewise have its characteristic modes of expression. But where there exists that degree of genius and talent which entitles a writer to aim at the honors of a poet, the very *act* of poetic composition *itself* is, and is *allowed* to imply and to produce, an unusual state of excitement, which of course justifies and demands a correspondent difference of language, as truly, though not perhaps in as marked a degree, as the excitement of love, fear, rage, or jealousy.
>
> (1907: II, 55–6)

Although the process of destroying and reinventing language is seminal to all Romantic poetry, and somehow both Coleridgean and Wordsworthian poetic texts attest to the fact that, in fabricating a new and unconventional speech replacing the 'disorganized' medium (i.e. the words which become 'through time, signs for portions or classes of thoughts instead of pictures of integral thoughts' (Shelley 1954: 278)), the creative artist enters the plane on which passion is converted into thought and vice versa, there is, I believe, a fundamental diversion of opinion between the two poets concerning the function of the impassioned state. For Wordsworth, passion *speaks*, i.e. it is transformable into λόγος, and this logos is ποίησις – whether uttered by the poet proper or the rustic, innocent of formal requirements. Still, 'it is impossible for the Poet to produce upon all occasions language as exquisitely fitted for the passion as that which the real passion itself suggests' (1974: I, 139); this is the 'poetry of common speech' to which not enough attention has been paid. Coleridge sustains the view that emotional intensity creates the conditions for poetic logos, but is by no means the origin and source of language – passion remaining a 'dumb' thing, and poetry resting on prior linguistic competence. 'Neither is the case rendered at all more tenable by the addition of the words, *in a state of excitement*', Coleridge continues his critique of Wordsworth's theory of 'REAL language of men' or 'natural language':

> For the nature of a man's words, where he is strongly affected by joy, grief, or anger, must necessarily depend on the number and quality of the general truths, conceptions and images, and of the words expressing them, with which his mind has been previously stored. For the property of passion is not to *create*; but to set in increased activity.
>
> (1907: II, 42)

Despite his professed Platonism, Coleridge seems here to reject the tenet of ποιητὴς ὁ Ἔρως and the view of poetry, particularly lyric poetry, as a transformative 'cry', a sign of a spontaneous overflow of passion breaking through, the 'hymn' of a human being possessed by divine power. In wishing, however, to retain the autonomy of the imagination from the associative limitations of its 'memorial' counterpart, fancy, he introduces a wedge between 'image', which is free and unconditioned, and 'word', expressive of conceptual structures embedded in memory:

> Could a rule be given from *without*, poetry would cease to be poetry, and sink into a mechanical art. It would be μόρφωσις, not ποίησις. The *rules* of the IMAGINATION are themselves the very powers of growth and production. The *words*, to which they are reducible, present only the outlines and external appearance of the fruit.
>
> (1907: II, 65)

The 'rule' of the imagination, as explicated elsewhere, is the integrative force that 'forms all into one graceful and intelligent whole', activating the entire soul of man, fusing the faculties through 'that synthetic and magical power' stimulated by 'will and understanding', and remaining throughout under the 'gentle' control of the rational drive, revealing itself 'in the balance or reconciliation of opposite or discordant qualities'; paradoxically, the 'conciliatory' process entails a hierarchical subjection of one term of the dialectical polarity to the other, and although the whole operation is conducted under the surveyance of the rational 'understanding', 'while it blends and harmonizes the natural and the artificial, still subordinates art to nature' (1907: II, 12–13).

The ending of the dedicatory poem 'To William Wordsworth' is an instance of the poetic reluctance to draw categorial distinctions such as 'art' and 'nature', conceptual compartments into which to fit 'emotional thought'. The whole composition of the lyric betrays awareness of a subjective experience that resists taxonomy and to which the terms 'aesthetic', 'philosophic', and even 'religious' are equally applicable:

> Scarce conscious, and yet conscious of its close
> I sate, my being blended in one thought
> (Thought was it? or aspiration? or resolve?)
> Absorbed, yet hanging still upon the sound –
> And when I rose, I found myself in prayer.
> (ll. 108–12)

The absorption and the lingering, the 'momentum' and 'stasis' of the 'still' and 'still hanging' oneness of 'thought' – something apprehended not as an abstract proposition but as a sort of eternal present 'space' into which time and causation do not enter, a sense of concrete reality from which the 'processional' element has been cancelled out – indicates that mind has gained to a new totality from which contradiction and confusion (time components) have vanished.

Both aspects of πάσχειν, suffering receptivity and passionate activity, are components of the Shelleyan concept of 'love':

> Love, from its awful throne of patient power
> In the wise heart, from the last giddy hour
>   Of dread endurance, from the slippery, steep
> And narrow verge of crag-like agony, springs
> And folds over the world its healing wings.
> (*Prometheus Unbound*, IV, 557–61)

'Love' is also climatic hedonism:

> One passion in twin hearts, which grows and grew,
> Till like two meteors of expanding flame,
> Those spheres instinct with it become the same,
> Touch, mingle, are transfigured; ever still
> Burning, yet ever inconsumable.
> (*Epipsychidion*, ll. 575–9)

'Passion' for Shelley carries the ambivalence that is also found in Wordsworth's presentation of the term – and representation of the experience; although being 'Nature's sacred power' (*The Revolt of Islam*, VII, 2867), it may lead through sensual intensity to the annihilation of the sensuous: 'And from her lips, as from a hyacinth full / Of honey-dew, a liquid murmur drops, / Killing the sense with passion; sweet as stops / Of planetary music heard in trance' (*Epips.*, ll. 83–6). Or, conversely, to a transfiguration of the senses – passion generating a heightened sensation: 'Such mighty change as I had felt within / Expressed in outward things' (*Prom.*, III, iv, 129–30).

What is the nature of the regenerative action of passion? When man wakes up from his egotistical 'dream', what does life feel like? This is the rhetorical question (rhetorical in the sense that it does conceal its own answer in accepting passion as 'poetic' agent) that underlies Shelley's poetry and thought. S. Rogers, in his discussion of the influence of classical Greece on the poetry of Shelley, proposes the adoption of the Platonic 'out of time' ἐξαίφνης as an interpretative model for Shelleyan apocalyptic / poetic occurrences: 'In Shelley's lyrical transformations, which have roughly paralleled the conversion of the Platonic philosopher and his spiritual discipline of "dying into life," the "moment" would seem to account for the change by which a simulated death carries the poet to a heightened vision'. In the world of poetic creativity, Rogers argues, such an experience replenishes the 'lyric gap': 'At the heart of this power lies the capability of passing, not merely into the eternity of nonexistence, but also into an absolutely creative dimension of time. This is the capacity for the irrational leap by which the philosopher transcends hypotheses and the poet transforms his consciousness' (1974: 113–14). Shelley's poetic rendering of the metamorphic effects of the 'moment', awareness of the 'nowness' and 'presence' of reality, points in two ways, one epistemological – that 'learning' means being active in the present – and the other psychological – that the process is grounded in personal intensity.[6]

In the creation myth of *Adonais* the 'quickening life' of 'change and motion' renews existence; it 'flashes' energy and 'kills' death: 'Shall that alone which knows / Be as a sword consumed before the sheath / By sightless lightning? – the intense atom glows / A moment, then is quenched in a most cold repose' (ll. 177–80). In an exact sense, the only thing that can be 'studied' in life is the 'moment'. The lyric 'instant', however, though related to tragic awareness, 'Woe is me! / Whence are we, and why are we? of what scene / The actors or spectators?' (ll. 183–5), is slightly but significantly different from the realization of the struggle and conflict of human 'beings' on the verge of death, or 'non-being'. The 'poetic' moment transforms the historical perspective, the drama of existence, by looking upon the world of suffering from the viewpoint of the 'observing' audience, not from the standpoint of interacting characters. The alternative to 'spectator' is not only 'actor', as suggested in the above cited lines from *Adonais*; the phrase in *The Triumph of Life*, 'from spectator turn / Actor or victim' (ll. 305–6) is a more faithful rendering of the acting / being acted upon, as an expression of the deepest mystery of the life force (the Platonic οὐσία) in which creation, destruction, change, and re-creation are but differential aspects in a unitary process of dramatic interplay.

The alternative to the actor / victim relation suggested by Shelley, to the ποιεῖν / πάσχειν dualism of existence, seems to be 'spectating' – the ἰδεῖν (of ἰδέα) – life seen as a stage show, a θέατρον. Sharpness of attention which is total awareness of the present (putting the accent not so much on the things seen but emphasizing the seeing itself) is an important step to accepting living situations as they are, thus transforming them. Noticing what is happening in the 'instant', not allowing the mind to become 'forgetful', keeps consciousness gathered and collected in λόγος that leads to εἶδος. Thus a balance is achieved and a deep and penetrating knowledge develops revealing many aspects of who, whence, and why we are – the persisting questions of Shelleyan metaphysics. Unlike the actor, the alert, watchful, observant spectator participates in the situation by merely taking note of it, without any interference; his ποίησις is in the looking, the intensity of his gaze. The moment when the centre of gravity has been displaced from the 'dramatic' personality to the 'theoretical' view of consciousness, the fixity of total seeing finally 'burns' up (eliminates) the observer / observed distinction; there is only attention, a choiceless and unbiased silent carefulness, a heightened state of being. The perceiving subject turns into an unrestricted openness in which time and space and action arise and vanish – the emptiness or field where the forms of objects appear and disappear; the θεατής becomes the open dimension, the θέατρον in which life comes and goes.

Comparing the function of imagery in the poetry of Shelley to that of Keats, W. J. Bate extends the usual assumption of a contrastive pattern of 'motion' vs. 'stasis', by suggesting the presence of a 'latent dynamism' as the dominant metaphor of Keats' imaginative constructs. Bate attributes the powerful completeness of Keats' craftsmanship to 'his highly dynamic power, caught momentarily in repose, and restrained and imprisoned still further in the bonds of art' (1918: 64). Keats himself has often expressed his views on the causal relation between 'passion' and 'poetry', in prose articulations of his aesthetic theory and in his poems. Statements like, 'the excellence of every Art is its intensity, capable of making all disagreeables evaporate, from their being in close relationship with Beauty & Truth' (1958: I, 192), the 'Idea of all our Passions' as 'creative of essential Beauty' (1958: I, 184), or 'the passion poesy' of the opening lines of *Endymion* (I, 29) indicate acceptance of a condition of fluidity that permits the open trafficking between πάσχειν and ποιεῖν. Passion as intensity is correlative to 'beauty', the sense of inward feeling of extraordinary elation which comes when there is complete cessation of mental motion or 'consequitive' thinking – the 'out of thought' condition; the essence of the content of consciousness being 'thought', and if 'but a moment's thought is passion's passing bell', the implication is that discursive consciousness must be effaced so that there is a totally different scope altogether. It is only in that dimension, Keats suggests, that there can be creativeness – the transformative power of intensification being destructive / creative; man 'does' or 'suffers' changes only when there is great passion, and it is only this fermentation that can effect 'another' kind of life in the individual and in the world. Πάσχειν and ποιεῖν for Keats share in the substratum of δύναμις, the common dynamic presence of power often in latent form, unmanifested or partly revealed to habitual consciousness: 'A drainless shower / Of light is poesy; 'tis the supreme of power; / 'Tis might half slumb'ring on its own right arm' (*Sleep and Poetry*, ll. 235–7). The phenomenology of poetic power aroused from latency is characterized by a light / sound correlation; the presupposition for its awakening from the 'half slumb'ring' mode in which it abides is paradoxically the reduction of consciousness to a state of 'sleep'.

In *Sleep and Poetry* the dependence of creativity on the receptive and vigilant mental condition of a 'Most happy listener!' (l. 16) is stressed – 'listening' implying the alert attentiveness that accompanies indolence, the 'doing nothing' that results in a perceptual capacity extended to its utmost potential, and awakening the power of ποίησις:

> What is it? And to what shall I compare it?
> It has a glory, and naught else can share it:
> The thought thereof is awful, sweet and holy,
> Chasing away all wordliness and folly;
> Coming sometimes like fearful claps of thunder,
> Or the low rumblings earth's regions under;
> And sometimes like a gentle whispering
> Of all the secrets of some wond'rous thing
> That breathes about us in the vacant air;
> So that we look with prying stare,
> Perhaps to see shapes of light, aerial limning,
> And catch soft floatings from a faint-heard hymning.
> (ll. 23–34)

The data surrounding the 'poetic' experience are: emptiness of mind ('vacant air'), suppression of thought ('But what is higher beyond thought than thee?'), the flashing of light and bursting of sound ('A glowing splendour round about me hung, / And echo back the voice of thine own tongue'), annihilation of the habitual self through intensification of the physical apparatus ('that I may die a death / Of luxury'), and illumination, the birth into the state of νοῦς or pure awareness, the ontological modality called 'Apollo': 'and my young spirit follow / The morning sun-beams to the great Apollo / Like a fresh sacrifice' (ll. 19–61). The power of μεταμόρφωσις inherent in elemental passion – an 'immortality of passion' (*End.*, II, 808) – whether gradual or instantaneous, dominates Keats' thought;[7] transformation always involves and affects the body, 'every sense / Filling with spiritual sweets to plenitude, / As bees gorge full their cells' (*End.*, III, 38–40). A powerful sensuous and emotive charge is expected to become the vehicle to Apollonian enlightenment; passion's energy used in escalating mind and expanding sensibility may lead, however, not to a condition of light / silence but to one of darkness / sound, the 'But here there is no light, / Save what from heaven is with the breezes blown / Through verdurous glooms and winding mossy ways' of the 'Ode to a Nightinghale' (IV).

The disjunction of the two aspects of πάσχειν (πάθημα and πάθος) that is effected in Keats' last work, *The Fall of Hyperion*, is indicative of an uneasy relation between the two states; the Poet's rejection of poetic magic for an 'unmediated' confrontation with human suffering, finally brings into the open the ironic tensions inherent in Keats' conception of πάσχειν. The wedge driven between πάθημα and πάθος also affects the nature of ποιεῖν. Creative insight, it is suggested, can be gained by 'those to whom the miseries of the world / "Are misery, and will not let them rest' (I, 148–9), those who 'are no dreamers weak, / "They seek no wonder but the human face; / "No music but a happy-noted voice' (I, 162–4) – and precisely those who sojourn in a life of clean and clear-cut oppositions, the earth where 'every creature hath his home; / "Every sole man hath days of joy and pain, / "Whether his labours be sublime or low – / "The pain alone; the joy alone; distinct' (I, 171–4). On the contrary, the Poet is characterized by Moneta as 'a dreaming thing, / "A fever of thyself', a visionary who, ignorant of and indifferent to the 'giant agony of the world', 'venoms all his days, / "Bearing more woe than all his sins deserve' (I, 168–76). The distinction into two kinds of suffering, the pain inflicted by circumstances on the one hand and self-induced 'poisoning' on the other, is retained throughout the dialogic encounter of Prophetess and Poet, 'medicin'd / "In sickness not ignoble' (I, 183–4). The ambiguity of poisoning / healing is carried forward by the Poet's presumptuous assumption that 'sure a poet is a sage; / "A humanist, physician to all men' (I, 189–90), immediately undermined by Moneta's answer, whereby it is not the bard / sage relation that is abruptly negated – the possibility of a 'rapport' between poetry and philosophy – but the nature of poetry itself that is put under interrogation: ' "Art thou not of the dreamer tribe? / "The poet and the dreamer are distinct, / "Diverse, sheer opposite, antipodes. / "The one pours out a balm upon the World, / "The other vexes it" ' (I, 197–202). This is a recognition that comes very close to the Platonic rejection of 'all the poetic tribe, beginning with Homer', for casting a 'mighty spell' on the human soul through the lyric colouring of their words and imitative antics. Not only, Plato asserts, is imitation 'a form of play not to be taken seriously', but poetry enhances perceptual confusion, as 'do jugglery and many other such contrivances' (*Rep.*, X, 600e–602d).

An invocation to Apollo that follows in the Keatsian text – to exterminate 'all mock lyrists' – presents the problematic of the nature and function of the poet in a different light; 'dreamers' are equated to proud versifiers, 'self worshippers', the 'fanatics' of the opening stanza of Canto I. 'Fanaticism', as a separatist and 'exclusive' vision of life, is here contrasted to the 'inclusiveness' of poetry; and the image of poet / physician is introduced, based on the healing effects of 'utterance', whereby the correlation of λέγειν, ποιεῖν, and πάσχειν acquires a 'medical' or linguistic power, turning the horror of speechless muteness into articulate sound. The discursive introduction to the dream world, where Keats 'sings' not only 'by his own eyes inspired' but certainly through his own tongue expressed, presents an a priori reconciliation of the faculties, and powers, that the imaginative sequel puts under question – the properties of ποίησις, πάθος, and λόγος.

The enthusiastic mind and its 'poems', far from being sealed off from communication and therefore from any possibility of curing social ills, confirm the poet's humanitarian function in the assumption that every man is a 'poet' in potential; the word-magic that poetry exercises is a therapy, in saving from 'dumb enchantment' not only the poet himself, but those inarticulate victims of affectivity for whom πάθημα cannot easily be translated into ποίημα. For who can question the poetic identity, ' "Thou art no Poet – may'st not tell thy dreams?" / Since every man whose soul is not a clod / Hath visions, and would speak, if he had loved, / And been well nurtured in his mother's tongue' (I, 12–15). Keats' 'poet kings' (*Sleep and Poetry*, l. 267), like Plato's philosopher kings, become carriers of a transformed awareness, expressed in religious terms as a sense of possible identification of the 'human' and the 'divine', in psychological terms as integration of the soul, and in epistemological terms as cognition of reality. In N. Frye's words, 'The most comprehensive and central of all Romantic themes, then, is a romance, with the poet for hero. The theme of this romance form is the attaining of an expanded consciousness, the sense of identity with God and nature which is the total human heritage, so far as the limited perspective of the human situation can grasp it'. Resting on the correlation between romance proper and its allegorical transference ('as in the old romances' – the etymological rootage of 'Romanticism') Frye identifies 'the great Romantic theme' as 'the attaining of an apocalyptic vision by a fallen but potentially regenerate mind. Such an event, taking place in the individual, may become a sign of a greater social awakening'; metaphorically, 'social change is symbolized by a psychological change: mankind is treated as a single gigantic individual, which Prometheus represents' (1968: 37–8).

The centre of Romantic mythological epics (or lyrics portraying dramatic encounter in an ironic fashion) is an 'ego' which, like the world it comes to represent, is 'in process', a person whose identity is in crisis; so it appears that the dialectical model of a life based upon contradictions does not in itself present man as simply a 'unit' in conflict with other 'units', but reflects a being caught in psychological tensions that must be resolved within the individual before a large scale social renovation can be attempted. Transformation necessarily precedes reformation, and a competent dealing with inner contrarieties is suggested as the only mediation to political and cultural frictions. The major Romantic myths portray a paradoxical state of conflict, in that a 'fluid' self or subject is confronted with a 'rigid' object, system, or civil organization – an ironic encounter of psychological 'anarchy' and social 'order'.[8] Romantic narratives represent subjective states of ψυχομαχία where the antithetical polarities engaged in 'debate' can no longer be resolved within the traditional conceptual structures and public codes of conduct. Unaided by any universally held contemporary mythology – due to the devastating intervention of two centuries of 'scientific' thinking – Romantic transformational patterns are not only opposed to a degenerated theocratic creed, but in establishing 'transformation' as a basic psychological – and ontological – event, they reintroduce a view of the world as metamorphic and organic, which is *the* mythical / paganistic view. Having rejected not only the Christian reality model, but its orthodox vocabulary of describing spiritual encounter as a mystical union of depraved man with his almighty lord, the Romantic mind, seeking to cast the out-of-normal experience it has arrived at in secular terms, should be expected to return to alternative documentations of human transactions with 'being'. The Romantic movement does not so much initiate a 'change' in 'cosmic grammar' but the 're-collection' of a forgotten or suppressed typology, which establishes a radical epistemological (and often ethical) transvaluation. The prevailing Christian doctrine of patriarchal kingship – promoting a discriminating, authoritarian, and controlling 'ego' – asserting and effecting a 'distancing' which turns divinity into an 'abstraction' that conceptualizes the primal 'shudder' of the sacred into speculation and dogma – ceases to be the only mode of experiencing, and expressing, 'otherness'.

The problem that the Romantics face, i.e. the interpretation of un-common states of consciousness in non-theological terms, makes the technique of subverting known habits of association as fundamental a premise in Romantic μῦθος as it was for the Platonic λόγος. To the extent that Romanticism can be considered as a 'Dionysian' movement, a reaction of 'chthonic' powers against the 'solar' divinities of Christian – and scientific – rationalism, it might also be seen as undermining what is normally considered the 'enlightened' and 'static' frame of reference of the Platonic school. Yet, a closer study of Plato's work has proved, I believe, that the two 'movements' have more similarities than differences, in their parallel deconstruction of the 'given' categories of the real, which makes 'transformation of consciousness' as much the Romantic as the Platonic archetypal story. The concern with 'self-knowledge' for the purpose of 'self-transcendence' is a common paradox in both Platonic and Romantic texts; in fact, my conviction is that it is not so much the mythology and symbology of the Platonic tradition that the Romantics were attracted to, as Plato's method of investigation of the 'unaided intellect' (*Phaedo*, 65e) delivered from the authority of ideas – assumptions, beliefs, ideologies, presuppositions – which is the 'past' dominating the 'present'. It is not surprising that both Romantic and Platonic myth – and drama – should concentrate on the individual human figure as the locus of unification of logos and mythos – Plato's dialogues being full not of 'ideas' but 'people'. The Platonic / Romantic shift that turns its attention to the text of the human body, translates the centrifugal search for 'being' into a centripedal one. Close analysis of the Platonic and Romantic work reveals a constant awareness of physicality, the observing and listening to somatic structure as an experience, or employing it as paradigmatic metaphor. The body is the vessel in which the transformative process takes place, spontaneously overflown by 'powerful feelings', or thoughts; sensation, πάθημα, always tears at the body, and the light of νοῦς presupposes the heat of μανία.

Μεταμόρφωσις as the central ontological and mythical event (Plato's ὁμοίωσις θεῷ), takes the place of the Christian ἐνσάρκωσις (incarnation). In the Platonic / Romantic view, the world 'participates' (κοινωνεῖ) in divine madness and is a manifestation of the holy – or 'ideal'; the sacred is not alienated from the human, the body, physical activity. Rather than humanizing the divine, the Romantics, as much as the Grecian Plato, divinize the human. The Romantic diversion from traditional modes of experiencing and articulating 'reality' lies not only in the attempt to ground metaphysics in the human mind, but also to translate the symbols of the so-called 'mystical' encounter into the profane linguistics of ordinary perception – and expression – the 'familiarization' of the 'unfamiliar' and its depiction in the 'natural language' of men.

To put it very simply, the Romantics refuse, I believe, to exclude the 'body' from the transformative experience and insist that metamorphosis to be genuine and complete should incorporate the natural. The myth of the dialectic between 'nature' and 'imagination', the great Romantic theme of the divided and re-united self, may be seen as nothing more, or less, than a new 'science' of listening to the 'bodily' element – mind becoming aware of certain physical processes and organic happenings habitually conducted subliminally or below normal understanding. Such 'readings' or 'recordings' appear to induce a mind–body unity and become a doorway to a new, expanded realm of self-unfolding in altered states of sensibility. Maximal mind–body intimacy (which presupposes a model of body-in-mind as much a mind-in-body) is usually the condition that precedes the peak experience in poetry, and generates a qualitative alteration of awareness. The Romantic transformation of consciousness is dual, like the Platonic: it encompasses a pattern of stages of growth to maturity (gradual), together with an instantaneous, almost miraculous, conversion (sudden new being). Yet although the suffering of the agonies of μεταμόρφωσις is a component present in both 'systems', the possibility that the transgression of boundaries may be 'horrific' rather than 'ecstatic' – a further gradation in πάσχειν rather than a transition from πάθημα to ποίημα – is much more pronounced in the Romantic than the Platonic work. Hence the often 'ironic' rather than 'symbolic' mode of Romantic poetry which maintains tension, discontinuity, and dialectical structure to breaking point, often cracking into 'fragments', in place of the carefully constructed 'chaos' of the Platonic dialogue. And if 'None of the romantic poets was able to achieve a serene affirmation of the conditions of human life, a sense that "ripeness is all" ' (Perkins 1959: 295), one could

TRANS-FORM-ATION

almost argue as convincingly that at the end of a Platonic dialogic drama the 'stage' is strewn with intellectual 'bodies' which, having been shaken to 'nothingness', totter away under the heavy shadow of the Socratic ordinance to 'think well' about the truth of 'being' (and life) – which is to dwell in the uncertainty of the question, the 'to be or not to be' whose hermeneutical range is obviously far wider than a mere contemplation of suicide.

4

ΠΑΘΗΜΑ AND ΠΟΙΗΜΑ
Being in the Romantic Texts

THE PRELUDE

The difference between transcendental experience as portrayed in the Platonic myth of Socrates and in its Romantic counterparts, the mythic 'heroes' of the Wordsworthian Poet, Coleridgean Mariner, Shelleyan Prometheus, and Keatsian Apollo, would be the distinction which is best expressed (quite unexpectedly, or perhaps justifiably so) by Keats, the poet of 'sensations rather than thoughts', in a letter to Reynolds:

> An extensive knowledge is needful to thinking people – it takes away the heat and fever; and helps, by widening speculation, to ease the Burden of the Mystery: a thing I begin to understand a little, and which weighed upon you in the most gloomy and true sentence in your Letter. The difference of high Sensations with and without knowledge appears to me this – in the latter case we are falling continually ten thousand fathoms deep and being blown up again without wings and with all [the] horror of a ‹Case› bare shoulderd Creature – in the former case, our shoulders are fledge‹d›, and we go thro' the same ‹Fir› air and space without fear.
>
> (1958: I, 277)

Keats' implicit recognition of Wordsworth's contribution to the 'en-light-enment' of the 'burden' of the mystery which is life, is repeated more explicitly by many modern critics, among them M. Sherwood, whose voice I choose to incorporate precisely because it very conveniently bridges the gap between the two poles of the present investigation – Platonic philosophy and Romantic poetry:

'One wonders', she remarks, referring to *The Prelude*, the Wordsworthian lyrical epic of the 'I', 'whether such scrutiny of the inner life, such reverent study of man's consciousness, had been made since the days of Socrates and Plato. Confessions, diaries, autobiographies', she admits, 'there had been, but never, before, or since, such a study of the growth of a genius, in singling out that which nourished, fostered the development of his mind and imagination, as he became more and more of an individual. As Pater says of Socrates: "The very thoroughness of that sort of self-knowledge he promoted had in it something sacramental" ' (1934: 159).

'Development' of mind (with all its scientific and economic overtones) is probably not the best manner to render the naturalness of the organic image that the word 'growth' used by the poet, emits. The term is misleading in yet a second way: it presupposes a process which is both continuous and additive, whereas the 'growth' of consciousness in *The Prelude* (and the other lyrical epics) reveals a mathematics of psyche that incorporates subtraction, multiplication, and division – as well as the psychologically 'catastrophic' shock of 'geometric progression', the blitz of transformation. The dynamism present in innate 'growth' (but not in externally induced 'development') is rooted in the interplay of Wordsworth's central polarities, 'nature' and 'mind', the reciprocal action upon one another of 'outer' and 'inner'. As an ἐναντιοδρόμια, the swinging back and forth of energy between the perceptive / emotive and emotive / intellective functions brings to completion, to closure, to a natural integrative ending, what has been 'developing' but left hanging or in fixed conflict; as one thing becomes another, blocks are removed and the whole process flows freely, the total situation moves forward of itself. The mediatory role of 'passion' or πάσχειν is pronounced in the following statement – one among many of its kind: 'For with Wordsworth's repeated assertion of the significance of passion for perception, the passionless judgment bespeaks not only the emptiness of the external forms but also a complementary, perhaps primary, emptiness within the perceiving eye' (Ferguson 1977: 140).

The nuptials of *The Prelude* – or Wordsworth's project of marrying man to nature – rests on the acceptance of certain latent affinities between the physical world and the human mind (or rather consciousness of 'physicality' and consciousness of 'self'), which precipitate the union and transformative action.[1] The relation of mind–nature is simultaneously analogical and homological; the mind is 'mono-form', yet variable like a mountain, 'flowing', yet constant like a river – a miniature universe, as the universe is the image of mind. There is a multi-dimensional interaction of the powers called 'mind' and 'nature', whose isomorphic structure allows not only the rhetoric of μεταφέρειν but also that of συμβάλλειν. The methodology and teleology of such operation is most clearly expressed in the Preface to *The Excursion*:

> Paradise, and groves
> Elysian, Fortunate Fields – like those of old
> Sought in the Atlantic Main – why should they be
> A history only of departed things,
> Or a mere fiction of what never was?
> For the discerning intellect of Man,
> When wedded to this goodly universe
> In love and holy passion, shall find these
> A simple produce of the common day.
> – I, long before the blissful hour arrives,
> Would chant, in lonely peace, the spousal verse
> Of this great consummation . . .
>
> (ll. 47–58)

The 'hierogamy' of mind–nature, i.e. the conjunction of intelligence and sensation through affectivity, is only a novel version of a long tradition of ἱερὸς γάμος, in its religious aspect being an ecstatic union with god experienced as an initiation into death; in its psychological mode it signifies the interaction of conscious and unconscious, and in its mythical expression exemplifes the bond of male and female forces in the archetype of the androgyne. As M. H. Abrams observes, 'It begins to be apparent that Wordsworth's holy marriage, far from being unique, was a prominent period-metaphor which served a number of major writers, English and German, as the central figure in a similar complex of ideas concerning the history and destiny of man and the role of the visionary poet as both herald and inaugurator of a new and supremely better world' (1971: 31). Far from being a period-metaphor and the herald of a new world, I would add, hierogamy is one of the root models in archaic culture, the remnant of an old tradition resurrected for Romantic purposes searching for ready myth in which to embody their experience with reality.

The process of androgynous transformation is one of the constants present within the mythical / religious / metaphysical perspective that runs through western culture. Commenting on 'union' in Neoplatonism and Christianity, J. M. Rist emphasizes that on the way to total transcendence, mystics go through the annihilatory intimacy of divine love and marriage, in which they become ravished spouses of the godhead: 'The soul is likened to a maiden yearning with a noble love . . . a total submergence of the Self in the Ἔρως of the One . . . For in the *unio mystica* nothing is outside the Self, since the Self, by giving itself up, has become both the whole and the part of the One' (1964: 102–4); hierogamy as a polarity between the individual man and God becomes 'a private matter between the Bridegroom and the Bride, between the Logos and the Soul of the believer' (1964: 212). In Greek religion, ἱερογαμία was apparently celebrated in the Eleusinian mysteries as part of the orgiastic rite of Dionysus – or the Goddess (Harrison 1903: 562–4) – a ceremonial marriage to the divine, an evocation of profound energies below the illumined surface of individual finite consciousness. In both pagan ritual and Christian mysticism, ἱερος γάμος appears as a *mysterium transformationis*, a participation of the human in the sacred, a rite of holy union – or 'holy passion' as Wordsworth calls it – where human and personal limits are overcome, and a 'real presence' – theophany, epiphany, parousia – can, under certain conditions, be aroused in man.

The basic distinction in the hierogamy model between older religions and Christianity is, as I see it, that those traditions deal with integration through a female principle, in which an 'invisible woman' or Goddess is shown as the giver of life, wisdom, salvation, redemptive and transformative power; Christianity, by centring on an exclusively male triadic divinity (or two parts male and one neuter), obviously adopts a type of marriage that necessitates a 'female' human soul as bride to the divine bridegroom. The fusion, or confusion, which is inevitable as a result of the coexistence of archaic and Christian marriage models, can be seen most clearly I think, in historical periods when the urge to revive old paradigms and practices conflicts with a more or less strongly held Judaeo-Christian ideology – such as the Renaissance or Romantic period. An instance of such aberration can be seen in that unorthodox passage from Shakespeare's *Richard II*, presenting the duality of male / female forces not in cosmic or religious but in psychological terms, and also inverting the accepted Christian pattern of a soul-bride and God-bridegroom in a manner that revolutionizes the articulation of inner dramas of mind: 'My brain I'll prove the female to my soul, / My soul, the father; and these two beget / A generation of still-breeding thoughts' (V, v, 6–8). The discourse, or rather intercourse, of father / soul and mother / intellect – seed and matrix, action and sufferance, ποιεῖν and πάσχειν – has a striking resemblance to Wordsworth's 'wise passiveness'.

The symbolism of androgyny and hierogamy in *The Prelude* portrays an ambivalence concerning sexual, archetypal, and grammatical gender – as the active / receptive polarity between mind and nature is constantly shifting, introducing a metaphor whereby a potentially androgynous mind interacts (or 'intercourses') with a potentially androgynous nature. The poem exemplifies, I think, a dual allegiance to cultural and mythological value systems that present contrasting evidence as to the sex traits of the power behind creation. The worship of divinity as male or female expresses not only a religious orientation, but a hierarchy of priorities that have an immediate existential, psychological, social, and political impact. The male / female opposition – like that of light / darkness, πέρας / ἄπειρον – belonging among the most basic representations of the experience of dualism, makes the adoption of relevant imagery and classification expressive not only of psychic 'moods', but indicative of the specific cultural orientation within which a text (or its writer) operates.

The Prelude opens with an image of 'male' visitation that recalls the father-soul of the Shakespearean play:

> O there is a blessing in this gentle breeze,
> A visitant that while he fans my cheek
> Doth seem half-conscious of the joy he brings
> From the green fields, and from yon azure sky.
>
> (I, 1–4)[2]

It equally alludes to the Platonic ἔρως streaming into the soul and taking possession of it. The mind's condition of expectant perception and openness to the 'call' is suggested through the reponsiveness of the 'wandering cloud' metaphor, and the

ΠΑΘΗΜΑ AND ΠΟΙΗΜΑ

receptivity of matrix or womb:

> Trances of thought and mountings of the mind
> Come fast upon me: it is shaken off,
> That burthen of my own unnatural self,
> The heavy weight of many a weary day
> Not mine, and such as were not made for me.
>
> (I, 19–23)

The transformative effect of a wind which although 'gentle' can 'shake off' the burden of 'self', is defined as a process of 'naturalizing' man (rather than 'humanizing' nature) by a violation and destruction of 'unnaturalness'. There is a marked absence of the female gender in a scene where a male visitor upon a male 'I'-consciousness discards an obviously neuter it / burden / self. The 'correspondent breeze'[3] awakened by the 'sweet blow' of the 'breath of heaven' is also spoken of in terms of neutral energy, in the meteorological metaphor of 'tempest'. The significance of the visiting πνεῦμα is magnified in the 1850 version, where it is presented as a collaborator to the poetic activity – 'Thanks to both, / And their congenial powers, that, while they join / In breaking up a long-continued frost' (I, 38–40) – which in the 1805 *Prelude* was the product of the 'corresponding mild creative breeze' alone, the role of the visitor being restricted only to that of instigator to creativity. The image of the interaction of 'winds' is next translated to that of reciprocation of sounds – 'the mind's / Internal echo of the imperfect sound; / To both I listened' (I, 55–7). The aeolian harp metaphor of l. 96 further subverts the activity of the 'correspondent breeze' by presenting a model of mind utterly receptive to natural force; as such, it is entirely in accord with the pronounced emphasis on the femininity of mind that is clearly suggested through the repeated use of the pronoun 'she' and 'her': 'if my mind / . . . / Vain is her wish; where'er she turns she finds / Impediments from day to day renewed' (I, 127–31).

The Platonic image of Poet / Lover (ll. 135–6) offers a view of consciousness as 'possessed' by 'unmanageable thoughts'; the following lines, however, create a puzzling complexity of archetypes and loyalties:

> his mind, best pleased
> While she as duteous as the mother dove
> Sits brooding, lives not always to that end,

> But like the innocent bird, hath goadings on
> That drive her as in trouble through the groves;
> With me is now such passion, to be blamed
> No otherwise than as it lasts too long.
>
> (I, 139–45)

The editorial note to these lines attributes the imagery to a possible Miltonic influence, in that 'The human mind initiates the creative process by brooding, as the Holy Spirit in Milton's Christian epic had brooded over Chaos' (1979: 36), which suggests a series of interesting analogies in Wordsworth's cosmological, psychological, and metaphysical universe: the Miltonic Holy Spirit / Chaos polarity, a mind-mother / abyss dualism (the 'dove' metaphor being the connective link), is later symbolized in the Snowdon episode through the moon-mind / abyss-infinity iconography, 'the emblem of a mind / That feeds upon infinity, that broods / Over the dark abyss' (XIV, 70–3). The mind's feminine gender is repeatedly affirmed in the text, although often presented as involved in active occupations: 'Baffled and plagued by a mind that every hour / Turns recreant to her task . . . / . . . / . . . her hopes' (I, 257–60).

The femininity of nature is equally accentuated in *The Prelude*, as for instance in the discursive interlude between the 'raven's nest' and 'stolen boat' episodes, both inducing unknown modes of being under the intensity of anxiety, fear, or guilt; the 1805 version is more dramatic in its imagery, though both emphasize the overpowering dynamism of inscrutable machinations to which the human mind is exposed, beyond comprehension or resistance:

> But I believe
> That Nature, oftentimes, when she would frame
> A favored being, from its earliest dawn
> Of infancy doth open out the clouds
> As at the touch of lightning, seeking him
> With gentlest visitation; not the less,
> Though haply aiming at the self-same end,
> Does it delight her sometimes to employ
> Severer interventions, ministry
> More palpable – and so she dealt with me.
>
> (1805, I, 362–71)

The peculiar coexistence of aggression and meekness implicit in the 'gentle' 'touch of lightning', is repeated in the 1850 text in forms which alleviate what might otherwise be thought of as a potentially destructive eruption; 'fearless visitings', 'soft alarm', 'hurtless light', 'peaceful clouds', become vehicles of an inexorable trend for transformation in terms of a mind–nature interaction. Such intercourse can hardly be called a 'marriage' in the customary sense of the word – and the event – if a female 'intellect of man' is wedded to an equally female 'goodly universe', unless of course one reverts to the Platonic notion of the 'hermaphrodite' in the *Symposium* which allows for three primordial couples, the androgyne proper and the two homosexual matings (190a–b).

A more detailed depiction of this matrimonial metaphysics, the 'image of man and nature', is given in Book II; the correspondence is between a 'plastic power' dwelling or 'abiding' with the poet, 'devious' and 'rebellious' to normal patterns of conduct, 'a local spirit of his own' (a possible equivalent to the Socratic δαίμων), which although nonconformist to social custom and 'at war / With general tendency', proved 'Subservient strictly to external things / With which it communed' (II, 365–8) – the submission being a simultaneous exercise of control, a 'dominion' over the phenomenal world. Meanwhile, the mind's wilful awareness was occupied with a practice 'more poetic as resembling more / Creative agency', i.e. 'observation of affinities / In objects where no brotherhood exists / To passive minds' (II, 381–6). The result of such process whereby the percept receives intense attention while the mind refrains from 'analysing', i.e. employing its faculties for abstract categorization and thought, is that intellection is amplified by means of perception. This perceptual mode of receptive intensity seems to precipitate a change in the functional character of the percept or image, reversing the process from conceptual activity back to an engrossment with the sensuousness and vivacity of the thing itself.

The phenomenon of 'unity' or 'sympathy' experienced can be viewed as a de-differentiation that merges all boundaries, until the 'I' is no longer felt as a separate entity, and customary cognitive distinctions between Self / Other are no longer applicable:

>   the power of truth
> Coming in revelation, did converse
> With things that really are; I, at this time,
> Saw blessings spread around me like a sea.
> Thus while the days flew by, and years passed on,
> From Nature overflowing on my soul,
> I had received so much that every thought
> Was steeped in feeling; I was only then
> Contented, when with bliss ineffable
> I felt the sentiment of Being spread
> O'er all that moves and all that seemeth still.
>   (II, 392–402)

Such a 'holistic' view of the world, where all phenomena perceived by the senses are interrelated, connected, and are but different aspects or manifestations of the same power – forever in motion – spiritual and material at the same time, leads to a rhapsodic exaltation of the senses as mediators to the 'conjugal' state of mind:

>   the gift is yours,
>   Ye winds and sounding cataracts! 'tis yours,
>   Ye mountains! thine, O Nature! Thou hast fed
>   My lofty speculations; and in thee,
>   For this uneasy heart of ours, I find
>   A never-failing principle of joy
>   And purest passion.
>   (II, 445–51)

Nevertheless, there seems to be an alternative to this mind–nature marriage rite celebrated in sensory experience, a shift from an external focus of attention to an internal one – reflexive rather than perceptive – a turning down of the awareness of environment that keeps all outer sources of stimulation to a minimum. Such an inversion of attention away from sensation, a close parallel to the Platonic περιαγωγή, would seem to divert the 'marriage' metaphor into one of 'divorce':

>   Or turning the mind in upon herself
>   Pored, watched, expected, listened, spread my thoughts
>   And spread them with a wider creeping; felt
>   Incumbencies more awful, visitings
>   Of the Upholder, of the tranquil soul,

> That tolerates the indignities of Time,
> And, from the centre of Eternity
> All finite motions overruling, lives
> In glory immutable. But peace! enough
> Here to record I had ascended now
> To such community with highest truth.
>
> (III, 116–26)

As a result of this temporary 'turning off' of sensory input, the return to nature is freed from conceptual barriers and classifications of phenomena, granting a heightened sensitivity to the immediate situation; 'getting away' from and 'turning back' to perception seems simultaneously to de-automatize mind and de-familiarize nature; everything is 'fresh', 'new', 'different':

> A track pursuing, not untrod before,
> From strict analogies by thought supplied
> Or consciousness not to be subdued,
> To every natural form, rock, fruit, or flower,
> Even the loose stones that cover the high-way,
> I gave a moral life: I saw them feel,
> Or linked them to some feeling: the great mass
> Lay bedded in a quickening soul, and all
> That I beheld respired with inward meaning.
>
> (III, 127–35)

The 'newness' consists in a further breaking down of constructs which maintain an isolated personal consciousness, and a transition from the analytic mode to apprehension of a 'holistic' power-field and the erotic interplay of its components:

> For I, bred up 'mid Nature's luxuries,
> Was a spoiled child, and rambling like the wind,
> As I had done in daily intercourse
> With those crystalline rivers, solemn heights,
> And mountains . . .
>
> (III, 354–8)

The nuptials of *The Prelude* reveals a pattern of constant dialectic of a love / hate, excursive / discursive motion of mind, opening up to and withdrawing from the sensory world – an alternation of the marriage / divorce institutions or the wedding / funeral ceremonies. It is characteristic of a passage where the consummation scene is cast in imagery of unmistakable Christian mysticism,[4] and the mind's, or better soul's, femininity is most pronounced, that 'Nature' is absent and substituted by the more appropriate – at least as far as sex and gender goes – 'God': 'Gently did my soul / Put off her veil, and, self-transmuted, stood / Naked, as in the presence of her God' (IV, 150–2); yet surprisingly, 'Of that eternal scene which round me lay, / Little, in this abstraction, did I see; / Remembered less' (IV, 160–2). The possibility of reconciliation of the two models, 'perceptive' and 'reflexive', is suggested in the opening of Book V, where paradoxically the union or identification of mind / nature in the artistic activity of ποιεῖν – 'Thou also, man! has wrought, / For commerce of thy nature with herself, / Things that aspire to unconquerable life' (V, 18–20) – also proves to be the point of maximal tension or alienation:

> Oh! why hath not the Mind
> Some element to stamp her image on
> In nature somewhat nearer to her own?
> Why, gifted with such powers to send abroad
> Her spirit, must it lodge in shrines so frail?
>
> (V, 45–9)

The mind–nature relationship is structured not only 'dialectically' but also 'hierarchically'; it is shown to hold a changing position in a gradational scale of 'loves' and interests, unexpectedly 'absent' from the 'animal' activities of childhood – what in 'Tintern Abbey' is referred, 'For nature then / (The coarser pleasures of my boyish days, / And their glad animal movements all gone by) / To me was all in all' (ll. 72–5): 'Nature herself was, at this unripe time, / But secondary to my own pursuits / And animal activities' (VIII, 342–4). The reduction or sublimation of 'nature' to something distinct from what might be considered as its primal manifestations: creature-being, motion-joy, impulse-freedom undermines Wordsworth's theory of childhood as the 'communicative' state par excellence; in the exclusiveness of 'Nature, prized / For her own sake' (VIII, 346–7), the reference hints at a view of nature that is centripetal rather than centrifugal, and sets the motion / emotion complex as the unfolding or surface display of a deeper reality. There are two versions of what this reality or enfolded presence might be; the early pantheism of 'God and Nature's single sovereignty' is later substituted by a model which, although more consistent with orthodox Christian dogma in making God transcendent, still allows Nature its share in power and supreme rule, 'To presences of God's mysterious power / Made manifest in Nature's sovereignty' (IX, 234–5).

That intercourse or courtship with Nature does not seem to have begun until the time of youth or puberty, adds a strong sexual component to the spousal story of match-making between the 'human' and the 'physical':

> When I began in youth's delightful prime
> To yield myself to Nature, when that strong
> And holy passion overcame me first,
> Nor day nor night, evening or morn, were free
> From its oppression. . . .
>
> (X, 416–20)

The reverential tone of the passage and the ceremonial solemnity suggested by terms such as 'ritual', 'worship', 'service' bear witness to an indissoluble bond between religious emotion and eroticism – the intensity of 'holy passion' compounded of piety and sensuality. It is through 'adolescence' also that the 'politics' of natural power becomes operative, as

> Youth maintains,
> In all conditions of society,
> Communion more direct and intimate
> With Nature, – hence, offtimes, with reason too –
> Than age, or manhood even. To Nature, then,
> Power had reverted: habit, custom, law,
> Had left an interregnum's open space
> For *her* to move about in, uncontrolled.
>
> (XI, 27–34)

The ambivalent character of the nuptials between mind and nature brings the whole operation closer, I believe, to a human marriage than an hierogamy; the loveplay exhibits subtle tensions of 'authorial' domination leading to a 'perceptual' war, where nature subverts the dominant visual function through a coalescence of the senses – or synaesthesia. The apostrophe to Nature in Book XII, impressive as it might be, is expressive of an ambiguity concerning 'sensation' – nature's primal mode of manifestation – and suggests the possibility of a balance in the

ΠΑΘΗΜΑ AND ΠΟΙΗΜΑ

tripartite structure of consciousness, the 'eye / ear', 'heart', and 'unfolding intellect':

> O Soul of Nature! that, by laws divine
> Sustained and governed, still dost overflow
> With an impassioned life, what feeble ones
> Walk on this earth! how feeble have I been
> When thou wert in thy strength! . . .
> (XII, 102–6)

This weakness of mind is caused by an attitude that may be termed arrogant, analytic, comparative, and critical – in short 'egotistical' – measuring, calculating, and judging under the authority of the 'eye', the most powerful cognitive organ:

> I speak in recollection of a time
> When the bodily eye, in every stage of life
> The most despotic of our senses, gained
> Such strength in *me* as often held my mind
> In absolute dominion. Gladly here,
> Entering upon abstruser argument,
> Could I endeavour to unfold the means
> Which Nature studiously employs to thwart
> This tyranny, summons all the senses each
> To counteract the other, and themselves,
> And makes them all, and the objects with which all
> Are conversant, subservient in their turn
> To the great ends of Liberty and Power.
> (XII, 127–39)

Liberation from the 'tyrannical eye' lies not in 'blinding' it but in its substitution by a 'loving eye', the ability to perceive freed from normal patterns – a condition of 'direct' or non-selective attitude where all possible categories are simultaneously held, a non-restrictive vision in which everything happening in the present moment enters into awareness. The poet admits to an 'impassioned' look: 'I loved whate'er I saw: nor lightly loved, / But most intensely' (XII, 176–7), and then wonders, how,

> could I submit
> To measured admiration, or to aught
> That should preclude humility and love?
> I felt, observed, and pondered; did not judge,

ΠΑΘΗΜΑ AND ΠΟΙΗΜΑ

Yea, never thought of judging; with the gift
Of all this glory, filled and satisfied.
(XII, 185–90)

The degradation of custom and habit, conventional modes of perception, induces a transformative shift from analytic consciousness containing separate, discrete objects, to a second mode, an experience of παρουσία of nature and ἔνστασις of mind. The 'reunion' of mind–nature is effected through the 'imaginative power' which acts as a matchmaker or catalyst (a possible analogue to Platonic 'beauty' facilitating the act of 'parturition'):

I had known
Too forcibly, too early in my life,
Visitings of imaginative power
For this to last: I shook the habit off
Entirely and for ever, and again
In Nature's presence stood, as now I stand
A sensitive being, a *creative* soul.
(XII, 201–7)

The direct cognition of Nature or reality, attained by means of an alien visitation that undoes the normal construction of experience, is spoken of in terms of a subjugation of sense-perception (nature) to 'mind', 'Profoundest knowledge to what point, and how, / The mind is lord and master – outward sense / The obedient servant of her will' (XII, 221–3); it marks the transition from a linear, temporal mode of intellection (following the logical development of one idea at a time) to the synchronicity of a spatial, intuitive mode – a 'spot of time'. The grammatical (and ontological) incongruity of the phrase – a 'female' mind that, by imposing 'her' will upon (a female) sense, becomes 'lord and master' rather than 'lady and mistress' – is indicative, I think, of the inner tension caused in the poet's mind, and text, by the parallel adoption of a patriarchal authoritarian model, and the recognition of the 'feminine' values of affect and emotion – a simultaneous repression and exaltation of femininity.

That 'Such moments / Are scattered everywhere, taking their date / From our first childhood' (XII, 223–5), brings to the surface the problematics around the point of origination of the mind–nature 'awareness' of each other as prospective lovers – and spouses. This interaction the 'Immortality Ode' (romantically) places at the dawn of consciousness:

> There was a time when meadow, grove, and stream,
> The earth, and every common sight,
> > To me did seem
> > Apparelled in celestial light,
> The glory and the freshness of a dream.
>
> (ll. 1–5)

only to (platonically) subvert and modify it:

> > Our birth is but a sleep and a forgetting:
> > The Soul that rises with us, our life's Star
> > > Hath had elsewhere its setting,
> > > And cometh from afar:
> > Not in entire forgetfulness,
> > And not in utter nakedness,
> > But trailing clouds of glory do we come
> > > From God, who is our home:
> > Heaven lies about us in our infancy!
> >
> > (ll. 58–66)

Nature as a force-field penetrates mind in that it is the source of affectivity, of the dual psycho-physiological states of excitability and tranquillity, an influx causing mental diversity and restlessness or making the mind quiet, attentive, and reflective – energy consumption and energy conservation, creativity and receptivity. Under a harmonious dialectic of dynamic polarities the mind is able to do intellective, constructive work; mental agitation and mental calmness go together to 'bring the philosophic mind'. The 'togetherness' or reciprocity of affects or energy flows is given through the metaphor of 'sister horns', a characteristic pagan symbol of power and of the Moon-Goddess, creatrix of the phenomenal world:

> > From Nature doth emotion come, and moods
> > Of calmness equally are Nature's gift:
> > This is her glory; these two attributes
> > Are sister horns that constitute her strength.
> > Hence Genius, born to thrive by interchange
> > Of peace and excitation, finds in her
> > His best and purest friend; from her receives

> That energy by which he seeks the truth,
> From her that happy stillness of the mind
> Which fits him to receive it when unsought.
> (XIII, 1–10)

Human mind is presented as the principle of eternal activity embedded in supreme power – nature or 'right reason', the 'logos' of things. The psychomental phenomena arise from natural creativity, but consciousness is only a display, 'busy dance / Of things that pass away' (XIII, 30–1), of a process that slowly evolves mind to maturity.

Nature's dual function as 'evolver' and 'destroyer', at once promoting and inhibiting mind enlargement, is a theme that occasionally surfaces in *The Prelude* though not to the extent that it conditions the dialectics of the 'Immortality Ode': here the poet, in his 'heart of hearts' feels the regenerative 'might' of 'Fountains, Meadows, Hills, and Groves' (l. 191) and is aware of the cognitive function of sensation, as to him 'the meanest flower that blows can give / Thoughts that do often lie too deep for tears' (ll. 206–207) – a correlation of sensing / thinking that can alleviate emotional distress. Yet, Wordsworth plays 'nature' against 'nature' when this same world of sensation is shown to induce the withdrawal of 'celestial light' from 'every common sight', and 'The homely Nurse doth all she can / To make her Foster-child, her Inmate Man, / Forget the glories he hath known, / And that imperial palace whence he came' (ll. 77–84). In *The Prelude*, the poet wonders: 'What bars are thrown / By Nature in the way of such a hope? / Our animal appetites and daily wants, / Are these obstructions insurmountable?' (XIII, 89–92). Nature is not a blessing but a curse, 'If man's estate, by doom of Nature yoked / With toil, is therefore yoked with ignorance' (XIII, 175–6). The spiritual light does not come from the material universe but through a de-naturalization of mind, 'to Nature's self / Oppose a deeper nature' (XIII, 200–1), or of nature itself – which not only makes 'nature' pluralistic but teeming in collisions and self-contradictions (characteristic, I think, of the poet's multiple allegiance to mutually exclusive reality models). Conversely, nature and mind are presented as not antithetical but coextensive forces, even potentially equiprimordial and equally revered, as for instance 'To Nature, and the power of human minds, / To men as they are men within themselves' (XIII, 225–6) veneration should be shown. Nature is not only to be opposed but to be trusted:

> And that the Genius of the Poet hence
> May boldly take his way among mankind
> Wherever Nature leads; that he hath stood
> By Nature's side among the men of old,
> And so shall stand for ever. . . .
>
> (XIII, 295–9)

Recognition of the function of the poet as a follower of and spokesman for the 'natural way', the interaction of 'passion' with 'passion', the reciprocity that locates the transformative experience of spiritual awakening within the material – and linguistic – body rather than outside it, makes of a poem a ποίημα – 'Creative and enduring, may become / A power like one of Nature's' (XIII, 311–12).

The overall pattern of Mind–Nature (or vice versa) courtship in *The Prelude* as presented by Wordsworth exhibits the formal structure of traditional romance, going through the stages of meeting, separation, and reconciliation, 'the old, Romantic tale of his own mind's freedom, enslavement, and reliberation' (Kroeber 1964: 23). The period of estrangement, 'a time / When Nature, destined to remain so long / Foremost in my affections, had fallen back / Into a second place, pleased to become / A handmaid to a nobler than herself' (XIV, 256–60), was superseded when the blockage was cleared, 'and the stream / Flowed in the bent of Nature' (XIV, 370–1). The end of the poem leaves the 'great spousals' very much in progress. The poet has received glimmerings of visionary power's capacity to transform the reality perceived by bodily eye. He defines himself as a 'Prophet of Nature' yet his rhetoric is not one of marriage, equality, union – of 'A motion and a spirit, that impels / All thinking things, all objects of all thought, / And rolls through all things' of 'Tintern Abbey' (ll. 100–2), or the equal sharing in the phenomenology of spirit introduced earlier in *The Prelude*, where,

> A gracious spirit o'er this earth presides,
> And o'er the heart of man: invisibly
> It comes, to works of unreproved delight,
> And tendency benign, directing those

Who care not, know not, think not what they do.
(V, 491–5)

or even reverence for 'natural' language, 'The ghostly language of the ancient earth' whence he drank 'the visionary power' (II, 309–11).

The concluding argument of the poem momentarily 'freezes' the dialectic of mind / nature into a structure of hierarchy, where nature (this earth) is finally subordinated to mind – twice 'more' and once 'alone' exalted, paradoxically by a poet who, seeing himself as a consort and high priest of 'nature', yet instructs mankind 'how the mind of man becomes / A thousand times more beautiful than the earth / On which he dwells, above this frame of things' – aesthetically, morally, and spiritually superior: 'In beauty exalted, as it is itself / Of quality and fabric more divine' (XIV, 450–6). In the metaphysical ascendancy accredited to νοῦς over φύσις, 'mind' and 'nature' are not only 'divorced' but presented as different modalities of being – with a strong quantitative distinction that is possibly a qualitative one. The greater 'divinity' of mind is dis-engaged from the psychomental flux and the bodily sensations. Between Nature and Mind there seems to be a difference of an ontological order; 'substance' and 'spirit' appear in a relationship of false solidarity or competitive 'egotistical' self-assertion, where 'beauty is truth' is subjected to 'truth beauty', and intelligence withdraws from the 'body' of natural facts in an autonomy of 'truth' that is perhaps 'imageless'.

THE RIME OF THE ANCIENT MARINER

The Romantic myth of μεταμόρφωσις, although exhibiting a common need to transcend historical consciousness, assumes a variety of forms in the work of the four poets or phenomenologists of mind who have been the object of the present study, not only in formal features but in emphasizing different stages and mutations in the single tremendous 'fiction' of 'self': the 'self-remembrance' of *The Prelude*, the 'self-assertion' of *The Ancient Mariner*, the 'self-forgiveness' of *Prometheus Unbound*, and the 'self-forgetfulness' of *Hyperion* and *The Fall of Hyperion*.

The attempt at a 'marriage' between Platonism and Christianity[5] – which I see as Coleridge's lifelong futile endeavour – constantly surfaces in his poetic and philosophical utterances, betraying his

Thy melodies of woods, and winds, and waters,
Till he relent, and can no more endure
To be a jarring and a dissonant thing,
Amid this general dance and minstrelsy;
But, bursting into tears, wins back his way,
His angry spirit heal'd and harmoniz'd
By the benignant touch of Love and Beauty.
                    ('The Dungeon', ll. 20–30)

The experience of estrangement from the song and dance of nature is to be cured by the sensuous intervention of nature; through an intensification of the senses (seeing, hearing, touch, smell, motion), he seeks to be re-integrated into the rhythm of the natural world. The poet's abstention from the 'bodily' is presented more as a self-inflicted condition rather than a result of circumstance or custom (as is the case with Wordsworth); in a paradoxical self-splitting, he implores nature to intervene and make him (addressed in the third person as 'nature's child') 'relent', relieve him from suffering. The common origin of disease and remedy, poison and cure, present in the Greek word φάρμακον, is vaguely invoked here. The precise character of Coleridge's equivocal attitude towards the physical world is detected throughout his life and writings, not least when he refers to 'the poor Heathen who represents to himself the divine attributes of wisdom, justice, and mercy, under multiplied and forbidden symbols in the powers of Nature' (1969: I, 279–80).

The structure of *The Ancient Mariner* embodies the perils of a transformational 'grammar' of consciousness, and language, where 'self' passes from subject-creative to object-receptive position through 'verb' – action or ποιεῖν; it also portrays the reverse process which is effected through πάσχειν in both senses of the word, suffering and passion. The poem is open, I think, to two parallel readings – historical and ritualistic: the first interpretation would see the 'journey' as a 'fall' from myth into history (and the concomitant 'rise') in both the individual consciousness of the Mariner / poet and the collective consciousness of mankind; the second would explain the various stages of the Mariner's penitentiary process as 'rites of passage' in an already undertaken initiation of 'return'. Whatever the case, the reality of πάσχειν remains functional – the ordeal of extremities of heat and stagnation where the elements of 'fire' and 'earth' have gained absolute ascendancy over those of 'water' and 'air'. My point is that the Mariner's voyage may be concurrently read as the story of the 'construction' of ego, as well as its 'deconstruction'. The central event of 'shooting' – though apparently unmotivated – as an act of 'transfixing the albatross into definite form', an 'urge towards fixity and definiteness' (Beer 1977: 167–8), generates a syllogistic world of causal relations, and a dryness of intellect cut off from the imaginative apprehension of unity with nature. The unpremeditated act of aggression is a 'sin' – or shift – not in action, but in perception; it introduces the modern, i.e. post-mythical or post-magical concept of 'thing', which sees it primarily in its epistemological relation to 'understanding' and its technological relation to 'will' – cognizance not of *the thing as it is,* but of the thing in its instrumentality to human aspirations.

Symbolic of 'ego power' as the capacity to 'affect' other bodies through volition, the Mariner's act epitomizes the separation of humanity from its instinctive, left, 'maternal' side; it portrays the tearing loose from 'nature' (whether as 'mother', 'goddess', or 'agency') for the sake of an independent sense of 'separate' identity introduced by patriarchal cultures. Mind had to 'kill' or subdue 'being' and make it serve the 'I' for the functioning of a complex 'technocratic' society. As R. Haven observes – translating historical or psychomental events into the imaginative and linguistic world of the poem – the shooting of the albatross introduces a new rhetoric of awareness: ' "I" discover myself by discovering the difference between "I" and "it," by opposing, resisting, killing, "it" ' (1969: 29). From 'At length did cross an Albatross, / Thorough the fog it came; / As if it had been a Christian soul, / We hailed it in God's name' (ll. 63–6), to ' "God save thee, ancient Mariner! / From the fiends, that plague thee thus! – / Why look'st thou so?" – With my cross-bow / I shot the ALBATROSS' (ll. 79–82), the interim is ('Like a phantasma or a hideous dream' (*Julius Caesar*, II, i, 65)) a change in perception – and 'attitude' – that is not 'fair'. The act of shooting with the 'cross-bow' the creature that 'crossed' the fog to serve as a guide through the 'wondrous cold' world of emerald green ice, rather than being a liberation from rational order may be seen as an emerging into the dryness and sterility, the 'waste land' of habitual causality: 'The Mariner does not intend. He does not begin to think or feel until he has acted. He and his fellows judge his act only as they become aware of its consequences. The act of violence that tears apart the self from the not-self is like the casting of the date-pit: only the results prove its significance' (Haven 1969: 34–5).

The Mariner's crime has been interpreted by the majority of Coleridge readers as a sin of ignorance – which is, of course, the basic root of evil, according to Plato; the etymological archaeology of the Greek word ἁμαρτία (sin) – to miss the point – unexpectedly relates, if in inverted manner, to the target-hitting of the poem's central act. The 'what' and 'wherefore' of the event have become a source of endless speculation in Coleridgean criticism. J. L. Lowes, having explored the wide expanses of Coleridge's transmutation of reading materials into poetic thoughts, declares that the albatross is a δαίμων in the Greek / Platonic rather than Christian sense of the term: 'For a *daemon* and a *demon* are not one and the same thing. And it is daemon, in its Platonic sense of a being intermediary between gods and men – not demon, with its Judaeo-Christian import of an unclean, evil, or malignant spirit – that we must keep in mind'. Lowes furthers his argument by introducing an intermediary – realistic this time – figure between Plato and Coleridge, that of the Platonist Thomas Taylor: 'Taylor the English pagan quotes, in his commentary on the *Phaedrus*, from the Platonic Hermias: "But there are other daemons transcending these, *who are the punishers of souls, converting them to a more perfect and elevated life.*" And Taylor was one of Coleridge's "darling studies," and that is the function of the polar daemon in the poem' (1927: 213–16).

The extinction or historical elimination of the mediational link, the connective potential, is seen by M. H. Abrams as an alienation from nature (1971: 273). Parallel interpretations stress the estrangement of man from nature, through an act whose significance – despite its apparent non-motivation, or precisely because of it – seems to be the wish of 'I' to achieve 'heroically' by imposing the will on the natural order, by transforming or transfixing (killing) it, thus turning a reciprocal relationship into the hierarchical polarity of I-It, ἔνθεη φύσις into dead matter.[6] In the light of what I have called a 'historical' interpretation of the poem – the 'fall' of individual and collective consciousness from the pagan worship of the divinity within nature to the 'spiritualization' of Christianity, or the 'voiding' of the sacred from the bodily element – the Mariner's sin can be 'called a "corruption of consciousness" and not some mistake to be corrected by a moral lesson' (Kessler 1979: 49). Coleridge's simultaneous awareness of the personal and transpersonal, literal and paradigmatic, dimensions of the song or 'rime' of the 'ancient' mariner, is discussed by a number of readers explicating the problem of 'freedom' of the human will as generator of causality[7] – a 'free will' which in the poem, as I see it, takes the form of aggressive violence in control of nature, a power-drive that seeks domination and self-assertion. The poem portrays a communicative model of interaction between ego / otherness as the central pivot around which the poet's life dialectic moved. Coleridge's own adoption of a 'heroic' model which he applied to Self-Other transactions, does not only become apparent in the frequent reiterations of the 'I Am' formula in the *Biographia* and elsewhere, but also in the statement that 'whatever part of the *terra incognita* of our nature the increased consciousness discovers, our will may conquer and bring into subjection to itself under the sovereignty of reason' (Barfield 1971: 113).

The problematics of perception and action, the relation between 'thing' and human 'intentionality', provide focal points of reference in the poem. 'Why does the Mariner kill the albatross?', G. H. Hartman wonders, before launching into an exploratory exegesis of the engineering of motivation and its consequences, referring us to Coleridge's polarized distinction from *Aids to Reflection*, which identifies 'will' with 'spirit' versus 'nature'. Suggesting a possible analogy between mental derangement and the imaginative events of the poem, Hartman emphasizes the urge for integration that at once coexists with and cancels the separatist impulse (1975: 75–6). The forging of an absolute gulf between 'I' and 'Other', or mind and nature, is attributed by Hartman to the 'poetics' of will or 'revelation' of self: 'The new distance betwen self and other, which the self experiences in "coming out," is part of a separation anxiety which exaggerates the other into a quasi-supernatural or spectral otherness' (1975: 36). As a depiction of entry into 'ordinary' mentality, the Mariner's journey 'down' – or 'up' – the stream of history, portrays a modality of being that is self-centred (or object-centred, which is the same) – the selective, active, analytic separation of oneself from other things and organisms, resulting in the construction of a stable, solid, and fixed world in

ΠΑΘΗΜΑ AND ΠΟΙΗΜΑ

which man can differentiate things, isolate them, and act upon them. The upward (if 'fortunate' and certainly fortune-making) fall into rational consciousness, whose chief parameters are time, spatiality, and causality, may serve as a point of departure in the hermeneutics of the transformational horrors in the *Ancient Mariner*, where the 'sun' of 'enlightened' reason becomes, as R. P. Warren most suggestively describes it, echoing Coleridge, 'the "mere reflective faculty" which partakes of "Death" ' (1969: 29–30).

The 'normality' of common discursive intellection, the 'burthen' of the 'habitual self' (to use Wordsworth and Keats jointly in an attempt to interpret Coleridge) is pictorially portrayed in the poem as an oppressive heat of ratiocination and a stagnation or paralysis of life-flow, after the Mariner's admission that he 'had killed the bird / That made the breeze to blow' (ll. 93–4). For a signification of the term – and experience – of 'breezing' in Coleridge's imaginative universe, we may consult his own writings at moments when the lucidity of his prose provides interpretative insights into the density of his poetry; in a letter to Robert Southey he proclaims:

> Believe me Southey! a metaphysical Solution, that does not instantly *tell* for something in the Heart, is grievously to be suspected as apocry[p]hal. I almost think, that Ideas *never* recall Ideas, as far as they are Ideas – any more than leaves in the forest create each other's motion – The Breeze it is that runs thro' them / it is the Soul, the state of Feeling –.
> (1956–71: II, 961)

The drying up of the source of vitality and motion simultaneously cancels 'wind' and (ironically) 'water', allowing only extremities of 'fire' and 'earth':

> Down dropt the breeze, the sails dropt down,
> 'Twas sad as sad could be;
> And we did speak only to break
> The silence of the sea!
>
> And in a hot and copper sky,
> The bloody Sun, at noon,
> Right up above the mast did stand,
> No bigger than the Moon.

> Day after day, day after day,
> We stuck, nor breath nor motion;
> As idle as a painted ship
> Upon a painted ocean.
>
> Water, water, every where,
> And all the boards did shrink;
> Water, water, every where,
> Nor any drop to drink.
>
> (ll. 107–22)

Water stagnation into a 'painted ocean' is an analogue to the immobility or 'freezing' of the breeze. All flow is suspended, as the 'cross-killed' bird that had 'crossed' the fog has been immobilized, pendent like a 'cross' – possibly in the Mariner's attempt to turn the inconstancy of 'wind' or 'water' into the permanence of 'picture' or 'object'.

Piercing through motion and rendering it immobile – due to desire or fear – involves the substitution of a rigid world of fixities and securities in place of flowing energy, the accommodation of the 'I / my' system and its defence mechanisms of aggression and control; the ego imposes a kind of 'frozenness' which hinders any authentic being. The need for 'identity', with its primal imperative of historical continuity (with or without 'natural piety') and stability, interrupts the flux of life and creates a stationary pool, or sluggish ocean where no waves rise, heavy with scum and slime. Inertia and decay, the 'rotting sea' that is called existence, betrays the 'stilling' of motion (a 'hindrance' which, in Plato's words, is the cause of all evil (*Cratylus*, 417d–421b)). The ordeal of stasis in the poem signifies the paralysis of arrested 'change', inherent in a search for safety within the given structure of social, religious, and conceptual reality, safeguarding the urge for preservation – the 'having' and 'doing' so well expressed in the closing lines of the 'Eolian Harp'.

That the human condition imaginatively rendered in the poem as the experience of physiological and psychomental extremities of fire / earth – 'heat' and 'heaviness' – may not only pertain to the 'boredom' of a rational existence trapped away from the free-moving energies of life (through its carefully constructed 'veil of perception'), but the 'horror' of a backward look 'into' the prohibitive functional patterns of such a consciousness, we have Coleridge's own testimony in the *Notebooks*, proclaiming:

> I would make a pilgrimage to the burning sands of Arabia, or &c &c to find the Man who could explain to me there can be *oneness*, there being infinite Perceptions – yet there must be a *one*ness, not an intense Union but an Absolute Unity, for &c
>
> (1957: I, 556)

In the light (or 'darkness') of such a reading, the 'stasis' and 'burning' may be seen not as symbolic manifestations of the 'understanding' or dry intellectualism, but as necessary steps in an initiatory process, a 'rite of passage' away from the cluster of a discursive, scientific, analytic, controlling approach – the logic of common sense and competitive competence. The two interpretations of the *Ancient Mariner*, which I have termed 'historical' and 'ritualistic', indicative of ego-structuring and ego-destructuring respectively, incorporate into one mythical plot the dual archetype of paradise lost / paradise regained (in Christian-Miltonic terms), or Prometheus bound / Prometheus unbound (in Greek-Romantic terms).

The historical 'diachronic' approach would see the setting off from 'home' as the starting of the cyclic journey of the soul, the fall from paradise or golden age into the vicissitudes of chronological existence through the 'sin' of bird-killing, and the return or 'homecoming' to an unfallen paradisal consciousness through the snake-blessing. The ritualistic 'synchronic' approach would read the starting from 'home' as a withdrawal from the historically conditioned self by means of a morally equivocal and imaginatively ambiguous act of bird-killing, a travelling through the scorching anguish of initiation, and a return or homecoming to historical existence through snake-blessing – which introduces not a different world but a different mode of perceiving the old world. Metamorphosis being the central event in both readings, the former would be built on an underlying pattern of there / here / there, whereas the latter would rest on a structural organization of here / there / here – the transformational hinges remaining the same: bird-killing and snake-blessing. In the second case, bird-killing can be seen as either the definitive action that triggers the initiatory experience, or perhaps a 'wrong' move on the part of the initiate into the 'mysteries' of life (and love), which translates the smoothness and ease of the process through 'otherness' into an ordeal of spiteful resistance and death, turning the 'friendly' partner of the game of chess (or dice) into a dangerous opponent.

As an archetypal myth of regeneration, the Mariner's journey portrays the ritual passage from boredom to near-glory through horror. The 'horror' stage indicates the typical regression into 'cosmic night', a disintegration of the old personality, a condition of 'madness' which annuls historical existence; the internally consistent logic of the poem, as entirely divorced from the causal systems operative in normal awareness, may be said to follow the formal crisis schema from 'chaos' to 'creation', from πάσχειν to ποιεῖν. In the paradigmatic rebirth process, the images of boat and wind may be taken to symbolize, respectively, the individual and the life-flow or force of circumstances. By handling it with care and skill, the initiate can cross over the waters of the underworld, the vast reaches that intervene between 'ego' and 'other'. The desert crossing (alias engulfment into water or sea-monster) emblemizes a characteristic phase of all ritual quests: the devastating sense of spiritual 'thirst' and desolation that comes when all certainties and securities are gone, and one has to abandon 'inspiring' ideas that have turned into 'static' concepts; here the initiate suffers from the unbearable heat of the sun, the uncomfortable knowledge of his own weaknesses, the repulsive 'dark' aspects of existence that had been conveniently suppressed.[8] No longer 'protected' by the 'shade' of comforting illusions and habits, he must endure the painful exposure to the searing heat of 'reality'. The moon is suggestive of the impulse towards coolness and enlightenment; when the latent potentiality is awakened, it feels like a refreshing, soothing liquid (drunk from an urn?) that drenches the body and revives the spirit, thus enhancing the progress toward liberation. Association with bird figures is also a common element in the iconography of ceremonial practices; the bird denotes rising, activation, change, vitality – symbolic of 'soul' or an intelligent 'being' collaborating with man.

The act of shooting the 'wind-bird' (whether seen as the blessing of supernatural πνεῦμα or the curse of 'spiritual' conditioning, daemon or demon) induces a state of unnatural immobility and heat, internal as well as external, which simultaneously denotes the separation of 'inner' feeling from 'nature', as well as their possible homology. Hartman's allusion to the poem observes that 'A link is already made, here, between a stasis in nature and a stasis in the soul. Selfhood manifests its weight, and . . . an external deliverance – "a breeze," an action of grace or nature – is needed before the spell can be broken even in part' (1964: 133). The horrific sensation of scorching paralysis, instituted by the combination of focused attentiveness and ego surrender, considered as necessary for experiencing existence at this fundamental level, the tyranny of πάσχειν in both its senses as πάθος and πάθημα, intensity and receptivity, are also noted by Hartman: 'Death or self-forgetfulness is not allowed: the Mariner becomes "A man by pain and thought compelled to live" ' (1964: 132). The Mariner departs from the mode of rational activity which forms the basis of personal and cultural life, the normal process of linearity, the 'stream' of consciousness consisting of objects and people. He 'moves' from a temporal sequence of consecutive events in which we habitually operate, into the fixed locality of a 'painted' present – or ocean. In the linear modality, time is directional, a duration or succesion carrying man from the past into the future, the present moment always fleeting away. In the spatial mode, however, the present 'exists' and is all that exists. The 'terror' of the present-centred moment, the static infinite 'now' out of time progression and space diversity, the immobility of the one-pointed existence that the poem embodies so dramatically, presents the metaphysics of 'pure presence' or *nunc stans* as neither so 'pure' nor so desirable, if 'The very deep did rot: O Christ! / That ever this should be! / Yea, slimy things did crawl with legs / Upon the slimy sea' (ll. 123–6).

The categories of temporality and spatiality, although operative as a 'frame', partake of the evasiveness and preternatural condition of 'once upon a time' – and 'place'. The Mariner's excursion outside the institutionalized categories of a given ontology, is characterized at once by a 'fixity' of awareness and a 'fluidity' which allows an unending series of shifts between 'subject' and 'object', in an organic whole where barriers have collapsed. 'He not only sees impossible *things*', Haven notices; 'He experiences extremes of agony and ecstasy, of alienation and communion which have no place in a Cartesian view of reality' (1969: 23). The perils to consciousness in stepping out of time-sequence and space-variety, inherent in a complete 'suspension' of the human intentionality which becomes passive and receptive to powers outside itself, are emphasized by N. P. Stallknecht and D. Simpson, respectively concentrating on the phenomenological and verbal symptoms of a process that does away with the 'filters' controlling the contents of normal functioning – (conceptual) language, (Aristotelian) logic, and (social) convention. Discussing man's experience of time, Stallknecht refers to the 'tendency toward automatism that we find in ourselves as we relinquish the effort to maintain our active mentality – that is, our decision and our freedom. If we live largely in the immediate present, we lose sight of possibility and we thus fail to profit by our past – we simply continue to repeat it. But when we try to "pull ourselves together," we attempt to recapture a steady vision of possibilities. We try to recapture the future' (1954: 231–2). Simpson's reference to the prison-house of presentness, although relating to Keats' poetry, provides a pertinent analysis of the mariner-experience: 'Unable to achieve a metacomment, we are trapped in a perpetual present, where causality and temporality are completely suspended'; Simpson connects the 'imagery of immobility and thraldom' to 'another common preoccupation of the period, the so called "animal magnetism" or somnambulism'; such attitudes 'can be seen to embody loss of will, of consciousness, and of control', and, generally, 'The somnambulist condition is marked by the fusion and confusion of pleasure and pain . . . of inner and outer . . . and by the loss of the ability, if not the urge, to speak' (1979: 197–8):

> With throats unslacked, with black lips baked,
> We could nor laugh nor wail;
> Through utter drought all dumb we stood!
> I bit my arm, I sucked the blood,
> And cried, A sail! a sail!
>
> (ll. 157–61)

The protracted sojourn outside 'time' and 'language', defined as an extreme of agony and ecstasy, is imaginatively – and physiologically – recorded as an intensity of shivering and burning, the 'wondrous cold' of ice and the 'glorious sun' of the 'copper sky'. Traditionally, contact with the properties of severe cold or excessive heat indicate that the initiate has gone beyond the ordinary human parameters and is now a participant in the sacred world. Eliade points out in his discussion of the syndromes of ritual practices and their vocabulary, that we are 'in the presence of a fundamental magico-religious experience, which is universally documented on the archaic levels of culture: access to sacrality is manifested, among other things, by a prodigious increase in heat'. A comparative study of various religions and cults furnishes ample proof, he contends, that an unnatural rise in temperature indicates 'that the human condition has been abolished and that the shaman, the smith,[9] or the warrior participate, each on his own plane, in a higher condition' (1958: 86). The report that the 'Ancient' Mariner unfolds to the reluctantly detained and will-less Wedding Guest is perhaps a tale of such archaic states of unencumbered vision and unmediated confrontation with the 'hot' and 'bloody' sun (or fire) of sacred power:

> The western wave was all a-flame.
> The day was well nigh done!
> Almost upon the western wave
> Rested the broad bright Sun;
> When that strange shape drove suddenly
> Betwixt us and the Sun.
>
> And straight the Sun was flecked with bars,
> (Heaven's Mother send us grace!)
> As if through a dungeon-grate he peered
> With broad and burning face.
>
> (ll. 171–80)

In his commentary on 'magical heat' Eliade observes that the rousing of bodily temperature in order to achieve fire-mastery is common to shamans and mystics the world over; the Buddha is 'burning'[10] and 'the Mohammedans believe that a man in communication with God becomes "burning hot." Anyone who performs miracles is called "boiling" ' (1958: 86). These *mystiques* of magical fever exhibit a 'mastery of fire' that manifests itself in the handling of heat and resistance to cold. However, as Eliade affirms, 'the meaning of all these techniques of "mastering fire" lies deeper: they indicate the attainment of a certain ecstatic state, a non-conditioned state of spiritual freedom. But a *sacred power* experienced as an intense warmth is obtained by other means besides shamanic and mystical techniques. It may come from the forces aroused during military initiations' (1960: 148). The phonetic kinship in the Greek language of Ἔρως / Ἄρης, gods of love and war, is probably indicative of the common ground of the erotic experience (the shuddering / warmth alternation described in the *Phaedrus* as preliminary to the wing-growing of the soul (251a–c)) and the martial arts – although no such mention is made by Plato, whose four types of μανία or divine rage encompass the prophetic, mystic, poetic, and erotic / philosophic aspects of the approximation of the human to the sacred. 'This "fury" ', Eliade testifies, is an uncustomary experience; 'there is nothing "ordinary" or "natural" about it, it belongs to the syndrome of possession by something sacred. Being a *sacred energy*, it can be transformed, differentiated, subtilised by a further process of integration or "sublimation" '. The ambivalence inherent in the human reaction to the incursion of sacrality – a composite of attraction / repulsion, a fascination with abomination – is also emphasized in Eliade's account of the transactions between men and gods: 'As one would expect, however, the "fury" and the "heat" aroused by a violent and excessive access of *power* strike fear into the majority of mortals'. Eliade's subsequent etymological interpretation of the word *shânti* which, among other things, concludes Eliot's *Waste Land*, is apocalyptic: 'The term *shânti*, which in Sanskrit means tranquillity and peace of soul, absence of passion and suffering relieved, is derived from the root *Sham*, which originally included such meanings as the extinguishing of "fire", and the cooling-down of anger or, indeed, of the "heat" aroused by demonic powers' (1960: 149).

The heat of divine possession or reception of a sacred force that underlies the dissolution process of the 'body' of the *Ancient Mariner*, is variously interpreted by Coleridge critics, J. Beer offering one of the most interesting readings; the 'ethical' and 'rationalistic' emphasis of the interpretation is emphasized in a passage affirming that 'The Sun remains unchanging as a symbol of the divine Glory. Psychologically, it is the divine Reason in mankind, which the unenlightened understanding of the guilty experiences only in the heat and wrath of conscience' (1959: 168). Exemplifying the anguish and solar torment in terms of 'glory' violates, I think, the internal logic of the poem and minimizes the stage, or state, of 'dark' and troubling crisis, the 'death' that precedes rebirth or the 'horror' that mediates between 'boredom' and 'glory'. In her documentation of the 'rebirth' archetype, M. Bodkin sets the structural dialectic of the *Ancient Mariner*, particularly the pattern of downward and upward motion, within the larger context of psychoanalysis and eastern mysticism, the

Freudian death-instinct and Nirvana condition in conflict with the life-instinct or ego-preservation: 'This accounts for the fact', she argues, 'that the emotional effect of the imagery of fixity and stagnation in the poem is an experience of effort and tension' (1934: 69).

As the imaginative immobility 'moves' towards the second climax, tensions – psychological, moral, aesthetic – become more pronounced: 'The many men, so beautiful! / And they all dead did lie: / And a thousand thousand slimy things / Lived on; and so did I' (ll. 236–9). The unmistakable identification of 'I'-'slimy' points towards a self-loathing and self-hatred whose origin lies in the Mariner's reluctance to accept 'slime' as a 'necessary' composite of his own make up – indeed of all existence. As such, the force of resistance can only be overcome, and spiritual growth towards an organic wholeness of the personality effected, through acceptance of the 'slimy thing', and recognition of (to use a Shakespearean analogue) 'this thing of darkness I / Acknowledge mine' (*The Tempest*, V, i, 275–6) – the 'slime out of the depths' that contains, as Jung 'calls such contents', 'not only "objectionable animal tendencies, but also germs of new possibilities of life" ' (Bodkin 1934: 52). The ego's fear of the transformative dimension apparently reduces it to a destructive function which evokes depression and self-hate, metaphorically and physiologically rendered in the poem as inertia and paralysis.

The 'sacrifice' exacted from the Mariner is to accept his own reality and to commit himself to what he discovers himself to be, even though by the prevailing social standards this may be regarded as ugly and repulsive. The second, or positive, transformation in the poem, the way out of agony and stagnation, although iconographically depicted as a reconciliation of opposites on many ontological levels – sun / moon, fire / water, red / white, shadow / light, calm / motion – is essentially activated by the antecedent factor of acceptance of reptile 'slime' as an inevitable component of life:

> Her beams bemocked the sultry main,
> Like April hoar-frost spread;
> But where the ship's huge shadow lay,
> The charmèd water burnt alway
> A still and awful red.

> Beyond the shadow of the ship,
> I watched the water-snakes:
> They moved in tracks of shining white,
> And when they reared, the elfish light
> Fell off in hoary flakes.
>
> Within the shadow of the ship
> I watched their rich attire:
> Blue, glossy green, and velvet black,
> They coiled and swam; and every track
> Was a flash of golden fire.
>
> (ll. 267–81)

The aesthetic intuition of the 'beauty of ugliness', recognition of the splendour of spiral serpentine energies, is also a moral victory over conflict and suffering, resting on inclusiveness of the 'shadowy', 'abysmal', 'decaying', and 'repulsive' – or rather a 'seeing through' the abominable aspect of existence to its root power and essential magnificence. The transformative vision is divided into two phases, the first effected through 'distancing', the second through 'participation': 'Beyond the shadow of the ship / I watched the water-snakes' expresses an optical dynamics of detachment that reveals the 'shining white', a possible analogue to Shelley's 'white radiance of Eternity'; the second stage suggests an 'inside' view: 'Within the shadow of the ship / I watched their rich attire', which transmutes the white brilliance into 'Blue, glossy green, and velvet black', the 'many-coloured glass' of life (in the Shelleyan *Adonais*) or the 'dazzling hue, / Vermilion-spotted, golden, green, and blue' of the homologous 'snake', the Keatsian Lamia.

The Mariner's process to the 'sea of beauty' both parallels and inverts the Platonic ascent to the πέλαγος κάλλους: rather than physical beauty arousing love which leads to the vision of transcendental beauty, ἐκεῖνο τὸ καλόν, it is the perception of the ultimate beauty of reality, the one 'shining white' within whose 'elfish light' the water-snakes danced, that generates enchantment and love for the multi-coloured and multiform phenomenal existence. As a manifestation or 'flash' of 'golden fire' disclosing blessings spread around him like a sea, everything on which he beheld became full of blessings.[11] 'Blessing' is precisely the speech act that substitutes the ineffability of the aesthetic experience – 'no tongue / Their beauty might declare' –

and marks the turning point of the discharge of waters, the spontaneous overflow that follows immediately upon the luminosity of insight. 'The Mariner's release', S. Prickett observes, 'comes through blessing "unawares" the slimy and horrible water-snakes that until then had filled him with loathing and disgust. He had to learn to love and see beauty in what frightened and nauseated him'; evidently, 'It was this very ambivalence of his own experience that he had to accept before he could be restored, cleansed, to the world of men' (1970: 24–5). That the unaware 'blessing' was as unpremeditated as the will-less 'shooting' indicates, I think, that restoration is a usurpation upon the Mariner's wilful intentions as much as the 'heroic' action of ignorance. The miracle of metamorphosis, in both its negative and positive aspects, can only intensify the mystery of an a-causal (from the human perspective) sequence, yet hinting towards its antecedents – the conditions appearing to precipitate the transformative occurrence: recognition of an uninterrupted 'continuity' binding all forms of existence. The triadic ritualistic pattern of Greek mysteries – 'I saw', 'I said', 'I did', i.e. perception, expression, enactment – is almost detectable in the codification of the Mariner's ecstasis, in the structural sequence of 'I watched', 'I blessed', 'I dreamt'.

The only form of representation that can render the beauty and love experienced seems to be 'blessing' / 'praying', pointing towards the paradoxical relatedness that is discovered by Heidegger in the etymological kinship of 'thanking' and 'thinking': 'The Old English *thencan*, to think, and *thancian,* to thank', he asserts, 'are closely related; the Old English noun for thought is *thanc* or *thonc* – a thought, a grateful thought, and the expression of such a thought; today it survives in the plural *thanks*'; because of its correspondence to 'thinking', 'thanking' is also related to memory, yet a form of memorizing or commemorating that connects it not to 'pastness' but 'presentness'. The absence of intention or artful contrivance in this type of thinking / thanking is further exemplifed by Heidegger: 'The things for which we owe thanks are not things we have from ourselves. They are given to us'; above all, 'the thing given to us, in the sense of this dowry, is thinking'. That the 'act' of thinking is a 'gift', passively received and acknowledged, bestowed and reflected, consists one of the most daring, I believe, of Heidegger's astonishing pronouncements – echoing, of course, the ξυνὸς λόγος ('shared account') of Heraclitus; 'Pure thanks is rather that we simply think – think what is really and solely given, what is there to be thought' (1968: 139–43). On the testimony of the *Notebooks*, a parallel investigation was undertaken by Coleridge himself, whose linguistic sensibility had embarked upon a similar course of exploring the diachronic, and trans-national, etymologies of 'thinking' – and of course 'being':

> Σωμα ψυχοπλαστον ψυχη σωματοπλαττουσα Reo = reor probably an obsolete Latin word, and res the second person singular of the Present Indicative – If so, it is the Iliad of Spinozo-Kantian, Kanto-Fichtian, Fichto-Schellingian Revival of Plato-Plotino-Proclian Idealism in a Nutshell *from* a Lilliput Hazel. Res = thou art thinking. – Even so our 'Thing': id est, thinking or think'd. Think, Thank, Tank = Reservoir of what has been *thinged* – Denken, Danken – I forget the German for Tank / . . .
>
> (1962: II, 2784)

The Mariner's coercion to speak, following upon the horrors of aphasia, indicates an attempt to put into language the experience he underwent with language – or its absence. Having come back from the heart of darkness (or 'heated' void), he seems to find the proper mode of his existence in 'words', in the compulsive repetition of his 'tale', the instant reenactment of the event in the symbolic form of verbal utterance:

> Since then, at an uncertain hour,
> That agony returns:
> And till my ghastly tale is told,
> This heart within me burns.
>
> I pass, like night, from land to land;
> I have strange power of speech;
> That moment that his face I see,
> I know the man that must hear me
> To him my tale I teach.
>
> (ll. 582–90)

The conversational relation between 'experienced old man' and 'inexperienced youth', and the emphatic one-sidedness of the 'dialogue' counteracted only by silent noddings, is not a very distant analogue (excepting the urges to escape) to the educational situation as presented in the Platonic dialogues – with two basic differences: the association of 'wisdom' with 'sadness', which emphasizes the ominous element of the experience over and above the intuitive apprehension of 'happiness' in living things, and the introduction of a greater measure of 'difference' or 'otherness' between instructor and instructed, by placing their encounter on chance acquaintance rather than sustained fellowship.

As Eliade comments in reported speech, citing external authority, ' "the real treasure, that which can put an end to our poverty and all our trials, is never very far; there is no need to seek it in a distant country. It lies buried in the most intimate parts of our own house; that is, of our own being'. Giving a more specific locus to this domestic phenomenology of spirit, Eliade (or rather H. Zimmer) continues in a manner that strongly recalls Plato's definition of οὐσία as ἑστία, the hearth of the household: 'It is behind the stove, the centre of the life and warmth that rule our existence, the heart of our heart, if only we know how to unearth it. And yet', he enunciates, 'there is this strange and persistent fact, that it is only after a pious journey in a distant region, in a new land, that the meaning of that inner voice can make itself understood by us'; 'otherness' is doubly present in that 'he who reveals to us the meaning of our mysterious inward pilgrimage must himself be a stranger, of another belief and another race" ' (1960: 246).

Unlike the Platonic dialogues (with 'minor' exceptions), the poem fulfils the condition of estrangement rather than familiarity, and an asceticism and alienation from 'nature', suggested not only by the disrupted nuptials of the frame-story, but in the hierarchical preference which makes walking 'to the kirk' 'sweeter than the marriage-feast'. As the 'loud uproar bursts from that door! / The wedding guests are there' (ll. 591–2), and the maidens sing in the garden-bower, the Mariner withdraws to offer his pious worship to God, following the bidding of the 'vesper bell'. Such 'divorce' which makes joviality and solemnity, erotic desire and religious emotion mutually exclusive, at once portrays the reality model that pervades Coleridge's imaginative construction, and unwittingly recalls the 'ending' of the *Symposium*, whose alternative resolution is made more manifest by the striking similarity of circumstance. There (to remind ourselves of the scene), as the initiating procedure came to a close, 'a whole crowd of revellers came to the door and finding it open' entered and joined the party; soon 'the whole place was in an uproar'; and, as the ('wedding') guests actually partook of the 'loving' conviviality of 'man and bird and beast' rather than merely 'understanding' it theoretically, 'decency and order went by the board, and everybody had to drink the most enormous quantities of wine' (223b). Here, as 'the Wedding-Guest / Turned from the bridgegroom's door' (*Ancient Mariner*, ll. 620–1), he 'married' wisdom to sadness under the aegis of a paradigm – the Judaeo-Christian 'unhappy consciousness' (to use Hegel's observation) – that exults human suffering rather than human joy, and requires the repression of spontaneous needs and urges, or taints them with guilt.[12]

PROMETHEUS UNBOUND

The atonement of guilt not through 'prayer', individual or communal, which bids,

> To walk together to the kirk,
> And all together pray,
> While each to his great Father bends,
> Old men, and babes, and loving friends
> And youths and maidens gay!
> (*Ancient Mariner*, ll. 605–9)

but through its 'unspeaking' – the deconstruction of the conceptual categories which 'nominate' it, and the destruction of the defence mechanisms which promote it – is the theme of Shelley's *Prometheus Unbound*, and particularly of the first Act of this drama 'drawn from the operations of the human mind' (1905: 205). The 'play', I believe, is the embodiment of the Platonic creation myth,[13] 'Intelligence Persuading Necessity', which is dramatized in the triptych of Prometheus-Asia-Demogorgon, or, to retain the structure of the prototype (ἀνάγκης ἡττωμένης ὑπὸ πειθοῦς ἔμφρονος (*Timaeus*, 48a)), 'Demogorgon Asia-ed by Prometheus' – the etymological identity of ἔρως / ῥῆμα (through their common rootage in ἐρῶ – to love / to say, and their kinship to ῥέω, to flow) providing a linguistic support to cosmogony. In his assessment of the relation between the Shelleyan drama and its Aeschylian original, and in a manner that strongly echoes Shelley's own intentionality, S.

Rogers remarks: 'As we examine Shelley's reconstruction of the Prometheus myth, we shall see how he adapted the treatments which Aeschylus and Hesiod gave this myth to suit his Platonic allegory of the soul, and how the wish to believe that guilt is proportionate not to passion, but to intelligence, found support in a reading of this Greek tragedy'; the curative or therapeutic function of language (also present in the Platonic text through Socrates' identification of his dialectical method as θεραπεία) is, in Rogers' view, definitely employed by Prometheus who 'knew that words are physicians if applied at the critical moment', and so 'by means of words he controls his suffering' (1974: 73–4).

The opening scene of the drama exposes Προμηθεὺς κατηγορούμενος (the word employed in its dual Greek usage, as 'defendant' and 'predicate' i.e. holding 'object' position, both of which are applicable to the specific Promethean condition of endurance) in a direct verbal confrontation with his eternal foe who, although a character of the Greek Olympian pantheon, is introduced in his 'historical' translation of the Roman 'Jupiter':

> Monarch of Gods and Daemons, and all Spirits
> But One, who throng those bright and rolling worlds
> Which Thou and I alone of living things
> Behold with sleepless eyes! regard this Earth
> Made multitudinous with thy slaves, whom thou
> Requitest for knee-worship, prayer, and praise,
> And toil, and hecatombs of broken hearts,
> With fear and self-contempt and barren hope.
>
> (I, 1–8)

That the signifier 'Jupiter' points towards a signified which comprises the Father-in-Heaven patriarchal God of Judaeo-Christianity,[14] as well as the deified analytical 'reasoning', has been a point of convergence in Shelley critical evaluations.[15] *Prometheus Unbound* is a myth about authoritarian kingship in both its religious and political aspects, and about that particular form of consciousness engendered and ratified by patriarchy, a consciousness permeated by a calculative, abstracting, and despotic 'I am' – ambivalently introduced by the Platonic hierarchy of λογιστικόν over the other functions of the soul, and securely established by the Cartesian *cogito ergo sum* as the only type not only of 'cognizing' but of 'existing'. On all planes of existence – epistemological, theological, social, psychological, mythic – the ego's dictatorship enforces the fiction of its being not only supreme but exclusive ruler; the values of competitiveness, aggression, conquest, and possession 'dictate' the creation of 'adversaries' that have to be overpowered under the auspices of the heroic ideal. When Prometheus admits, addressing Jupiter, 'Whilst me, who am thy foe, eyeless in hate, / Hast thou made reign and triumph, to thy scorn, / O'er mine own misery and thy vain revenge' (I, 9–11), he perceives his involvement in a power-game of conflict, violence, and hatred – or rather self-hatred. The mind's awareness of having instituted a censor, evaluator, judge who wants to conquer or subjugate the other 'images' or psychic functions, has to be 'realized' within the codes of conduct, categories, and behaviour patterns instituted by the tyrannical authority – ego-consciousness itself.

The critical moment in the play, Prometheus' 'unspeaking' of his curse[16] upon Jupiter, is a recognition of ego strategies, and a refusal to 'play' by the rules of ego's game; by negating the 'warlike' way of confrontation / victory, he suddenly 'falls out' of the very conceptual system that sustains ego rule. The paradox of rejecting authority in 'accepting' it – giving up resistance and defiance – lies at the core of Shelley's version of the Promethean myth: 'I speak in grief, / Not exultation, for I hate no more, / As then ere misery made me wise. The curse / Once breathed on thee I would recall' (I, 56–9). The revocation of his malediction is an un-speaking of 'hatred',[17] which amounts to an insight into the nature of self-hatred, that dismantles psychological 'patronage' from its power and initiates the process of bringing a total revolution within the structure of the psyche. The eradication of malice from 'memory' and 'wish' – past experiences and future expectations – is the delivery from a constructed model that installs and sustains 'authority':

> If then my words had power,
> Though I am changed so that aught evil wish
> Is dead within; although no memory be
> Of what is hate, let them not lose it now!
> What was that curse? for ye all heard me speak.
>   (I, 69–73)

In surrender 'of' rather than 'to' enmity, Prometheus begins to undo the basic structure of ego / Jupiter – which, as he admits, is of his own creation – entering on a process of stripping, opening, and giving; he transcends ego tactics not by opposing or vanquishing them, but by 'seeing through' them. As with all great Romantic myths of transformation, *Prometheus Unbound* rests upon a perceptual revolution deconstructing the conceptual order, showing that the main point of any spiritual practice is to 'clear out' of ego's bureaucracy; the real solution lies in the disappearance of the system, not in its elimination or suppression.

Prometheus recognizes the groundless quality of 'I', the 'frail and empty phantom', which presents a unique semantic peculiarity in that its meaning, unlike that of other nouns and pronouns, does not rest on a stereotype correspondence with an ontological 'object', but on the speaking 'subject' itself, the very seat of signification. As such, it does not refer to 'one' thing, but a complex – and complicated – pattern of interlocking forces continually shifting, whose pluralism and fluidity introduces a constant split between signifier and signified. Seeing through the illusory nature of the 'I' and its projections, of which 'no thought inform thine empty voice', Prometheus realizes that his own hatred for his eternal foe is precisely what feeds and sustains, in fact 'protects' a bubble that could burst at any moment. The ritual recantation of his curse is the result of a long period of suffering in 'burning cold', reminiscent – though in a shift of emphasis to the 'polar' extremity rather than the 'equator' – of the interaction of ice / heat that constitute the symptoms / images of the Mariner's experience.

Prometheus has committed himself to the pain of 'exposing' himself – King Lear fashion; of taking off his clothes, his skin, nerves, heart, brain, 'liver', until he is open to the universe. This gradual elimination of habits, preconceptions, defences, culminates in the knowledge that self-hatred has become a kind of monolithic occupation, an absorption that has paralysed him; self-evaluation and self-criticism proves a great burden causing a strain or strife between what *he is* and the 'image' of his own making. So all he does, is let go of self-images, projections, and the tensions involved in upholding them. He just sits back and permits it all to unfold by itself, without any intervention, retribution, infliction, suppression, condemnation: 'It doth repent me: words are quick and vain; / Grief for awhile is blind, and so was mine. / I wish no living thing to suffer pain' (I, 303–5).

Resisting not only submission – 'bending his soul in prayer' – but the cherishing of future victory, he annihilates the very cultural economy within which hierarchy, control, and success are valid – and valuable – categories of experience. The subversion of rational censorship, the removal of the filters of perception (the 'choice' mechanism that had undertaken the role of purifier of consciousness) brings to the surface the 'slime', the emotional entanglements of fear and pain at the bottom of existence, which the mind now encounters with an ambient feeling of terrified welcoming, or fascination with abomination.

Dressed in the imagery of Greek mythology, Coleridge's 'slimy things' provoke the same ambivalence of 'contradiction' that is at once the starting point of the Platonic dialectical process, and the τόπος where sacred power manifests itself. Prometheus addresses them:

> Horrible forms,
> What and who are ye? Never yet there came
> Phantasms so foul through monster-teeming Hell
> From the all-miscreative brain of Jove;
> Whilst I behold such execrable shapes,
> Methinks I grow like what I contemplate,
> And laugh and stare in loathsome sympathy.
>
> (I, 445–51)

Unfiltered confrontation – or rather 'conversation' – with the images of the 'loud multitude' of the 'deep' is a novel horror, following immediately upon Prometheus' cancellation of the curse, which 'annuls' Jupiter or rather initiates the transformational process that will eventually 'incarnate' what is initially a tentative alteration in 'perception' – 'apophatically'[18] expressed. 'The removal of hate', E. R. Wasserman observes, 'is only a negative act; it can only prepare the way for Love to activate Power. Asia's retreat from the world of being into the realm of the potential, then, motivates the parallel withdrawal of Jupiter by Power into its own potentiality, and thus makes possible the release of the "natural" course of events, symbolized by Asia's flight from the realm of potentiality to active reunion with Prometheus' (1965: 133–4). The effects of Prometheus' 'uncursing' are similar to those of the Mariner's 'blessing': a release or unfreezing of flow, the translation of intense cold or heat – πάσχειν – into an effortless, spontaneous certainty, the ποιεῖν of events, inevitable and of great value.

The 'rupture' of plane that makes possible the passage from one mode of being to another through uncursing / blessing, is fundamentally the substitution of 'yes' for 'no', a choiceless acceptance of one's life and 'selfness'. In *Prometheus Unbound* the 'attitude' of revocation becomes the crucial move that revitalizes energy to 'her' heroic tasks, leading to the ultimate reunion of the 'divorced' couple, Prometheus and Asia, in the hierogamy of νοῦς ἐρων. Prometheus does not conform to the masculine ideal of conquering hero, like his mythical prototype; he rather plays the role of seeker, discoverer, passive observer. After his speech act at the opening section of the play, he entirely disappears from the stage only to return when the Asia–Demogorgon 'verbal' confrontation is over, and Jupiter dethroned. Having 'suffered', Prometheus does not 'act'. The technology of transformation that the poem dramatizes, reveals that 'meaning' is a perceptual issue; and the plot casts Prometheus in the role of ὑπο-κείμενον, awareness as the 'ground' of conscious life, the 'perception' that is the centre of all experience impassively witnessing the locomotion of Asia. Prometheus' apathetic or receptive mode to the unfolding of events in the play is an aspect not of 'impotence' but 'potency'. From a different point of view, though, loss of dynamism may also be said to characterize the term of his torment, which is the result of his separation from energy – the enlivening force of Asia from whom he had been 'divorced' through the intervention of the 'shadow' Jupiter. The enforced split between νοῦς / ἔρως (or why not ὄνομα / ῥῆμα – the ὑποκείμενον / κατηγόρημα or subject / predicate division of linguistic, and perhaps ontological, grammar), can only be healed through the complete negation of Jupiter / ego, and the subsequent encounter of 'loving energy' with 'eternal power'. In performing the role of daemonic mediator between Prometheus and Demogorgon, Asia becomes the feminine 'counterpart' of her husband, duplicating the historical / mythical role of Prometheus as the 'go-between' the human and the divine. That Prometheus has no direct communication with Demogorgon except through the intervening 'persuasiveness' of Asia, is emphasized both by the imaginative and structural set up of the poem; 'Since mind has no immediate access to Power, Prometheus cannot be the agent to rouse Demogorgon from his sleep ... Only Asia, generative love, serving as agency of the One Mind and acting under the compulsion of Necessity, can retreat into potentiality and awaken it' (Wasserman 1965: 133).

Any hermeneutical exploration of the lyrical drama must address itself to the form – or formlessness – of Demogorgon. The name of Demogorgon is apparently the product of the conjunction of two Greek words, Δαίμων and Γοργώ (the Gorgon, the grim one, deriving from the epithet γοργός, grim, fierce, terrible); δαίμων is god or goddess irrespectively, deity or divine power. The interrelation of the two seems to be a linguistic concoction for the concretization of that 'awful power' that haunts the Shelleyan mind – and text.[19] As for the 'archaeology' of the component δαίμων, the term has a dominant presence in the Platonic dialogues, where it appears in three functions: supernatural (*Epinomis*, 984e–985b), metaphysical (*Symposium*, 202d–e), psychological (*Apology*, 31d; *Tim.*, 90b–d). The etymological investigation in the *Cratylus*, gives us the root meaning of the word as deriving from δαήμων (knowing or wise) – hence: the wise one (398b–c).

That the battling of Jupiter and Demogorgon is a renewed figuration of the perennial conflict between the forces (and code systems) emblemized respectively by Eagle and Serpent, is made manifest in the verbal exchange between the two combatants as they encounter each other in Act III. To Jupiter's question 'Awful shape, what art thou? Speak!' Demogorgon replies 'Eternity' (i, 51–2), which is an echo of earlier imaginative representations – 'the vast snake Eternity', or 'the snake that girds Eternity'. At the moment of his fall, Jupiter interprets his annihilation in symbolic terms that precisely reveal the archetypal conflict of the two powers so clearly depicted in *The Revolt of Islam*: the Evil / Comet / Eagle and the Good / Star / Serpent: 'Sink with me then, / We too will sink on the wide waves of ruin, / Even as a vulture and a snake outspent / Drop, twisted in inextricable fight, / Into a shoreless sea' (*Prom.*, III, i, 70–4). That Demogorgon, despite its apparent disappearance into water, does not conform to the wishful thinking of Jupiter and perish with him, is attested to by its re-emergence at the closing moments of the drama in full power, and its pronouncement of the concluding lines, 'a universal sound like words'. In Demogorgon's assessment of events and forces interlocking in the play, love is accorded its due as the chief factor of transformative regeneration, in that 'from its awful throne of patient power' it can effect the conquest of Conquest.

The first mention of Demogorgon in the poem is made by the Earth in Act I, when referring to the two worlds of 'life' and 'death' – the phenomenal one, object of the senses, and the super-(under-)natural, where exact 'copies' of living things may be found, 'And Demogorgon, a tremendous gloom' (l. 207). Asia's journey / descent to the dwelling place of the dark power is made in terms of following or pursuing a 'sound', a throng of voices that invite, incite, and instruct: 'In the world unknown / Sleeps a voice unspoken; / By thy step alone / Can its rest be broken; / Child of Ocean!' (II, i, 190–4). Possibly the 'darkness' and 'gloom' of the place refer to this quality, or condition, of 'unknowing latency', 'inarticulateness' – in other words the 'negativity' or 'emptiness' into which Asia and her companion enter. The dormant state of the static 'voice' can only be 'awakened' or rendered operational by the 'dynamism' of Asia. It is the flight, or flow, of creative Love that can break the 'rest', passivity, of the sleeping mightiness, 'the gloom divine'. The approach to Demogorgon is primarily 'sonar', in a way that strangely corresponds to Keats' 'Ode to a Nightingale', another instance of musicality that drowns vision.

The downward motion of Asia is more 'enforced' than freely chosen or followed, attracted and impelled 'By Demogorgon's mighty law'. The last signpost before entrance into the cave or abyss of Demogorgon is a 'pinnacle of rock among mountains'; the 'realm of Demogorgon' having been reached, the two sisters stand over 'the mighty portal',

>   chasm,
> Whence the oracular vapour is hurled up
> Which lonely men drink wandering in their youth,
> And call truth, virtue, love, genius, or joy,
> That maddening wine of life, whose dregs they drain
> To deep intoxication; and uplift,
> Like Maenads who cry loud, Evoe! Evoe!
> The voice which is contagion to the world.
>   (II, iii, 3–10)

The passage carries a moral ambivalence that may be somewhat abated if one brings to mind the vocal utterances of the 'wilderness' in 'Mont Blanc'; in any case, the landscape or rather 'inscape' scenery is the same, as Asia's descent has paradoxically landed her on a mountain summit (the natural form which, when translated into its geometrical equivalent, gives the triangle, and into its achitectonic counterpart, the pyramid). The problem remains the nature of this 'spirit', because the notion of 'power' seems irreconcilable to 'weak and beautiful' – unless, of course, one connects it to other statements where the unorthodox conjunction of weakness and strength is effected, as in,

> Resist not the weakness,
> Such strength is in meekness
> That the Eternal, the Immortal,
> Must unloose through life's portal
> The snake-like Doom coiled underneath his throne
> By that alone.
> (II, iv, 93–8)

The capacity of 'patient power' to induce 'eternity', to activate and incarnate 'doom' by allowing it entrance into life, is precisely the 'drama' that is acted out in the middle section of the poem. The relation of Eternity to the Serpent is here presented in slightly different terms from its other manifestations in Shelley's poetry. The Snake neither 'is' nor 'girds' Eternity but is 'coiled' underneath Eternity's throne, who is characteristically of a masculine sex and gender, as in Canto I of *The Revolt of Islam* – and unlike Act IV (ll. 565–7) of *Prometheus Unbound*. The coiled position of the serpentine power in its 'inertia' aspect suggests both stasis and latency. The spiral shape of the sleeping force implies a form of dormant dynamism, within that 'repose' and finality which are attributes of the circle proper; the 'coil' conceals an actual potency present, which when released can effect tremendous changes. The rest of Act II, and the first scene of Act III, trace precisely the process of dynamization of the snake-like, spiral-form power or energy, its ascent, its encounter with Jupiter, and the final absorption of 'power' into greater 'power'.

When the cave of Demogorgon is entered and Panthea asks 'What veiléd form sits on that ebon throne?' (II, iv, 1), 'power' is placed 'on' a throne rather than 'underneath' one. Probably the change suggests the alteration in the physical position of the observer-questioners, who are now situated below the mountain throne of Eternity, in the 'underneath' itself. The falling of the veil, or the cleansing of the witnesses' perceptive faculty,

ΠΑΘΗΜΑ AND ΠΟΙΗΜΑ

uncovers the double paradox of a 'dark luminosity' and 'formless formation':

> I see a mighty darkness
> Filling the seat of power, and rays of gloom
> Dart round, as light from the meridian sun.
> – Ungazed upon and shapeless; neither limb,
> Nor form, nor outline; yet we feel it is
> A living Spirit.
>
> (II, iv, 2–7)

The answers that Demogorgon pronounces to Asia's 'overwhelming' questions are nothing but reflections, or projections of Asia's thoughts: 'I spoke but as ye speak', the Serpent-power admits, and Asia realizes that 'my heart gave / The response thou hast given' (II, iv, 121–2). So the replies to 'Who made the living world?' and 'Who made terror?' carry no 'objective' validity and give no 'new' information, but are images (or echoes) of the already formulated conceptions of Asia's 'historical' consciousness. To the first interrogation which, although it purports to include 'all' the world contains, is actually an inquiry into 'Who made goodness' (thought, passion, reason, will, and imagination being 'good' things), the answer is 'God' – a noun, a name, a substantive. The author of 'evil' is not 'named' as such, but defined by a verb – energy, action, lacking in 'substantiality'. Demogorgon does not take long to uncover the futility of this intellectual game that Asia is trying to impose on their encounter:

> If the abysm
> Could vomit forth its secrets. . . . But a voice
> Is wanting, the deep truth is imageless;
> For what would it avail to bid thee gaze
> On the revolving world? What to bid speak
> Fate, Time, Occasion, Chance, and Change? To these
> All things are subject but eternal Love.
>
> (II, iv, 114–20)

The 'two woes of speaking and beholding' (I, 647), language and perception – anything that thought operates on, or fabricates, or reflects about – is a reality conditioned; the 'revolving world' of sensation and the 'speech' of discursive thought, should be pierced by the 'eternity' of Love. Perception and thought are seen as the ephemeral appearance of images interspersed with words. That the 'deep truth' is imageless, or better 'conceptless', is a verbal gesture in the direction of uncovering thought's incapacity to encompass reality, the implication that propositional thinking can never answer any tremendous question. The 'old' mind, burdened with knowledge of the 'past' and past memories, cannot solve the immediate problem of 'present' living because comprehension of a new, 'unremembered' fact, is not 'reality' to thought. Still, Demogorgon finds a way to communicate to Asia its cryptic message, penetrating the business and speed of Asia's constant stream of analytic consciousness, through gaps in her awareness – her 'aporetic', questioning attitude.

Although 'a voice is wanting' and 'the deep truth is imageless', Demogorgon 'speaks' – and 'shows'. That Shelley allows some form of utterance to the ineffable (in the paradox that it speaks but cannot be spoken of), can be seen in the following lines from 'Mont Blanc', where the voice of 'Otherness' annuls convention – religious dogmas and political ideologies:

> The wilderness has a mysterious tongue
> Which teaches awful doubt, or faith so mild,
> So solemn, so serene, that man may be,
> But for such faith, with nature reconciled;
> Thou hast a voice, great Mountain, to repeal
> Large codes of fraud and woe; not understood
> By all, but which the wise, and great, and good
> Interpret, or make felt, or deeply feel.
>
> (ll. 76–83)

So the problem with the 'wilderness' or 'abysm' is not 'speechlessness' but 'interpretation', or perhaps the establishment of a common communicative ground. The void of the deep truth is probably the vacancy of a mind that has finished with all the movement of consciousness – perceptive, emotive, discursive. Demogorgon's 'negation' initiates a sceptical 'belief' in *nothingness*,[20] i.e. in something that has no form and no colour, something which exists before all forms and colours and sounds appear. The 'imagelessness' of Demogorgon's deep truth, in that it lacks conceptualization, is actually voicelessness – a mental condition that annihilates all chattering and prejudice. Formlessness and silence are necessary in order to go beyond the limitations of intellection; an insight into 'deep truth', Shelley implies, does not come out of conceptual or imaginative conditioning, but as an intuition of the 'silent' mind, a sudden apprehension of how, or what, things are. Love, whether in its 'passive' or 'intensive' aspect, is presented as the necessary presupposition to this concept-less emptiness, inducing a receptivity without involvement in value judgements or actions of seizing / rejecting. In that the 'deep truth' is imageless, it is naked, formless, empty – the openness of the field (τόπος or χώρα?)[21] where forms appear, a spacious dimension of being which Heidegger calls 'the heightening of consciousness': 'The Open is the great whole of all that is unbounded. It lets the beings ventured into the pure draft draw as they are drawn, so that they variously draw on one another and draw together without encountering any bounds' (1971a: 106), remaining outside the 'customary consciousness of calculating production' (1971a: 128). Truth, Shelley believes, is empty (of images, preconceptions, judgements, categories, interpretations); and obviously – to borrow Keats' chiastic structure – emptiness is true.

The linguistic game between Asia and Demogorgon ends not with symbolic but realistic action, a performative utterance:

> That terrible shadow floats
> Up from its throne, as may the lurid smoke
> Of earthquake-ruined cities o'er the sea.
> Lo! it ascends the car; the coursers fly
> Terrified: watch its path among the stars
> Blackening the night!
>
> (*Prom.*, II, iv, 150–5)

The dormant power, activated through the presence (and logos) of Asia (and Panthea), is aroused and takes an upward course; its ascent leads it precisely to the throne of Jupiter / Eagle, its eternal rival. Jupiter is acutely conscious of the stages, and the effects, of the ascensional process, as a τόκος (birth) not 'in beauty' but in terror. Hence he speaks of the forthcoming event, whose inevitability he recognizes, as his own 'child' (a denomination also adopted by Demogorgon), and draws the comparison between his own present experience of 'alien' power to the words spoken by Thetis ('bright image of eternity') expressing 'her' experience of 'his' power: 'I sustain not the quick flames, / The penetrating presence; all my being, / . . . / . . . is dissolved, /

Sinking through its foundations' (III, i, 38–42). His last words before the final and irrevocable extinction are a metaphor for his opponent: 'And, like a cloud, mine enemy above / Darkens my fall with victory! Ai, Ai!' (III, i, 82–3).

The concluding speech made by Demogorgon at the end of the poem puts the whole question of the power of 'Nature' or nature of 'Power' in another perspective, and brings forth the use of the root metaphor that Shelley's imaginative explorations 'Into the mysteries of the universe' (III, iv, 105) have focused upon, the central 'Form' emblemizing 'Power' or 'Being': that of the 'serpent' – with or without its binary opponent, the 'eagle' (IV, 554–69). The passage, while instrumental in that it brings together concepts and symbols crucial to Shelley's poetic thought and metaphorical representation, is also, I think, notoriously difficult in mixing and dividing personages and roles in a manner that is unprecedented in Shelley's text: 'Heaven's despotism' presents no problem, as it suggests a clear relationship to both its mythical and symbolic counterparts, Jupiter and the vulture (eagle); Eternity / Mother is also present, ready to free 'the serpent that would clasp her with his length'. 'Eternity' and 'serpent' are evinced as different metaphysical entities, or at best variant ontological modalities of the same being; and to complicate matters more, the whole speech is uttered by Demogorgon, who in the drama is a bearer of both the 'eternal' and the 'serpentine' attributes.

In *Prometheus Unbound* the daemonic element is incarnated in the Demogorgon / Asia complex, which may be taken to represent respectively the two aspects of the Dionysian Delphic dragoness, the fluid darkness prior to form, and fire – the receptive abyss of the maternal ground and its kinetic counterpart which mysteriously activates the dormant power. Thus, in this drama, a rapport of tensions is introduced as an expression of the transformative dynamics of life force, in which creation, destruction, change, and recreation are but variations of a unitary process, and 'play' of form with formlessness. The poem expounds an awareness of the presence of the cosmic force in her repellent no less than her beautiful aspect. However, it is worth noting that in this poetic construction of 'marvels', it is the woman (in the mythical figure of Asia) who actually subjects herself to the allure and perils of darkness, who confronts 'otherness', endangerment, and terror with a respectful, if not loving, acceptance. It is she who asks the ritual questions and 'persuades' Demogorgon to assume an active role that transforms the given structure of things.

The part of the female lover is closer to that of 'quester' than 'temptress', and Asia serves as a mediator – or mediatrix – into the daring venture of becoming consciously aware of one's depth, and of life as an undivided whole. She undergoes this initiatory challenge for the 'man', but also for herself – the call to look and listen to the 'abyss'. Asia becomes a carrier of all the positive attributes of the primordial principle, I believe, while the negative ones are attributed to the 'awful gloom' of Demogorgon. Asia is the dynamic energy in constant motion, the 'electron' (to speak in the scientific idiom so beloved by Shelley), to which Demogorgon is the static counterpart, the nucleus, the latent form of energy 'acting' as the background to the dynamism of Asia (although, contrarily, it is the static form of electricity that is named 'positive' and the dynamic that is called 'negative'). It is the successful polarization of the two energies in the poem, Asia's 'dynamism' and Demogorgon's 'static support' that effects the fateful inversion, i.e. the dynamization of Demogorgon and the consequent 'withdrawal' of Asia, which results in the dethroning of Jupiter and the release of a new form of consciousness.

The first mention of Asia in the drama is made by Prometheus in a recollection of what seems to be the 'original fall' in its pre-Christian, Platonic version – the splitting of the 'one' hermaphrodite being into 'two': 'I wandered once / With Asia, drinking life from her loved eyes' (I, 122–3). A regenerative 'flow' of energy seems to be experienced by the separated lovers, which comes to replace the stillness / stagnation that weighs heavily on both. Prometheus laments: 'and thou art far, / Asia! who, when my being overflowed, / Wert like a golden chalice to bright wine / Which else had sunk into the thirsty dust' (I, 808–11). The unexpected reversal of the metaphor connects Asia with the 'cup', the container – traditional symbol of femininity. In similar terms, Panthea stresses the present condition of the repressed female principle in a world where paralysis, inertia, or depression, dominate. The Morning Star (alias Serpent) is also present in the imaginative depiction of the exiled Goddess: 'but the eastern star looks white, / And Asia waits in that far Indian vale' (I, 825–6). Asia's opening lines, an invocation to spring treating April as the cruellest month, throws bridges of recognition backwards and forwards into cultural history – to the waste land of the Grail legend and its modern revival in the Eliotic version. Shelley's text provides a middle link and should probably be read as *The Waste Land* and the *Four Quartets* together:

> As suddenly
> Thou comest as the memory of a dream,
> Which now is sad because it hath been sweet;
> Like genius, or like joy which riseth up
> As from the earth, clothing with golden clouds
> The desert of our life.
> (II, i, 7–12)

Paradoxically, the erotic consummation of Prometheus and Asia in the poem is effected 'by proxy', the mediation of Panthea who is the one that actually experiences the Promethean 'fire'. In the only scene in which the two lovers are brought together (III, iv), not only are they surrounded by a host of witnesses – Panthea, Ione, and the spirit of the Earth – but they hardly address each other. This 'distancing' in union, first becomes manifest in the narration of Panthea's dream, in whose eyes Asia can see reflected not only her own 'fairest shadow imaged there', but 'A shade, a shape' beyond their inmost depth. So the only place where Prometheus and Asia are 'seen together', or 'felt together', is literally in the mirror-like eyes of Panthea[22] who transmits to Asia the effects on her body of the 'titanic' visitation:

> I saw not, heard not, moved not, only felt
> His presence flow and mingle through my blood
> Till it became his life, and his grew mine,
> And I was thus absorbed, until it passed,
> And like the vapours when the sun sinks down,
> Gathering again in drops upon the pines,
> And tremulous as they, in the deep night
> My being was condensed . . .
> (II, i, 79–86)

Asia's descent into the underworld of daemonic gloom, as we have seen, has all the characteristics of a νέκυια or κάθοδος εἰς Ἅδην that are encountered in the epic stories of heroic adventure – with a difference, which brings the poem closer to the Grail quest rather than to the myths and rituals of 'ego' enhancement: its objective is not 'conquest' but 'questioning'. The immersion in formlessness presages a renewal of life, if consciously suffered through. In waiting, and in listening to the images – or imagelessness – of the deep, a new awareness of acceptance is developed which, of itself inactive, sets a transformative process going. Asia's 'active receptivity' to Demogorgon is expressed in her submissive and unquestioning following of the 'sound', the fearless confrontation with the 'mighty darkness', and the asking of the ritual questions of origination, 'Who made?'. The woman is presented as the conscious seeker who dares to pronounce the socially forbidden interrogation, 'What does it all mean?' or 'What is life?'. It is in the meeting with the dark, death aspects of reality – the terrifying $\Delta\alpha\acute{\iota}\mu\omega\nu$ $\Gamma o\varrho\gamma\acute{\omega}$ whose sight turns people into stone – that the release of 'flow' is generated. It is of course true that the original ceremonial event that marks the transformative process is Prometheus' speech act, the 'unsaying' of his curse upon Jupiter. Yet, the quest itself, in a deviation from the classical myths, is undertaken not by the hero, but the heroine. Throughout the 'action' of the drama the male 'component', as already suggested, remains isolated, almost indifferent, a mere inactive spectator. Having initiated action, the 'unmoved mover'[23] sits and waits for things to take their course; autonomous, static, non-productive, contemplating activity in a sort of metaphysical 'wise passiveness'.

Asia's act of persuasion is at once 'erotic' and 'rematic', the employment of 'love' and 'verbum' in the channelled awakening of the latent or dormant 'primal Power'; 'Voice is precisely what Asia must valorize and recover, making her task a parallel to, perhaps a purer form of, Prometheus' task in Act I. There he recovers voice literally when the words of his curse are returned to him. Asia must find the limits to the projection of voice outside the self, and in that discovery, cleanse voice of its deleterious powers of mystification' (Brisman 1978: 154). The metaphysics of the poem gives us a 'close up' of the rhetoric of persuasion, as it becomes manifest that questioning activates potency, which indeed discloses not only the hermeneutical but also the ontological priority of the question – the 'inquiring' state of awareness or 'open' dimension of being. Asia 'has realized that Demogorgon is not an oracle but an echo'; as such 'The oracle sees no more than its interrogator. And that is why oracles tell the truth. To see something is to make it true, for everything exists as it is perceived' (Cronin 1981: 152–3). And everything answered as asked. The 'question' motivates Demogorgon, and generates the flow or upsurge of overpowering fury from the volcanic centre of dormant potential – Demogorgon who is 'accurately described in terms of shapeless molten magma or lava' (Matthews 1957: 221); in fact 'The cave of Demogorgon is located in the crater of a volcano and the action by which he brings about the downfall of Jupiter can be equated with a volcanic eruption which has been energised by Asia and Prometheus' (Webb 1977: 220). Regeneration does or does not come – one can only make it possible for it to happen; the transformative potentiality has been there all along and will move of its own accord when mind is 'ready', when the power of the censoring tyrant has been repealed. Such 'readiness' or 'ripenness' – which is 'all' – is suggested in the poem by the wakeful expectation shared by all four protagonists, creating a chain of 'waiting' in which the totality of the human mind is revealed: Prometheus waits upon Jupiter (I, 3–4), as Asia 'waits in that far Indian vale, / The scene of her sad exile' (I, 826–7); Jupiter awaits the birth of the impregnated event, 'That fatal child, the terror of the earth, / Who waits but till the destined hour arrive, / Bearing from Demogorgon's vacant throne / The dreadful might of ever-living limbs' (III, i, 19–22); finally, Demogorgon remains as a power in abeyance, the 'snake-like Doom coiled' (II, iii, 97), potency subsisting in latent form, the primal source of life that underlies all existence.

The 'change', which Panthea is the first to observe both in Asia and in nature – 'Hearest thou not sounds i' the air which speak the love / Of all articulate beings?' (II, v, 35–6) – is the outcome of a recognition effected through the 'suffering' of Demogorgon's 'actuality' by Asia – 'love' associated with 'darkness' as well as with the beauty of the world; love or compassion is related with 'what is', and hate, violence, terror *are* as much as their desired opposites. What Asia learns through experience is that in order to develop love – universal love, cosmic love – one must accept the whole situation of life, both light and darkness, form and formlessness; one must open itself to 'being', communicate with it and its 'necessity': 'Common as light is love, / And its familiar voice wearies not ever. / Like the wide heaven, the all sustaining air, / It makes the reptile equal to the God' (II, v, 40–3). The whole world seeks Asia's sympathy, the inanimate winds are 'enamoured' of her; this passion seems to be a vast store or centre-less energy, a kind of dance of phenomena, the universe making love to itself. It appears to have two characteristics, as becomes evident in the disembodied song that fills the air: a 'fire' quality of warmth, and a tendency to 'flow' in a particular pattern, in the same way in which flame consists of spark as well as the air which contains the spark:

> Life of Life! thy lips enkindle
>   With their love the breath between them;
> And thy smiles before they dwindle
>   Make the cold air fire; then screen them
> In those looks, where whoso gazes
> Faints, entangled in their mazes.
> Child of Light! thy limbs are burning
> Through the vest which seems to hide them.
>   (II, v, 48–55)

The 'liquid splendour' is equally projected and received; more specifically, Asia emanates radiance and experiences fluidity, or sonority:

> My soul is an enchanted boat,
> Which, like a sleeping swan, doth float
> Upon the silver waves of thy sweet singing;
>   And thine doth like an angel sit
>   Beside the helm conducting it,
> Whilst all the winds with melody are ringing.
>   It seems to float ever, for ever,
>   Upon that many-winding river,
>   Between mountains, woods, abysses,
>   A paradise of wildernesses!
>   (II, v, 72–81)

Her heart responds to the controlling hands that steer the boat, she trusts in the river, the flow of life which, paradoxically, moves backwards rather than forwards, as has been already pointed out; from adulthood to youth to infancy, she floats through birth to a reborn state, a 'calm wilderness' of vaulted labyrinths 'Peopled by shapes too bright to see' (II, v, 108).

It is in one such 'vault' all overgrown and screened with vegetation that the two lovers will spend the rest of their life after their reunion, in the company of relatives and friends. Their practices will not be erotic but discursive; Asia – addressed by Prometheus as 'light of life, / Shadow of beauty unbeheld' – will participate, together with the others, in a game, not of chess, but of careful balancing of opposites, and 'metaphorical' exchanges of categories:

> A simple dwelling, which shall be our own;
> Where we will sit and talk of time and change,
> As the world ebbs and flows, ourselves unchanged.
> What can hide man from mutability?
> And if ye sigh, then I will smile, and thou,
> Ione, shall chant fragments of sea-music,
> Until I weep, when ye shall smile away
> The tears she brought, which yet were sweet to shed.
> We will entangle buds and flowers and beams
> Which twinkle on the fountain's brim, and make
> Strange combinations out of common things,
> Like human babes in their brief innocence.
>
> (III, iii, 22–33)

Shelley's iconography of 'Eternity' bears strong resemblances to other celebrated renderings of the modality of being 'outside' time and conflict: the chess-playing of Ferdinand and Miranda in *The Tempest*, the Lear–Cordelia exchange of 'We two alone will sing like birds i' th' cage', talking about 'Who loses and who wins; who's in, who's out – / And take upon's the mystery of things / As if we were God's spies' (*King Lear*, V, iii, 9–17), and Yeats' golden bird singing to the gentry of Byzantium of 'What is past, or passing, or to come' ('Sailing to Byzantium', IV).

What 'is passing' in the drama has no resemblance whatsoever to what is 'passed'. The natural transformation which uncovers 'mild and lovely forms / After some foul disguise had fallen, and all / Were somewhat changed' (III, iv, 69–71), filters through social structures, and de-activates violence and repression. The liberation of man from the evils of authority and terror is specifically presented by Shelley in terms of the emancipation of woman. Going to the core of the problem, the devaluation of femininity as an intrinsic feature of the dominant patriarchal culture, Shelley recognizes that owing to its theological, or rather metaphysical, nature, this debasement has modified the woman's own self-image as strongly as it has man's attitude to her; in responding to a vicious role created for her, woman has been to some extent responsible for her subordination. Shelley views the freedom conferred upon society not as something done, but as something 'undone': the lifting or 'en-lightening' of a burden, the oppression of the (female) population:

> None talked that common, false, cold, hollow talk
> Which makes the heart deny the *yes* it breathes,
> Yet question that unmeant hypocrisy
> With such a self-mistrust as has no name.
> And women, too, frank, beautiful, and kind
> As the free heaven which rains fresh light and dew
> On the wide earth, past; gentle radiant forms,
> From custom's evil taint exempt and pure;
> Speaking the wisdom once they could not think,
> Looking emotions once they feared to feel,
> And changed to all which once they dared not be,
> Yet being now, made earth like heaven; nor pride,
> Nor jealousy, nor envy, nor ill shame,
> The bitterest of those drops of treasured gall,
> Spoilt the sweet taste of the nepenthe, love.
>
> (III, iv, 149–63)

A subtle modification in the politics of power is observed here; its exercise is separated from despotism and used consciously and responsibly, not for ego inflation and 'self' aggrandisement at 'other's' expense. Wisdom, the forbidden γνῶσις of the serpent, now comes into the open through its natural emissary, the female, who has moved from 'not be' to 'being now', perfectly aware of herself – a 'presence' in the present situation. Σοφία, as expressed through its feminine signifier, seems to be a very 'domestic' affair indeed.

By resuming a positive attitude of non-hatred and non-condemnation, Prometheus energizes a whole series of latencies, and enhances the envigorating process whose ultimate objective is the reunion of the divorced ἀνδρόγυνον, androgyny being 'an archaic and universal formula for the expression of *wholeness*, the co-existence of the contraries, or *coincidentia oppositorum*. More than a state of sexual completeness and autarchy, androgyny symbolizes the perfection of a primordial, non-conditioned state' (Eliade 1960: 176). Their conjunction emblemizes a psychological and cosmic integration, the ἱερὸς γάμος that transmutes individual misery and 'poverty' into communal 'plenitude'; Asia

> rugged once
> And desolate and frozen, like this ravine;
> But now invested with fair flowers and herbs,
> And haunted by sweet airs and sounds which flow
> Among the woods and waters, from the aether
> Of her transforming presence, which would fade
> If it were mingled not with thine. . . .
> (I, 827–33)

And if Mary Shelley's testimony is to be trusted – identifying Asia with 'Venus and Nature' – the nuptials of *Prometheus Unbound* constitutes a solid marriage without any of the separatist tendencies found in the relevant hierogamies of *The Prelude* and *The Rime of the Ancient Mariner*, based, I think, upon Shelley's shift of 'tyranny' from the 'eye' itself to the conceptual structures that inform the eye, the egotistical illusion or defence system that safeguards 'identity'.

Denial – in fact 'forgiveness' – of the self which creates division, automatically re-establishes within the imaginative content of the poem the broken spousals between the 'man who suffers' and the 'mind which creates',[24] the πάσχειν / ποιεῖν that constitute the 'power' of 'being'. As R. Woodman affirms, 'The Promethean myth is a variation of the myth of Dionysus. Its fundamental assertion is that the creative power of the gods properly belongs to man and that through the recovery of this power man can restore his lost divinity'; he specifies that 'In Orphism the creative power is Eros, the infinite yearning in man to recover his own divine form, to remove all the veils which separate him from Dionysus, the archetype of his divine nature' (1964: 70). To the extent that the drama embodies the successful rapprochement of mind as a witnessing presence, and life force – and portrays the condition beyond the mechanical, 'artificial' intelligence of conditioned ego – it seems to me to incorporate in its 'enstatic' discourse the archetypes of Apollo and Dionysus, precisely in the way that the Platonic *Symposium* does. An interesting, though opposite view, which proposes the broken dialectic of the Apollonian / Dionysian forces in sustaining an identification of Apollo with the Shelleyan Jupiter (on the grounds of their common Olympian origin, I suppose), is offered by Woodman again, who asserts that the 'constellated androgyne' of Prometheus / Asia is an expression of Shelley's 'vision of an androgynous universe' (1981: 247), but interprets the bridal reunion as a release of 'the human mind from its enslavement to Apollo's *cyclic* domain'; in his opinion, 'The cosmos constellatt in the love union of Asia and Prometheus casts off the painted veil of the male disguise it assumes in the eye of Apollo to recover its androgynous form' (1981: 241).

In his explicit identification of the rational, analytic aspect of mind with Jupiter, and the intuitive, synthetic one with Prometheus, Shelley does not implicate Apollo into his psychic dialectics, and it is very likely that he considers the god of prophecy homologizable to Dionysus by virtue of their sharing patronage of divine madness (together with the Muses and Eros) in the fourfold schema introduced by Plato in the *Phaedrus*. The Delphic myth that presents Apollo as the slayer of the Dionysian Python does not detract, as we have seen, from the historical cohabitation of the two gods in Greek culture, of which Shelley was certainly aware when he composed his twin hymns of *Pan* and of *Apollo*, celebrating 'dance' and 'song' respectively: to Pan's 'I sang of the dancing stars, / I sang of the daedal Earth, / And of Heaven' (ll. 25–7), is juxtaposed Apollo's:

> I am the eye with which the Universe
>   Beholds itself and knows itself divine;
> All harmony of instrument or verse,
>   All prophecy, all medicine is mine,
>   All light of art or nature; – to my song
> Victory and praise in its own right belong.
>
> (ll. 31–6)

HYPERION / THE FALL OF HYPERION

Keats' poetry provides the opportunity to study the Τιτανομαχία, the dialectical engagement of Titans / Olympians, under a new model of discourse. The fact that Keats chooses Apollo as the prime mover of his conceptual and mythical system[25] indicates an a priori allegiance to the Olympian mode, probably made within the qualifying condition best expressed by Schelling who claimed that 'the "point of absolute difference" between self and the outer world was Jupiter; the ideal world was Apollo' (Wimsatt

1957: III, 376). Nevertheless, unlike the imaginative and moral clarity that invests the confrontation of Prometheus–Jupiter, which allows no margin for misinterpretation of their basic functions, the Keatsian manner of presenting his own ψυχομαχία, the Apollo–Hyperion controversy, is 'loaded' with a strong ambiguity of signification. Both 'Hyperion' poems – paradoxically named after the adversary rather than the protagonist – indicate a shift in the focus of attention that can be fully realized if we were to think, for instance, that Shelley might entitle his drama 'The Fall of Jupiter', rather than *Prometheus Unbound*.

The mythic action – or 'inaction' – of the 'Hyperions', whose structural set-up carefully refrains from bringing into direct opposition the two 'light' gods – Hyperion and Apollo – is in fact conducted in a 'limbo' or state of paralysis, a 'freezing' in-betweenness of 'not quite fallen from power' and 'not yet come into power'. Ironically, suspension of motion seems to be the chief characteristic of the progress, the 'grand march of intellect', from the Titanic to the Olympian state, expressive, I think, of the poet's attitude of equivocalness toward the transcendental forces – and human experiences – that the two gods represent. That the simplistic attitude which views the function of Hyperion 'as the Titan sun god, a power of nature which must yield to the infinitely superior Apollo, the light of the mind' (Hungerford 1941: 154) is not tenable in the poem, is amply proved not only by Keats' reluctance to bring the conflict into a culminating confrontation, but also by the poem's fragmentariness (twice). Myth having failed to act as mediator or resolver of antinomies, it allows itself to be decomposed into that strongest instance of ironic rupture, the fragment. The ambivalence underlying Keats' moral and imaginative loyalties concerning the substitution of the Olympian for the Titanic mode, his reluctance to clearly pronounce it a 'fortunate' or 'unfortunate' fall, is also reflected in the contradictory critical views that have been tackling the problematics of the 'Hyperion' poems. Against a series of 'post-lapsarian' interpretations,[26] there are a host of 'evolutionist' approaches; recognition of the historical development of consciousness from the Titanic to the Olympian, the progressive change 'from a lower to a higher order', is a constant in variant readings that focus on 'perfectibility' as the thematic core of the poems.[27] Such antithetical exegeses suggest that the mythical transformation embodied in *Hyperion* and *The Fall of Hyperion* may be one simultaneously from / to 'culture' and 'history'.[28]

The structure of both 'Hyperion' poems betrays a complexity of motion, a dual directionality that cannot be identified simply with the forward process of evolution: it is regressive as much as progressive, oriented towards teleology as much as cosmogony – looking forward and backward to ends and beginnings. In fact one might argue that action has reached a 'zero' point, as 'progress' and 'regress' cancel each other establishing an 'inscape' where pictorial, and physical, components are those of inertia, paralysed motion, gloom, and alternate extremities of the sensations of cold and heat. In its acute preoccupation with 'origins' – modalities of 'being' prior to the one currently experienced – Keats' version of the Hyperion myth exhibits his concern for 'grounding', the retrospective attitude of mind, as well as the Romantic obsession with return to origination (whether on the personal or collective level). The paradox of the desired condition, a return to the unconscious, emphasizes the anxiety and dilemma of the Romantic thinker when he comes to reconcile 'myth' with his intense awareness of 'historicity', to translate an 'either / or' situation into a 'both / and'. Having to choose between pre-reflective unconsciousness through identification with nature, and expansion of self-consciousness through self-reflection – the Dionysian and Apollonian modalities of ecstatic and enstatic experience – the Romantic poet, and specifically Keats, opts for a dialectical synthesis that far from establishing a firm conceptual – and experiential – bond between the two reponses, leads to contradiction and confusion. In his choice of this specific moment from the Τιτανομαχία, the one I have termed as the convergence of the 'not quite' and the 'not yet', Keats mythologizes the condition of his own mind, the ψυχομαχία or conflict between the needs to 'grow up' and 'grow down', which results in 'growing still'. Images of depth, listlessness, and 'frozen' power are the dominant iconography of the Hyperion story as such, whether in its first 'fragmentary' version, or its second 'dreamlike' one. The rhetorical shift of 'fragment' into 'dream' suggests a transference from a world of divisible objects to a state of composite fluidity. Yet not even the 'chameleon' fluctuations of the dream vision, where the boundaries between categories and modes of being are melted, can effect the desired event of Hyperion's 'fall' (apparently a venture unparalleled to the analogical 'fall' of Jupiter in *Prometheus Unbound*) since the poem 'ends', despite its title, with Hyperion 'flaring on'.

But to take the story from the beginning, or rather the *media res* into which Keats' narration plunges us:

> Deep in the shady sadness of a vale
> Far sunken from the healthy breath of morn,
> Far from the fiery noon, and eve's one star,
> Sat gray-hair'd Saturn, quiet as a stone,
> Still as the silence round about his lair;
> Forest on forest hung about his head
> Like cloud on cloud. No stir of air was there,
> Not so much life as on a summer's day
> Robs not one light seed from the feather'd grass,
> But where the dead leaf fell, there did it rest.
> A stream went voiceless by, still deadened more
> By reason of his fallen divinity
> Spreading a shade: the Naiad 'mid her reeds
> Press'd her cold finger closer to her lips.
>
> (*Hyp.*, I, 1–14)

The portrayal of 'stony' images populating the deep shade of this dead land, the voiceless stream and stir-less air, the depraved gods deprived of power, 'deadened more / By reason', or 'by reason of' their 'fallen divinity', indicate a mental landscape analogous to the sluggishness of the 'horror' stage of the Mariner's transformative journey, and the terrors of Prometheus' imprisonment (not to mention the lifelessness and emptiness of later 'waste lands' and 'hollow men').

The novelty that *The Fall of Hyperion* establishes, besides the change in title and the distancing from reality that the subtitle implies, is a narrative technique which, rather than effecting the expected 'difference' – in being a report of someone in a dream, who dreams that he is listening – 'enters' the observer, and the speaker (Poet / Goddess) of the frame-story into the 'history' or plot of events that are being represented. The emphasis on the conversational mode that the remodelled version of the poem introduces, has quite the opposite effect from the expectations of a dream condition; by anchoring dream on the actuality of daily human transactions, it familiarizes the unfamiliar. Without suggesting an influence (though by no means excluding the possibility), the paradigmatic fictional relation that *The Fall of Hyperion* 'copies' in its Poet–Priestess initiatory encounter, is the

Socrates–Diotima one. Keats' Hyperion allegory may be seen to mirror the Platonic text in yet an additional manner: it exhibits the emotional ambivalence of attitude to, and evaluation of, the age of Cronus that is characteristic of Plato's treatment of the 'titanic'.

The unfolding of the 'cosmic story' by the Stranger to the young Socrates in the *Statesman*, distinguishes between two periods in human history, the 'Titanic' (under the government of Cronus) and the 'present' – known as 'Olympian' – (under the rule of Zeus). The quality of life in each period is radically different: Cronus' age is described as one of paradisal existence, God being 'supreme governor in charge of the actual rotation of the universe', and a 'heavenly daemon' being the shepherd of 'every herd of living creatures' (271d). And when the age of Cronus came to 'its destined end', 'the pilot of the ship of the universe . . . let go the handle of its rudder and retired to his conning tower in a place apart. Then destiny and its own inborn urge took control of the world again and reversed the revolution of it' (272d–e). Hence all daemons withdrew from their appointed regions, as 'A shudder passed through the world at the reversing of its rotation, checked as it was between the old control and the new impulse which had turned end into beginning for it and beginning into end' (273a). As the bodily element, Plato continues his μῦθος, took dominion over the world, the 'primal chaotic condition', the root of all wrongs and evils, began to reassert itself – the 'ancient condition of chaos' looming threateningly, and 'forgetfulness of God' setting in. Nevertheless, God's concern for the created world – lest it might 'be dissolved again in the bottomless abyss of unlikeness' – induces him, at some point before utter disintegration has liquidated existence into formlessness, to take 'control of the helm once more', and heal its 'former sickness' (273b–e). That Plato should present the 'Olympian' stage of world history as a degradation from the 'Titanic' – as an era 'bereft of the guardian care of the daemon'[29] – has perhaps induced Shelley to make his astonishing declaration that the model for *Prometheus Unbound* is not Aeschylus but Plato (1905: 207).

The 'cosmic crisis' of Keats' Hyperion myth, the peak experience of the transition from the 'old' to the 'new' order, is a state of suspended animation attributed to a sense of 'loss', fragmentation, fall from power. In the first of the seven intrusions that interrupt the narration in *The Fall of Hyperion* version, coming precisely after l. 3 of the earlier work, the Poet is confronted with a saying / showing situation that speaks of an eternal 'sitting', waiting, and passive suffering:

> Onward I look'd beneath the gloomy boughs,
> And saw, what first I thought an image huge,
> Like to the image pedestal'd so high
> In Saturn's temple. Then Moneta's voice
> Came brief upon mine ear – 'So Saturn sat
> When he had lost his Realms –' . . .
> (I, 297–302)

The strong feeling of depression that is imparted from the scene back to the observers is stressed in the second critical intervention, after l. 25 of the original text: 'Then came the griev'd voice of Mnemosyne, / And griev'd I hearken'd' (*Fall*, I, 331–2). Saturn's hand is seen lying 'nerveless, listless, dead', and in Thea's face 'there was a listening fear'; language itself has been de-energized, dropping to a minimal articulatory capacity: 'O how frail / To that large utterance of the early Gods!' (*Hyp.*, I, 50–1), Thea laments.

Saturn, the 'poor old King', is the ailing king of a waste land, awaiting liberation through the intervention of Hyperion, the only one of the old divinities still 'empowered'. The debasement of all the elements is emphasized: the earth is 'afflicted', ocean 'pass'd', air 'emptied', lightning 'scorches and burns', and time is 'aching'. The ambiguity in signification of time 'in pain' and 'moments big as years' – the agony of disease but also of labour – points toward the dualism of πάσχειν as repressive destruction or creative possibility. The psychic dynamics of 'arrest' that the myth dramatizes as 'freezing' may be taken to portray both annihilation and latency: 'And still these two were postured motionless, / Like natural sculpture in cathedral cavern; / The frozen God still couchant on the earth, / And the sad Goddess weeping at his feet' (*Hyp.*, I, 85–8). The 'still' does not convey the stillness of repose in fulfilment of desire, but a condition of paralysis induced by fear.

The commentary in *The Fall of Hyperion*, interpolated precisely at this point, is even more revealing, as it marks an withdrawal of the projected mental suffering from the mythical correlative to its existential source, where the fixity of imagery is revealed for what it really is: the unbearable tension of a soul in pain:

> A long awful time
> I look'd upon them; still they were the same;
> The frozen God still bending to the earth,
> And the sad Goddess weeping at his feet,
> Moneta silent. Without stay or prop,
> But my own weak mortality, I bore
> The load of this eternal quietude,
> The unchanging gloom, and the three fixed shapes
> Ponderous upon my senses, a whole moon.
> For by my burning brain I measure sure
> Her silver seasons shedded on the night,
> And ever day by day methought I grew
> More gaunt and ghostly. – Oftentimes I pray'd
> Intense, that Death would take me from the Vale
> And all its burthens – gasping with despair
> Of change, hour after hour I curs'd myself.
> (I, 384–99)

The metaphorical language not only rings ominously close to the metaphysical, and physical, climate of the *Ancient Mariner* – with the only difference of substituting an alternating pattern of cursing / praying for the sequential one of Coleridge's poem – but carries distinct echoes of some of the key themes of Keats' poetic thoughts as expressed most clearly in his letters: the concern with intensity, heaviness, self-forgetfulness. The 'burning brain' appears in an early letter of 1817, where Keats refers to his intellectual passion: 'thought so much about Poetry so long together that I could not get to sleep at night . . . Another thing I was too much in Solitude, and consequently was obliged to be in continual burning of thought as an only resource' (1958: I, 138–9). The words 'load' and 'quietude' that characterize the dark and heated immobility of the poetic experience point in two directions, which invert the negative connotations of the phrase: the 'Cave of Quietude' in *Endymion*, the 'Happy gloom! / Dark Paradise', whose 'silence dreariest / Is most articulate' (IV, 537–40), as the place where is effected the transmutation of suffering into poetry, πάσχειν into ποιεῖν; similarly, Keats affirms in his prose writings that the 'load' weighing on mortality is transformable to its opposite: 'the feverous relief of Poetry

seems a much less crime – This morning Poetry has conquered
. . . And I am thankful for it – There is an awful warmth about
my heart like a load of Immortality' (1958: I, 370).

The analogy between the mythical vale of the fallen Saturn, the theological 'vale of tears', and the existential 'vale of Soul-making' – one of the most original of Keats' philosophical conceptions – is made clear in the discursive passage from *The Fall of Hyperion* just cited, where the prominence of 'Vale / And all its burthens' relates Titanic to human suffering. Keats' unorthodox ontology turns psyche from metaphysical entity to historical process – the product of the interaction of 'intelligence' and 'heart' in the context of 'world' (1958: II, 102). Keats not only dismantles soul of its divine origin, but through identifying it with subjectivity, the individualism of personality, makes it one with ego, or the sense of separate self. The paradox of a 'soul-less' poet, as an existent that has no 'identity' and hence no personal history – 'A Poet is the most unpoetical of any thing in existence; because he has no Identity – he is continually in for – and filling some other Body' (1958: I, 387) – is indicative, I think, not of a lack of 'proper action of *Mind and Heart* on each other for the purpose of forming the *Soul* or *Intelligence destined to possess the sense of Identity*' (1958: II, 102), but of its possibly remaining unrecorded in memory.

Saturn characteristically speaks of his destitution as a loss of identity: 'I am gone / "Away from my own bosom: I have left / "My strong identity, my real self, / "Somewhere between the throne, and where I sit / "Here on this spot of earth' (*Hyp.*, I, 112–16). The ardent desire for the reinstatement of lost identity (and power), is further devitalized in the second version of the poem, where the admonition 'Search, Thea, search' is rephrased into the invocation 'Moan, Cybele, moan!'. The narrative practice of commentatory intrusion in *The Fall of Hyperion*, makes stronger at this point the thinly covered metaphor of 'human' affliction in its 'divine' impersonation:

> Methought I heard some old man of the earth
> Bewailing earthly loss; nor could my eyes
> And ears act with that pleasant unison of sense
> Which marries sweet sound with the grace of form,
> And dolorous accent from a tragic harp
> With large-limb'd visions. – More I scrutinized:

> Still fix'd he sat beneath the sable trees,
> Whose arms spread straggling in wild serpent forms,
> With leaves all hush'd . . .
>
> (I, 440–8)

The realization of an impassable gulf between 'dolour' and 'vision', suffering and creativity, πάθημα and ποίημα, is also the theme of Saturn's speech; even though 'This passion lifted him upon his feet', it seems that passion can do no more than produce an utterance of dejection at the loss of the creative potential: ' "But cannot I create? / "Cannot I form? Cannot I fashion forth / "Another world, another universe, / "To overbear and crumble this to nought? / "Where is another chaos? Where?" ' (*Hyp.*, I, 141–5).

The point of Saturn's and Thea's departure for visiting the prison-house of the fallen Titans, marks not only a thematic and structural transition (indicated by the blank space in *Hyperion*, and the transfer from Canto I to Canto II in *The Fall of Hyperion*) but, most importantly, a psychological or ontological one into altered forms of consciousness, or 'other' modalities of being beyond the threshold – a transportation from the antechamber of πάθημα to the inner chamber of πάθος:

> Ere I could turn, Moneta cried, 'These twain
> 'Are speeding to the families of grief,
> 'Where roof'd in by black rocks they waste, in pain
> 'And darkness, for no hope.' – And she spake on,
> As ye may read who can unwearied pass
> Onward from the Antichamber of this dream,
> Where even at the open doors awhile
> I must delay, and glean my memory
> Of her high phrase: – perhaps no further dare.
>
> (*Fall*, I, 460–8)

Moneta's 'high language', as she herself explains in the opening lines of Canto II, is a sustained metaphor which translates 'Word' into 'word' (the Platonic mythical method of 'tales of approximation'); it is 'likeness' that marries the 'other' to the 'same', the unknown to the known – speaking not of what things 'are' but what they 'are like' – as approach to the object is made imperfectly and by a series of analogies:

ΠΑΘΗΜΑ AND ΠΟΙΗΜΑ

> 'Mortal, that thou may'st understand aught,
> 'I humanize my sayings to thine ear,
> 'Making comparisons of earthly things;
> 'Or thou might'st better listen to the wind,
> 'Whose language is to thee a barren noise,
> 'Though it blows legend-laden thro' the trees. –
> (*Fall*, II, 1–6)

The 'metastasis' annunciated in the various rhetorical devices that have been mentioned, is not one from 'gloom' to 'gloom', but from 'darkness' to 'light' – or better 'fire' – the section's opening line, 'Meanwhile in other realms', serving only as a brief transference / introduction to the 'high argument'. The expression 'but one' of l. 13 (*Hyp.*, I, 164), emphasizes the exceptional condition of exclusiveness cast upon its bearer, but also the equivocal precariousness in power – of one who 'still kept', 'still sat', 'still sniff'd', 'yet unsecure' – in the dialectic of still / yet that constitutes the structural organizing principle of the poem:

> But one of the whole mammoth-brood still kept
> His sov'reingty, and rule, and majesty; –
> Blazing Hyperion on his orbed fire
> Still sat, still snuff'd the incense, teeming up
> From man to the sun's God; yet unsecure:
> For as among us mortals omens drear
> Fright and perplex, so also shuddered he –
> (*Hyp.*, I, 164–70)

The alternation of a tensive pattern of fear / anger or deflation / inflation marks the contractive / expansive motion, ebb and flow of power, as 'horrors, portion'd to a giant nerve, / Oft made Hyperion ache'; it is a 'horror', however, accompanied by 'glory', as 'His palace bright / Bastion'd with pyramids of glowing gold, / And touch'd with shade of bronzed obelisks, / Glar'd a blood-red through all its thousand courts, / Arches, and domes, and fiery galleries' (*Hyp.*, I, 175–80).

Hyperion is a wrathful sun whose anger stems from fright; savouring 'poisonous brass and metal sick' instead of 'spicy wreaths / Of incense', 'Amaz'd and full of fear', he transmutes his imminent destruction to an immanent fierce destructiveness. The imaginative introduction into the scene of a second doorway, the western 'passage' from light to darkness – 'Hyperion leaving twilight in the rear, / Came slope upon the threshold of the west'

ΠΑΘΗΜΑ AND ΠΟΙΗΜΑ

(*Hyp.*, I, 203–4) – paradoxically induces an inverted condition of 'dawning' to the initiate of *The Fall of Hyperion*, who at this point makes his last – and final – entry into Moneta's stream of narrative:

> Now in clear light I stood,
> Reliev'd from the dusk vale. Mnemosyne
> Was sitting on a square-edg'd polish'd stone,
> That in its lucid depth reflected pure
> Her priestess-garments. – My quick eyes ran on
> From stately nave to nave, from vault to vault,
> Through bow'rs of fragrant and enwreathed light,
> And diamond-paved lustrous long archades.
> Anon rush'd by the bright Hyperion;
> His flaming robes stream'd out beyond his heels,
> And gave a roar, as if of earthly fire,
> That scared away the meek etherial hours,
> And made their dove-wings tremble. On he flared.
>   (II, 49–61)

If the fervent action of the Titanic sun in a way duplicates the burning horrors of the Typhonic sun in the *Ancient Mariner*, Hyperion's fearful language subsumes all the characteristic images of the Promethean confrontation with the Furies:

> 'O dreams of day and night!
> 'O monstrous forms! O effigies of pain!
> 'O spectres busy in a cold, cold gloom!
> 'O lank-ear'd Phantoms of black-weeded pools!
> 'Why do I know ye? Why have I seen ye? Why
> 'Is my eternal essence thus distraught
> 'To see and to behold these horrors new?
> 'Saturn is fallen, am I too to fall?
>   (*Hyp.*, I, 227–34)

The mental – and physical – 'space' that Keats calls 'Hyperion' is an inscape of alternate sensations of fire and frost, severe warmth and ice-cold, extremities of burning and freezing. The 'blaze', the 'splendour', the 'fiery frontier', are counterpoised by 'Phantoms pale', 'thrice horrible and cold'. Serpentine convulsions and 'palpitations' 'frenzy' the 'bright Titan' – 'primeval God' – not only into 'Actions of rage and passions', but into sufferings of panic and pain:

And from the mirror'd level where he stood
A mist arose, as from a scummy marsh.
At this, through all his bulk an agony
Crept gradual, from the flesh into the crown,
Like a lithe serpent vast and muscular
Making slow way, with head and neck convuls'd
From over-strained might. . . .
(Hyp., I, 257–63)

The distress of violent muscular spasms to which Hyperion is subjected through the presence of excessive power – 'from over-strained might' – possibly indicates the god's intoxication by the Dionysian presence within (Dionysus' dismemberment and devouring by the Titans being one of the major events in the relevant myth), as his bodily motions and postures 'imitate' the jerking necks and tossing heads of maenadic possession. 'Releas'd', Hyperion goes about his normal route of sky activities and rotations, 'signifiers' of a forgotten archaic language,

> hieroglyphics old
> Which sages and keen-eyed astrologers
> Then living on the earth, with labouring thought
> Won from the gaze of many centuries:
> Now lost, save what we find on remnants huge
> Of stone, or marble swart; their import gone,
> Their wisdom long since fled. . . .
(Hyp., I, 277–83)

Book II of *Hyperion* introduces a new area of 'middle earth' where two correlated movements converge: the upward 'icy' progress of Saturn and the downward 'fiery' progress (or regress) of Hyperion; the place of 'meeting' is the prison-house of the Titans lying in unimaginable poses that suggest a violent distortion of 'nature': 'Lock'd up like veins of metal, crampt and screw'd; / Without a motion, save of their big hearts / Heaving in pain, and horribly convuls'd / With sanguine feverous boiling gurge of pulse' (ll. 25–8). The 'fallen tribe' includes – to mention only the most familiar or relevant ones – Typhon, Asia, Atlas, Phorcus ('the sire of Gorgons'), Oceanus and Tethys, Themis and Ops, all mingled in a shadow world of non-differentiation, 'No shape distinguishable, more than when / Thick night confounds the pine-tops with the clouds' (II, 79–80).

It is to this darkness and suffering that Saturn and Thea have climbed 'from a depth / More horrid still' (II, 85–6). To this unthinking desolation Saturn brings the 'light' of rationality, as his voice loaded 'With thunder and with music' seeks the causality that necessitated the present condition – in the twice repeated clamorous realization: ' "Can I find reason why ye should be thus' – to which (unlike Plato's theory of cosmic periodicity (*Statesm.*, 269–70)) he finds no corresponding law of evolution, having studied 'Nature's universal scroll'.

The debate initiated by Saturn affords the opportunity for an ardent exposition of evolutionism and perfectibility (Aristotelian, Christian, and rationalistic in its origin), furnishing a teleogical model within which the 'fall' of the Titanic element must be interpreted. Oceanus becomes the spokesman for the law of growth, the 'eternal truth' of a 'grand march of intellect', the progressive change from a lower (chaotic) to a higher (structured) mode of existence. Reassuring the grudging Titans that ' "We fall by course of Nature's law, not force / "Of thunder' (II, 181–2), he traces the unfolding of consciousness from its earliest beginnings, as a dynamic pattern of irreversible advancement:

>'And first, as thou wast not the first of powers,
>'So art thou not the last; it cannot be:
>'Thou art not the beginning nor the end.
>'From chaos and parental darkness came
>'Light, the first fruits of that intestine broil,
>'That sullen ferment, which for wondrous ends
>'Was ripening in itself. The ripe hour came,
>'And with it light, and light, engendering
>'Upon its own producer, forthwith touch'd
>'The whole enormous matter into life.
>   (II, 188–97)

Evolutionism is presented in the manner of a gradual change, or idealization process, from chaos / darkness to form / light, bearing the unmistakable 'signs of purer life' – solidity, beauty, freedom, friendship. The linear transition from primitivism and unconsciousness to consciousness and 'soul-making', Oceanus proclaims, compels the displacement of the 'less' by the 'more' perfect:

> 'So on our heels a fresh perfection treads,
> 'A power more strong in beauty, born of us
> 'And fated to excel us, as we pass
> 'In glory that old Darkness: nor are we
> 'Thereby more conquer'd, than by us the rule
> 'Of Shapeless Chaos. . . .
>
> (II, 212–17)

The joining of 'beauty' and 'power' in the verbal formation of ' "That first in beauty should be first in might' (II, 229), confirmed in Oceanus' oration, finds its 'transcendental signified' in the succeeding speech of Clymene, 'embodying' concept into image: the abstract beauty is concretized in a 'new blissful golden melody' that converts Titanic 'roar' into Apollonian 'music'. In her tale of annunciation, the Titaness recounts how she was made,

>   sick
> 'Of joy and grief at once. Grief overcame,
> 'And I was stopping up my frantic ears,
> 'When, past all hindrance of my trembling hands,
> 'A voice came sweeter, sweeter than all tune,
> 'And still it cried, "Apollo! young Apollo!
> ' "The morning-bright Apollo! young Apollo!"
> 'I fled, it follow'd me and cried "Apollo!"
>
> (II, 288–95)

Her utterance of mixed feelings of enchantment, aversion, and alarm is literally shaken by the earthquake explosion of Enceladus whose 'inductive' speech becomes the fervent introduction – all 'flames', 'burning', 'fierceness', and 'fire' – to the radiant appearance of Hyperion who rose 'suddenly a splendour, like the morn' – a light in sound, a sound-like power in light:

> And all the everlasting cataracts,
> And all the headlong torrents far and near,
> Mantled before in darkness and huge shade,
> Now saw the light and made it terrible.
> It was Hyperion: – a granite peak
> His bright feet touch'd, and there he stay'd to view
> The misery his brilliance had betray'd
> To the most hateful seeing of itself.
>
> (II, 363–70)

A light made 'terrible' by what is reflected in it, a terrible beauty which in its turn 'betrays' the perceiver by illuminating an ugliness that cannot possibly be tolerated, makes 'crude and sore / The journey homeward to habitual self!' and 'Cheats us into the swamp, into a fire, / Into the bosom of a hated thing' (*End.*, II, 275–80).

The empty 'space' that intervenes between Books II and III of the mythical epic of *Hyperion* is not just optical and structural; it denotes a chasm or break, a missing link in the evolutionary chain of developmental process, a leaping over or 'out' of the μεταξύ condition. The presence of an 'error' in the mechanism of transformation that is to convert the 'titanic' into the 'olympian' – a lower to a higher mode of consciousness, πάσχειν into ποιεῖν – is amply indicated in the rhetorical impass that results in fragmentation, turning re-membering into actual dis-membering. The poet intentionally disentangles himself from the world of alternate fury and calm, with a sense of uselessness and repulsion for 'old darkness' – an attitude probably to be expected from someone who admits, 'I did wed / Myself to things of light from infancy' (*End.*, IV, 957–8):

> Thus in alternate uproar and sad peace,
> Amazed were those Titans utterly.
> O leave them, Muse! O leave them to their woes;
> For thou art weak to sing such tumults dire:
> A solitary sorrow best befits
> Thy lips, and antheming a lonely grief.
> Leave them, O Muse! For thou anon wilt find
> Many a fallen old Divinity
> Wandering in vain about bewildered shores.
>   (*Hyp.*, III, 1–11)

Between past 'amazement' and future 'bewilderment', the imagery that occupies the 'meantime' introduces an amalgamation of music – 'Delphic harp' and 'Dorian flute' – and proceeds with detailed depiction of a landscape that expresses a rising crescendo or intensification of all the senses: rose glows intense, air warms, clouds float in voluptuousness, wine boils cold, labyrinthine shells turn vermilion (the scarlet form of mercuric sulphide), and the maid is flushed with erotic expectation in the passionate intensity that makes all disagreeables evaporate – when 'every sense had grown / Ethereal for pleasure' (*End.*, II,

671–2). As the 'pleasure thermometer' rises, the transcendence of past modalities of existence is triumphantly announced in 'Apollo is once more the golden theme! / Where was he, when the Giant of the Sun / Stood bright, amid the sorrow of his peers? / Together' (*Hyp.*, III, 28–31). The 'togetherness' is a misleading configuration, as it refers to Apollo's mother / sister complex and not to the expected direct confrontation between the rival gods; it is as if the two light-gods inhabit different realms of being – ontologically secluded or psychologically divided by an unbridgeable chasm.

The need of mediation recognized, the mediator appears in the personage of 'an awful Goddess', the Titaness Mnemosyne, one of the very few still free 'to roam about' and stray the world. The recognition scene that follows is a powerful symbolic projection of the encounter between 'new heroism' and 'old desertion' – Mnemosyne characterizing herself as 'an ancient Power / "Who hath forsaken old and sacred thrones / "For prophecies of thee, and for the sake / "Of loveliness new born!" ' (III, 76–9). The goddess' role as primordial memory and source of inspiration is well defined in the mythology of remembering / forgetting. As Eliade remarks, 'The Goddess Mnemosyne, personification of "Memory," sister of Kronos and Okeanos, is the mother of the Muses'; so 'When the poet is possessed by the Muses', he reminds us, 'he draws directly from Mnemosyne's store of knowledge, that is, especially from the knowledge of "origins," of "beginnings," of genealogies'. Past knowledge, Eliade affirms, is not a chronicle sought for its own sake, but as the birthplace of the present, the womb where generation takes place; 'recollection does not seek to situate events in a temporal frame but to reach the depths of being, to discover the original, the primordial reality from which the cosmos issued and which makes it possible to understand becoming as a whole' (1963: 120).

The paradoxical element in the dialogic exchange between Mnemosyne and Apollo is the 'unborn' god's referring to himself as an already 'fallen' being – subject not to unknowing innocence but knowledgeable forgetfulness; the myth of 'memory' and the myth of 'loss' seem to be inextricably linked:

> For me, dark, dark,
> 'And painful vile oblivion seals my eyes:
> 'I strive to search wherefore I am so sad,

> 'Until a melancholy numbs my limbs;
> 'And then upon the grass I sit, and moan,
> 'Like one who once had wings. . . .
>
> (III, 86–91)

That the need for memory is in fact a remembrance of forgetfulness and quest for origins, is enhanced by the Platonic image of the wing-less soul, the mystery of deprivation. Apollo, however, speaks from within the Christian awareness of 'damnation', himself a link in a long chain of malediction, at once patient and agent of denunciation: 'O why should I / "Feel curs'd and thwarted, when the liegeless air / "Yields to my step aspirant? why should I / "Spurn the green turf as hateful to my feet?' (III, 91–4). In an attitude of 'nothing is but what is not' (*Macbeth*, I, iii, 141), Apollo yearns for things that are 'absent', that have disappeared from the world of phenomena.

The desire to substitute 'absence' (un-remembered event) for 'presence' (visible fact) is more of a yearning for 'another presence' undetected by the senses, the annihilation of the temporal and spatial; he seeks 'some unknown being', 'other regions', 'the way' to metempirical experience – all subsumed in his overwhelming 'imperial' question: 'Where is power?'. Apollo's cognitive expedition is in fact not philosophical but political, not a search after knowledge *per se*, but knowledge instrumental as the awakening of, or to, 'power'. Interaction with power is effected through the 'reading' of 'silence', in which the 'mute' face of Mnemosyne plays the role of 'text' – or that reflexive text, the mirror. Although language as such is bypassed, the 'linguistic' is one of the signifiers chosen for the encoding of the experience, the other being the 'intoxicant':

> 'Mute thou remainest – mute! yet I can read
> 'A wondrous lesson in thy silent face:
> 'Knowledge enormous makes a God of me.
> 'Names, deeds, grey legends, dire events, rebellions,
> 'Majesties, sovran voices, agonies,
> 'Creations and destroyings, all at once
> 'Pour into the wide hollows of my brain,
> 'And deify me, as if some blithe wine
> 'Or bright elixir peerless I had drunk,
> 'And so become immortal.' . . .
>
> (III, 111–20)

ΠΑΘΗΜΑ AND ΠΟΙΗΜΑ

The passage depicts the ecstatic excitement of the speaker at this sudden – and 'collective' – re-collection of the past, the instantaneous recreation of a forgotten world by encapsulating events spaced out in time into the coincidence of synchronicity – 'creations and destroyings all at once'.

What deserves our unwavering attention from this point to the end – or rather sudden interruption – of the poem, is, I believe, the phenomenology and physiology of the metamorphic process that Keats records in minutest detail. The signs and symptoms of Apollo's 'rebirth' are primarily occurences of contortion and muscular spasms, as if the body were caught in the grip of a rending, undulatory force: the transfixing of 'enkindled' gaze, the agony of extreme cold transmuted into unbearable heat, his 'eager neck' convulsed. In the emphasis given to the physical aspect of metamorphosis, very little is known of the spiritual component of the regenerative process, except that it is a death 'into life':

>   Thus the God,
> While his enkindled eyes, with level glance
> Beneath his white soft temples, steadfast kept
> Trembling with light upon Mnemosyne.
> Soon wild commotions shook him, and made flush
> All the immortal fairness of his limbs;
> Most like the struggle at the gate of death;
> Or liker still to one who should take leave
> Of pale immortal death, and with a pang
> As hot as death's is chill, with fierce convulse
> Die into life: so young Apollo anguish'd:
> His very hair, his golden tresses famed
> Kept undulation round his eager neck.
> During the pain Mnemosyne upheld
> Her arms as one who prophesied. – At length
> Apollo shriek'd; – and lo! from all his limbs
> Celestial
>   (III, 120–36)

The 'fierce convulse' and intense warmth induced by a violent and excessive surfacing of sacred power, as the would-be god, dying to the human condition, is initiated into 'life'; the aching horrors that shake his nerves, the flushed limbs and frenzied gestures, the anguish of wrath and the fury of passion; the stormy influx of energy manifested in spontaneous physical movements, the rippling and shaking of the body, the contortions of the head; finally, the culmination of agony in a sudden outburst that tears his inner being, coercing the 'shriek', shrill cry or wild laugh – are unmistakable signs of the supreme ontological irony of Apollo's transformation into Hyperion.

As a regress towards the origins of life, or 'being', such μεταμόρφωσις is 'into' rather than 'away from' the primeval, the chaotic, the titanic – the Dionysian. In a process that is 'involutionary' rather than evolutionary (and certainly revolutionary rather than developmental) rebirth becomes a *regressus ad uterum*, a return to the dynamic source of which Hyperion is the last-but-one manifestation. In his discussion of 'the orgiastic, Dionysiac mood' Cassirer stresses its underlying attitude which 'feels the I only as a violent rending away from the primal source of life, and what it strives for is a return to that source'; from this perspective, individuality can only be seen as 'the factor of tragic isolation', and is 'directly represented in the myth of Dionysius–Zagreus, who is torn to pieces and devoured by the Titans' (1955b: 197). The cosmic story that Mnemosyne disclosed to Apollo must of necessity have taken him to 'creations and destroyings' far beyond the portion of myth incorporated in the *Hyperion* fragment, to the 'point' before the fall of the 'wicked Titans, who trapped the infant Dionysus, tore him to bits, boiled him, roasted him, ate him, and were themselves immediately burned up by a thunderbolt from Zeus; from the smoke of their remains', we are informed, 'sprang the human race, who thus inherit the horrid tendencies of the Titans, tempered by a tiny portion of divine soul-stuff, which is the substance of the god Dionysus still working in them as an occult self' (Dodds 1951: 155). A reading of the poem that sees the whole transformation process as the transfiguring of Apollo into Hyperion / Dionysus rather than vice versa, justifies, I believe, both the title of the work and its abrupt inconclusiveness, betraying Keats' inability to handle a poetic situation of insurmountable ambivalence which, expressive of an intentionality to turn πάσχειν into ποιεῖν, finds itself drawn into the existential metaphysics of passion and μανία – a state that has no place in the progress of enlightened humanitarianism, the grand march of intellect that Keats 'seems' to endorse as the ideological core of the poem.

In his exposition of regressive myths and techniques, the sailing upstream in the flow of time, history, and – inevitably – memory, Eliade draws a distinction that can be used as the informative model exemplifying the structural and stylistic divergences of the two 'Hyperion' poems, beyond the obvious connotations of 'fragmentation' and 'elusiveness' that their subtitles imply. Eliade points out that 'there are several ways of "going back," but the most important are: (1) rapid and direct re-establishment of the first situation . . . and (2) progressive return to the "origin" by proceeding backward through Time from the present moment to the "absolute beginning" '. The first mode of transformation, he notes, is characterized by a sudden 'instantaneous abolition of the Cosmos', an immediate transition to 'chaos', 'seed', or 'embryon'; conversely, 'In the second case – that of gradual return to the origin – we have a meticulous and exhaustive recollecting of personal and historical events'. A new time register is introduced in that a detailed and laborious retrospection into the incidents of one's own personal history is essential, 'for it is only by virtue of this recollection that one can "burn up" one's past, master it, keep it from affecting the present'. He continues: 'The difference from the first method, whose model is instantaneously abolishing the World and re-creating it, is obvious. Here *memory* plays the leading role. One frees oneself from the work of Time by recollection, by *anamnesis*.[30] The essential thing is to remember all the events one has witnessed in Time' (1963: 88–9). In this second-type regression, private history is the material that has to be grappled with and related to.

Both the narrative technique and the title of *The Fall of Hyperion. A Dream* suggest an inversion of process that substitutes 'involution' for evolution in an 'enfolding' rather than unfolding of mind, analogous to the Platonic περιαγωγή (the turning round and looking back), rather than a teleological 'march of intellect'. The historical progression and heroic dimensions of the earlier epic having collapsed – in the final recognition of the survival of nuclei of 'darkness' (fire and fury) in supposedly 'enlightened' forms of being – evolutionism surrenders to a dreamy retrogression – dreams and the way of thinking peculiar to dreams revealing, according to Jung, regressive states of mind characteristic of earlier phases of life. The myth proper, the narration of the fallen state of the Titans, does not begin in this remodelled version until l. 294, and covers only about one third of the text. The introductory section or sections of Canto I consist primarily of two structural units – the first expository, the second imaginative – initiating the transition from the reality principle to the dream world. Despite their difference in context and discourse, the exterior world of logic and activity and the interior world of psychic continuum are constructed on the same dialectical opposition expressed in a variety of forms, as fanatic / poet, poet / sage, and poet / dreamer. The distinctive feature of the first unexpected antithetical pair should be sought in the definition of a 'fanatic' as one possessed by an excessive enthusiasm for, or devotion to, a theory, belief, line of action; as the opposite pole to the 'exclusive intentionality' of the 'fanatic', the 'poet' is construed as the expounder of 'inclusive extensiveness', making of his mind a thoroughfare for all beliefs and dogmas – which accords with Keats' theory of the 'camelion Poet' whose lack of solid identity and absence of 'self' renders him a passive recipient to all that is, living 'in gusto, be it foul or fair' (1958: I, 387).

The second binary opposition, that of poet / sage, is initially given not as a contrast but an equation – 'sure a poet is a sage' – and receives an internal definition from within the text, where poet equals sage equals humanist / physician. The correspondence of 'philosopher' to 'healer' of humanity is one of the central metaphors of the Platonic dialogues, and Socrates repeatedly refers to his method as a θεραπεία, one of whose aspects is 'midwifery' or the assisting to 'birth' of the attendant soul. The third polarity, that of poet / dreamer is also subjected to minute analysis in the poem – the former presented as the one who 'pours out a balm upon the World', the latter as he who 'vexes' the world. Here the healing metaphor is retained, the properties of 'therapist' transferred from philosopher to poet – as the distinction is made within the same cultural genre, that of ποίησις – yet translating moral presuppositions into aesthetic ones: the poet being the 'good' poet, the dreamer an inferior versifier out of touch with 'reality'. The 'vexing' that Keats speaks of, and the whole concept of poet-instigator, is of course a central motif, and basic ground, as we have seen, for Plato's 'infamous' debasement of poetry which 'waters and fosters' the feelings of 'sex and anger' (i.e. the black and white unruly forces of the mortal soul), 'when what we ought to do is to dry them up'

(*Republic*, X, 606d). Consequently, Plato proclaims, 'we can admit no poetry into our city save only hymns to the gods and the praises of good men. For if you grant admission to the honeyed Muse in lyric or epic, pleasure and pain will be lords of your city instead of law' (*Rep.*, X, 607a). Poetry, by exercising a 'spell' and 'magic' on the soul due to its rhythmic metrical form, induces a 'letting go' that relaxes the guard of reason; hence, 'in its exploitation of this weakness of our nature falls nothing short of witchcraft' (*Rep.*, X, 602d).

The Fall of Hyperion becomes an attempt to differentiate 'dream' from 'dream', and to revoke the sentence on poetry by precisely inverting the relation of 'poetry' to 'witchcraft': 'For Poesy alone can tell her dreams, / With the fine spell of words alone can save / Imagination from the sable charm / And dumb enchantment' (I, 8–11). The double function of 'magic' is a close analogue to the Greek use of φάρμακον as poison / cure; the verbal charm releases the mind from a possession of 'aphasia', λόγος becomes the 'white' magic – the incantatory power inherent in the magical formula of words – that can dissolve the bewitching of the soul. This is mainly effected in the poem through the 'discursive' recapturing of past experience, the contents of memory. The unexpected relation of 'muteness' and 'speech' is the characteristic feature of the confrontation between 'speaker' and Mnemosyne (Memory) in both 'Hyperion' poems. In the first, two 'silent' states – the Goddess' 'mute countenance' and Apollo's 'reading' – end in a ravishing experience that falls short of verbalization. In the reconstructed version, the Poet penetrates beyond surfaces – the 'silent face' of the Prophetess – venturing inside,

> to see what things the hollow brain
> Behind enwombed: what high tragedy
> In the dark secret chambers of her skull
> Was aching, that could give so dread a stress
> To her cold lips, and fill with such a light
> Her planetary eyes . . .
>
> (I, 276–81)

'Seeing' is simultaneously a 'hearing' – as 'I look'd' is immediately succeeded by 'Then Moneta's voice / Came brief upon mine ear' (I, 300–1). This conjunction of the verbal and perceptual functions has nowhere received a more memorable utterance, I believe, than in Heidegger's: '*The essential being of language is Saying as Showing*' (1971b: 123).

The imagery of the opening section of the dream experience beginning with the words 'Methought I stood' – with its roses, fruits, shells, wine – is analogous to the introductory part of Book III of the first *Hyperion*. The sense of plenitude common to both is heightened in the second poem by the magical (rather than metaphorical) function of 'intoxication' – the liquid drunk, whose nature remains unidentified. Recognition of the potion's potency in 'That full draught is parent of my theme', and the destructive / creative effects of the poison / elixir, introduce yet a third dimension of distancing from actuality, precisely depicting the state so often encountered in Plato's dialogues. Another differentiating characteristic is not only the 'coexistence' of natural and cultural forms that we find in the relevant scene of the first *Hyperion*, but their 'confusion'; the *regressus ad uterum* approach to the 'thing enwombed' in Moneta's skull is a return to the chaotic and primeval – 'So old the place was, I remember'd none / The like upon the Earth' (I, 65–6). An extraordinary correlation of τάξις and ἀταξία is conveyed through the image of 'the eternal domed Monument' and the objects it contains, 'All in a mingled heap confus'd there lay / Robes, golden tongs, censer and chafing-dish, / Girdles, and chains, and holy jewelries' (I, 78–80).

The τέμενος that the Poet has entered, and which he tries to make familiar by 'fathoming' it in all directions, is a 'space' bordered by 'nothingness' – 'ending in mist / Of nothing' – northwards and southwards, imprisoned by 'black gates' on the eastern side, visibility and exit being located only westwards where besides the inanimate objects – an 'image', an 'altar', and a staircase – there stood 'One minist'ring'. The ceremonial flame lit, the 'sacrifical fire' made – whose incense 'spread around / Forgetfulness of everything but bliss' (I, 81–104) – forgetfulness of bliss is immediately effected by the 'language pronounc'd' which invites the Poet to the ritual ordeal of 'ascent'. That 'forgetfulness of everything' is not an intoxication but a dis-intoxication, is stressed by the command to an 'anagogical' process above the habitual self rather than a 'catagogical' relapse below:

> I heard, I look'd: two senses both at once,
> So fine, so subtle, felt the tyranny

ΠΑΘΗΜΑ AND ΠΟΙΗΜΑ

>Of that fierce threat and the hard task proposed.
>Prodigious seem'd the toil; the leaves were yet
>Burning – when suddenly a palsied chill
>Struck from the paved level up my limbs,
>And was ascending quick to put cold grasp
>Upon those streams that pulse beside the throat:
>I shriek'd, and the sharp anguish of my shriek
>Stung my own ears – I strove hard to escape
>The numbness; strove to gain the lowest step.
>
>(I, 118–28)

The Poet's agony of transformation, compared to that of Apollo in the older version, reveals as its distinctive feature the suffering of 'cold numbness' to that of 'fierce convulse'. The value scales of hot / cold are inverted, as the burning / cooling of *Hyperion* is translated into freezing / warming. The liberating action is a 'stepping up' by only one small degree (step) from the marble level that thrusts upwards the 'stifling, suffocating' paralysis consuming life. The short distance travelled, the mounting up achieved, 'life seem'd / To pour in at the toes' (I, 133–4).

The Poet's 'second birth' is followed by a gradual ascent / approach to the dualism of 'horned shrine' and the equivocation of Moneta's language, who, to his aesthetic request for perceptual purgation of the 'mind's film', retorts the moral imperative of acceptance of suffering, the titanic 'giant agony' of the world. Moneta's admonition presents 'life' not as a lyrical wonder where everything we look upon is blessed, but an alternative vision of tragic realization of disjointed and warring opposites: ' "The pain alone; the joy alone; distinct' (I, 174). The dreamer's condition is not however one of unconscious bliss; his state of constant intensity – 'fever' – is, in Moneta's view, an alienation from happiness in refusing to accept the alternation of 'joy' and 'pain': ' "Only the dreamer venoms all his days, / "Bearing more woe than all his sins deserve' (I, 175–6). In demanding the substitution of one form of 'woe' for another – the transference from 'passion' to 'suffering', from πάθος to πάθημα – Moneta (whether she is conscious of it or not) still moves within the ontological – and psychological – realm of πάσχειν.

The primary intention of the initial stage of their dialogue appears to be 'purgatorial', in the sense that the 'High Prophetess' finally reduces her interlocutor to a state of violent distrust of all he had formerly held true about himself and his 'profession'. Like an expert dialectician, she goes through the preparatory stage of 'disputation' and 'confutation' which tears into pieces common assumptions (τάς ὑποθέσεις ἀναιροῦσα (*Rep.*, VII, 533c)) and habitual patterns of thinking, and encourages the rise above conventional modes of 'seeing' – and 'being'. Moneta's ἔλεγχος, her cross-examination, is a purificatory process in that it simultaneously delivers from opinions held (the fanatic's way) and enforces humility upon the arrogant, knowledgeable subject (now more appropriately 'object'). The dialectical 'steps' are easily recognizable: to Moneta's climax of refutation and mortification, 'Such things as thou art', the Poet answers in modesty and self-effacement, admitting his 'unworthiness' – which is a long distance travelled from his initial assertive 'arrogance' of 'being' and 'professing'. The ultimate effect of intellectual disproof is reduction to existential nihilism, as the Poet enters a condition of complete bafflement and utter negation – ' "That I am none I feel' (I, 191) – recalling in its tragic (or ironic) awareness the Socratic ἓν οἶδα ὅτι οὐδὲν οἶδα. Out of the sheer 'nothingness' of this position the first glimmerings of self-knowledge begin to emerge, in the form of ritual questions that express a 'hermeneutical' attitude to existence: ' "What am I then?' and ' "What tribe?', followed by the interrogative shower of:

> 'Majestic shadow, tell me where I am,
> 'Whose altar this; for whom this incense curls;
> 'What image this whose face I cannot see,
> 'For the broad marble knees; and who thou art,
> 'Of accent feminine so courteous?'
> (I, 211–15)

The 'courteousness' attributed to Mnemosyne is partly a euphemism, since her attitude to the Poet so far has been overtly hostile. His 'successful' (if the paradox of utter defeat may be thought of as victory) undergoing through the various 'rites of passage' of which his initiation consists, entirely alters the relational situation of Prophetess / Poet; her 'hostility' removed by his 'negation', she 'opens up' the contents of her 'globed brain' for his reading, offering the total, inclusive knowledge that she contains within. It is her own transformation into an 'object' or 'text' that grants the poet subjective or 'authorial' stance (and following upon his own prior 'objectification'); despite minor inconveniences, the transition (for the protagonist) from πάσχειν into ποιεῖν has been structurally effected:

> 'The sacrifice is done, but not the less
> 'Will I be kind to thee for thy good will.
> 'My power, which to me is still a curse,
> 'Shall be to thee a wonder; for the scenes
> 'Still swooning vivid through my globed brain,
> 'With an electral changing misery,
> 'Thou shalt with those dull mortal eyes behold,
> 'Free from all pain, if wonder pain thee not.'
>
> (I, 241–8)

Moneta's transmission of knowledge will be a transfusion of power – and a transmutation of 'curse' into 'wonder' (a cognate of 'blessing'). The 'curse' is the recording of scenes, paradoxically 'swooning vivid', in their 'electral' process; the 'wonder' is the 'reading' of this 'flux', the backward look through memory (and time), which 'structures' the flow and reveals its function.

As one by one the 'veils of perception' are lifted, the Poet encounters Moneta's naked 'wan face' before his final plunge into her 'hollow brain':

> This saw that Goddess, and with sacred hand
> Parted the veils. Then saw I a wan face,
> Not pin'd by human sorrows, but bright-blanch'd
> By an immortal sickness which kills not;
> It works a constant change, which happy death
> Can put no end to; deathwards progressing
> To no death was that visage; it had past
> The lily and the snow . . .
>
> (I, 255–62)

The ambivalence of an 'immortal sickness' is intensified by the incongruity of 'constant change'; Moneta uncovers herself as an endless succession of moments, the experience of the flow of impermanence, the basic and inherent insecurity of existence which does away with the solidity and stability of historical identity. She discloses the illusion of permanence, the truth of transiency or mutability, a paradoxical 'being' condemned to perpetual motion – time or immortality. Moneta's message is that without accepting the fact of 'constant change' man cannot find rest; because humans cannot welcome the condition of ephemerality, they suffer. So the root of pain seems to be the negation of this reality; her teachings of 'suffering' and 'change' appear as the dual aspects of one and the same truth. Her 'sickness' and 'curse' – the intimation that there is nothing enduring, everything arising and vanishing continually – is simultaneously the 'wonder' and the 'cure': seeing the inconstancy of all phenomena marks for the Poet the beginning of freedom.

Unlike the Mnemosyne / Apollo confrontation, where the god had 'steadfast kept' his gaze upon the goddess with a sheer force of will, here the Poet becomes captive to Moneta's viewless eyes that 'held him back' in 'blank splendour'. Moneta's glance becomes the door of perception that allows entry behind the facade, the 'wan face', into the 'dark secret chambers'. The penetrating movement from 'visage' into 'skull', is a simultaneous translation of the linearity of change and succession to the realization of a dialectical interplay of forces, whose interaction and conflict generates 'high tragedy': the mechanism of 'suffering' is disclosed as that of 'drama'. The Poet's initiation into the 'play' acted in the shadowy unknown recesses of memory (archaic or historical, collective or personal) is about to begin. The 'what' that 'ferments to and fro' (I, 290) becomes the clue to an ontological explanation, whose modern philosophic utterance is to be found in Gadamer's *Truth and Method*; it assesses, as already discussed, the to and fro movement of play as a self-generating motion, effortless and purposeless, engulfing the player into its ebb and flow and thus relieving him from 'the burden of the initiative, which constitutes the actual strain of existence' (1975: 94).

All the Poet has to do is sit very attentively and 'become' the flow of 'acting' – going along with the pattern of memory, or stream of consciousness, without interfering. He begins to watch those 'swooning vivid' scenes as they come to show themselves, seeing 'history' as if from a little distance, witnessing thoughts as they pass before, or rather below, his observation post, the bare attention of his inner eye or ear:

> Then Moneta's voice
> Came brief upon mine ear – 'So Saturn sat
> When he had lost his Realms –' whereon there grew
> A power within me of enormous ken
> To see as a god sees, and take the depth

ΠΑΘΗΜΑ AND ΠΟΙΗΜΑ

Of things as nimbly as the outward eye
Can size and shape pervade. The lofty theme
Of those few words hung vast before my mind,
With half-unravel'd web. I set myself
Upon an eagle's watch, that I might see,
And seeing ne'er forget. . . .

(I, 300–10)

The enlarged awareness reported – 'seeing as a god sees' – a replica of phenomenal perception, is an echo (or more than an echo) of the Platonic ἀνάμνησις, when ἰδέα had not yet been abstracted but was still something to be 'seen'.

5

ON RE-COLLECTION

The myth of memory that dominates Romanticism follows, both chronologically and causally, upon the Enlightenment's concern with the phenomenology of 'reminiscent' consciousness; the, apparently crucial, proposition of G. Poulet in his *Studies in Human Time*, that 'The great discovery of the eighteenth century is the phenomenon of memory', is taken as the starting point for two explorations into the Romantic 'remembered existence in time' – and particularly that of Wordsworth – initiated by C. Salvesen and H. Lindenberger. The latter continues his citation from Poulet with ' "it is the greatness of the eighteenth century to have conceived the prime moment of consciousness as a generating moment and generative not only of other moments *but also of a self which takes shape by and through the means of these very moments*" '; to which he adds his own commentary that 'memory, because of the double perspective in which it sets the past, becomes a unique instrument in revealing knowledge about the self' (1963: 139–40). Salvesen defines the 'characteristic Romantic awareness of time' as a 'completely unself-conscious self-consciousness . . . as the state of being alert – over-alert – to one's own existence: for Wordsworth, it was enough to be aware of his being' (1965: 3–4). It is my view that it is precisely such 'alertness' to the incessant stream of remembered images that constitutes what I would call the dual function of memory: that of creating the unity-of-self in time and that of seeing through – in the sense of 'exposing', or 'exploding' – the strategies by means of which the image of a unified, solidified 'self' is fabricated.

The paradoxical activity of memory, destructive in its creation and creative in its destruction, or more appropriately de-construction, is the ambiguous Romantic dialectic that finds one of its most rememberable pronouncements in Wordsworth's 'Ode: Intimations of Immortality from Recollections of Early Childhood'. There, infantile 'memorilessness' becomes the point of departure – and the goal of return – in an existence whose desire is for 'days to be bound each to each' by the structure of individual continuity, the connective link between the 'I' of yesterday and the 'I' of the present moment (with a projecting inclusion of the 'I' of tomorrow) – *and* the diffused sense of 'being' enjoyed by the childhood 'consciousness' prior to its 'growth' into personal identity. The whole problematics of a simultaneous 'terror of discontinuity' (Hartman 1964: 274) and desire for dissolution is encapsuled, I believe, in the epigraph to the 'Ode', which, in making the 'Child' *father* to 'Man', introduces a conceptual model of patriarchal authority (or 'egotistical sublime') that by instituting hierarchy – and hence rationality – acts as a barrier to the retroactive *regressus ad uterum* into an ambivalent, receptive, holistic, and unclassified 'childish' state where the personal is subsumed into the transpersonal. The centrality of Wordsworth's concept of, and attitude to, memory is also manifested in less celebrated lines, as for instance: 'Memory, like sleep, hath powers which dreams obey, / Dreams, vivid dreams, that are not fugitive; / How little that she cherishes is lost!' ('Bothwell Castle', ll. 12–14). The metaphorical equation of memory to sleep, as a twilight stage, a mediator, a threshold between 'self' and 'other', becomes the 'shore' image where the children of the 'Ode' 'sport' or play:

> Hence in a season of calm weather
> Though inland far we be,
> Our souls have sight of that immortal sea
> Which brought us hither,
> Can in a moment travel thither,
> And see the Children sport upon the shore,
> And hear the mighty waters rolling evermore.
> (ll. 165–71)

'Inland' seclusion is simultaneously an 'inclusion', since man is granted brief glimpses of that πέλαγος (κάλλους) 'excursing' there 'in a moment'. Admittedly, the visual experience is only of the 'signifier', the children-at-play, and not of the sea itself; but the incessant 'rolling' of 'mighty waters' gushing forth from the abyss' mouth can be distinctly heard – and comprehended.

Coleridge's attitude to memory, though fundamentally empiricist in its assumption of a mechanical causal process based upon the association of ideas – making of 'Fancy' a 'mode of Memory' which, 'equally with the ordinary memory' 'must receive all its materials ready made from the law of association' (1907: I, 202) – allows for instances of 'paramnesia', where fancy operates quite erratically and subverts the very 'law' it is supposed to obey:

> Oft o'er my brain does that strange fancy roll
>   Which makes the present (while the flash doth last)
>   Seem a mere semblance of some unknown past,
> Mixed with such feelings, as perplex the soul
> Self-questioned in her sleep; and some have said
>   We liv'd, ere yet this robe of flesh we wore.
> ('Sonnet, Composed on a Journey Homeward . . .', ll. 1–6)

In a note to the poem, the reference to the doctrine of pre-existence is not made directly to Plato (or his Orphic sources) but to later commentators, 'Almost all the followers of Fénelon'; Coleridge touches upon the equivocal relation of 'memory' to 'dream' by admitting that 'The first four lines express a feeling which I have often had – the present has appeared like a vivid dream or exact similitude of some past circumstances' (1912: 154), where, although the location of 'past experiences' is not defined, its metempirical (pre-existent) nature is fairly obvious.

One of the most evocative of Shelley's allusions to memory is made within the mythical 'context' of Mnemosyne, the goddess presiding over the poetic process as the mother of the Muses. In Stanza XXII of *Adonais*, although a dual 'mothering' is introduced – the Muse Urania also invoked in her motherly role as a 'childless Mother' (because of her deprivation in Adonais' death) – Shelley refrains from referring to the 'mother' of the mother in the traditional 'anthromorphic' terms: 'And all the Echoes whom their sister's song / Had held in holy silence, cried: "Arise!" / Swift as a Thought by the snake Memory stung / From her ambrosial rest the fading Splendour sprung' (ll. 195–8). The metaphorical analogy between psychology and myth, and the ambiguity of 'stinging' as both lethal and redemptive, are not the only characteristics of Shelley's peculiar version of a traditional story. By enlisting 'memory' within the 'serpent' code of his imaginative fabrications, he makes it a cognate of 'the vast snake

Eternity', the 'green serpent' grasped by the eagle, the 'wounded Serpent', the 'dire Snake', the 'snake that girds Eternity', the 'snake-like Doom', the 'serpent that would clasp' Eternity with his length and, finally, the serpent that is 'shut out from Paradise' – to mention only a few examples from Shelley's extensive ophidian iconography.

Keats' association of 'memory' and 'dream' finds other 'locales' besides *The Fall of Hyperion*; unconscious dreaming and conscious remembering merge in the state of reverie, where 'trains of peaceful images', his 'store of luxuries', are mingled with the reminiscence of biographical data, 'when I 'gan retrace / The pleasant day, upon a couch at ease' (*Sleep and Poetry*, ll. 340–53). Wordsworth's 'shore' image emerges again in *Endymion*, as the 'Wide sea, that one continuous murmur breeds / Along the pebbled shore of memory!' (II, 16–17). Another sea image, this time of oceanic depths, occurs in Book I of *Endymion*, where the 'dream within dream' encounter of the protagonist with the moon-goddess – the retrogressive plunge into the raw materials of primal memory – is presented through the contrasting functions of forgetting / remembering, and the contradictory images of falling / rising: 'Methough I fainted at the charmed touch, / Yet held my recollection, even as one / Who dives three fathoms where the waters run / Gurgling in beds of coral: for anon, / I felt upmounted in that region' (ll. 637–41).

The maritime imagery that dominates the Romantic 'landscapes of memory', concretizes the view that consciousness does not create itself – and that despite Keats' 'soul-making' – but wells up from unknown depths, from an 'unconscious' condition (though not necessarily unconscious in 'itself'), which makes of 'being' the 'trace' or 'sign' of 'non-being' (in the Plotinian saying of τὸ γὰρ ἴχνος τοῦ ἀμόρφου μορφή). The language of poetry constantly employs the 'sea' in its imaginative representation of the 'mysteries' of the human mind; D. A. White, in his assessment of Heidegger's transactions with the poetic logos, affirms that 'The sea as sea becomes the appearance of the sea as the giver and taker of memory. The poetized sea thus becomes a temporal as well as a spatial entity: it is the earthly counterpart to the time involved in remembering the past in the present, and the movement required to transcend the present and recall that moment in the past which is to be remembered'; analogically, 'Memory is of *one* time just as the immediate configuration of waves is of *one* sea' (1978: 103).

Awareness of eternity in temporality, 'being' in 'time', or 'idea' in 'presence' is a conceptual and imaginative constant that spans the philosophical and poetic horizon from Plato to Heidegger (to use the two poet-philosophers as landmarks). Heidegger defines memory as the 'gathering of thought', (thought of the 'upholder' – as in Wordsworth's expression): 'Thought of what holds us, in that we give it thought precisely because It remains what must be thought about' (1968: 4). Memory is a gift, he propounds, and the 'thinking' of the gift is recollecting forgetfulness; the dual-sided process of forgetting / remembering is constitutive of man's existential, transient 'being'. 'The word "memory" originally means this incessant concentration on contiguity', he affirms; 'In its original telling sense, memory means as much as devotion'. The introduction of the concept of 'devoutness', in both senses of religious piety and epistemological attentiveness, leads to the conjunction of thinking / thanking (already discussed) as activities embedded in the 'memorial' attention to what 'is being'. But memory in this 'originary sense', Heidegger underlines, 'later loses its name to a restricted denomination, which now signifies no more than the capacity to retain things that are in the past'. The transition or 'fall' of memory, as the German philosopher sees it, is from the 'concentrative' to the 'retentive' function: 'But if we understand memory', he urges, 'in the light of the old word *thanc*, the connection between memory and thanks will dawn on us at once. For in giving thanks', he concludes, bringing his argument to apocalyptic pitch, 'the heart in thought recalls where it remains gathered and concentrated, because that is where it belongs. This thinking that recalls in memory is the original thanks' (1968: 145).

Hartman interprets Heidegger's intense awareness of a 'forgetfulness of being' as one more instance of reconstruction of the Platonic doctrine of ἀνάμνησις – memory as a potential of returning to a forgotten state of 'presence' or plenitude. He continues with a pertinent comment that gathers together all specific loci of interest in the present book: 'Plato's myth', Hartman asserts, 'is revived in all its potency in the Romantic period; there is hardly a great writer, from Novalis to De Quincey, who does not explore both the existential and metaphysical implications of – shall we say – sleep'; it is persistently reiterated in the period that 'Human life in its freedom is a transcendence toward Being, but always as this Nothing, this eclipsed or veiled form' (1970: 98–9). Heidegger's interpretation of 'absence' is not nihilistic, nevertheless: 'Whatever withdraws, refuses arrival. But – withdrawing is not nothing'; as man *points* toward what withdraws', he is in his 'essential nature' a 'pointer' or sign awaiting interpretation. Using a line from Hoelderlin – 'We are a sign that is not read' – Heidegger reverts to the hermeneutic act of poetizing: 'This is why poesy is the water that at times flows backward toward the source, toward thinking as a thinking back, a recollection. Surely', he protests, 'as long as we take the view that logic gives us any information about what thinking is, we shall never be able to think how much all poesy rests upon thinking back, recollection. Poetry wells up only from devoted thought thinking back, recollecting' (1968: 9–11) – or, to translate Heideggerian into Wordsworthian diction, 'poetry is the spontaneous overflow of powerful feelings: it takes its origin from emotion recollected in tranquillity' (1974: I, 149).

Heidegger's mentioning of the titles in the various drafts of the Hoelderlin hymn – 'The Serpent', 'The Sign', 'The Nymph', and 'Mnemosyne' – (besides supporting in an unquestionable manner the problematic relation between the 'memorial' and the 'serpentine' that we witnessed in Shelley's *Adonais*) leads on, according to the celebrated Heideggerian norm of dealing with 'words', to an exploration of the etymological archaeology of the term, since 'For the Greeks, to tell is to lay bare and make appear'. He affirms: 'This Greek word may be translated: Memory. And since the Greek word is feminine, we break no rules if we translate "Dame Memory" '; the brief introduction is followed by the genealogy of the Titaness Μνημοσύνη. Not easily satisfied with mythical externalities, Heidegger probes into deeper layers of implication, contesting that 'the word means something else than merely the psychologically demonstrable ability to retain a mental representation, an idea, of something which is past. Memory – from Latin *memor*, mindful – has in mind something that is in the mind, thought'. The verbal game over a memory that 'speaks' – in Latin – its own signification of 'mindfulness' to mental contents, is followed by a deeper dive into origins: 'But when it is the name of the Mother of the Muses, "Memory" does not mean just any thought of anything that can be thought'; memory, in this maternal or primordial sense, 'is the gathering and convergence of thought upon what everywhere demands to be thought about first of all'. At this point the remembering faculty attains to the status of Platonic ἀνάμνησις: 'Memory is the gathering of recollection . . . – the thinking back to what is to be thought is the source and ground of poesy' (1968: 10–11). The 'poem' becomes a paradigmatic model of commemorating the memorable function of ἀνάμνησις; as in Plato's theory of recollection, the philosopher (poet) comprehends all things and re-members them in the creative act of ποιεῖν.

Plato's use of a language full of erotic overtones to describe the manner of approach to the vision of essential 'being' through recollection, is probably justified (among other things) by the etymological aura around the anamnestic process: ἀνά-μνησις, as a 'calling to mind', is a derivation from μνάομαι – to be mindful of, to turn one's mind to, to woo for one's bride, to court. As 'courtship', ἀνάμνησις or mindfulness, must win the love of its 'object' – therefore it must be observant, care-ful, and alert; it must offer an attention of extensive solicitude and exclusive interest, never letting the prospective 'bride' out of the focus of its caring attentiveness, accepting and respecting her whims and erratic moods. 'Remembering' as 'courtship' is seeking the favour of the 'beloved', endeavouring to 'please' by constant 'attentions'; not allowing the mind to become forgetful (of itself), ἀνάμνησις keeps it grounded and collected (a collectedness also expressed in the 'gathering' and 'laying' of λέγειν / λόγος) and becomes itself a purifying force. Ἀνάμνησις means infinite care for learning what 'being' is, the νοῦς ἐρῶν that cultivates a devoted and non-criticizing attitude; it becomes the energy itself that solves the riddle of 'being'.

The other kinship of μνάομαι, that to μνᾶ (unit of money), would probably have escaped notice were it not for Moneta's (the Latin version of Μνημοσύνη) glaring 'monetarism'; the fact that Roman coinage was minted in her temple emphasizes a relation that in its Greek version remains less obtrusive. So 'money', like all 'real' symbols, appears to have an ambivalent nature; it signifies not only the 'selfish and calculating principle', as suggested in Shelley's, 'poetry, and the principle of self, of which money is the visible incarnation, are the God and Mammon of the world' (1954: 293); as 'means of exchange', the thing, the

Goddess, as well as the mental function may be said to express a principle of relatedness, and also an attitude of 'giving' for 'taking', of 'paying', of necessary sacrifice. As money is the motivating force behind all human transactions, the energy that keeps the world spinning, Μνημοσύνη may be seen as the inner energy, the state of attention which is total intensity, the potency that is the highest form of human intelligence. In a transference from psychology to metaphysics via the metaphor of 'currency', one could refer to the Heraclitean 'fire' as the substance of universal exchangeability, in his dictum: 'All things are requital for fire, and fire for all things, as goods for gold and gold for goods' (Heraclitus 1979: 47). The transformative value of memory is recognized by the Greek mind that places it in the same linguistic code with money; similarly, the cosmological analogue of fire as the 'one' principle of bartering for the pluralism of existence, makes an interesting cluster of memory / money / flame as correlatives in the same ontological power-field.

When attempting to trace Plato's myth of memory, we must stop first at his own account of the etymological origination of the term; then we discover that μνήμη (also derivative from μνάομαι) is one of the relatively few words that Plato employs in the *Cratylus* to prove not the theory of natural signification, but its opposite – that names are products of custom and convention. Having built his argument of the 'naturalness' of language on the assumption that 'all things are in motion and progress and flux', which 'idea of motion is expressed by names', he finds the name of 'memory' a clear transgression of the rule, as indicative of stasis: 'then again, μνήμη (memory), as anyone may see, expresses rest in the soul, and not motion' (*Crat.*, 436e–437b); thus memory becomes the touchstone for the refutation of the whole theory of 'authentic' language or, conversely, for the inclusion of immobility as a mode of reality. Plato assumes that the etymology of the word falsifies natural nomination, rather than admitting 'stasis' as the essential nature of memory – which would entail seeing memory in its relation to 'eternity' rather than to 'time'. Plato, at least in the *Cratylus*, is reluctant to concede that the mind of man can perceive the immortality of the 'moment' which is seemingly caught in an incessant flux; rather than accepting this – or perhaps only for the sake of balancing the proposition with a counter-thesis – he prefers (or pretends) to explode the whole edifice of the semantic theory proposed.

We may divide Plato's approach to the problematics of memory into four categories: linguistic, metaphorical, mythical, phenomenological. In his symbolic rendering of the psychological function of memory, he uses the image of a 'block of wax' which the soul employs deliberately in order to retain impressions – the obvious implication being that mind is 'selective' of what it chooses to record or not record (*Theaetetus*, 191c–e). Plato also employs the metaphor of 'aviary' (*Theaet.*, 197c–e) to suggest the process of recalling the recorded materials; unlike the permanence and solidity implied in 'wax' and 'stamping', the mobility and restlessness of 'wild birds', even confined within the enclosed space of a cage, points towards a displacement of the correspondence between the collective and re-collective faculties. To remember Yeats again – the mind indeed appears to be a 'rage' rather than a 'storehouse'. In the myth of Er that concludes the *Republic* – one of the strongest manifestations in the dialogues of a personalist view of immortality – the vicissitudes of the human soul between two existential incarnations are depicted with the exactness and clarity of a geometrical theorem. The final stages of the return journey back into human time, and space, are described in the imaginative idiom of 'heat' and 'thirst' whose thoughtless and rash satiation induces the burden of forgetfulness (X, 621a–b).

Plato attempts a systematic examination of the phenomenology of memory in the *Philebus*. Memory presupposes a prior contact between sensation and soul; what remains 'undetected' by the soul at the moment of perception – the soul being 'indifferent' or inattentive ($ἀπαθῆ$) to the disturbance of the body – is experienced but not recorded (33d). He distinguishes between two conditions of 'memorilessness', as becomes evident in his argument, the state of 'nonsensation' and that of 'forgetfulness': 'forgetting [$λήθη$] is the passing away of memory' (33e). The proposition connects Platonic psychology with Greek semantics in a significant correlation, as the word for truth, $ἀ$-$λήθεια$, paradoxically designates a 'negative' condition – that which is 'not forgotten' – or, if we go into the heart, or better root, of the matter, the initial verb $λανθάνω$, as 'that which does not escape notice, the unconcealed'. To those experiences ($παθήματα$) which move soul and body together, the term 'sensation' is ascribed – and memory ($μνήμη$) is the 'preservation' of sensation. Plato here desynonymizes the two derivatives of $μνάομαι$ – $μνήμη$ and ἀνάμνησις, memory and recollection. From a differential definition – 'Then by "recollection" we mean, do we not, something different from memory?' (34b) – he moves into exposing the subtlety of the distinction: both cases being a recapturing of sensation, memory involves a soul–body experience, whereas recollection excludes the body altogether. In a passage that carries intimations of recollection from Wordsworth's 'the soul, / Remembering how she felt, but what she felt / Remembering not' (*Prelude*, II, 315–17), Plato proceeds to give a dual interpretation of the phenomenon of ἀνάμνησις; first, 'When that which has been experienced by the soul in common with the body is recaptured, so far as may be, by and in the soul itself apart from the body, then we speak of "recollecting" something' (34b–c). The second definition refers to ἀνάμνησις in a way that clearly makes it not the synonym but the antonym of μνήμη: 'And further, when the soul that has lost the memory of a sensation or what it has learned resumes that memory within itself and goes over the old ground, we regularly speak of these processes as "recollections" ' (34c).

Clearly then, ἀνάμνησις is a 'leap' over distance and discontinuity, whereas μνήμη rests on continuity in time and uninterrupted preservation; ἀνάμνησις necessarily entails a previous condition of loss or repression – the 'absence' of something that has withdrawn from awareness. The conjunction of present consciousness with the experience (πάθημα) that has slipped from memory, constitutes re-collection or re-cognition, ἀναγνώρισις. Gadamer asserts recognition to be 'the central motif of Platonism', and detects the resemblance of the state of 'revelation' to the imitative representation of 'play'; artistic creation, in bringing to light paradigmatic structures, transforms the conventional into the original. His conjoining of Platonic metaphysics to a theory of aesthetics defines, as we have already seen, recollection as a heightened awareness of presence, a concrete perception of life here and now, unveiling a new dimension of existence (1975: 103).

The process of Platonic ἀνάμνησις begins at the beginning, i.e. with recollection of 'forgetfulness', or the problem of retrieval of 'disappearance', which raises the epistemological – and ontological – paradox, 'how does something come out of nothing?'. Restoration of latent anamnestic contents into conscious experience presupposes partial cognizance of their 'retreat' or repression – their 'withdrawal' from noetic grasping. The Platonic ritual of commemoration actually begins with the question of how knowledge can come of ignorance, how what has vanished as substance can still be retained as sentient mode. In the *Theaetetus* Plato, attempting to reach a solution through a parallelism between remembrance and perception – and using his favourite method of analogical thinking – argues that as memory is to perception so is recollection to memory, since shutting one's eyes does not automatically eliminate from the mind the image of the percept (163e–164b). The question characterized as 'the most formidable poser of all', 'Can the same person know something and also not know that which he knows?' (165b), reveals the complex games that the human mind is playing with itself. The root of this recollective recognition lies for Plato in the state of perplexity or ἀπορία (*Meno*, 80c), which brings the inquiring attitude to the edge of a mental precipice; α-πορία is yet another deprivative word, α-πόρος / περάω denoting inability to drive through or across space, dispossession of the means of passing – absence of the 'ferryman', Πόρος, who also happens to be the father of Ἔρως (*Symposium*, 203b). C. P. Bigger offers a very interesting interpretation of the dialogue through investigating the etymology of the name 'Meno' as μένειν, to stay as before, to stay put. The sophisticated Meno, who was 'too blind to see', was ultimately 'shown by his own slave with the help of Socrates another kind of memory, that which breaks through custom and convention and habit and shows what is as it is'; recollection, the critic contends, 'is part of the Platonic strategy against Sophistry. It is within this context that *idea* unfolds its meanings' (1968: 19).

Plato seems to be toying with his doctrine of ἀνάμνησις whose other side is called 'immortality' – ἀθανασία – in founding recollection on pre-existence (*Meno*) as much as he grounds pre-existence on recollection (*Phaedo*). It would seem that ἀνάμνησις is the symbolizing process or the capacity to recognize structural constants (Ideas) beyond the randomness of experiential data; since the soul is imperishable, Plato contends, it 'has learned everything that is', and consequently can remember everything (*Meno*, 81c–d). The question-and-answer technique, Socrates maintains, opens the path to recollection by initiating a procedure which transforms 'ignorance of knowledge' into 'knowledge of ignorance' – to the final 'knowledge of knowledge' (84a–85e). The state of ἀπορία (wonder) – the condition of intellectual void or subversion of cognitive security – is the necessary stage of transition, the 'infection' as Socrates calls it, through which the mind must pass, before desire for cognition of truth can be stimulated. As presented in the *Meno*, remembrance of 'forgotten' ratios, geometrical theorems, has about it a 'dream-like quality' (85c) which, translated into poetic terms, sounds quite close to the capacity of 'being in uncertainties, Mysteries, doubts, without any irritable reaching after fact & reason' (Keats 1958: I, 193). The paradox of a logical process that is steeped in the uncertainty of dream emphasizes the haziness of the newly aroused faculty, whose essential nature is the perception of 'relationship' and λόγος among things that seemed randomnly conjoined.

The Platonic poetics of memory as expressed in the *Meno*, in pronouncing all cognition to be re-cognition, turns the slightest instance of understanding into a revelatory act. The knowing mind as a re-membering mind is an intelligence that instinctively 'connects', and realizes 'patterns' or exemplary models. That 'knowledge will not come from teaching but from questioning' (85d), establishes the 'question' at the outset of epistemological and ontological priorities – the initiator of a long process that leads to remembrance as the presupposition of immortality. Inverting his earlier stance (which made of immortality the precondition to reminiscence), Plato now argues that 'if the truth about reality is always in our soul, the soul must be immortal, and one must take courage and try to discover – that is, to recollect – what one doesn't happen to know, or, more correctly, remember, at the moment' (86b). By investing the void with plenitude – or detecting potential 'presence' in actual 'absence' – Plato confirms the possible retrieval of an unconscious, involuntary, or collective memory buried deep in each individual. That such a dormant latency may exercise a dynamic influence on human life, even prior to its becoming instrumental to the awakened mind, is evidenced by those 'men divine who with no conscious thought are repeatedly and outstandingly successful in what they do or say' (99c) – namely priests, prophets, and 'poets of every description. Statesmen too, when by their speeches they get great things done yet know nothing of what they are saying, are to be considered as acting no less under divine influence, inspired and possessed by the divinity' (99d). The operation of a transpersonal 'presence', even though apparently 'absent' from awareness, makes 'thought' and 'action' a mystery to be intuited and accepted as a transcendent 'otherness' living through human psychic structures. Thus ἀνάμνησις becomes a recognition of παρουσία whose 'presencing' constantly evinces more or less clearly in the acts and thoughts of the amnesiac mind.

The Platonic ambivalence towards pre-existence and recollection in the *Meno* – which, in trying to solve the paradox of questioning and seeking after an 'absence' whose signs are hardly traceable, makes ἀνάμνησις concurrently the premise and conclusion of the dialectical procedure – is 're-presented' in the *Phaedo*: immortality is inferred from recollection, itself a hypothesis in need of 'proof' (73e–74a). Plato's characteristic form of deducing immortality of the soul from the intellectual, cognitive process – ' "to know" means simply to retain the knowledge which one has acquired, and not to lose it' (75d) – is extended to perception, i.e. a prior state of existence is reconstituted from the recognition of beauty and splendour investing phenomena with 'other presence', and not vice versa:

> And if it is true that we acquired our knowledge before our birth, and lost it at the moment of birth, but afterward, by the exercise of our senses upon sensible objects, recover the knowledge which we had once before, I suppose that what we call learning will be the recovery of our own knowledge, and surely we should be right in calling this recollection.
>
> (75e)

The experiential basis for Plato's conviction of ἀθανασία is not very far from Wordsworth's intimations of immortality from recollections of sensation – as both rest on a kind of 'anamnestic perception'.

The emphasis on the κοινωνία (participation) of phenomenal objects in 'beauty' (and other forms) as given in the *Phaedo* – a dialogue where, above all the others, 'dying' to the sensory and sensuous is an essential presupposition and a life-task for the philosopher – is largely responsible, I believe, for making Plato's attitude to the body and sense perception as ambiguous as, for example, Wordsworth's. And though the surface argument postulates a clear distinction between mortal body and divine soul (anxiously awaiting its deliverance from the captivity of incarnate prison), the presence of the spiritual in the sensual makes their symbiosis a 'tale of approximation'. The proof of immortality as investigated in the *Phaedo* is based mainly on two premises: that of polarity and that of recollection; according to the first formula an existent is produced from its opposite, so life derives from death as its complementary counterpart, in that things 'come one from the other, and that there is a process of generation from each to the other' (71b). Death being the opposite of life, soul (being 'life') cannot partake of death – which makes of 'soul' and 'death' mutually exclusive provinces. The other arguments are subsumed under the basic presupposition of the existence of Ideas, archetypal structures, and the soul's ability to recall them. Recollection of Ideas is presented as a procedure analogical to the association of ideas, based on the principle of resemblance or contiguity:

> Are we also agreed in calling it recollection when knowledge comes in a particular way? I will explain what I mean. Suppose that a person on seeing or hearing or otherwise noticing one thing not only becomes conscious of that thing but also thinks of something else which is an object of a different sort of knowledge. Are we not justified in saying that he was reminded of the object which he thought of?
>
> (73c–d)

The example offered as an instance of the 'different sort of knowledge' triggered by 'noticing one thing', although it appears randomly chosen is, I believe, carefully selected: it depicts the synecdochic relation of part / whole or object / possessor that becomes manifest in the context of erotic attraction:

> Well, you know what happens to lovers when they see a musical instrument or a piece of clothing or any other private property of the person whom they love. When they recognize the thing, their minds conjure up a picture of its owner. That is recollection.
>
> (73d)

Thus, recollection seems to rest upon a dialectic of presence / absence, i.e. presence of 'thing' but absence of 'owner' of the thing – in this case the Ideas of which Plato very often speaks as 'possessors' of objects, 'things which are compelled by some form which takes possession of them' (104d). Imaginative representation of a forgotten or 'absent' reality induced by sensory evocation of its 'properties', is the epistemological process that underlies philosophic, as well as poetic, recollective practices – which makes as much a Platonist of Wordsworth, as a Wordsworthian of Plato: 'Recollection of the soul's immortal power is dependent in Wordsworth upon its absence; it must fade and be diminished before the soul can recognize its nature' (Sherry 1980: ix).

Although the proof of immortality in the *Phaedrus* does not rest upon ἀνάμνησις (as in the *Phaedo* and *Meno*) but upon the permanence of motion – 'All soul is immortal, for that which is ever in motion is immortal' (245c) – the very iconography of the fallen soul 'burdened with a load of forgetfulness and wrong-doing' because of which it 'sheds her wings and falls to the earth' (248c–d), points to the metaphorical relation of the two conditions – by translating arrest of motion into heaviness of being, and that into amnesia. We have already noted that when Plato discusses remembrance in the *Phaedo*, he describes the incident of the recollection of Ideas from sense objects as a 'conjuring up', an almost magical activity of invoking hidden powers to manifest themselves; in the *Phaedrus*, the same event is depicted as a moment of passionate experience analogous to that of erotic attraction (250a, 251a). In the *Phaedo*, a sense object is said to be essential for the initial step to remembrance; by a slight shift of meaning in the *Phaedrus* from 'body' (i.e. material) to 'body' (i.e. carnal), Plato turns an epistemological argument into an experiential event. Sense objects remind us of Ideas – their 'owners' or 'possessors'; similarly, human bodies remind us of the 'gods' by which they are suffused (252e–253a).

The cognitive and erotic aspects of μνάομαι (remember) are clearly married in the *Phaedrus*: memory of divine partnership – or 'dancing' (252d) – becomes the instinctual power, ἔρως, compelling the growth of the shrunken wings that are stimulated by the perception of beauty in the phenomenal world. Eros, the attraction towards a condition of forgotten fellowship with essence, is very closely associated with the Platonic doctrine of ἀνάμνησις. The instant of recollection, when imagination spellbinds, i.e. transforms the materials of memory (or rather of 'forgetfulness') into immediate experience, is equally a moment of ποίησις and understanding, 'and such understanding is a recollection of those things which our souls beheld aforetime as they journeyed with their god, looking down upon the things which now we suppose to be, and gazing up to that which truly is'

(249b–c). 'To see as a god sees' possibly implies a simultaneous duality of vision of generation / immortality, appearance / reality, time / eternity; then the theory of recollection is not quite a polemic against a sensationalist epistemology, but only an expansion of perception to incorporate the 'up' and the 'down' – namely the way 'structure' is ingredient in motion, 'pattern' in the senso-mental flux of historical consciousness. 'Neither Plato nor Wordsworth', R. Kuhns argues, 'can explain how the awareness of the individual becomes so enlarged'; such spatialization of the temporal – Plato's γεωμετρεῖν of reality and Wordsworth's 'spots' of time – the critic believes to be enhanced by the artistic consciousness which 'contributes to the furnishing of that realm of memory to which Plato gave the name anamnesis' (1971: 112–14).

For Plato, as he extensively demonstrates in the *Phaedrus*, this is the concern of the philosopher who, making 'right use of such means of remembrance [ὑπομνήμασιν]' and always approaching 'to the full vision of the perfect mysteries [τελέας ἀεὶ τελετὰς τελούμενος]' (249c), may gain access to 'that which truly is'. The ὑπόμνημα – reminder – of the Ideas is passionate perception, i.e. perception under the compulsion of ἔρως – divine possession or mediation, whereby the lover 'as soon as he beholds the beauty of this world, is reminded of true beauty' (249e). Affective vision is at once intelligent vision, furnishing the beholder with the token and reassurance of the sacredness of phenomena, what Wordsworth called 'intimations of immortality':

> Few indeed are left that can still remember much, but when these discern some likeness of the things yonder, they are amazed, and no longer masters of themselves, and know not what is come upon them [πάθος] by reason of their perception being dim.
>
> (250a)

Such philosophical or aesthetic discernment is developed when the stream of erotic attention (μνάασθαι) is directed towards οὐσία. The mind which sees clearly, penetrating deeply into that which is, experiences the arising and passing of phenomena very distinctly; it becomes luminous, and consciousness begins to shine forth, as 'for beauty alone this has been ordained, to be most manifest to sense' (250d).

The intensity and 'extensiveness' of the cognitive act is the non-knowledge and forgetfulness. Memory and truth cannot be separated', Derrida concludes in his close, non-interpretative rendering of the text's intentions: 'The movement of *alētheia* is a deployment of *mnēmē* through and through. A deployment of living memory, of memory as psychic life in its self-presentation to itself' (1981: 105). Derrida's reinstatement of 'writing' as the root metaphor for existence, cuts through the pride of λόγος by supporting that all language (verbal a well as iconic) is already a distancing from the presence of primal being (persistently refusing to 'present' itself). The 'deadness' that Plato ascribes to the 'written discourse' as contrasted to the 'living speech' (*Phaedr.*, 276a) is seen as the distinctive property of *any* and *all* forms of language.

Plato's condemnation of γράμματα in the *Phaedrus* as 'epitaphs' of memory (and 'being') should be read, I think, in conjunction with that other 'Egyptian story' in the *Philebus*, whose protagonist is again Theuth, called by Derrida the 'father of logos'. The narrative once more concerns γράμματα, not in their optical but their acoustic or phonemic aspect, and is the second 'tale of approximation' furnished by Plato in this dialogue, in an attempt to give the language of symbolic logic a concrete embodiment. The myth of Theuth is preceded by the myth of Prometheus, both being imaginative renderings of man's awareness of the ontological interplay between the primal duality, πέρας and ἄπειρον:

> There is a gift of the gods – so at least it seems evident to me – which they let fall from their abode, and it was through Prometheus, or one like him, that it reached mankind, together with a fire exceeding bright. The men of old, who were better than ourselves and dwelt nearer the gods, passed on this gift in the form of a saying. All things, so it ran, that are ever said to be consist of a one and a many, and have in their nature a conjunction of limit and unlimitedness.
>
> (16c–d)

Investigation of a thing's nature, Plato enunciates, should concentrate on the 'intermediate' forms, between its 'one' and its 'unlimited many' – on the actuality lying between eternal possibility and infinite potentiality. Transcendence of the conventional seems to lie precisely in the intimate 'occupation' with the conventional, which bears the character not of 'oneness' or 'unlimitedness', but of 'number':

> It is only then, when we have done that, that we may let each one of all these intermediate forms pass away into the unlimited and cease bothering about them. There then, that is how the gods, as I told you, have committed to us the task of inquiry, of learning, and of teaching one another . . .
> (16d–e)

His interlocutor's inability to understand the 'one-and-many' problem of 'being' – even though concretized into a legendary story – enforces Socrates to proceed from the mythical to the metaphorical method, from the 'godly' to the 'godlike'. The medium is going to be γράμματα, as he asserts: 'My meaning, Protarchus, is surely clear in the case of the alphabet; so take the letters [γράμμασιν] of your school days as illustrating it'; and then he opens his teaching with 'The sound that proceeds through our mouths . . .' (17a–b).

The paradox of a 'visual sound' (γράμμα deriving from γράφω, to scratch, to represent by lines drawn, to express by written characters) is not a Socratic deviation, but is inherent in the etymology of the very word used – φωνή; the 'voice' which, being rooted in φάω (to give light, to shine), indeed recognizes a 'light in sound' or a 'sound-like power in light':

> The unlimited variety of sound was once discerned by some god, or perhaps some godlike man; you know the story that there was some such person in Egypt called Theuth. He it was who originally discerned the existence, in that unlimited variety, of the vowels – not 'vowel' in the singular but 'vowels' in the plural – and then of other things which, though they could not be called articulate sounds, were noises of a kind.
> (18b–c)

Theuth's γραμματικὴ τέχνη – 'the expression "art of letters," implying that there was an art that dealt with the sounds' (18d) – is shown to be as much an art of speaking as of writing, embedded however in the optical, 'light' metaphysics of 'voice', which indeed makes of speech a kind of 'writing', something to be 'seen' or 'shown'. Socrates' pupils, still amazed, 'comparing the illustrations with one another', are possessed by the 'same dissatisfaction', wondering about 'the relevance of it all' (18d).

Such relevance is best manifested when the γραμματικὴ τέχνη of the *Philebus* becomes the ontological grammar of the *Statesman*, which in its turn is translated into the humble domestic occupation, 'the art of weaving woolens' (279b). Γραμματικὴ τέχνη is offered as a paradigmatic model that not only parallels the structures of the real, but is a discipline whose skilled exercise can lead to their recollection. The Stranger portrays the 'strange human plight', the general condition where 'Every one of us is like a man who sees things in a dream and thinks that he knows them perfectly and then wakes up, as it were, to find that he knows nothing', and its θεραπεία (remedy) in a constant μεταφορά, the translation of codes or systems of classification into each other – as 'example' is always 'found to require an example' (277d). In his discussion on metaphor Ricoeur, referring to Aristotle's presupposition that 'to make good metaphors is to contemplate likeness – *theorein to omoion*', emphasizes that 'To see *the like* is to see the same in spite of, and through, the different', pronouncing the 'tension between sameness and difference' to be the 'logical structure of likeness' (1978: 147–8).

Metaphor, in its interplay of differences and resemblances, becomes the very 'model' of reality as well as the 'pursuit' for reality – truth and method. This anagogic practice is allegorically presented through the teaching of 'learning to read' to 'young children':

> Take them to the syllables in which they have identified the letters correctly; then set them in front of the syllables they cannot decipher; then place known syllables and unknown syllables side by side and point out to them the similar nature of the letters occurring in both.
>
> (*Statesm.*, 278a–b)

The structural analogies which ground metaphorical insight, and allow the passage from one category to the other in an 'isomorphic' context, become therefore 'examples' of a unity underlying and connecting all phenomena: 'Would we be surprised, then', the instructor asks, 'to find our own mind reacting in the same way to the letters with which the universe is spelled out?' (278c–d).

The 'morphological' transformation that metaphor allows, the *μετα-μόρφωσις* of *μετα-φορά*, rests on the same possibility of transfer within an 'open' or relational world, in which the *γραμματικὴ τέχνη* can operate as an ontological grammar of 'being'. Heidegger's saying that 'The metaphorical exists only within the metaphysical' – speaking of *μετά* not only as the 'after' of sequence but the 'with' of togetherness – multiplies the possibilities of transgression of boundaries, and liberates the semantic motion (*φορά*) of metaphor tending from the 'known' to the 'unknown', which is not necessarily always a transition from the empirical to the metempirical. Because the mind, the Eleatic Stranger continues in the *Statesman*, even though familiarized with the forms or 'letters with which the universe is spelled out', making 'a right judgment of a particular combination of elements' and knowing the patterns of their interaction, 'when it sees the same elements transferred to the long and very difficult syllables of everyday existence, it fails to recognize again the very elements it discerned a moment before' – to which the young Socrates pertinently replies, 'One cannot wonder at it' (278d).

NOTES

1 THE DIALOGUE FORM: APOLLO AND DIONYSUS IN DISCOURSE

1 We should not forget that in this dialogue the roles are reversed: the young Socrates plays 'pupil' to the renowned Eleatic master.
2 All Platonic textual references, unless otherwise stated, are to *The Collected Works of Plato*, ed. E. Hamilton and H. Cairns. The Greek words and phrases interspersed in the English text are cited from *Platonis Opera*, ed. I. Burnet.
3 Probably Plato's assumption of a radical divergence in the philosophy of his venerable predecessors, Parmenides and Heraclitus, is undertaken in his usual spirit of contesting a proposition from both sides. He deliberately ignores that Heraclitus' ξυνὸς λόγος ('shared account' or common intelligence) is the unifying principle, the measure or pattern within the flux of things – which introduces a metaphysics of permanence behind a physics of flux – thus absolutely conforming with the basic demand of what E. Cassirer calls 'the metaphysics of all times', presupposing 'a unitary and single being, because and insofar as truth could be thought of only as unitary and simple'. Cassirer refers to Heraclitus rather than Parmenides as the chief exponent of this 'one', single, simple being that constitutes 'truth': 'In this sense the ἓν τὸ σοφόν of Heraclitus became the watchword of philosophy: it was an admonition to seek the one, unbroken light of pure knowledge behind the variegated colours of sensory experience, behind the multiplicity and diversity of the forms of thought' (1957: 1).
4 The problem of the relationship of the 'one' and the 'many' is a constant that crops up in a number of places, yet always within a somewhat similar pattern; in the *Philebus* it is asserted that an identical 'oneness' is found simultaneously in unity and in plurality (15b), or that the 'one' is 'many' and the 'many' are 'one' (14c). The proposition that Platonic reality is itself pluralistic, is put forward by R. L. Hart, in 'Plato never abandoned his pluralism. Real Being is constituted by a plurality of dimensions: no one may be reduced to another nor may all be reduced to one, no matter whether the

reduction be attempted ontologically or mythologically' (1965: 453).
5 It should be noted here that in a number of dialogues this primal becoming and movement of all that 'is', is identified with 'soul'. 'Soul' is the self-mover, and the essence of soul is 'motor'; it is that which gives breath, that which carries and moves, and its alleged immortality appears to be due to its mobility, as 'All soul is immortal, for that which is ever in motion is immortal' (*Phaedr.*, 245c). It is the prime source of all transformations in things and traverses the whole universe in ever-changing forms.
6 M. Murray clarifies the distinction between (Chomskyan) 'psychological linguistics' and (Heideggerian) 'ontological linguistics': 'For Heidegger's part', he argues, 'what language itself says and reveals – how it discloses the world – is more basic than and prior to the speaking of the subject'. Heidegger, he remarks, 'shares with the French structuralists the decentering of the subject which assigns primacy to the "saying" of language over the "speaking" of the individual speaker'; but from this point on, a diversion is introduced, because 'As stress on speaking leads analysis back to the speaking subject, so does a stress on the primacy of saying lead reflection to what is said' (1978: xv).
7 Heidegger is an obvious exception to this proposition. Derrida's 'mimesis' of the Platonic method in *Glas* as an optical left / right column correlation of two discourses – one on Hegel (dialectical philosopher) and the other on Genet (homosexual artist) – is an intentional parody, I think, of the Platonic text rather than an attempt to revive the mechanics which allowed – despite ironic tensions – the blending of two ways of relating to language, 'thinking' and 'poetizing'. As G. H. Hartman also comments, 'Where Gadamer, claiming to follow both Hegel and Plato, sees language as "fusing horizons" through dialogue exchange, Derrida sets column against column, signifier against signified, and the act of writing against homogeneous discourse' (1980: 138).
8 The domestic occupation of 'sifting' and 'straining' is a reiterated motif in many fairy tales, and the initial task imposed on the soul in Apuleius' fable of 'Amor and Psyche'.
9 W. V. Spanos makes a clear and very informative distinction between 'Derridean deconstructive' and 'Heideggerian destructive' practices, the differentiating character being that of 'absence' vs. 'presence': Derrida, Spanos asserts, 'Does not subscribe to this projective "step back" to the pre-Socratics, claiming that they – and thus Heidegger – are "within the lineage of the logos" insofar as they posit the "original and essential link" between *logos* and *phone* [voice]' (1976: xiv).
10 'The return to a more ontological approach to poetry', K. Harries maintains, 'has found its most vigorous spokesman in Heidegger' who proclaims that poetry uncovers 'being' in establishing a 'world' as a 'space of meanings'; Ricoeur, in Heidegger's wake, translates ontology into hermeneutics by transposing 'world' into the experience of 'text'. So metaphor, Harries remarks, 'is discussed in

NOTES

the context of this methodological interpretation' (1978: 88–9).
11 As Gadamer puts it, 'What we learned from Heidegger was above all the pervasive unity of the metaphysics originated by the Greeks and its continued validity under the subtly altered conditions of modern thought' (1978: 45).
12 Discussing Heidegger's relation to – and employment of – the dialogic mode, E. Donato states that 'Heidegger's discourse has to submit itself to the form of a *Zwiesprache*, a dialogue, a dramatization, that is to say a literary form par excellence' (1977: 5).
13 S. Rosen actually sees the dialogue form as a 'threeness' in the metaphysical schema of Monad and Dyad: 'The Three is the dialogue, and so the community, between the One and the Two, which makes speech about the entity possible. It makes the entity visible' (1963: 432).
14 In R. Kamber's words, 'The largest and most prominent class of technically non-assertive works in the domain of philosophy is the class of philosophical dialogues in which the author does not appear as a speaker. Included in this class are the dialogues of Plato' (1977: 342).
15 In his comparative study of Plato and Heidegger, H. G. Wolz traces a relation of continuity in both philosophies, in their lack of finality, a temporality which 'in turn, leads to transcendence'; he maintains that 'if we look at the dialogues from the perspective of Heidegger's philosophy, we find that the inquiry does not come to rest, even if we have managed to resolve the paradoxes'; in fact, 'Heidegger takes up the problem where Plato leaves it and carries it a significant step further' (1981: 22–3).
16 The attitude portrayed in Gadamer's playing consciousness bears a close resemblance to the poetic consciousness as exhibited in both Keats' 'negative capability' (1958: I, 193) and Coleridge's 'willing suspension of disbelief' (1907: II, 6).
17 Defining irony as 'a conscious attempt to mediate between the various elements of discourse', C. Hamlin contends that 'In Romantic theory, as also in Platonic philosophy, this mediation is defined as a dialectical process, which interrelates the parts and the whole'; irony becoming itself 'a measure of the incommensurability of language in its efforts to achieve such a union of opposites', it employs the dialogue form demonstating that 'the art of mediation can only be approximate, as indicated by the effort to communicate through the dialectical process, which requires both a differentiation of voices (Socrates and his interlocutors) and an extension in time (as implied dramatic performance,' (1976: 6).
18 The allusion is to J. Conrad's *Heart of Darkness* where the 'fascination of the abomination' (5), the 'incomprehensible' and 'detestable' mystery, is a running theme throught the novel; the phrase – and its signification – has become one of the focal points around which this work has been constucted.
19 See Plato's account of the revolution of '"sleeping" circles' which, in achieving a blending of 'sameness' and 'difference' in rotation,

'becomes a source of all sorts of marvels' (*Laws*, X, 893c–d). The 'wondrous' effect that results from the equalizing of the 'lesser' (different / non-being) and 'greater' (same / being) is investigated from a slightly different perspective, that of 'sound' (another form of motion), in the *Timaeus*; the discussion probes into the interrelation between 'swift' and 'slow' sounds (the equivalent to 'high' and 'low' velocities), and the emotional response they excite in man (80a–b). Such a 'musical' dialogue between the two kinds of revolution (ταὐτόν / θάτερον) in the soul, gives to the harmonizing process a pulsating pleasurable effect whose rhythm, Plato admits, approximates human motions to divine vibrations.

20 C. Jung draws upon the work of A. Kuhn to point out the tentative etymological kinship between the Greek verb μανθάνω, the root of Προμηθεύς (προ-μηθής / μαθεῖν / μανθάνω) and the Sanskrit verb '*manthāmi*, "to shake, to rub, to bring forth by rubbing." Kuhn relates this verb to Gr. μανθάνω, "to learn," and has also explained', Jung points out, 'the conceptual relationship between them. The *tertium comparationis*', Jung emphasizes, 'may lie in the rhythm, the movement to and fro in the mind. According to Kuhn', he continues, 'the root *manth-* or *math-* leads, via μανθάνω (μάθημα, μάθησις) and προ-μηθέομαι, to Προμηθεος, the well-known Greek fire-robber'. Investigating into the ambivalent etymological parentage of 'Prometheus', Jung asserts that 'The only thing that can be established with any certainty in this complicated situation is that we find thinking, precaution, or foresight somehow connected with fire-boring, without there being any demonstrable etymological connections between the words used for them' (1956: 145–7).

21 Plotinus informs us that ' "The Pythagoreans refer symbolically to The One as 'Apollo' " – that is, as "Not (*a*) Many (*pollon*)" ' (O'Brien 1964: 19).

22 For a full treatment of the subject see Chapter X on 'Orphic and Dionysian Mysteries', in J. E. Harrison (1903: 478–571).

23 For a parallel ritualistic / meditative reading of the poem, see E. Wasserman (1953: 37–8), B. Blackstone (1959: 330–1), and D. Perkins (1959: 236–41).

24 'By the Pythagorean equation of silence and celestial harmony inaudible to man', L. Spitzer affirms, 'Keats is able to resolve the paradox of the silent but "speaking" urn and also to find the transition from things seen (with the eyes) to things heard (with the "spirit")' (1955: 211–12).

25 The 'shape' of the urn, it has been argued, 'bears a haunting resemblance to the curving lines of the feminine body' (Patterson 1954: 211).

26 The allusion is to J. L. Weston, *From Ritual to Romance*; her argument, which traces the thematic and structural continuity between archaic initiatory rites and medieval mythical narratives, may be extended to incorporate modern artistic constructs – the 'name' of Romanticism defining itself 'as in the old romances'. For a detailed discussion of the etymology of the term, see Eichner (1972: 3–16).

27 A similar reading is offered by A. E. Dyson and J. Lovelock (1973: 206–17).
28 M. Murray affirms that 'The ancient question of the interconnection between the poem, the poet, and the interpreter reached its highest classical expression in the *Ion* of Plato', and looks upon this dialogue as the originating point of the investigation into the hermeneutical experience – and practice (1975: 13–22).
29 The conjunction of 'coldness' and warm 'pastoralism' has stimulated an intense critical speculation; I quote a few representative 'attitudes': ' "Cold Pastoral!". Here perhaps for all that earlier longing and enthusiasm, is the poet's realisation that the Greek view of life and the art that expressed it were not for him, that they demanded on his part an ultimate renunciation' (Godfrey 1965: 50–1); ' "Cold Pastoral!" It remains untouched by the fury and the mire of phenomenalistic introspection and the insoluble question of the relation of self and other; untouched, in fact, by the whole problem of knowledge as it was so keenly apparent to the philosophers of the eighteenth century' (Simpson 1976: 266); 'Cold Pastoral! – unfeeling, imperturbable, the figures etched on its surface frozen, requiring a meeting of the mind, an active imagination, to give them warm life' (Wigod 1957: 115).

2 EROS IN LOGOS: SYMPOSIA ANCIENT AND MODERN

1 I borrow Wordsworth's statement from the *Preface* (1974: I, 138) because I find it exquisitely fitted to a daily situation at once so far from 'low and rustic life' but also so close to a language that 'the real passion itself suggests'.
2 The common etymological root $\Lambda\varepsilon\chi$ in $\lambda\acute{o}\gamma o\varsigma$, $\lambda\acute{o}\chi o\varsigma$ (ambush), and $\lambda\acute{\varepsilon}\chi o\varsigma$ (marriage) may be seen to carry the conceptual kernel of the dramatic situation.
3 In what he calls the 'imperialism of *theoria*' – and always within the premise of his equation, Same=Being=Ego – Derrida stresses the continuity between Platonic ontology and modern phenomenology: 'More than any other philosophy, *phenomenology*, in the wake of Plato, was to be struck with light. Unable to reduce the last naïveté, the naïveté of the glance, it predetermined Being as object' (1978: 84–5).
4 The prefatory essay, like the translation, was never published by Shelley, and because of the delicacy of its topic it appeared in fragmentary form (due to censorship exercised by Shelley's father and the publisher) in Mary's edition of 1840. The complete essay, together with the translation, was first published under the title *A Discourse on the Manners of Antient Greeks Relative to the Subject of Love* in 1931 (1954: 216).
5 J. Barrel contends that 'Plato came to represent Greek thought to Shelley, the thought of that civilization to which, as Shelley says, we owe our civilization' (1947: 118).
6 The editor's note to the letter informs us that Shelley was very upset

by this loss and that he recovered the manuscript at Pisa a few days before his death (1964: II, 342).
7 The suggestion that this 'own Symposium' might be *The Triumph of Life* is also made by W. Cherubini (apparently adopting the view of W. M. Rossetti), who, however, does not specifically associate it with the Platonic work, as he concedes that 'Shelley's use here of "Symposium" is ambiguous. What cannot be doubted is his intention to write an extended poem, of great scope, which should at the same time be human and warm'. He also refers to three letters by Shelley to Charles Ollier during 1821 (16 and 22 February, and 23 September) where the poet announces his employment 'in high and new designs in verse . . . the labours of years, perhaps', a 'production of a far higher character [i.e. than *Charles the First*]', whose 'execution' will 'require some years', followed by the later announcement (or rather annunciation): 'I am full of great plans' (1942: 559).
8 The allusion is to T. S. Eliot's *Hollow Men* (IV).
9 For an exploration into the personal experiences that form the context of the poem, see also G. M. Matthews (1961: 40–8), and D. H. Reiman (1963: 536–50).
10 In his article on 'Mysticism and Philosophy', A. Moore provides the equation of fear=ego, sustaining that the 'ego is acquired . . . at the same time as fear and is fear; the self is what one is fearful for, what one has learnt to protect'; so, if individuality *is* tension, he concludes, 'then it is literally and not just metaphorically true that we can relax into the All' (1976: 502).
11 'Traditional' interpretations (including readings that could be engrafted within the 'deconstructive' critical approach) see the poem as fragmentary, as a disillusioned version of Shelley's idealistic aspirations, as a transvaluation of his earlier positions – a dialectic between vision and actuality, with the definite ascendancy of the latter. More specifically, see Bloom (1959: 223), Miller (1979: 234), Rajan (1980: 59–60); also Bostetter (1963: 9), Holmes (1974: 718), Chernaik (1972: 177–8). The poem's darkness and defeatism is emphasized by Butter (1954: 31) and Kurtz (1933: 323); Abrams discusses the poem's theme as 'the unrelieved tragedy of the defeat of human potentiality' (1971: 441–2), while Reiman affirms that 'The problem for Shelley, as for all idealists, was to maintain his vision of the Ideal while living effectively within the limitations of the sublunary, actual world' (1965: 84–5) – an interpretation whose 'Platonic' overtones are more openly emphasized by Gutteling (1922: 134).
12 To connect Shelley's statement with the thematics of his prototype, 'Diotima, then, needs to be taken seriously in her account of the identity of the person; on her account there is no underlying metaphysical "self", but rather a collection of qualities. This at once legitimizes her extensions of the notion of "immortality", and her notion of love's being properly of qualities' (Warner 1979: 338).
13 For a comparison of Asia's retrograde journey with the Platonic

NOTES

theory of cosmic revolutions, see I. H. Chayes (1961: 358–69).

14 Emerald is not only the sacred stone of Aphrodite, goddess of love, but is traditionally associated with the legendary father of alchemy, Hermes Trismegistus who in his magic text, the *Emerald Table* or *Tabula Smaragdina*, calls alchemy the 'operation' of the sun; the *Emerald Table* has been a point of reference for later alchemists, quoting from or alluding to its maxims; for instance the 'As Above so Below' is frequently cited as a clue to the interpretation of reality.

15 As G. M. Matthews appropriately observes, 'The Shape blots and tramples out Rousseau's existing thoughts because, however bright their sparks (or fires), she is incomparably brighter, and like the stars at daybreak they are no longer needed' (1968: 356).

16 In the chapter called 'The Greek Shamans and Puritanism', E. R. Dodds tentatively interprets Orphism as a manifestation of the shamanic tradition in Greece; he argues that 'Orpheus is a Thracian figure of much the same kind as Zalmoxis – a mythical shaman or prototype of shamans' (1951: 147).

17 The severe criticism of Shelley's 'single recorded judgement of the *Confessions*', Reiman claims, has discouraged the tracing of a possible influence, or the 'close parallels' identified have not been thought satisfactory (1963: 545). The reference to Rousseau appearing in a letter to Thomas Hogg in the spring of 1811 ('The Confessions of Rousseau are . . . either a disgrace to the confessor or a string of falsehoods, probably the latter' (1964: I, 84)), cannot in any way be considered binding, it seems to me, of the poet's attitude in the spring of 1822.

18 The allusion is to Conrad's *Heart of Darkness* (84).

19 T. Webb stresses the significance of Euripides not only for Shelley, 'since Euripides was the only tragic dramatist whom Shelley translated', but for the larger Shelley circle; both Peacock and Hogg appear to be deeply affected by the thematic as well as the formal features of the dramatist's work (1976a: 56–7).

20 I am, of course, aware of the poem's 'actual' incompleteness, the final lines reading (I quote from D. H. Reiman's critical edition (1965: 210): ' "Then, what is Life?" I said . . . the cripple cast / His eye upon the car which now had rolled / Onward, as if that look must be the last, // And answered. . . . "Happy those for whom the fold / Of'. My point is that the poem has an integrative unity, which is paradoxically best expressed through its open-endedness; and although speculation is futile and possibly dangerous, I believe that Shelley must have been close to completion. The presence of the word 'fold' (G. M. Matthews' emendation for 'gold') refers us to the δαίμων of *The Daemon of the World* – 'the world's supremest spirit' that 'Beneath the shadow of her wings / Folds' all the maiden's memory (I, 78–80) – the 'lady' of *Alastor* – who 'Folded his frame in her dissolving arms' (l. 187) – the 'love' of *Prometheus Unbound* – 'Love, from its awful throne of patient power / . . . springs / And folds over the world its healing wings' (IV, 557–61) – and the 'comet' of *Epipsychidion* – the 'Comet beautiful and fierce', the one power

before the schism in two, whose reappearance Shelley invokes: 'Oh, float into our azure heaven again! / Be there Love's folding-star at thy return' (ll. 373–4). For a detailed discussion of the textual problematics of the poem, see Matthews (1960: 271–309, and 1962: 104–34).
21 I believe that Keats' concept of serpent and 'demon' (as the spelling also betrays) retains enough of the Christian component of depravity – despite assertions to the opposite, as for instance the proposition that 'the first source of the daemonic in Keats's poetry is one of several pre-Christian Greek conceptions of daemonic creatures before Christian theology debased all daemons together into hellish beings and fallen angels' (Patterson, Jr. 1970: 4).
22 Shelley, too, speaks of 'the reveries of Plato and the reasonings of Aristotle' in his notes on *Queen Mab* (1905: 820), and Coleridge suggests a dual reconciliation of opposites in his 'The sunny mist, the luminous gloom of Plato' (1895: 31). Wordsworth, again, in what appears to be a very unorthodox metaphor, associates Plato with the imaginative rather than the rational faculty (although for him reason and imagination are homologizable) by speaking about the 'lunar beam / Of Plato's genius' ('Dion' ll. 8–9) rather than the expected 'solar' one.

3 TRANS-FORM-ATION: THE DIALECTICS OF Πάθος AND Ποίησις

1 The paradoxical conjunction in the signification of ἄτοπος of concepts denoting 'amazement' and 'disgust' may be accounted for by the mythical designation of divinity as has been expounded by Cassirer in the passage cited earlier (119–20).
2 Ἀγαθόν, although of derivation uncertain, phonetically unfolds out of the Ἀγ root that also produces ἄγος, signifying religious awe but also pollution and abomination.
3 The reference is to the well known nineteenth-century Platonic scholar whose contribution consists not only in the translation of the dialogues and his reappraisal of the Platonic work (the reading of the dialogues *as* literature, as well as an interpretation of Plato based on Hegel) but also in the raising of scholarly status that he offered to the Greek philosopher (unlike the earlier translator, Thomas Taylor), which effected the re-entry of Platonic studies into the curriculum of Oxford and other British universities (Plato 1871: II, *Rep.*, IV, 436b–c).
4 We should also bear in mind, W. C. Greene reminds us, that 'Plato's own thoughts are actors in the drama, and make their exits and their entrances in accordance with the plot', adding that many of his pronouncements 'about poetry and inspiration and imitation are no more intended to be regarded as Plato's ultimate views than are the ironical and dialectic *obiter dicta* and *excursus* of his logical discussions' (1918: 3–4).
5 Notopoulos' analysis of the dialectical process is made along similar

lines: 'Dialectic destroys the fixation, the dogmatism of the limited perspective, and releases thought framed in any partial outlook', he asserts; 'It is the movement of thought which treats the image, the hypothesis, the theory not as a stopping point, but as a point of departure' (1936: 73).

6 In yet another 'anti-Platonist' attack, H. Bloom proclaims that 'The most obvious and absolute difference between Plato and Shelley is their rival attitudes toward aesthetic experience. Shelley resembles Wordsworth or Ruskin', he affirms, 'in valuing so highly certain ecstatic moments of aesthetic contemplation precisely because the moments are fleeting'; consequently, 'For Shelley these are not moments to be put aside when the enduring light of the Ideas is found; Shelley never encounters such a light, not even in *Adonais*' (1970: 382).

7 M. L. D'Avanzo, making an imaginative exploration of the Keatsian premise emphasizing 'the absolute necessity of passion or excitement as "the only state for the best sort of poetry" ', suggests a cluster of four metaphors (mania, flower dew, laurel and oak, wine) to represent 'that state of poetic excitement which Plato termed "madness" and which Shakespeare described as "a fine frenzy" '; these metaphors, he suggests, 'are expressive of varieties of poetic stimulants not unlike aphrodisiacs, for each has the special power of raising the poet to transcendent passion, which Keats identifies as Platonic lunacy' (1967: 92).

8 Romantic 'subversion' of tradition is discussed by I. J. Swingle who maintains that 'Romantic thought is preoccupied, first of all, with competing systems' (1978: 272), and that Romantic poetry attempts 'to disrupt a reader's equilibrium, to break down his sense of order and cast doubt upon the doctrines he holds when he comes to the poetry' (1971: 1977).

4 ΠΑΘΗΜΑ AND ΠΟΙΗΜΑ: BEING IN THE ROMANTIC TEXTS

1 Hartman considers the poet as 'the matchmaker, his song the spousal verse'; the natural landscape, he suggests, is the empowered scene that carries the signification of the 'marriage of heaven and earth': 'An awful power rises from the mind's abyss, disowning nature; another descends from Abyssinian clouds. He seeks his earthly paradise not "beyond the Indian mount" but in the real Abyssinia – any mountain-valley where poetry is made' (1964: 69).

2 The substitution of the masculine gender 'he' for the neuter 'it' of the 1805 version could offer a starting point for speculation on the poet's intentions, were it not for the editor's note informing us that there is no manuscript authority for the neuter gender of the first edition, suggesting that the original 'he' was probably deleted by Christopher Wordsworth, Jr. (later to become Bishop of London) in order to 'remove the characteristic but unorthodox Wordsworthian animism' (1979: 29). If one were to accept the alternative assumption, i.e. that the emendation is the poet's own, it could possibly mean two things:

NOTES

either, that the poem opens with a neuter 'nature' as it ends with a neuter 'mind' (in both versions), or, that the poet, consistent with his later 'Christianization' of *The Prelude*, introduced a masculine force calling upon the correspondent 'gentle' breeze.

3 M. H. Abrams, after pointing to 'the symbolic equations between breeze and breath', expresses the view that the Romantic ideal 'is that of a controlled violence, of a self ordering impetus of passion' (1957: 129), which sounds very close to the Platonic ὀρθῶς μαίνεσθαι of the *Phaedrus* (244e) and the ὀρθὸς ἔρως of the *Republic* (III, 403 a–b).

4 '*Spiritual marriage* is another metaphor of union with the divine', W. Embler affirms; so, 'the metaphor of the Bridegroom and the Bride becomes of profoundest meaning when, as was not uncommon in the Middle Ages, it stands for God's own pursuit of the unwilling soul, the reverse of the self's quest for the Absolute' (1974: 275).

5 One aspect of Coleridge's longing to reconcile the two reality models can also be detected in his interest in the Cambridge Platonists of the seventeenth century which he looked upon as his spiritual 'home'. What he apparently sought to find in the doctrine provided by the 'native' Platonists, was an answer more congenial to his own mental constitution; he turned to them looking for support and evidence in what he felt was an imperative need to 'desynonymize' between 'reason' and 'reason', or, as D. Newsome remarks: ' "reason" as the *Aufklärung* had defined it needed to be put into the proper relationship with the quality which the Platonists had described as "higher reason" or intuitive faculty' (1974: 92). The key position that the Cambridge Platonists held for Coleridge is that, at a time relatively close to his own age, and within his own culture and language, they attempted to bring about a fusion of Greek / Platonic and Judaeo-Christian premises.

6 See Bate (1968: 58), Warren (1969: 28), Brett (1960: 100).

7 See for example Boulger (1965: 451).

8 That the *Ancient Mariner* may bring 'into play Coleridge's conception of the modes by which a consciousness might be changed and sleeping faculties awakened' (Beer 1977: 157) has been a running theme in the poem's hermeneutics. To begin at the beginning, 'The imagery of ice introduces a feeling of lethargy in which actual fears tend to merge and diminish as in a fainting-fit' (Matthey 1974: 7), and the language of the opening stanzas 'suggests an atmosphere of striking beauty and of great dreamlike energies abroad: it is "wondrous" cold; the ice is "green as Emerald"; the sounds are reminiscent of noises projected from within oneself during a swoon' (Beer 1977: 167).

9 Whether the royal 'golden smithies' in Yeats' 'Byzantium', or less exalted craftsmanship.

10 Within or without the Eliotic *Waste Land*.

11 The allusions are respectively to *The Prelude* (II, 395) and Yeats' 'Dialogue of Self and Soul' (II).

12 J. H. Muirhead maintains that Coleridge's religious quest was for a

schema of ' "Judaism+Greece". While in Greece the Personality of God is the esoteric doctrine, the infinite whole the exoteric, in Christianity it is the reverse. That this side of his philosophy', Muirhead continues, 'obtained exaggerated emphasis in the later years of his life owing to his personal craving for a god who "answers prayer" and *forgives* is . . . traceable to the morbid bent in his own character' (1930: 36).

13 As L. Abbey claims, 'Although the subject of Shelley's Platonism is unfashionable at the moment, the Platonic cast of much of his writing is undeniable' (1979: 75).

14 T. Webb maintains that 'Shelley's vision of Greece is intrinsically beautiful but it must also be recognized as part of a dialectic', in that the 'full significance of Shelley's Greece becomes clearer when it is set against Christianity . . . God the Father against the Apollo of Belvedere', adding that it is in *Prometheus Unbound* where the 'opposition between the religion of Greece and the system of orthodox Christianity is perhaps clearest' (1976b: 365–6).

15 For a limited selection of such reviews, see Webb (1977: 131–3), Curran (1975: 116), Woodman (1964: 112–13), Bodkin (1934: 250–8), Allsup (1976: 87), and Wasserman (1965: 35).

16 The 'unspeaking' has been interpreted as a 'change in Prometheus' understanding of language', where 'Promethean voice is always reclaiming speech from a language of reference' and 'where words are assumed to have stronger relations to the objects and thoughts they represent than to one another' (Brisman 1977: 56–9).

17 Prometheus' 'renunciation of hate', W. H. Hildebrand asserts, 'like a reversible reaction in chemistry, set in motion the process of remembering the words of the curse. And that remembering becomes, in the mythic structure of the drama, a literal recalling of the words' (1983: 192).

18 The term is a transcription of the Greek word ἀπόφασις which, in its archaic signification, means both 'negation' (opposite to κατάφασις) and 'decision' – thus collecting into one word the precise nature of the Promethean act.

19 It is notable that the term 'Demogorgon' is also employed by Coleridge in his poem 'Limbo' written in 1817, that is one year prior to the composition of *Prometheus Unbound*. The use that Coleridge makes of the concept, and its symbolism, is somewhat similar to Shelley's, bringing out the paradox of a positive negativity inherent in the horror inspired by this power – closely analogous to the Shelleyan 'luminous gloom'.

20 C. E. Pulos, defending Shelley's 'intellectual coherence' against charges that interpret the poet's thought as lacking a 'unified tendency' and 'characterized by basic and irreconcilable contradictions', sees an answer to the (hypothetical) confusion of the poet's philosophical presuppositions, in his reconciliation of scepticism and Platonism; in fact, he argues, 'The sceptical tradition prepared the way for Shelley's acceptance of Plato by resolving the objection to Plato held by the *philosophes* and by depicting Plato as a

NOTES

kind of sceptic himself – or as, at least, a forerunner of scepticism'. Erecting yet another 'defence' for Shelley, Pulos avows that 'Shelley, then, is not a pseudo-Platonist but a Platonist in the sceptical tradition' (1954: 2–3, 69, 88).

21 E. Casey makes an interesting suggestion of analogy between the Platonic χώρα and the Romantic imagination: 'Like Plato's Receptacle, the indeterminacy of imaginal space demands the ordering element of form' (1975: 258).

22 That Panthea is an embodiment of the androgynous experience in the manner of the Platonic hermaphrodite, is suggested by W. H. Marshall (1959: 121–3).

23 Aristotle's definition for νοῦς.

24 T. S. Eliot's terms are employed only to be used in an inverted manner.

25 Hartman complains about 'the tyranny of Greece over England' not yet properly described, and asserts that Keats' 'quest for authorial identity' raises 'the vexed question of a modern or "northern" equivalent to Greek objectivity' (1974: 2). The literary allusion to Greek 'oppressiveness' is, I suppose, to the prototype of E. M. Butler, *The Tyranny of Greece over Germany*.

26 As, for instance, Sperry (1973: 182).

27 Sherwood (1934: 260–1); Thorpe (1926: 139) couples together what he calls the 'evolutionary' myths of Keats and Shelley, also hinting at a possible influence. The likelihood that the myths, far from indicating a parallel evolutionism, might be a complete inversion of each other in that they move in opposite directions – Keats' from the Titanic to the Olympian, Shelley's from the Olympian to the Titanic modes of consciousness – is, I believe, a crux that cannot be overlooked.

28 Hepworth (1978: 208), Hungerford (1941: 142), Kroeber (1964: 138–9).

29 Yet, Plato's treatment of the mythical age of Cronus and the Titanic condition is not unambiguous. The automatic and effortless nature of 'paradisal' existence when 'all good things come without man's labor' (*Statesm.*, 271d), an 'age of bliss' when 'all life needs was provided in abundance and unsought' (*Laws*, IV, 713c), is paradoxically to be feared and avoided as a relapse into chaos; in the 'reckless excess of liberty' instigated by the practice of poetry, the 'spectacle of the Titanic nature of which our old legends speak is re-enacted; man returns to the old condition of a hell of unending misery' (*Laws*, III, 701b–c).

30 A similar reading is offered by A. J. Harding who maintains that 'the confrontation with tradition can be an empowering as well as a humbling experience. In Platonic terms it resembles the moment of anamnesis, the moment when the truth that we know already, but have not been permitted to recall, floods into the mind and transforms us' (1986: 84).

NOTES

5 ON RE-COLLECTION

1 P. Ricoeur, dealing with the question of writing / reading in both its ontological and historical perspectives, emphasizes its positive aspect as a '*φάρμακον*', in its capacity to overcome temporality and cultural alienation: 'Reading is the *pharmakon*, the "remedy," by which the meaning of the text is "rescued" from the estrangement of distanciation and put in a new proximity, a proximity which suppresses and preserves the cultural distance and includes the otherness within the oneness' (1976: 43).

BIBLIOGRAPHY

Abbey, L. (1979) *Destroyer and Preserver: Shelley's Poetic Scepticism*, Lincoln and London: University of Nebraska Press.
Abrams, M. H. (1957) 'The correspondent breeze: a Romantic metaphor', *Kenyon Review* 19: 113–30.
—— (1971) *Natural Supernaturalism: Tradition and Revolution in Romantic Literature*, New York: Norton.
Allsup, J. O. (1976) *The Magic Circle: A Study of Shelley's Concept of Love*, Port Washington, N.Y., and London: Kennikat Press.
Barfield, O. (1971) *What Coleridge Thought*, Middletown, Conn.: Wesleyan University Press.
Barrel, J. (1947) *Shelley and the Thought of his Time: A Study in the History of Ideas*, New Haven: Yale University Press.
Bate, W. J. (1918) *Negative Capability: The Intuitive Approach in Keats*, 2nd edn 1939, Harvard University Press; rpt 1976, New York: AMS Press.
—— (1968) *Coleridge*, Macmillan; rpt 1969, London: Weidenfeld & Nicolson.
Beach, J. W. (1944) *A Romantic View of Poetry*, University of Minnesota Press; rpt 1963, Michigan: Scholarly Press.
Beer, J. (1959) *Coleridge the Visionary*, London: Chatto & Windus.
—— (1977) *Coleridge's Poetic Intelligence*, London: Macmillan.
Bigger, C. P. (1968) *Participation: A Platonic Inquiry*, Baton Rouge: Louisiana State University Press.
Blackstone, B. (1959) *The Consecrated Urn: An Interpretation of Keats in Terms of Growth and Form*, London: Longmans, Green, and Co.
Bloom, H. (1959) *Shelley's Mythmaking*, Yale University Press; rpt 1969, Ithaca: Cornell University Press.
—— (1970) 'The unpastured sea: an introduction to Shelley', in H. Bloom (ed.) *Romanticism and Consciousness: Essays in Criticism*, New York: Norton.
—— (1973) *The Anxiety of Influence: A Theory of Poetry*, New York: Oxford University Press.
Bodkin, M. (1934) *Archetypal Patterns in Poetry: Psychological Studies of Imagination*, London: Oxford University Press.

BIBLIOGRAPHY

Bostetter, R. L. (1963) *The Romantic Ventriloquists: Wordsworth, Coleridge, Keats, Shelley, Byron*, Seattle and London: University of Washington Press.

Boulger, J. D. (1965) 'Christian scepticism in *The Rime of the Ancient Mariner*', in F. W. Hilles and H. Bloom (eds) *From Sensibility to Romanticism: Essays Presented to F. A. Pottle*, New York: Oxford University Press.

Brett, R. L. (1960) *Reason and Imagination: A Study of Form and Meaning*, London: Oxford University Press.

Brisman, L. (1978) *Romantic Origins*, Ithaca and London: Cornell University Press.

Brisman, S. H. (1977) ' "Unsaying his high language": the problem of voice in *Prometheus Unbound*', *Studies in Romanticism* 16: 51–86.

Butler, E. M. (1935) *The Tyranny of Greece over Germany*, Cambridge: Cambridge University Press.

Butter, P. (1954) *Shelley's Idols of the Cave*, New York: Haskell House Publishers.

Casey, E. (1975) 'Imagination and repetition in literature: a reassessment' *Yale French Studies* 52: 249–67.

Cassirer, E. (1944) *An Essay on Man: An Introduction to a Philosophy of Human Culture*, New Haven and London: Yale University Press.

—— (1946) *Language and Myth*, trans. S. Langer, Harper and Brothers; rpt 1953, New York: Dover Publications.

—— (1955–57) *The Philosophy of Symbolic Forms*: trans. R. Manheim, (1955a) *Vol. I. Language*, New Haven and London: Yale University Press; (1955b) *Vol. II. Mythical Thought*, New Haven and London: Yale University Press; (1957) *Vol. III. The Phenomenology of Knowledge*, New Haven and London: Yale University Press.

Chayes, I. H. (1961) 'Plato's *Statesman* myth in Shelley and Blake', *Comparative Literature* 13: 358–69.

Chernaik, J. (1972) *The Lyrics of Shelley*, Cleveland and London: The Press of Case Western Reserve University.

Cherubini, W. (1942) 'Shelley's "own Symposium": *The Triumph of Life*', *Studies in Philology* 39: 559–70.

Coleridge, S. T. (1895) *Anima Poetae: From the Unpublished Note-Books of Samuel Taylor Coleridge*, ed. E. H. Coleridge, London: William Heinemann.

—— (1907) *Biographia Literaria*, ed. J. Shawcross, 2 vols, Oxford: Oxford University Press.

—— (1912) *Poetical Works*, ed. E. H. Coleridge, London: Oxford University Press.

—— (1956–71) *Collected Letters of Samuel Taylor Coleridge*, ed. E. L. Griggs, 6 vols, Oxford: Clarendon Press.

—— (1957–73) *The Notebooks of Samuel Taylor Coleridge*, ed. K. Coburn, (1957) *Vol. I, 1794–1804*, New York: Pantheon Books/Bollingen Series; (1962) *Vol. II, 1804–8*, London: Routledge & Kegan Paul/Bollingen Series; (1973) *Vol. III, 1808–19*, Princeton: Princeton University Press/Bollingen Series.

—— (1969) *The Friend*, ed. B. E. Rooke, 2 vols, London:

Routledge & Kegan Paul; Princeton: Princeton University Press/Bollingen Series.
    (1972) *Lay Sermons*, ed. R. J. White, London: Routledge & Kegan Paul; Princeton: Princeton University Press/Bollingen Series.
Conrad, J. (1960) *Three Short Novels: Heart of Darkness, Youth, Typhoon*, New York: Bantam Books.
Cosman, L. A. (1976) 'Platonic love', in W. H. Werkmeister (ed.) *Facets of Plato's Philosophy*, Assen/Amsterdam: Van Gorcum.
Cronin, R. (1981) *Shelley's Poetic Thoughts*, London: Macmillan.
Curran, S. (1975) *Shelley's Annus Mirabilis: The Maturing of an Epic Vision*, San Marino, Ca.: Huntington Library.
D'Avanzo, M. L. (1967) *Keats's Metaphors for the Poetic Imagination*, Durham, N.C.: Duke University Press.
De Man, P. (1984) *The Rhetoric of Romanticism*, New York: Columbia University Press.
Demos, R. (1939) *The Philosophy of Plato*, Charles Scribner's Sons; rpt 1966, New York: Octagon Books.
Derrida, J. (1973) *Speech and Phenomena, And Other Essays on Husserl's Theory of Signs*, trans. D. B. Allison, Evanston: Northwestern University Press.
    (1974a) *Glas*, Paris: Editions Galilée.
    (1974b) *Of Grammatology*, trans. G. C. Spivak, Baltimore and London: Johns Hopkins University Press.
    (1978) *Writing and Difference*, trans. Alan Bass, London: Routledge & Kegan Paul.
    (1979) 'Living on', in H. Bloom *et al.* (eds) *De-construction and Criticism*, London: Routledge & Kegan Paul.
    (1981) *Dissemination*, trans. B. Johnson, Chicago: University of Chicago Press.
Dodds, E. R. (ed.) (1944) *Euripides, Bacchae: Edited with Introduction and Commentary*, 2nd edn 1960, Oxford: Clarendon Press.
    (1951) *The Greeks and the Irrational*, Berkeley: University of California Press.
Donato, E. (1977) 'The idioms of the text: notes on the language of philosophy and the fictions of literature', *Glyph* 2: 1–13.
Dyson, A. E. and Lovelock, J. (1973) *Masterful Images: English Poetry from Metaphysicals to Romantics*, London: Macmillan.
Eichner, H. (ed.) (1972) *'Romantic' and its Cognates: The European History of a Word*, Toronto and Buffalo: University of Toronto Press.
Eliade, M. (1958) *Rites and Symbols of Initiation: The Mysteries of Birth and Rebirth*, trans. W. R. Trask, New York: Harper & Row.
    (1960) *Myths, Dreams, and Mysteries: The Encounter between Contemporary Faiths and Archaic Reality*, trans. P. Mairet, Harvill Press; 2nd edn 1968, Glasgow: William Collins & Sons.
    (1963) *Myth and Reality*, trans. W. R. Trask, New York: Harper & Row.
Eliot, T. S. (1932) *Selected Essays*, new edn 1960, New York: Harcourt, Brace & World.

(1933) *The Use of Poetry and the Use of Criticism*, 2nd edn 1964, London: Faber & Faber.
 (1935) *Murder in the Cathedral*, 4th edn 1938, London: Faber & Faber.
 (1963) *Collected Poems, 1909–1962*, London: Faber & Faber.
Embler, W. (1974) 'The metaphors of mysticism', *ETC: A Review of General Semantics* 31: 272–87.
Euripides (1954) *The Bacchae and Other Plays*, trans. P. Vellacot, 2nd edn 1973, Harmondsworth: Penguin.
Evert, W. H. (1965) *Aesthetic and Myth in the Poetry of Keats*, Princeton: Princeton University Press.
Ferguson, F. (1977) *Wordsworth: Language as Counter-Spirit*, New Haven and London: Yale University Press.
Findlay, J. N. (1974) *Plato: The Written and Unwritten Doctrines*, London: Routledge & Kegan Paul.
Fletcher, A. (1964) *Allegory: The Theory of a Symbolic Mode*, Ithaca: Cornell University Press.
Fontenprose, J. (1959) *Python: A Study of Delphic Myth and its Origins*, Berkeley: University of California Press.
Friedländer, P. (1958) *Plato: An Introduction*, trans. H. Meyerhoff, 2nd edn 1969, Princeton: Princeton University Press/Bollingen Series.
Frye, N. (1968) *A Study of English Romanticism*, New York: Random House.
Gadamer, H.-G. (1975) *Truth and Method*, trans. W. Glen-Doepel, 2nd edn 1979, London: Sheed and Ward.
 (1978) 'Plato and Heidegger', in M. Sprung (ed.) *The Question of Being: East-West Perspectives*, University Park and London: Pennsylvania State University Press.
 (1980) *Dialogue and Dialectic: Eight Hermeneutical Studies on Plato*, trans. P. C. Smith, New Haven and London: Yale University Press.
 (1985) *Philosophical Apprenticeships*, trans. Robert R. Sullivan, Cambridge, Mass. and London: MIT Press.
Gittings, R. (1954) *John Keats: The Living Year*, London: Heinemann.
Godfrey, D. R. (1965) 'Keats and the Grecian urn', *Hermathena* 100: 44–53.
Gould, T. (1963) *Platonic Love*, London: Routledge & Kegan Paul.
Greene, W. C. (1918) 'Plato's view of poetry', *Harvard Studies in Classical Philology* 29: 1–75.
Gutteling, J. F. C. (1922) *Hellenic Influence on the English Poetry of the Nineteenth Century*, rpt 1972, New York: Folcroft Library Editions.
Hamlin, C. (1976) 'Platonic dialogue and Romantic irony: prolegomenon to a theory of literary narrative', *Canadian Review of Comparative Literature* 3: 5–26.
Harding, A. J. (1986) 'Speech, silence, and the self-doubting interpreter in Keats's poetry', *Keats–Shelley Journal* 35: 83–103.
Harper, G. M. (1961) *The Neoplatonism of William Blake*, Chapel Hill: The University of North Carolina Press; London: Oxford University Press.

Harries, K. (1978) 'Metaphor and transcendence', *Critical Inquiry* 5: 73–90.
Harrison, J. E. (1903) *Prolegomena to the Study of Greek Religion*, 3rd edn 1962, London: Merlin Press.
Hart, R. L. (1965) 'The imagination in Plato', *International Philosophical Quarterly* 5: 436–61.
Hartman, G. H. (1964) *Wordsworth's Poetry, 1787–1814*, 2nd edn 1971, New Haven and London: Yale University Press.
—— (1970) *Beyond Formalism: Literary Essays 1958–1970*, New Haven and London: Yale University Press.
—— (1974) 'Spectral symbolism and the authorial self: an approach to Keats's *Hyperion*', *Essays in Criticism* 24: 1–19.
—— (1975) *The Fate of Reading and Other Essays*, Chicago and London: University of Chicago Press.
—— (1980) *Criticism in the Wilderness: The Study of Literature Today*, New Haven and London: Yale University Press.
Haven, R. (1969) *Patterns of Consciousness: An Essay on Coleridge*, Massachusetts: University of Massachusetts Press.
Heidegger, M. (1959) *An Introduction to Metaphysics*, trans. R. Manheim, New Haven and London: Yale University Press.
—— (1968) *What is Called Thinking?*, trans. J. G. Gray, New York: Harper & Row.
—— (1971a) *Poetry, Language, Thought*, trans. A. Hofstadter, New York: Harper & Row.
—— (1971b) *On the Way to Language*, trans. P. D. Hertz, San Francisco: Harper & Row.
—— (1972) *On Time and Being*, trans. J. Stambaugh, New York: Harper & Row.
Hepworth, B. (1978) *The Rise of Romanticism: Essential Texts*, Manchester: Carcanet.
Heraclitus (1979) *The Art and Thought of Heraclitus: An Edition of the Fragments with Translation and Commentary*, ed. C. H. Kahn, Cambridge: Cambridge University Press.
Hildebrand, W. H. (1983) 'Naming-day in Asia's vale', *Keats–Shelley Journal* 32: 190–203.
Holmes, R. (1974) *Shelley: The Pursuit*, Weidenfeld & Nicolson, 2nd edn 1976, London: Quartet Books.
Hungerford, E. B. (1941) *Shores of Darkness*, Columbia University Press; rpt 1974, Gloucester, Mass.: Peter Smith.
Jung, C. (1956) *Symbols of Transformation: An Analysis of the Prelude to a Case of Schizophrenia*, trans. R. F. Hull, 2nd edn 1967, Princeton: Princeton University Press/Bollingen Series.
Keats, J. (1956) *Poetical Works*, ed. H. W. Garrod, London: Oxford University Press.
—— (1958) *The Letters of John Keats, 1814–1821*, ed. H. E. Rollins, 2 vols, Cambridge, Mass.: Harvard University Press.
Kessler, E. (1979) *Coleridge's Metaphors of Being*, Princeton: Princeton University Press.
Krell, D. F. (1975) 'Female parts in *Timaeus*', *Arion* 2: 400–21.
Krieger, M. (1971) *Visions of Extremity in Modern Literature. Vol. II.*

BIBLIOGRAPHY

The Classic Vision: The Retreat from Extremity, Baltimore and London: Johns Hopkins University Press.

Kroeber, K. (1964) *The Artifice of Reality: Poetic Style in Wordsworth, Foscolo, Keats, and Leopardi*, Madison and Milwaukee: University of Wisconsin Press.

Kuhns, R. (1971) *Literature and Philosophy: Structures of Experience*, London: Routledge & Kegan Paul.

Kurtz, B. P. (1933) *The Pursuit of Death: A Study of Shelley's Poetry*, Oxford University Press; rpt 1970, New York: Octagon Books.

Liddell, H. G. and Scott, R. (1843) *A Greek–English Lexicon*, rev. 9th edn eds Sir H. S. Jones and R. McKenzie 1940, Oxford: Clarendon Press.

Lindenberger, H. (1963) *On Wordsworth's Prelude*, Princeton: Princeton University Press.

Lowes, J. L. (1927) *The Road to Xanadu: A Study in the Ways of the Imagination*, Boston: Houghton Mifflin.

Marshall, W. H. (1959) 'Plato's myth of Aristophanes and Shelley's Panthea', *Classical Journal* 55: 121–3.

Matthews, C. (1984) 'Sophia: companion on the quest', in J. Matthews (ed.) *At the Table of the Grail*, London: Routledge & Kegan Paul.

Matthews, G. M. (1957) 'A volcano's voice in Shelley', *Journal of English Literary History* 24: 191–228.

—— (1960) ' "The Triumph of Life": A New Text' *Studia Neophilologica* 32: 271–309.

—— (1961) 'Shelley and Jane Williams' *Review of English Studies* N.S. 12: 40–8.

—— (1962) 'On Shelley's "The Triumph of Life" ', *Studia Neophilologica* 34: 104–34.

—— (1968) ' "The Triumph of Life" ', *Essays in Criticism* 18: 352–6.

Matthey, F. (1974) *The Evolution of Keats's Structural Imagery*, Bern: Francke Verlag.

Miller, J. H. (1979) 'The critic as host' in H. Bloom et al. (eds) *Deconstruction and Criticism*, London and Henley: Routledge & Kegan Paul.

Moore, A. (1976) 'Mysticism and philosophy', *Monist* 59: 493–505.

Muirhead, J. H. (1930) *Coleridge as Philosopher*, London: George Allen & Unwin; New York: Macmillan.

Murdoch, I. (1977) *The Fire and the Sun: Why Plato Banished the Artists*, Oxford: Oxford University Press.

Murray, M. (1975) *Modern Critical Theory: A Phenomenological Introduction*, The Hague: Martinus Nijhoff.

—— (ed.) (1978) *Heidegger and Modern Philosophy: Critical Essays*, New Haven and London: Yale University Press.

Newsome, D. (1974) *Two Classes of Men: Platonism and English Romantic Thought*, London: John Murray.

Nietzsche, F. (1967) *The Birth of Tragedy and The Case of Wagner*, trans. W. Kaufmann, New York: Vintage Books.

Notopoulos, J. A. (1936) 'Movement in the divided line of Plato's Republic', *Harvard Studies in Classical Philology* 47: 57–83.

(1949a) *The Platonism of Shelley: A Study of Platonism and the Poetic Mind*, Duke University Press; rpt 1969, New York: Octagon Books.

(1949b) 'Shelley and the *Symposium* of Plato', *The Classical Weekly* 42: 98–102.

O'Brien, E. (ed.) (1964) *The Essential Plotinus: Representative Treatises from the Enneads*, New American Library; rpt 1975, Indianapolis: Hackett Publishing Co.

Parker, S. (1666) *A Free and Impartial Censure of the Platonick Philosophie*, 2nd edn 1667, Oxford: Printer to the University.

Pater, W. (1925) *Plato and Platonism: A Series of Lectures*, Macmillan; rpt 1969, New York: Greenwood Press.

Patterson, C. I. (1954) 'Passion and permanence in Keats's *Ode on a Grecian Urn*', *Journal of English Literary History* 21: 208–20.

Patterson, C. I., Jr (1970) *The Daemonic in the Poetry of John Keats*, Urbana: University of Illinois Press.

Perkins, D. (1959) *The Quest for Permanence: The Symbolism of Wordsworth, Shelley, and Keats*, Cambridge, Mass.: Harvard University Press.

Pettet, E. C. (1957) *On the Poetry of Keats*, Cambridge: Cambridge University Press.

Plato (1871) *The Dialogues of Plato, Translated into English with Analyses and Introductions*, ed. B. Jowett, 4 vols, 4th edn rev. 1953, Oxford: Clarendon Press.

(1900–1907) *Platonis Opera*, ed. I. Burnet, 5 vols, Oxford: Oxford University Press.

(1961) *The Collected Works of Plato*, ed. E. Hamilton and H. Cairns, Princeton: Princeton University Press/Bollingen Series.

Poulet, G. (1954) 'Timelessness and Romanticism', *Journal of the History of Ideas* 15: 3–22.

Prickett, S. (1970) *Coleridge and Wordsworth: The Poetry of Growth*, Cambridge: Cambridge University Press.

Pulos, C. E. (1954) *The Deep Truth: A Study of Shelley's Scepticism*, Lincoln: University of Nebraska Press.

Rajan, T. (1980) *Dark Interpreter: The Discourse of Romanticism*, Ithaca and London: Cornell University Press.

Randall, J. H., Jr (1970) *Plato: Dramatist of the Life of Reason*, New York: Columbia University Press.

Reiman, D. H. (1963) 'Shelley's "The Triumph of Life": the biographical problem', *PMLA* 78: 536–50.

(1965) *Shelley's 'The Triumph of Life': A Critical Study, Based on a Text Newly Edited from the Bodleian Manuscript*, University of Illinois Press; rpt 1979, New York: Octagon Books.

Ricoeur, P. (1976) *Interpretation Theory: Discourse and the Surplus of Meaning*, Fort Worth: Texas Christian University Press.

(1978) 'The metaphorical process as cognition, imagination, and feeling', *Critical Inquiry* 5: 143–59.

Rist, J. M. (1964) *Eros and Psyche: Studies in Plato, Plotinus, and Origen*, Toronto: University of Toronto Press.

Rogers, S. (1974) *Classical Greece and the Poetry of Chenier, Shelley,*

and Leopardi. Notre Dame, Ind.: University of Notre Dame Press.
Rosen, S. (1963) 'Ideas', *Review of Metaphysics* 16: 407–41.
Rousseau, J.-J. (1953) *The Confessions*, trans. J. M. Cohen, Harmondsworth: Penguin.
Ryle, G. (1966) *Plato's Progress*, Cambridge: Cambridge University Press.
Salvesen, C. (1965) *The Landscape of Memory: A Study of Wordsworth's Poetry*, London: Edward Arnold.
Shakespeare, W. (1951) *The Complete Works*, The Players Edition, ed. P. Alexander, London and Glasgow: Collins.
Shelley, P. B. (1905) *Poetical Works*, ed. T. Hutchinson, edn corr. G. M. Matthews 1943, London: Oxford University Press.
—— (1954) *Shelley's Prose, or The Trumpet of a Prophecy*, ed. D. L. Clark, corr. edn 1966, Albuquerque: The University of Mexico Press.
—— (1964) *The Letters of Percy Bysshe Shelley*, ed. F. L. Jones, 2 vols, Oxford: Clarendon Press.
Sherry, C. (1980) *Wordsworth's Poetry of the Imagination*, Oxford: Clarendon Press.
Sherwood, M. (1934) *Undercurrents of Influence in English Romantic Poetry*, Cambridge University Press; rpt 1971, New York: AMS Press.
Simpson, D. (1976) 'Keats's Lady, metaphor, and the rhetoric of neurosis', *Studies in Romanticism* 15: 265–88.
—— (1979) *Irony and Authority in Romantic Poetry*, London: Macmillan.
Spanos, W. V. (ed.) (1976) *Martin Heidegger and the Question of Literature: Toward a Postmodern Literary Hermeneutics*, Bloomington and London: Indiana University Press.
Sperry, S. M. (1973) *Keats the Poet*, Princeton: Princeton University Press.
Spitzer, L. (1955) 'The "Ode on a Grecian Urn," or content vs. metagrammar', *Comparative Literature* 7: 203–25.
Stallknecht, N. P. and Brumbaugh, R. S. (1954) *The Compass of Philosophy: An Essay in Intellectual Orientation*, Longmans, Green and Co.; rpt 1974, Westport, Conn.: Greenwood Press.
Stewart, J. A. (1905) *The Myths of Plato*, new edn ed. G. R. Levy 1960, Fontwell, Sussex: Centaur Press.
Swingle, I. J. (1971) 'On reading Romantic poetry', *PMLA* 86: 774–81.
—— (1978) 'The Romantic emergence: multiplication of alternatives and the problem of systematic entrapment', *Modern Language Quarterly* 39: 264–83.
Thorpe, C. D. (1926) *The Mind of John Keats*, New York: Russell & Russell.
Warner, M. (1979) 'Love, self, and Plato's *Symposium*', *Philosophical Quarterly* 29: 329–39.
Warren, R. P. (1969) 'A poem of pure imagination: an experiment in reading', in J. D. Boulger (ed.) *Twentieth Century Interpretations of The Rime of the Ancient Mariner: A Collection of Critical Essays*, Englewood Cliffs, N.J.: Prentice-Hall.

BIBLIOGRAPHY

Wasserman, E. R. (1953) *The Finer Tone: Keats' Major Poems*, Baltimore: Johns Hopkins University Press.
— (1965) *Shelley's Prometheus Unbound: A Critical Reading*, Baltimore: Johns Hopkins University Press.
Webb, T. (1976a) *The Violet in the Crucible: Shelley and Translation*, Oxford: Clarendon Press.
— (1976b) 'Shelley and the religion of joy', *Studies in Romanticism* 15: 357–82.
— (1977) *Shelley: A Voice Not Understood*, Manchester: Manchester University Press.
Weston, J. (1957) *From Ritual to Romance*, Cambridge University Press; rpt 1983, Gloucester, Mass.: Peter Smith.
White, D. A. (1978) *Heidegger and the Language of Poetry*, Lincoln and London: University of Nebraska Press.
White, N. P. (1976) *Plato on Knowledge and Reality*, Indianapolis: Hackett Publishing Company.
Wigod, J. D. (1957) 'Keats's ideal in the *Ode on a Grecian Urn*', *PMLA* 72: 113–21.
Wimsatt, W. K., Jr and Brooks, C. (1957) *Literary Criticism: A Short History*, 4 vols, new edn 1970, London: Routledge & Kegan Paul.
Wittgenstein, L. (1961) *Tractatus Logico–Philosophicus*, trans. D. F. Pears and B. F. McGuinness, London: Routledge & Kegan Paul.
Wolz, H. G. (1981) *Plato and Heidegger: In Search of Selfhood*, London and Toronto: Associated University Presses.
Woodman, R. G. (1960) 'Shelley's changing attitude to Plato', *Journal of the History of Ideas* 21: 497–510.
— (1964) *Apocalyptic Vision in the Poetry of Shelley*, Toronto: University of Toronto Press.
— (1981) 'The androgyne in *Prometheus Unbound*', *Studies in Romanticism* 20: 225–47.
Wordsworth, W. (1904) *Poetical Works*, ed. T. Hutchinson, rev. edn ed. E. de Selincourt 1936, London: Oxford University Press.
— (1974) *The Prose Works of William Wordsworth*, ed. W. J. B. Owen and J. W. Smyser, 3 vols, Oxford: Oxford University Press.
— (1979) *The Prelude 1799, 1805, 1850: Authoritative Texts, Context and Reception, Recent Critical Essays*, ed. J. Wordsworth, M. H. Adams, and S. Gill, New York: Norton.
Yeats, W. B. (1933) *The Collected Poems of W. B. Yeats*, definitive edn with the author's final revisions 1956, New York: Macmillan.

INDEX

Abrams, M.H. 190, 210
Adonais 69, 87–9, 221; and life 94–6; and memory 279; passion 178–9
Aeschylus 42, 226
Agathon 83
ambiguity, in *The Triumph of Life* 98, 106
ambivalence: Keats' in *Hyperion/Fall of Hyperion* 248, 265, 272; in *Lamia* 134–5; moral, in *Prometheus Unbound* 233; of passion 177–8; and recollection 280, 286; in *The Triumph of Life* 117
Anatomy of Melancholy 70, 125
Ancient Mariner see Rime of the Ancient Mariner
androgyny: in *Prometheus Unbound* 245; symbolism of 191, 192
Apollo: and Dionysus in *Lamia* 134, 137; and *Hyperion/Fall of Hyperion* 247, 259, 261–3, 265, 267, 272; and Keats 53–4, 60–2; and *Lamia* 126–8, 130; and Prometheus 246; in *Symposium* 78
Apology 156
Aristotle 294
Asia, in *Prometheus Unbound* 226, 230–42
authority, in *Prometheus Unbound* 225–7

Bacchae 116–17, 118–21, 128
Bacon, Lord 86
Barfield, O. 211
Bate, W.J. 179
Beach, J.W. 125
beauty: in *Hyperion/Fall of Hyperion* 259; in *Phaedrus* 99–100; in *Symposium* 79
Beer, J. 209, 219
Being: and dialogue 42; as form 2–5, 8; and Idea 5–6; and logos 9, 13, 20; and naming 10, 12; and not Being 9; in Plato 1–13, 27, 153–4; in *Prometheus Unbound* 237; and reality 7–8; and recollection 280, 290, 293; in *Symposium* 73; and time 149–50, 153–4
Bigger, C.P. 284
Blake, W. 110
Bloom, H. 61, 110
Bodkin, M. 220
body and soul in Plato's writing 154–5
Brisman, L. 241
Burton, R. 70, 125

Cassirer, E. 51; on holiness 119–20; and *Hyperion/Fall of Hyperion* 264; and *Lamia* 134–5; and mythical thinking 136, 140–1, 144–7; and 'Ode on a Grecian Urn' 62–3
change 143

INDEX

Christianity in Coleridge's work 206–7, 211
Clairmont, C. 88
coldness: in Keats' poetry 56; in *The Triumph of Life* 102, 106
Coleridge, S.T. 51; on Being 1–2; and contradictions 229; and dialectic 36; and memory 276; on passion 168, 174–6; on poetry 173; and *Ancient Mariner* 205–25; symbols 141–2; on Wordsworth 173–4
collectedness in Plato 139
combat in *Lamia* 130–1
Confessions, The 113–14
confrontation: of Apollo and Mnemosyne 262, 267, 272; of Prometheus and Jupiter 227–37
consciousness: in *Ancient Mariner* 212; and dialectic 39; in *The Prelude* 203; single pointedness of mind 134, 136, 169, 179
contradiction: in poetry 165–7; in soul 43, 45
Cosman, L.A. 5, 79
Cratylus 100, 213, 231; and being 11; and language 10, 19–20; and logos 19, 26; and memory 281; and motion 12–13; names 31; and non-being 9; and reality 151; and time 153
crisis: in *Hyperion/Fall of Hyperion* 251; of identity, in Romantic poetry 184
Cronin, R. 91, 97, 241

daemon: in *Ancient Mariner* 210; Demogorgon in *Prometheus Unbound* 231, 237–8; in *Statesman* 250
dance, in *The Triumph of Life* 116–19
Dante 111
De Man, P. 98
De Quincey, T. 278
Demogorgon, in *Prometheus Unbound* 226, 230–42
Demos, R. 78
Derrida, J.: on being and speaking 141; and logocentric tradition 35–6, 40; and Dionysus 62; on Idea 2; and memory 291–2; and play 47; and *The Triumph of Life* 98
dialectic: as art 38–9, 41; defined 34–5; and form 39; and language 36–7; in *The Prelude* 198–9, 205
dialectical method 5, 16–17
dialectical thinking 136
dialogue: and Being 42; as play 23–49; and romantic period 51; in *Symposium* 72–3, 75
Dialogues 28
difference 8; between Apollo and Dionysus 62
Dilke, C.W. 58
Dionysus: and Apollo in *Lamia* 134, 137; and Eleusinian mysteries 190–2; in *Hyperion/Fall of Hyperion* 257, 264–5; and Keats 60–2; in *Lamia* 126–8, 130–1; and Prometheus 245–6; and sexuality in man 120–1; in *Symposium* 74, 78, 80–1
division in Plato 139
Dodds, E.R. 116–21, 265
drama: and platonic dialectic 42–3; in Plato's writing 165; *Symposium* as 73–4, 82
Dungeon, The 208

Ego *see* Self
Eliade, M.: on androgyny 245; on mastery of fire 218–19; on memory 261, 265; on ritual death 63–4
Eliot, T.S. 121, 124, 219, 239
Endymion 69, 253; and Dionysus 66; and *Lamia* 125; love 60, 67, 70, 181; and memory 277; opposites 55; and passion 180
energy: in Keats' poetry 54–5; in *The Triumph of Life* 108
epics, mythological, and Romantic poets 183–5
Epinomis 44, 163, 231
Epipsychidion 87, 89, 93, 177

Eros: and soul 158–60; in logos 4, 72–135; in *Symposium* 72–83; see also love
Euripides 42, 116
Evert, W.H. 53
evil: and ignorance, in *Ancient Mariner* 210; *Lamia* as 125
Excursion, The 169, 190
existence *see* Being

Fall of Hyperion, The, see Hyperion
femininity: of nature in *The Prelude* 194–5; in *Prometheus Unbound* 238, 240, 242–4
Findlay, J.N. 40
Fletcher, A. 14
Fontenprose, J. 126–8
form: and Being 2–5, 8; distinctions between 8; and Grecian urn 66
Four Quartets 239
Friedländer, P. 15, 40
Frye, N. 183

Gadamer, H.-G. 27, 32–3, 41–2; and German romanticism 49–51; on hermeneutics 122; and memory 283; metamorphosis 146; Platonic dialogues 139; on play 46–9, 143
Gisborne, John and Mary 84, 86, 88–9, 90
Gittings, R. 71
Godwin, W. 86
Goethe, J.W. 88, 91, 109
Gorgias 23, 86, 163
Gould, T. 79
grammar and naming 22–3
Grecian urn *see* 'Ode on a Grecian Urn'
growth and *The Prelude* 189
guilt and *Prometheus Unbound* 225

Harper, G.M. 62
Harrison, J.E. 191
Hartman, G.H. 211, 216, 275, 278
hate and love in *The Prelude* 198

Haven, R. 209–10
heat: in *Ancient Mariner* 218–19; in *Lamia* 132–3
Heidegger, M.: and Being 27, 150–1; and consciousness 236; and language 35–6, 268; light and Being 45–6; and logos 9, 13, 20–2, 26, 126–7, 139–40, 145; on memory 147–8, 277–9, 290, 295; and metaphor 295; on thinking 222–3; on questions 123; and work of art 68
Hellas 87, 88, 89, 94
Heraclitus 11, 35, 80, 127, 144–5, 223, 281
hermeneutics 50; in 'Ode on a Grecian Urn' 49–71; play as Being 143; in *The Triumph of Life* 91
hierogamy: symbolism of 192–3; and Wordsworth 190–1
Hippolytus 120
Hoelderlin (poet) 279
Hogg, T. 86
homosexuality, and Shelley 84–5, 86–7
Hungerford, E.B. 247
Hunt, Leigh 85, 88
Huxley, A. 118
Hyperion/The Fall of Hyperion 122, 181, 206, 247–73; ambivalence of Keats 248, 265, 272; and beauty 259; crisis in 251; Dionysus in 257, 264–5; language of 252–3; and light 247, 256, 260; and memory 277; and metamorphosis 263–4; opposites in 266–7; regression in 264–5; structure of 248–9, 265; suffering in 253–4; tension in 255–6

Idea: and dialectical process 5; exploration of 1–2
ideal, in *The Triumph of Life* 97
image: of memory 277; of urn in Keats' work 56, 58
imagery in *Hyperion/Fall of Hyperion* 249, 261, 268

INDEX

immortality, and memory 284–6, 288
'Immortality Ode' 65, 203, 275
Ion 38, 68, 174; and poetry 163–5; and 'power' 156
irony: in Plato 14–15, 16; in *The Triumph of Life* 97

Jowett, B. 156
Jung, C. 29
Jupiter: and *Hyperion/Fall of Hyperion* 247, 249; in *Prometheus Unbound* 226–8, 230–1, 237, 240, 246

Keats, George 53
Keats, J. 122; and Coleridge 212, 217; creative process 54–5; and eros 72; heat and cold in poetry 56; *Hyperion/Fall of Hyperion* 247–73; imagery of 179; and *Lamia* 125–35; letter to Reynolds 58–9; and memory 277, 285; modes of thought 52–4; and 'Ode on a Grecian Urn' 64, 68–9; and 'Ode on Indolence' 59–60; and opposites 55, 57; on passion 168–9, 180–1; on poetry 183; spiritual and sensual state 60; views on sexuality 70–1
Kessler, C. 211
Krell, D.F. 4
Krieger, M. 61
Kroeber, K. 204
Kuhn, R. 289

Lamia 125–35, 221; ambivalence in 134–5; Dionysus in 126–8, 130–1; heat in 132–3; light in 127; 'moral' of 132–3; opposites in 129–30, 134; sexuality in 128–9; as a symposium 129
language: and *Ancient Mariner* 217, 223–4; and dialectic 36–7; in *Hyperion/Fall of Hyperion* 252–3; and metaphor 14; Plato's use of 13–14; and reality 9, 10;

and Romantic poetry 175–6; in *Symposium* 85
Laws 118, 149; and logos 18, 19; opposites 16, 17; and poetry 164–5, 166–7; and soul 156, 158
Letters 130, 135, 138; and logos 18, 19
life: in *Adonais* 94–6; concept of in Shelley's works 91–5; in *The Triumph of Life* 108–9, 125
light: in *Ancient Mariner* 221–2; in *Hyperion/Fall of Hyperion* 247, 256, 260; in *Lamia* 127; in poetry 174; in *The Triumph of Life* 94, 99, 101–3, 104–7
Lindenberger, H. 274
linguistics, bond with ontology 140–1
logocentrism 35–6, 40, 141
logos: and Being 9, 13, 20; and eros 4, 72–135; evolution of concept 33; in Heidegger's writing 20–2; and myth/mythos 13–27, 28, 31–2, 136–51; Plato's attitude to 18–19
love: and hate in *The Prelude* 198; in Keats' poetry 59–60; in *Prometheus Unbound* 230–1, 235–6, 238, 242; and soul 159–61; in *Symposium* 75–80, 83, 85; in *The Triumph of Life* 105; *see also* Eros
Lowes, J.L. 210

madness/mania: in *Phaedrus* 159; and poetry 163–5; in *Symposium* 74–5; and *The Triumph of Life* 114–15, 117
man and nature, married in *The Prelude* 189–90, 195, 199
marriage and metaphor in *The Prelude* 190–1, 195, 196–9, 204
Matthews, G.M. 123, 241
Medwin, T. 86
memory: images of 277; and immortality 284–6, 288; and metamorphosis 147–8; and money 280–1; as Mother of Muses 276, 279; and Plato

321

281–90; and Romantic poets 274–7; and time 274, 278; and writing 292–4
Meno 38, 164; and memory 284–6, 288
metamorphosis 136–51; and *Ancient Mariner* 205–6, 214–15, 222; in *Hyperion/Fall of Hyperion* 263–4; and memory 147–8; and Romantic poets 185–6; in *The Triumph of Life* 101
metaphor: and marriage in *The Prelude* 190–1, 195, 196–9, 204; in Plato 14, 23; and reality 294–5; in *The Triumph of Life* 99, 104–5
Metaphysics 151
Miller, J.H. 99
Milton, J. 54, 194
mind–nature relationship: hierarchy in 198–9; in *The Prelude* 190–1, 196; as romance 204–5
Mnemosyne: and *Hyperion/Fall of Hyperion* 261–3, 267, 271–2; and memory 276, 279
Moneta 254–5, 268–73
motion: in *Ancient Mariner* 213–14; as evil 12–13; as form 8; as good 11; in *Hyperion/Fall of Hyperion* 248; and language 12; as reality 11
Murdoch, I. 40
Muses, memory as Mother of 276, 279
myth/mythos: function of 138; and logos 28, 30–2, 136–51; and mythological world 142; and 'To J.H. Reynolds, Esq.' 59; in Plato's writings 28–32
mythical thinking 134–5, 136

naming: art of 22; and Being 10, 12; and definition 22–4; in Plato's writings 14–16; and poetry 26
narrative, of *Hyperion/Fall of Hyperion* 250, 266

nature: cognition 201; and Coleridge 208, 224; dual function of 203; and man, married in *The Prelude* 189–90, 195, 199; penetrating mind 202; power of in *Prometheus Unbound* 237
Nietzsche, F. 61
nothingness 8
Notopoulos, J.A. 83
Novalis (Hardenberg) 278

'Ode on a Grecian Urn' 52–71; and Beauty and Truth 69; as discourse 60–1, interaction of forms 63; metaphors 65–6; myth 59; opposites in 60–1; 'rape' of 64–5; sexuality in 64–5, 66–8; syntax of 66–7; urn, shape of 66
'Ode on Indolence' 59–60, 65, 68
On the Constitution of the Church and State 206
ontology, bond with linguistics 140–1
opposites/opposition: in *Hyperion/Fall of Hyperion* 266–7; in Keats' poetry 55, 57; in *Lamia* 129–30, 134; and 'Ode on a Grecian Urn' 60–1; in Plato's writing 16–18, 156–7; of poetry and philosophy 52

Parker, S. 74
Parmenides 2, 8, 9
Parmenides, and reality 152–3
passion: in *Ancient Mariner* 208–9; Plato on 151–68; and poetry of Romantic poets 168–87; and reason 170–1; and thought 171–2
Plater, W. 40, 189
Peacock, T.L. 84
Perkins, D. 187
Pettet, E.C. 70
Phaedo: and form 4; and memory 284, 286–8; and poetry 164; and reality 151; and Romantics 185; and the soul 44
Phaedrus 139; dialectic 38; and

INDEX

form 3; and logos 25; and madness 159; and memory 288–9, 292; and myth 28–9, 31; and 'Ode on a Grecian Urn' 61; and poetry 163–4, 168; and reality 152; and soul 157–9; and the soul 44; and *Symposium* 78; and *The Triumph of Life* 99, 100–1, 114; and words 23

Philebus 152, 154, 157–8; and memory 282, 292, 294; and 'Ode on a Grecian Urn' 61

philosophy and poetry: conjunction of in Plato 161; and romanticism 51

Plato: on Being and forms in 1–13, 153–4; dialogues as play 27–49; interaction of myth and logos 13–27; and irony 14–16; and Keats 129; and language 13–14; on logos 18–19; and memory 281–90; metaphor 14, 23; and movement 11; myths and logos, in dialogues 28–30, 32, 138–9; and Olympian age 250–1; and opposites 16–17, 156–7; on passion 151–68; on recollection 280–9, 292–3; and romantic period 49–50; and Rousseau 114; and *Symposium* 72–83

play: platonic dialogue as 27–49; and transformation 143–4

pluralism, of names 7–8

poetry: as art 163; contradictions in 165–7; criticism of 164; danger of 166–7; definition 162–3; of Keats 54–5; and madness 163–5; and naming 26; and passion of Romantic poets 168–87; and philosophy and romanticism 51; Plato on 151–68; and recollection 279–80

Poulet, G. 146, 274

power of nature in *Prometheus Unbound* 237

Prelude, The 101–2, 169–71, 172, 188–205; consciousness 203; love and hate in 198; and memory 283; metaphor of marriage in 190–1, 195, 196–9, 204; self in 189, 191, 193

'presentness' 146–8

Prickett, S. 222

Prometheus Unbound 92, 98, 100, 102–3, 104, 107, 178, 225–46, 249, 251; ambivalence in 233; and Being 237; love in 230–1, 235–6, 238, 242; nature, power of 237; self in 227–8, 245; submission in 228–9; tension in 238

prophecy 163

Protagoras 164

Python and *Lamia* 126–8

Queen Mab 91, 93

question: in Platonic dialogues 39–40; in *The Triumph of Life* 122–3

Randall, J.H. 32, 42, 138; and *Symposium* 73, 74, 81, 82

reality: and art 49; and Being 7, 9; defining 7; and idea 6; and language 9, 10; and metaphor 294; and naming 22–3; in Plato's writing 151–2

reason, and passion 1701

receptacle, formless 2–3

recollection 274–95; and Being 280, 290; and poetry 279–80; *see also* memory

regeneration in *Ancient Mariner* 215

regression in *Hyperion/Fall of Hyperion* 264–5

Reiman, D.H. 109

religion in Coleridge's work 207

Republic 267; dialectic 37–8; and dynamics of tension 16–17; and *Hyperion/Fall of Hyperion* 182; and ideas 4–5; and language 14–16; logos 19; love 160, 161; and memory 282; and poetry 164, 166–7; and reality 152; and the soul 43–5, 156, 158–9, 165

rest: as form 8; as good 12

323

Revolt of Islam, The 91, 177, 231, 233
Reynolds, J.H. 58–9, 188
Ricoeur, P. 294
Rime of the Ancient Mariner, The 101, 103, 205–25, 229–30, 245, 252, 256; consciousness in 212; daemons in 210; heat in 218–19; language in 217, 223–4; light in 221–2; metamorphosis in 205–6, 214–15, 222; motion in 213–14; passion in 208–9; regeneration in 215; self in 209, 210–11; structure of 208–9; time in 216–17
Rist, J.M. 191
ritual: as cultural form 63; Greek urn as 65, 67; and reasoning in *Symposium* 75; and play 41–2
Rogers, S. 178, 226
romance, in mind–nature relationship 204–5
Romantic poets/poetry: and language 175–6; and memory 274–7; and metamorphosis 185–6; and mythological epics 183–5; passion and poetry of 168–87; and philosophy 51–2; similarities to Plato 185–6; *see also Hyperion/The Fall of Hyperion; The Prelude; Prometheus Unbound; The Rime of the Ancient Mariner*
romanticism: and Keats 69; and Plato 50–1; and poetry and philosophy 51–2
Rousseau, J.J. 88, 91, 103–4, 106–7; in *The Triumph of Life* 109–15
Ryle, G. 40

Salvesen, G. 274
sameness 8
Saturn 251, 253–4, 258
Schelling, F.W.J. 21, 50, 62, 150, 247
Schleiermacher, F.E.D. 350
'Self-knowledge' 206
Self: in *Ancient Mariner* 205, 209, 210–11; in *Hyperion/Fall of Hyperion* 206; in *The Prelude* 189, 191, 193, 205; in *Prometheus Unbound* 205, 227–8, 245
sexuality: in *Lamia* 128–9; in man and Dionysus 120–1; in 'Ode on a Grecian Urn' 64–5, 66–8; in *Symposium* 75–6, 79–82
Shakespeare, W. 192, 209, 220, 228, 243
Shelley, Mary 84, 86, 90, 245
Shelley, Percy B. 26, 51, 247; choice of Rousseau 112–15; disillusionment 90, 91; and eros 72; imagery of 179; letters to Gisborne 84, 88–9; and logos 138; and memory 276; and money 280; on passion 175, 177–9; and poetry 164; and 'present' 89–90, 91; *Prometheus Unbound* 225–46; and *Symposium* 97, 106, 112, 117, 121; translation of *Symposium* 84–6; *The Triumph of Life* 87–125
Sherry, C. 288
Sherwood, M. 188
Sidney, P. 164
Simpson, D. 217
Sleep and Poetry 180, 183
Smith, H. 90, 91
Socrates 54, 109; and *Cratylus* 12–13; and dialectic 34–5; and eros 112; and form 2; and *Lamia* 129; and legend of Athens 30; and love 159; and myth 28–9; and Platonic dialogue 73; and reality 11; and recollection 284–5; relationships in *Symposium* 80–1; and Rousseau 114; in *Statesman* 250; and *Symposium* 74–5, 77–8, 80, 82
Sophist: and Being 6, 7, 9; blending of ideas 22; and dialectic 34; and nothingness 8–9; and poetry 162–3, 167; and 'power' 153–4; and reality 151–2; and soul 157